CARING FOR YOUR HISTORIC HOUSE

Dedicated to Ross R. Merrill for his visionary leadership

in the field of preservation and conservation.

Heritage Preservation is honored and proud to celebrate

with Mr. Merrill in this, our twenty-fifth anniversary year.

CARING FOR YOUR

HISTORIC HOUSE

HERITAGE PRESERVATION AND NATIONAL PARK SERVICE

CHARLES E. FISHER AND HUGH C. MILLER, GENERAL EDITORS

CLARE BOUTON HANSEN, PROJECT DIRECTOR

PREFACE BY ROBERT STANTON AND LAWRENCE L. REGER

FOREWORD BY HILLARY RODHAM CLINTON

INTRODUCTION BY RICHARD H. JENRETTE

WITH ESSAYS BY

GORDON BOCK, JAMES BOORSTEIN, RICHARD O. BYRNE, THOMAS A. COUGHLIN,

CHARLES E. FISHER, DAVID FLAHARTY, DALE H. FRENS, ANDREA M. GILMORE,

JEFFREY GREENE, MARILYN E. KAPLAN, JOHN LEEKE, T. K. MCCLINTOCK, HUGH C. MILLER,

RICHARD PIEPER, WILLIAM B. ROSE, MARY HARDING SADLER AND W. CAMDEN WHITEHEAD,

ROBERT SILMAN, DEBORAH SLATON AND TIMOTHY BARTON,

JOHN R. VOLZ, BARBARA WYATT

HARRY N. ABRAMS, INC., PUBLISHERS

EDITOR: HARRIET WHELCHEL

EDITORIAL ASSISTANT: RACHEL TSUTSUMI

DESIGNER: CAROL ROBSON

Library of Congress Cataloguing-in-Publication-Data

Caring for your historic house / Heritage Preservation and National Park Service ;
    foreword by Hillary Rodham Clinton ; introduction by Richard Hampton Jenrette ;
    with essays by Gordon Bock ... [et al.].
        p.   cm.
    Includes bibliographical references (p.   ) and index.
    ISBN 0–8109–4087–6 (hardcover).— ISBN 0–8109–2779–9 (pbk.)
    1. Dwellings—Maintenance and repair. 2. Historic buildings— Conservation
and restoration. I. Bock, Gordon. II. Heritage Preservation (Organization). III.
United States. National Park Service.
TH4817.C32   1998
690'.24—DC21   97–33266

Printed and bound in Japan

 Harry N. Abrams, Inc.
100 Fifth Avenue
New York, N.Y. 10011
www.abramsbooks.com

CONTENTS

PREFACE

ROBERT STANTON, DIRECTOR, NATIONAL PARK SERVICE,
AND LAWRENCE L. REGER, PRESIDENT, HERITAGE
PRESERVATION

*Watch an old building with an anxious care; guard it as best you may, and at
any cost, from every influence of dilapidation.*
— John Ruskin, *The Seven Lamps of Architecture*

In this passage, written in 1848, John Ruskin describes the sanctity of historic architecture and the need for vigilance regarding its care. Ruskin's warning is a clarion call for the necessity of maintenance.

Maintenance is the key to preserving historic houses. Heretofore, professional and popular publications emphasized the *restoration* of a historic house, while *preventive maintenance* might have been a secondary topic. The time has come to devote an entire book to the subject.

The National Park Service and Heritage Preservation embrace a shared mission to communicate the value of maintenance and ongoing care of historic homes and objects to the broadest public possible. We hope this book, co-produced by the National Park Service and Heritage Preservation, will excite and fortify you with its detailed information on the essential components of maintenance so that you may successfully preserve your own historic home.

This book is the result of the support of numerous professional groups and individuals. Foremost among them is First Lady Hillary Rodham Clinton. We offer the First Lady our inestimable gratitude for contributing the foreword. When she and the President announced the White House Millennium Program, the President asked, "What of our values and heritage will we carry with us? And what shall we give to the future?" By maintaining your historic house, you give something of the past to your family, your community, and your nation.

Caring for Your Historic House has a companion, *Caring for Your Collections.* This brainchild of Arthur W. Schultz focuses on preventive maintenance and care for objects. *Caring for Your Collections* alerts readers to the forces of deterioration that attack our cultural and personal treasures and explains how to control them. It promotes attentive care as a wise investment. Following the book's success, Mr. Schultz encouraged the publishing of *Caring for Your Historic House.* For all this, and for his continued support, we are deeply grateful.

The National Park Service, by protecting and maintaining twenty thousand structures in three hundred seventy-six park units, demonstrates how old buildings can survive and thrive with proper upkeep. In addition, through the Technical Preservation Services' publication program, the National Park Service has developed well over one hundred publications for use by property owners, design professionals, and public officials involved in the preservation and rehabilitation of more than six hundred thousand buildings listed in the National Register of Historic Places. As part of the continuing effort to provide sound preservation guidance, the National Park Service wishes to share its vast experience and information with you, the reader. In fact, the 1993 Interiors Exposition and Conference for Historic Buildings II, chaired by Charles E. Fisher of the National Park Service, prompted this book.

In its twenty-fifth-anniversary year, Heritage Preservation (formerly the National Institute for the Conservation of Cultural Property) wishes to express its gratitude to a distinguished and effective group, the President's Committee on the Arts and the Humanities, appointed by President William Jefferson Clinton and so ably chaired by the Honorable John Brademus. Special thanks to former Executive Director Ellen McCulloch-Lovell, now Deputy Assistant to the President and Advisor to the First Lady on the Millennium; current Executive Director Harriet Mayor Fulbright; and Deputy Director Malcolm Richardson. The Committee's important report, "Creative America," is successfully advancing the preservation of the nation's cultural heritage.

Special thanks to National Park Service staff, especially the Heritage Preservation Services Division of the National Center for Cultural Resource Stewardship and Partnerships, including Katherine H. Stevenson, de Teel Patterson Tiller, Charles E. Fisher, and the Technical Preservation Services Branch; the current Heritage Preservation chairperson, Inge-Lise Eckmann; as well as current and former Heritage Preservation staff, including Clare Bouton Hansen, Karen Groce, and Migs Grove. Thanks also to staff at Harry N. Abrams, Inc., including Paul Gottlieb, Harriet Whelchel, Carol Robson, and Rachel Tsutsumi.

In closing, we hope you will refer to this book often as you care for your own home. Historic houses are born anew, improve with age, and have ongoing lives only if they are well maintained.

Primer and finish coats are being applied to this nineteenth-century Stick Style house.

FOREWORD

HILLARY RODHAM CLINTON
THE WHITE HOUSE, WASHINGTON, D.C.

The privilege of living in the White House has been enjoyed by relatively few families in our country's history. From the family of John Adams, the first to occupy the White House, to our family today, each presidential family brings to the house interests and a style uniquely its own. Each family adds to the history and traditions of the house and each feels the responsibility to recognize and carry forward the traditions of the preceding families. The challenge—and the obligation—is to live a contemporary lifestyle and yet sustain the historic presence and integrity of this structure so appropriately called the *house of the people.*

Each year, more than 1.5 million people visit the White House. Touring the State Rooms is an experience unique to this country. Only the United States offers, on a regular basis, free public tours of the residence of its Chief Executive. As they walk through the magnificent rooms of this wonderful home, visitors are reminded of the history of our great nation. Each work of art, each lovingly polished antique table, every carefully restored architectural detail speaks of the care that is given to preserve and enhance this national treasure. A dedicated staff and talented craftspeople, some of them represented in this book, are able to maintain the delicate balance that respects the historic character of the collection and at the same time accommodates the present-day use and function of the house.

As you study this book, it is my hope that you will realize that consistent maintenance that is historically respectful and thoughtful can ensure lasting use and enjoyment of a historic treasure and a legacy that with loving and timely care will endure for generations to come.

Even the First Family must endure the inconvenience that sometimes accompanies restoration work and maintenance.

INTRODUCTION

Richard H. Jenrette

Restoring old houses to their former glory has been one of the great joys of my life. At last count, I have been directly involved with restoring sixteen old houses, six of which I now own personally and treasure. The rest belong to museum groups or to friends who give them the same loving care. In restoring these old houses, I feel I have played a role in helping preserve America's rich heritage of architecture. But the reality is that I did it for a personal reason—restoration is great fun.

While there is an excitement to restoring old houses to a pristine earlier state, *maintenance* is the real key to long-term satisfaction in owning an old house. There is no point in restoring a house to perfection and then letting it slide back into neglect. The adage "A stitch in time saves nine" has never been more apt than in the case of old houses. They require constant vigilance—repainting, repointing old brickwork, watching for water damage, insect infestation, human wear and tear—you name it.

While all this may sound like the "unfun" part of owning an old house, I have learned that there is no greater satisfaction than maintaining an old house with loving care. The more you polish it and care for it, the greater joy it will bring you. The restoration process goes on and on, but, since I like restoration, that simply means the joy of caring for an old house is unending.

Some of my preservation friends do the restoration and maintenance work themselves, which they find enhances their satisfaction while also saving money. I have usually been in the position of paying the bills for others to do the ongoing maintenance. In the process, I have made new friends among the artisans (I don't view them as "tradespeople") I have worked with. Most of these people love old houses and take great pride in their skills. Praise works even better than the almighty dollar when it comes to getting good results. Your own interest and involvement are contagious and can encourage others to take pride in the maintenance.

Good maintenance is absolutely essential, but it can also be fun. Your old house will just get better and better each year if you maintain it properly. This book will prove invaluable as you enjoy a long and happy life in your historic home.

Why Care about Your Historic House?

Hugh C. Miller

A historic house can mean many things to many people, but caring about it begins with an owner's identification with the historic values of the property. The house may be a museum-quality building associated with an important person or event, or representative of rare vernacular architecture, or an unusual surviving style of any historic period from colonial times up to mid-twentieth-century modernism. It may further represent a house of its period that has grown and changed in its own time to accumulate a unique history of design and use. The house may have been built in the country as an estate manor, plantation seat, or farm- or ranch house. It may be an urban mansion, town house, or part of a row terrace in old urban centers or their historic suburbs. Maybe it is in a small city or town. Today's historic houses include old homes of the wealthy, the middle class, and workers that have survived and been maintained, rehabilitated, and restored for continued use as residences.

A large universe of homes are on or eligible for listing on the National Register of Historic Places or are considered contributing buildings in historic districts. The fact that your house or neighborhood has never formally been designated does not mean that it is not historic. A house or neighborhood that is typical of its period of construction (usually more than fifty years old) can be considered historically significant in the context of its time and as a continuum of history if it displays integrity of design, location, setting, materials, workmanship, feeling, and association.[1] This association may include a historic connection to the homeowners' family that embodies a personal pride. Even where the previous owners of the house are anonymous, the building's past is part of the physical history of the place and thus connected to the history of the larger locality. All of these elements of significance and integrity combine to give your historic house its value.

A historic home also has an economic value that, like all real estate, is a function of location. This location encompasses micro- and macroenvironments that include neighborhood, setting, and environs as well as transportation routes and public services in either an urban or rural setting. A house in a historic setting or as part of an urban or rural historic district probably embodies a quality of life that can be quantified.

Caring for your historic house can have many components. There is *why* you care—why your house is valuable to you. This involves *what* you care about—the elements defining its architecture and character, the things you see and feel, including the details, texture, color, and workmanship that define the historic fabric of your house. There is *how* you care—reflected in when, how, why, and by whom maintenance and repairs are performed. Part of how you care is caring about the results as well as the cost.

Other than rehabilitating to meet the expectations of modern living or the urge to restore to recapture lost architectural splendor, owners of historic houses do not redecorate or remodel as often as do occupants of more modern homes. Homeowners' satisfaction with an older house usually reflects a recognition that the house has qualities that are hard to replicate in a new house or new location.

Details such as ornament and windows contribute to architectural character.

Historic fabric, such as the woodwork and stenciling of this staircase, lends significance, integrity, and value to the historic house.

The current doctrine of the National Park Service and many historic preservation organizations that "proper maintenance *is* preservation" is not a new statement of principle. In 1839 the French archaeologist A. N. Didron wrote: "It's better to preserve than to repair, better to repair than to restore, better to restore than to reconstruct." In the United States, these ideas came into focus in the early 1970s in response to repeated restoration campaigns on the same landmark and the heavy-handed removal of historic fabric to create an earlier appearance for which there was little documentation to justify restoration.

Today, treatments for historic houses are divided among preservation, rehabilitation, restoration, and reconstruction.[2] These words each describe a specific activity and have legal meaning as they relate to local, state, and federal preservation programs, grants, tax incentives, and project approvals. They should be used rigorously—avoid words like *renovate, remodel, redesign* when referring to work for the preservation of your historic house. (For further discussion of these terms, see page 23.)

The notion of *caring* is embodied in the definition of *preservation.* The principles of architectural conservation and preservation maintenance are in fact a restatement of ideas espoused in the nineteenth century during the "scrap–anti-scrap" debates. John Ruskin, one of the founders of the anti-scrap school of preservation in the mid-nineteenth century, wrote in *The Seven Lamps of Architecture:* "Take proper care of your monuments and you will not need to restore them. A few sheets of lead put in time upon a roof, a few dead leaves and sticks swept in time out of the water course, will save both roof and walls from ruin. Watch an old building with anxious care, guard it as best you may and at any cost from every influence of dilapidation."

Ruskin's descriptions of care and maintenance are straightforward and, if conscientiously applied, may be sufficient for the homeowner's needs. Unfortunately, the principles and practice of good preservation maintenance are an art and a science that require a mind-set, skills, and time that are rare and expensive in today's marketplace of housekeepers, trade mechanics, and contractors.

The popular concept that building-maintenance work is trite and demeaning is unfortunately widespread among service trades, and even among people who are committed to historic preservation. Yet preservation maintenance is essential and critical work that must be reinforced with planning and follow-through by a caring owner. It is important to determine that proper preservation maintenance is scheduled and proactive. The work to adjust, clean, or repair building elements that Ruskin talks about is not usually applied comprehensively to buildings. The maintenance schedules and inspection checklists routinely used for automobiles or furnaces, for example, are only now being developed for institutional building owners. Software is now on the shelf, but the available computer scheduling programs are often too demanding for most owners of historic houses. Caring homeowners may in fact do better armed with do-it-yourself knowledge and a willingness to communicate with housekeepers and trade mechanics for appropriate cleaning and timely repairs or replacement of defective building parts.

Good housekeeping practices that do not use harsh cleaning agents and provide a system for reporting changing conditions of the building are the critical beginning of "proper care." Routine inspections that include cleaning and adjusting anything that should move or tightening or fastening anything that should not move are the best preservation maintenance, since they are truly preventive.

THE WHOLE-BUILDING CONCEPT

An understanding of the house as a whole is essential to caring about its well-being. We should think of a house as a complex, six-sided system, with an inside and outside, stuck in the ground and exposed to the weather. The individual elements—envelope, structure, interior, infrastructure, and landscape, site, and environs—can be described as the house's anatomy and physiology. The *envelope* encloses the house from weather and external forces. In addition to its performance of these functional roles, the envelope also includes the facade, or "face," which defines the building's architectural character. The *structure* resists gravity with beams, columns, arches, trusses, and foundation and bearing walls that hold the house up. The structure is the "bones" of the house. The *interior* creates spaces for the functions of the house and, with design and finishes, inspires delight. It is the "soul" of the house. The *infrastructure* contains the heating, ventilating, air-conditioning, electrical, plumbing, and other systems that make the house habitable to meet today's expectations for living. These are the "arteries, veins, and nerves" of the house. Last, and not least, the *landscape, site,* and *environs* of the house are what define its context as a place. All these systems are physically and functionally intertwined. They possess varying degrees of permanence and resistance to change and the forces of deterioration.

In addition to these five systems are two layers that function as systems and are critical to the well-being of the house: people and their stuff. The owners, occupants, and users of a house bring with them furniture, fixtures, equipment, and collections of valuable and ephemeral things. Human activities with their movable things create expectations for the building systems' performance, demand space, and are agents of change, whether intended or not, to the house's well-being.

As one measures building performance and diagnoses and treats building ills, it is important to recognize that all these systems are related and respond to different forces in different ways. A problem in one system may show up as a sign of distress in another system and a failure of an element of a third or fourth system. A blocked downspout may spill water on the exterior wall, and resulting seepage of water may cause the interior plaster cornice to fall and the ceiling joist end to rot.

FORCES OF DETERIORATION

The forces causing houses to deteriorate can be divided into two broad categories: *intrinsic* forces, inherent *to* the house, and *extrinsic* forces, action *on* the house. Intrinsic forces include the house's location, site, geology, topography, soils, hydrology, and climate. These generally are given factors that allow little modification by the homeowner. The house's design for its environment can affect the intrinsic forces, however. The materials, workmanship, design, and details all play a role in the house's resistance to deterioration.

At this point one could ask, "What are the strengths and weaknesses inherent in the house's design and its component materials?" In some cases, the owner may have an option to change materials or details for better performance without changing the visual quality of the architectural or historic features. Drainage systems and surfacing materials of flat roofs may be changed to improve their function if this work will not change the architectural character of the house. However, changing the shape of a roof in a way that would

Natural disasters—in this case, Hurricane Hugo—can cause devastating damage to a historic house. Careful disaster-preparedness planning, adequate insurance, and appropriate structural reinforcing before, during, and after an event can save lives, mitigate damage, and provide the tools for restoring the house.

modify the house's architectural and historic appearance would not be acceptable. Adobe bricks and log walls have inherent material faults that are not easily mitigated. Repair and replacement of these materials "in kind" is an example of the commitment of love needed to preserve the architectural character of these building materials.

Extrinsic forces are natural, environmental, and human forces that act *on* the house. Gravity is the omnipotent natural force that acts continuously to cause the house and its elements to fall down. These physical and mechanical forces may be manifested in stress and strain that all intervene with building materials, causing them to fail, and may move structural elements up, down, or around to a point that the house can no longer support a load or itself and thus collapses.

Other natural and environmental forces are chemical, biological, and physical processes that act on materials to reduce them to their most basic state. Like gravity, these chemical, biological, and physical agents of deterioration are omnipresent. Changes in materials are ongoing but can be aggravated by the forces of wind, heat, humidity, and precipitation. Prolonged and continuous chemical, biological, and physical action erodes stone into sand; chemical and physical processes corrode steel back into its normal state of iron oxide (rust). Here the questions are, "What are the possible natural agents of deterioration that can affect the component materials?" and, "How can they be mitigated or circumvented?"

Natural disasters and events fortunately are occasional actions, but they unleash very strong and unusual forces that upset the house's equilibrium. The five major natural causes of damage to houses are floods, earthquakes, tornadoes, hurricanes (with high winds, rain, and sea surges), and downpours of rain that overload roofs. Other damaging natural events include thunderstorms, ice and snow, wildfires, and mudslides. To some extent, an owner of a historic house can plan for natural disasters and, with some luck, mitigate the damage.

Interestingly, most of the natural disasters causing major damage to houses involve water as a factor—flooding, hurricanes, downpours, mudslides, and ice-, snow-, and thunderstorms. Water is also a cause or factor in physical, chemical, and biological deterioration of materials. It must be present for rot to form in wood and is usually necessary for corrosion to occur in metals. Algae, moss, vines, and weeds need water to grow on houses. It can easily be said that water is the "villain" in most material deterioration and resulting building failures. In order to think about water as an agent of deterioration, we need to understand how it behaves in each of its three phases—liquid, solid, and vapor—what happens to water as it changes phase, and what happens to building materials with water on or in them.

After the forces of gravity, human forces are the most prevalent cause of building failure. Lack of adequate care is a major source of damage to houses. Changes to the house and its use, including alterations and additions, may induce the process of deterioration as well as change the house's architectural and historic character. Wear and tear, vandalism, and arson are obvious detrimental human activities. Accidents such as fires, explosions, and water leaks usually are related to some failures in the chain of human decisions or activities. Indirect human actions that are detrimental to the house include traffic vibrations, acid rain, and ground subsidence. If a house can overcome the forces of gravity, human activity or inactivity, and environmental or natural causes of decay, it can last forever. With proper care (and some luck), it will.

KEEPING HOUSES WELL

The care of houses has often been equated to the practice of medicine. Like medical specialists, old-house professionals and trade mechanics often think of "sick" houses. For owners of homes and those who work with them, however, the emphasis should be on keeping houses well.

The fact that you are living in your historic house and caring about it is a positive indicator of its well-being. That the house has survived fifty, seventy-five, or a hundred years or more is a tribute that many parts of the house have withstood the test of time and are still able to perform. When there is a failure to meet expectations, the problem or house's "ill" is usually related to one or more of its components or systems and the rest of the house is probably performing well.

Like the maintenance of your own personal health, you must understand the anatomy and physiology of houses in general and the history and physical condition of your historic house in particular. The "diseases" of the house are the forces that cause deterioration and failure. These diseases can be studied as the pathology of the house and analyzed with diagnostic tests. The old-house doctor (building conservator or maintenance professional) can make a prognosis about the severity of the disease and recommend treatments based on these tests and analyses. In a comprehensive house-care system, the treatment should be monitored and reevaluated regularly. Inspection of the entire house should be performed on a set schedule (see Establishing a Maintenance Program). These physical checkups are an essential part of keeping your house well.

The analytical approach to building preservation has been discussed as a philosophy for more than a hundred years, and many of today's techniques were well understood and used in Europe and England in the late nineteenth century. In the United States, however, the practice of architectural conservation and systems for preservation maintenance can be traced to the early 1970s. Initially, scientific and analytical methods were applied to building-restoration projects to determine the content of original materials such as paint or mortar. Dendrochronology or X ray was used to date materials. As the concepts of material conservation used for preserving museum objects were applied to buildings, it became less important to know the original color of a wall or the date of the floor joist, since conserving the whole building became the goal. Instead, what became important were the overall condition of the building, the function of all its interrelated elements and systems, and the methods and materials to use to preserve or repair its historic fabric. The result was architectural conservation practiced with preservation maintenance.

In the care of old houses, as with the practice of geriatrics, the intent is to understand the house's ills and treat them so that the whole house continues to function. The principles of extending life and doing the least harm are very applicable to historic houses. Minimum intervention may be preferred to major surgery. Historic houses have sags and bellies of old age and it may be preferable to accept them rather than perform an unnecessary face-lift. In the case of spalling masonry or peeling paint, for example, one must determine if the problem is critical to the well-being of the house or merely cosmetic. In some cases, as with spalling brick in a basement wall, it may be acceptable to treat the symptoms by replacing bricks rather than install an impervious waterproof barrier. Painting over wood rot, however, is a shortsighted cosmetic solution. The real cure is to remove the rot *and* its cause before the new replacement wood is painted.

PROBLEMS, PRIORITIES, AND SOLUTIONS

The difference between benign neglect and deferred maintenance is understanding at what point a "problem" is truly a problem. In the world of maintenance, knowledge of the preferred outcome is critical. Cost-benefit formulas that can equate the frequency of repairs and total replacement in the pure economics of the "life costs" may work for replacement of boilers and built-up roofs, but the deciding factors for care and preservation maintenance of historic fabric and architectural character are usually more subjective.

Problems and priorities can be defined in broad action categories of urgent; need to do; nice to do; watch it; and do nothing. Urgent problems are life-threatening or will result in major loss of property. Emergency action is often needed to protect or stabilize the house before appropriate corrective repairs are made. "Need-to-do" work requires corrective action of a problem that is progressive, like structural movement, signs of wood rot, and moisture migration. The rate of change is measurable and, if there is no intervention, the resulting deterioration could require urgent action. "Nice-to-do" work is often cosmetic and usually can be scheduled with routine or cyclical maintenance work. "Watch it" is an important priority and would apply to deterioration in the "need-to-do" and "nice-to-do" categories if the signs or symptoms of problems have not been fully diagnosed to determine the real cause. A monitoring system should be established to determine the rate of change or see if the problem gets worse, such as watching structural cracks to determine if they are active. Doing nothing may be acceptable if the problem, such as a leak, has been solved but the symptom, an old water stain, remains. If the problem has been diagnosed and found to be insignificant—if the floor squeaks, for example—doing nothing also may be acceptable. In both cases, the facts should be recorded in inspection reports so subsequent inspections can validate the decision to do nothing.

Solutions for your house ills may include (in addition to doing nothing) mitigating or circumventing the problem or reconstructing the damaged material or system. Mitigating involves removing the threat or agent of deterioration. Many of the best treatments of care are in this category—cleaning, adjusting, oiling, painting. They all should be routine. Removing a threatening tree branch or redirecting the outflow of downspouts is recognizing a real or potential problem and taking corrective action. In most cases, mitigating treatments are not long lasting and must be repeated.

Circumventing a problem usually involves altering the building material or system and/or the force or cause of deterioration or failure. This action is often undertaken to cure structural and infrastructural damage and may be applied to moisture problems. Ideally, the treatments, while they involve change, make the existing system "better" or stronger or like new, but not necessarily. Usually, these treatments have a long life if appropriately maintained.

Reconstructing the material or system involves major repair or replacement. The hierarchy of this treatment ranges from consolidation or repair in place, to repair with in-kind materials, to selected or complete replacement with similar or substitute materials. The principles of conservation specify the least intervention and retention of as much of the original historic fabric as possible. Conservators of buildings are concerned that systems and materials do not fix existing buildings "too well": envelopes (particularly walls and roofs) can be too tight. Structural systems should not be too rigid; rather, the dynamics of the building must be considered in the treatment. Imaginative treatments that incorporate existing elements where possible are suggested throughout the book.

The appropriate treatment of specific ills depends on many factors—the extent of the problem, the expected life of the treatment, its first cost and life cost, its visual impact on the historic fabric and architectural character, its

For a caring owner of a historic house, the management of water and its effects on materials and building systems are essential for the well-being of the building. Water in any of its phases adversely affects almost all building materials and building systems. Consequently, one needs to think of moisture systematically and symptomatically. Water sources and water damage are sometimes directly related, but, in many cases, causes and effects are not easy to identify and often involve water in different phases and moved by different transfer mechanisms, causing different types of damage. Where does water come from? Where does it go? And what does it do? These are complex system questions to be asked and answered before any treatment is undertaken.

Water is the cause of most material deterioration, as is evident in this eave.

Unwanted water can be transported into and through a building in several ways:
- falling or flowing—as accumulated water, ice, or snow
- rising in materials by capillary attraction
- condensing from water vapor to a liquid on surfaces or in cooler assemblies
- leaking or overflowing from rainwater, plumbing, or heating systems
- during construction or maintenance—while mixing plaster, concrete, or paint, or while washing up

Not only does this invading water damage building systems and materials by overloading wall and roof structural systems with the accumulation of water, ice, or snow, it also provides an environment for spores, rot, molds, mildew, and other biological agents and insects that attack wood, paper, or fabric. Excess water also
- dissolves adhesives and binders of composite wood materials, paper, plaster, clay products, concrete, and stone
- corrodes metals and saturates porous materials, filling voids in systems and causing performance failures
- freezes and expands in pipes, masonry, and other porous materials and wall or roofing assemblies
- dissolves salts and redeposits them in masonry, plastic, and concrete
- erodes and abrades material surfaces and changes dimensions or volume of many materials, such as wood or clay products, even soil

Symptoms of water problems can be observed with the senses of sight, hearing, smell, and touch, aided and verified by mechanical tests and monitoring. The most common problems to check for regularly are:
- free water flow, ponding, or ice from water penetration, leaks, or condensation
- surface wetting/dampness or stains from leaks, capillary attraction, or condensation
- salt deposits on plaster, masonry, and concrete, which usually indicates evaporation following capillary attraction. Caution: old water stains with salt deposit will give a "high wet" reading on a moisture meter.
- changes in dimension, surface, or performance of materials or systems (e.g., peeling paint, spalling masonry or concrete, corroding metals, rotting wood)
- visible molds or mildew and musty odors

The symptoms of water damage, like peeling paint, are often not considered a serious water problem, so it is important for caring owners not only to anticipate potential sources of water but also to understand the consequences of unwanted water in their buildings. The signs of moisture problems must be diagnosed systematically so that the actual cause can be treated. Too often, moisture problems, like interstitial condensation in a wall, are misdiagnosed, and expensive treatments of the symptoms, such as repainting a damaged exterior wall, do not solve the underlying problem. The following chapters will provide guidance in how to identify and repair specific problems as well as how to prevent their reoccurrence.

physical and chemical compatibility with the existing material or system, and its comparable weatherability or function. Health, safety, and environmental concerns as well as code requirements must also be addressed. Ease of installation, repairability, and reversibility are critical questions to ask about any treatment. Major intervention should be avoided if at all possible.

The decision to undertake a treatment should be in response to a quantifiable need to change or improve the performance of materials or systems. Hairline cracks in plaster can be repaired, and probably should be when a room is repapered or painted, but they will reopen. Developing a personal standard of expectations for your historic house should focus not on appearance but on protective maintenance. In North America, there is too much cleaning, repointing, and coating of masonry without a compelling reason. There is also probably too much metal polish, wax, and paint that says more about appearances than long-term protection of the historic fabric of the material. Proper maintenance involves caring about the appropriate treatment and the level of intervention. Caring is not a house-proud enthusiasm but a commitment to doing it "right" all the time with understanding and feeling. The following chapters speak to specific questions about how to care for your historic house.

Notes

1. "How to Apply the National Register Criteria for Evaluation," National Register Bulletin 15 (Washington, D.C.: National Park Service, U.S. Department of Interior, Government Printing Office, 1991).

2. Kay D. Weeks and Anne E. Grimmer, The Secretary of the Interior's Standards for the Treatment of Historic Properties with Guidelines for Preserving, Rehabilitating, Restoring & Reconstructing Historic Buildings (Washington, D.C.: U.S. Department of the Interior, National Park Service, 1995).

The retention of as much of the original historic fabric as possible with the least intervention is the main principle of conservation. This historic brickwork warrants thoughtful care and treatment to preserve it.

Most, if not all, historic homes have lead-based paint in one or more layers of exterior or interior paint coats. The presence of lead-based paint may or may not, however, present a health hazard. A hazard is present when paint has deteriorated or worn, creating chips or dust that can be ingested or breathed, particularly by young children who get this material on their hands, clothing, and toys. Restoration and maintenance processes that require sanding or heat or chemicals or cutting of painted surfaces can create toxic particles, dust, fumes, and residues that must be removed by thoroughly cleaning before the house is occupied.

When done properly, removing paint is time-consuming and may be expensive. Removing surfaces that contain lead-based paint can result in loss or modification of architectural features and finishes that is not appropriate for historic homes. Furthermore, well-intended efforts to remove lead-based paint can actually increase the hazard by creating dust or harmful pollutants from chemicals or heat. When there is an accumulation of old paint, debris should be treated with caution.

Intact painted surfaces are safe as long as they remain intact, but regular abrasion of the paint surface creates the potential for a hazard. Different types of surfaces have different probabilities of becoming a hazard. Friction surfaces (such as porch floors, stair risers, door and window edges), chewable surfaces (such as windowsills or shelves), and impact surfaces (such as baseboards and doorjambs) present more risk than other surfaces (such as flat walls) with good intact paint and lead-free topcoat. Federal, state, and some local laws that address lead hazards, primarily to protect the health of young children, have created a prevailing fear around the issue. Strict approaches to "eliminate the risk" of lead-based-paint hazards have been taken and more are under consideration as compliance requirements for some state and local building codes and some state and federal funding programs, such as those available through the Department of Housing and Urban Development. Final regulations of the Residential Lead-Based Paint Hazard Reduction Act went into effect in December 1996 to require owners to disclose knowledge about the presence of lead paint at the time of sale. This "due diligence" disclosure does not at this time require an owner of a private residence to remove or treat the lead-based paint.

It is important that an owner of a historic house be responsive to the health hazards and act responsibly to protect all occupants of the house and its architectural and historic character. Awareness of all the risks can help a homeowner control lead-based-paint health hazards. Good housekeeping that removes dust and paint particles, particularly around windows, doors, and other friction areas, is particularly important. Proper maintenance includes removal and careful disposal of loose and peeling paint and recoating with an appropriate modern paint. Various chapters in this book address specific aspects of lead-based paint management (see especially chapters on Wooden Windows and Exterior and Interior Paints). The National Park Service's *Preservation Brief No. 37: Appropriate Methods for Reducing Lead-Paint Hazards in Historic Housing* also presents a good discussion of the issues.

Hugh C. Miller/Clare Bouton Hansen

GETTING TO KNOW YOUR HOUSE

DEBORAH SLATON AND TIMOTHY BARTON

Owners of old houses are caretakers of history and tradition. As such, they have unique responsibilities. Owners must not only appreciate and understand a dwelling's past, but they must also maintain its physical structure. Houses have different levels of significance and appreciation: some may be recognized historic landmarks; others may have been designed by renowned architects or lived in by famous (or infamous) people. On a more personal level, some homes have special value to members of a family through long association with parents, grandparents, and other family members. Or, perhaps more typically, houses simply may have the inherent qualities of older design and materials that lend distinction. By their very nature, older homes demand thoughtful decision making in regard to repairs, alterations, and maintenance that will sustain their special meanings.

The distinctive character of older houses makes them increasingly valuable resources, on a personal level as well as for communities. Against the backdrop of the new construction that has dominated residential development for the last half century, preserving historic resources was long seen as a quaint activity undertaken by eccentrics. However, trends in architecture and community planning, such as the recent popularity of the New Urbanism, have underscored the value of traditional design for enhancing the quality of community living. Some areas have adopted design guidelines and designated historic districts in order to sustain the special features and visual continuity of older houses.

In planning the care and maintenance of an older or historic house, it is important first to identify the historic features and materials of the house and to decide what is significant. At the same time, the repair and maintenance requirements of the house need to be defined. This dual evaluation requires an understanding of the components of the house and its systems, as well as information about its history. All of these elements are considered together to determine how to best meet these needs while respecting the architectural and historic character of the house.

Part of getting to know your house is considering how it fits into the streetscape. These cottages line Gurney Street in Cape May, New Jersey.

UNDERSTANDING YOUR HOUSE AND ITS ARCHITECTURAL CHARACTER

The first responsibility of the owner of an older home is to understand and appreciate the house: to recognize its positive qualities in terms of character, design, materials, and construction. What are the special features of a house? What constitutes its special architectural character, and how can this be identified?

Perhaps the most important technique for getting to know one's house is living in it: looking at it every day, considering it from different viewpoints and in different lights, and thinking about its history and character and how it works with the present. The knowledge obtained by living in and looking at one's house is complemented by information gathered through research. Information about the house's history and construction and the stories of its designer, builder, occupants, and neighborhood add depth to our appreciation of the house and enhance the meaning of what we think of as home.

If available, historic photographs of the house—exterior or interior—and its setting are a wonderful guide and a font of information for comparison of original and existing features and appearance. Guides to architecture of a given period or style are also helpful in understanding which features of a house are original or historic. (For specific titles and for complete citations of titles referred to throughout, see Further Reading at the back of the book.) These guides include descriptions, sketches, and photographs of representative American architectural styles from the seventeenth century through the present. Even in the case of a house that does not adhere to a particular style, or that may be a hybrid of several styles, such guides are useful as starting points for interpreting the house's architecture.

We tend to identify a structure by the way it looks and to assign a style name to each building, but such analysis is too superficial to provide a true understanding of architectural character. In the National Park Service's *Preservation Brief No. 17,* Lee Nelson outlined a three-step process for assessing an older house through visual analysis. This process involves examining the building first from afar, in the context of its neighbors; then moving in close to study its exterior materials and workmanship; and finally examining the interior spaces and features in equal detail. Nelson also developed a useful "Architectural Character Checklist/Questionnaire" that lists the building characteristics to be reviewed in each step of the three-step process, a brief summary of which is given below.

STEP ONE: VIEW FROM AFAR

Examine the overall building shape, roof and roof features (such as cupolas, chimneys, and dormers), openings, projections, trim and secondary features (shutters, gables, railings), materials, and setting (fences, terraces, plantings, walkways).

As you observe the house from a distance, even if only from across the street, consider how it relates to the context of its streetscape. For example, how does it compare to adjacent houses in terms of size, setback, materials, and design? How is it similar to or different from its neighbors as a whole? If neighboring houses appear to be of the same vintage, they can provide clues as to the original design and configuration of elements of your house that may have been modified or lost over time, such as multilight windows or front-step details.

STEP TWO: VIEW AT ARM'S LENGTH

When one examines the exterior of a house as a whole, additions and alterations—both sympathetic and unsympathetic—become apparent. For example, aluminum siding or an aluminum storm door is easily recognized as a relatively recent addition to an older, wood-framed house. Differences in brickwork or wood-cladding styles may indicate different periods of construction.

Assess the materials and details of craftsmanship, such as texture, finishes, and patterns. Close-up exterior examination will yield clues as to what original features remain and which original features have been covered over. Screw holes in window frames can indicate where hinges were originally placed for shutters that have since been removed. A close look at the edges of a roof may reveal multiple layers of asphalt shingles that hide the original wood-shingle roofing. Do these changes contribute to the history and architectural character of the building? If so, they are important.

STEP THREE: VIEW FROM WITHIN

Evaluate the interior through the character of individual spaces, the relationship between those spaces, interior features (such as stairways, balustrades, archways), visible structural elements, and (close-up) surface finishes and materials.

In considering the interior of a historic house, it is often useful to organize the spaces and features in terms of their functional significance. For example, primary spaces such as living and dining rooms and bedrooms often have the most historic character and are usually the best candidates for preservation of original elements or restoration to a historic appearance. Kitchens and bathrooms may retain some interesting historic components, but are more likely to have been changed. If already significantly altered, these rooms are good candidates for renovation as needed to make them more serviceable. Secondary spaces such as basements, attics, closets, and cavities between interior walls usually permit significant changes to accommodate new uses and requirements.

The relationship of the rooms as part of the overall plan is also important. Consider the room relationships and ceiling heights. Look at how the spaces flow into one another vertically and horizontally. Consider the visual and functional relationships between the spaces, as they exist now and as they might have been in the past. Markings on an interior wall or floor may indicate the past location of a room partition, column, or window that has been removed or covered. Multiple layers of paint may disguise an original color scheme or wallpaper. Differences in the design and proportions of interior trim can also suggest later interior remodelings.

The overall design, materials, shapes and sizes of openings, and other elements combine to give a house its distinctive visual character. The appearance of this 1880s rowhouse, with its detailed stone facade, was changed dramatically with the removal of the cornice and the addition of aluminum siding. Not only do such cosmetic changes take away the visual interest, but they also may impose structural problems.

The goal of this three-step assessment, beyond identifying the distinguishing features of a historic property, is to discern the unity of the original design—how shape, materials, walls, and window and door openings interrelate. As diligent as homeowners may be in their research, information gaps may still exist. These gaps must be filled in by good judgment based on a thorough, almost intuitive, understanding of how the various parts of the design relate to each other.

Alterations to historic houses are often incompatible because they are not sympathetic to the original configuration. In deciding what to retain, the homeowner needs to consider whether later additions are in fact sympathetic to the original and whether they may have historical or architectural interest in their own right. (For example, the original architect may have also designed the later additions or alterations.) In deciding what to add, it is important to be historically accurate not just for history's sake, but also for the sake of a unified design.

As part of this process, it is important to distinguish historic *character* from historic *fabric*. Lee Nelson defined character as "all those visual aspects and physical features that comprise the appearance of every historic building. Character-defining elements include the overall shape of the building, its materials, craftsmanship, decorative details, interior spaces and features, as well as the various aspects of its site and environment."[1]

Historic fabric—the original materials of which the house is constructed—represents the work of the designer, craftsman, or worker who built the house. Where historic fabric remains, preservation standards recommend that it be retained and preserved or repaired. Where the existing fabric is too severely deteriorated to be repaired, or where the original material is missing, replacements can be considered. The first choice in any replacement in a historic house is to replace in kind, with the same material, but with the new elements carefully marked and dated to distinguish them from the original material. If

the same material is not available, or for cost or other reasons is not practicable, then substitute materials may be appropriate. Our understanding of the Secretary of the Interior's *Standards for the Treatment of Historic Properties* has recently been enhanced by a new publication by Kay D. Weeks and Anne E. Grimmer. This publication provides excellent definitions and a list of standards for each of four principal treatments: preservation, rehabilitation, restoration, and reconstruction.

The standards for *preservation* require retention of the greatest amount of historic fabric, along with the building's historic form, features, and detailing as they have evolved over time. The *rehabilitation* standards acknowledge the need to alter or add to a historic building to meet continuing or new uses while retaining the building's historic character. The *restoration* standards allow for the depiction of a building at a particular time in its history by preserving materials from the period of significance and removing materials from other periods. The *reconstruction* standards establish a limited framework for re-creating a vanished or nonsurviving building with new materials, primarily for interpretive purposes.

Preservation is defined as the act or process of applying measures necessary to sustain the existing form, integrity, and materials of a historic property. Work, including preliminary measures to protect and stabilize the property, generally focuses upon the ongoing maintenance and repair of historic materials and features rather than extensive replacement and new construction. New additions are not within the scope of this treatment; however, the limited and sensitive upgrading of mechanical, electrical, and plumbing systems and other code-required work to make properties functional is appropriate within a preservation project.

Rehabilitation is the act or process of making possible a compatible use for a property through repair, alterations, and additions while preserving those portions or features that convey its historical, cultural, or architectural values.

Restoration entails accurately depicting the form, features, and character of a property by means of the removal of features from other periods in its history and reconstruction of missing features from the restoration period. The limited and sensitive upgrading of mechanical, electrical, and plumbing systems and other code-required work to make properties functional is appropriate within a restoration project.

Reconstruction is, literally, new construction that re-creates the form, features, and detailing of a nonsurviving site, landscape, building, structure, or object for the purpose of replicating its appearance at a specific period of time and in its historic location.[2]

The components and systems of a house must be understood as parts of a whole: alterations to one part need to be considered as they will affect the entire house. The exterior of a house—the envelope that protects the interior against weather—consists not only of the walls and roof, but also of windows, doors, gutters and downspouts, trim, chimneys, porches, and stairs. The exterior relates to the setting of the house: sidewalks, drives, garden, landscape or streetscape, and environs. The interior of the house contains rooms to be lived in as well as support spaces such as closets, ducts, chases, and interstitial spaces between walls and between floors and ceilings; structural systems and elements; and mechanical, electrical, and plumbing systems.

Certain older or historic features may become outdated over time while other features retain their importance or even gain in value. For instance, historic woodwork may be removed as styles change, only to come back into style and become more desirable as time passes. Older wooden-framed structural systems may remain entirely serviceable over the life of the house, unless new additions to the house require supplementary structural supports. Conversely, older mechanical and electrical systems may require replacement for

Color treatment is an important aspect of houses and buildings. The accurate documentation of original paint colors—or stencils, where they exist—usually requires a specialist because paint can change its hue over time and with exposure to environmental factors. Here, an architect is uncovering a stencil design by architect Louis Sullivan, from the Auditorium Building in Chicago.

technical and performance reasons. For example, old knob-and-tube wiring may need to be replaced with safer wiring that can carry greater loads. Portions of the old, disconnected wiring can be retained in place as a record of the original wiring system. In some municipalities, building codes permit old fixtures or features such as knob-and-tube wiring to remain in use.

Although restorations and rehabilitations often conform to the initial appearance of a house, later additions do not necessarily detract from historic character. For example, many houses have had porches added several decades after construction. These porches have been in place so long that they have become part of the historic character of the house. Other alterations may be of architectural interest, or designed to harmonize with the original construction, and are therefore desirable additions to be retained in the rehabilitation project. The key to evaluating alterations and additions is identifying their place in the house's history as well as in its construction.

LEARNING YOUR HOUSE'S HISTORY

Older houses are part of history. They tell stories about individuals, communities, and even larger national trends. Unlike the rare museum artifacts often associated with studying the past, houses offer owners a tangible piece of history.

People undertake house histories for a variety of reasons. For homeowners who are rehabilitating an older house, a house history complements their own physical inspections of the property. This research is also necessary for those who are interested in landmark recognition, such as the National Register of Historic Places.[3] Most people, however, research their houses as an extension of their pride of ownership. For many homeowners, houses and their surroundings are akin to family, and finding out about a house is as rewarding as finding information about one's ancestors.

Most owners want to know basic information about their house: when it was built, when alterations were made, background on previous owners, who designed it. As a framework for their investigation, most researchers divide their study among three principal topics: the house and property, individuals who have lived there, and the relationship of the house to the community.[4] Several caveats are in order. Research usually takes a lot of time, especially compared with the amount of information turned up about a specific property. The effort, though, is worthwhile because the facts discovered add to a house's personality and heighten the owners' appreciation of it. In addition, the search frequently yields information about the history of the immediate neighborhood—for example, who founded and subdivided it, occupations of residents, and the dates of construction of neighboring houses. The search is also interesting for the experience of using government agencies and offices with which one may not otherwise have frequent contact.

Another cautionary note is that, as ideal as it would be to discover the design or construction drawings for a house, as a rule it is difficult to locate house plans if they were not conveyed with the house when it was purchased. It is worthwhile to check to see if the papers of the architect or builder have been collected by a historical society or retained by successor firms. In the absence of drawings, valuable clues can also turn up in alternative sources, such as maps or photographs.

A wealth of information—the history of a community, the character and significance of a historic home, or background information about the architect or construction of a dwelling—is available for those with access to the Internet. The National Park Service, for example, maintains a home page entitled Links to the Past. The Society of Architectural Historians provides valuable information concerning architects and building history and contains a catalogue of academic dissertations on American architectural history submitted over the course of the last

In planning the historic rehabilitation of some houses it is important to keep in mind that they can have later alterations that contribute to their historic character. This house was built in the late 1860s in a relatively austere style; architectural tastes changed, and by the 1880s its owners had enlivened it with a decorative sheet-metal bay and an ornate porch.

one hundred years. The Association for Preservation Technology International provides information and access to resources on historic building technology.

There are a number of resources in any area for researching house and community histories. Libraries sometimes have local-history collections or other materials relevant to house research. Librarians also may know of archives or research materials at nearby universities. State governments, as well as many local governments, have historic-preservation offices that may be able to provide information about local resources or determine if the property is documented in any historic-buildings surveys.

The owner of an unusual or old house has an inherent advantage in finding out about the house because it is likely to be the object of some community attention, in which case neighbors or previous occupants are often more than willing to talk about it. As valuable as this information is, however, it should be taken with the proverbial grain of salt as it may vary in accuracy. As a general rule, with oral history or any research, information should be verified by comparison with other documentation.

The most basic information about previous ownership and construction dates will come not from a library or historical society but from public records. Some owners receive an "abstract of title" when they purchase their house. This document lists all of the deeds, mortgages, liens, and other legal instruments relating to the property. The majority of owners, who do not have abstracts, would need to compile a similar chain of title.

The orderly recording of property transfers is a function of local governments, most often by a county recorder of deeds or county clerk. Ownership records are organized by either of two systems: the grantor-grantee index or the tract index. Under the grantor-grantee method (seller to buyer), for example, the current owner would find the previous property transfer by looking in the grantee index for the previous owner's name and then checking the corresponding grantor column to find the name of the previous seller. To find the remainder of the owners, the process is continued back to the original land grant from the federal government. A few states use the tract index, where conveyances are listed by legal descriptions (e.g., Lot 1 of Block 1 in Smith & Jones's Subdivision in Section 6, Township 39 North, Range 14 East). The legal description can be obtained from the tax assessor's office or the county clerk's office.

Both systems record the specific legal documents by which property has been conveyed or financed over time. Legal property conveyances include deeds, warranty deeds, quit-claim deeds, special-warranty deeds, sheriff's deeds, and deeds in trust. Property financing is accomplished through mortgages and trust deeds. In looking for mortgages and trust deeds, note that the owner is the grantor, and the bank or lending company is the grantee. Other instruments—such as easements, covenants, liens, or legal agreements—give further background about uses of and restrictions on property.

Although property records concern the land and generally do not give information about the construction of structures, building dates can sometimes be inferred from documents. With town houses, for example, owners record party-wall agreements with neighboring owners at the time of construction. The recording of a second mortgage when the land is purchased often reflects the financing necessary for home building.

When available, building-permit information is particularly valuable for facts related to the original construction as well as any additions. The data from building records typically includes the names of the original owner, architect, and builder; date and cost of construction; dimensions; and materials. Some municipalities may even have house plans. In some areas, this appears to have been undertaken only after film systems such as microfiche became available.

In some older eastern cities, drawings are available; however, they may be difficult to locate for a specific property.

    If building permits are not available, other records may point out construction activity. Permits for water and sewer hookups are alternatives. So too are address certificates, which are issued by municipalities for new construction. Tax-assessment records usually carry dates of construction, but are frequently only estimates of building dates. In many cities, from the mid-nineteenth into the twentieth century, weekly trade journals conveyed information about current construction projects.

    Probate records and wills are other useful public records. This material helps to trace descendants of previous owners, listing family names and locations at the time of the owner's death. To access this information, which is filed in county courthouses, the year of the person's death must be known.

    The most basic documentary source is the city directory, which can date from the mid-nineteenth century and is comparable to today's telephone directory. The entries are customarily very brief, but, depending on different publishers' practices, many provide additional data, such as individuals' occupations and whether residents owned the property. In using city directories, it is important to find out if the municipality's address system or street names have changed over the years, and, if so, to determine the appropriate address and street name for the year of the directory being examined.

A c.1890 postcard of the Hotel St. Benedict Flats, a Chicago landmark. Postcards are a valuable reference for documenting the early appearance of buildings. In addition to illustrating major structures, postcard companies also sold views of street scenes in small towns and city neighborhoods.

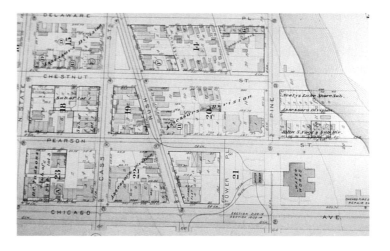

    Directories have two formats: alphabetical listings of occupants and listings by street address. The latter locational method, also referred to as reverse or crisscross listing, is particularly useful for giving details that might

The Hotel St. Benedict Flats was built in 1883 and was recently rehabilitated by its owners. The rehabilitation of vintage buildings requires careful documentation planning, and sometimes needs contractors who are familiar with traditional design and materials.

Opposite:
Fire-insurance atlases were made for cities and towns, beginning in the 1860s, throughout the country, giving detailed building information. They are useful for indicating materials, original house shapes, and features such as porches or bays. In the original, the Hotel St. Benedict Flats (on Chicago Avenue between Cass and Rush Streets) is shown in pink, indicating that it was constructed of brick. Nearby wooden-frame buildings are shown in a different color.

not otherwise be available. For example, even where an owner's name is known through a search of property records, the occupant of a house may have been a tenant, information not usually reflected in property records. Equally significant is that a reverse listing allows a researcher to determine the year of construction by tracing an address backward to its first appearance in a directory. Although more tedious, this can also be done with alphabetical listings in directories of smaller communities, where it is possible to scan the listings looking for the address.

Federal census data provides valuable biographical information about occupants of houses for the period from 1790 to 1920 (except the 1890 census, which was destroyed by fire). Federal law prohibits the release of census data from the most recent seventy-year period. The census lists the names of all dwelling occupants, in addition to their ages, occupations, and country of origin. It is available through the National Archives, but many university and research libraries have copies as well.

More biographical details can sometimes be gleaned from libraries or historical societies that have compiled files of prominent early citizens. Local histories, which were typically funded by residents' subscriptions, included biographies of the subscribers and others. If death dates can be obtained (through the public agency responsible for vital statistics), newspaper obituaries can also be used.

A good deal of historical background about an immediate area can be uncovered through local newspapers. Also, since house building was a popular news topic in smaller communities at the turn of the century, papers are often good sources for material about specific houses and their owners. Daily papers in larger cities sometimes have weekly real-estate or neighborhood sections. Also worth looking for are year-end-review columns that summarize or give comprehensive lists of construction. Scanning papers is time-consuming, but many people enjoy it for the broad historical background it affords.

Old illustrations of houses are as rare, unfortunately, as they are valuable. When all is said and done, most photographs of old houses (or families and friends in them) probably come from the houses' previous owners more often than any other source, thus underscoring the importance of documentary and public-records searches. Historic photograph collections are obvious gold mines where they exist. There are, however, several other avenues to pursue for visual records.

Photographs of picturesque residential blocks were popular images for post-cards sold by itinerant photographers during the 1900s and 1910s. Although some libraries and institutions have collections of them, many of these pictures are still in circulation as collectibles and are sold at flea markets and antique shows.

Many communities and builders advertised themselves through promotional materials. Some of these illustrate typical house types and plans, while others display photos of residential blocks and prominent buildings. "Bird's-eye views," which are large-scale perspective drawings of villages and towns published at the turn of the century, can also be useful for historical reference.

Where they are available, fire-insurance atlases identify information about the original size and materials of a house. These were large atlases compiled by different publishers (the Sanborn Map Company was the largest) that provided data about individual houses for insurance purposes. The atlases record building materials, types, and sizes in order to determine a building's fire resistance for insurance valuations. The volumes show the address, siting of the house on its lot, number of stories, and materials, as well as the placement of porches, chimneys, additions, and secondary structures. Publication of these books began in the mid-1860s and continues today; the current ones are published on microfiche. The maps were updated continuously, so comparing different editions can provide details about alterations. Check with local or state historical libraries for the availability of these maps.

The historic home is a special responsibility. Numerous sources of assistance are available to help the homeowner determine how to best care for a historic house. In many municipalities, local preservation commissions provide guidance and publications. State historic preservation agencies offer information, as do nonprofit advocacy groups. The National Park Service offers the aforementioned series of publications, *Preservation Briefs*, that address topics ranging from masonry repointing to lead-paint abatement to repairing historic concrete. The *Preservation Briefs* are available from the Government Printing Office at a very reasonable cost and are a wealth of information. In addition, useful information can be found through journals such as *Old-House Journal*, *Traditional Building*, and the Association for Preservation Technology International's quarterly technical journal, the *Bulletin*. Many television programs now offer advice to owners of historic homes, but be warned that home renovation is not always as easy as it looks on these shows.

Special federal, state, and local incentives are often associated with historic preservation. Different municipalities offer property-tax reductions, historic-rehabilitation grants and loans, exemptions from building-code requirements, zoning variances, and other incentives. Technical assistance may also be available for design matters. Contact your local landmarks commission, local and state preservation advocacy groups, or your state historic preservation officer for guidance.

Retaining the historic and architectural character of a house involves more care in planning and execution than the typical remodeling project; however, the inherent richness of forms and materials more than compensates for the extra attention. Carefully balanced, the goals of caring for a historic house are to protect the house's historic character, retain its historic fabric wherever possible, meet the needs of the occupants, and preserve the house for the future.

Notes

1. Lee H. Nelson, Preservation Brief No. 17: Architectural Character: Identifying the Visual Aspects of Historic Buildings as an Aid to Preserving Their Character (*Washington, D.C.: National Park Service, 1988.*).

2. Kay D. Weeks and Anne E. Grimmer, The Secretary of the Interior's Standards for the Treatment of Historic Properties with Guidelines for Preserving, Rehabilitating, Restoring & Reconstructing Historic Buildings (*Washington, D.C.: U.S. Department of the Interior, National Park Service, 1995*).

3. Information about listing a property on the National Register of Historic Places, or about properties already listed, is available from your state's historic preservation agency.

4. A very good checklist for research sources is provided in "A General Guide to Sources," in Researching a Historic Property, *a pamphlet by the National Park Service (National Register Bulletin No. 39). The pamphlet lists the sources and types of specific information available (such as abstracts of title and architectural drawings). It is available through your state's historic preservation agency or the National Park Service.*

ESTABLISHING A MAINTENANCE PROGRAM

DALE H. FRENS

Automobile owners are accustomed to practicing routine maintenance to extend the life of their investment—change the oil every five thousand miles, electrical tune-up every thirty thousand miles, and so forth. Indeed, factory warranties dictate following a written maintenance plan. Yet an automobile owner who lives in a historic house rarely has any form of a written plan for the maintenance and preservation of a much larger investment, a historic house.

A maintenance program for a historic house is the sequence of repeated activities that contribute toward the upkeep of the building. To be followed, the maintenance program must be a clearly understood and achievable process. The process should include a conditions assessment, maintenance plan, periodic inspections, maintenance activities, and annual report to reassess the program.

The formality of maintenance management is dependent on many factors—the significance of the building, sophistication of the owner, financial and legal constraints and obligations, and owner awareness and sensitivity to the building's inherent value. In the world of large cultural institutions, building maintenance is managed by a facilities-management department. In the world of your historic house, you are the maintenance manager—as well as the implementer.

Before discussing maintenance management, it is useful to consider the stages of the life of any building. The life stages of a building are as follows:

- Planning
- Construction
- Use
- Repair
- Rehabilitation
- Disposal

For a utilitarian building of no significance, economics largely determines the progression of the building through the sequence. For a historic house, the progression is more complex. Obviously, the planning and construction stages of the life of a historic building occurred far in the past. However, the design, detailing, and quality of materials and workmanship during those first stages greatly impact the cost and difficulty of current maintenance. For the historic house, the use, repair, and rehabilitation phases of the progression are extended in time, without using the yardstick of cold and rational economics ultimately to determine the length of the service life of the building.[1] The historic-house museum, which no longer serves as a dwelling, is conceptually beyond its functional service life and is operating in an aesthetic one of indefinite length, with a whole new set of requirements

Without cyclical maintenance, this house has fallen into extreme disrepair.

for maintenance. This chapter deals with maintenance needs of historic houses that continue to be lived in.

Because the maintenance program is cyclical, repeating itself each year, you can enter the process at any step of the way. Obvious maintenance work, for example, could be done prior to the preparation of a maintenance plan. Cyclical maintenance, such as semiannual gutter cleaning, should begin immediately upon acquiring (or beginning to maintain) a historic house and should not be postponed until after the completion of a conditions assessment. The important concept is to begin building maintenance and then to structure its management.

CONDITIONS ASSESSMENT

A conditions assessment summarizes the condition of the numerous systems and materials that constitute the historic house, and outlines recommendations for their maintenance and repair. The conditions assessment may be prepared by you if you are experienced in home maintenance, or, preferably, by a building-conservation consultant. Using the outline in this chapter, you may also prepare portions of the assessment, leaving unanswered questions for a consultant or specific trade specialist.

The conditions assessment is a baseline survey of the building, addressing both short- and long-term maintenance issues. Even for diligently managed maintenance programs, the conditions assessment should be updated every ten years (or less if the building has experienced severe conditions). Unless a greater level of detail is required by the owner, the assessment can reasonably be limited to immediate site conditions, the exterior envelope of the building, building structural elements, the interior, and mechanical and electrical systems.

The findings of each survey can be incorporated into the conditions assessment report as attachments. The following is a useful general outline for organizing the conditions assessment. Within the outline, each category can be further broken down by elements, with information recorded as "observations" and "recommendations" for each element.

A. Site
   1. Site Drainage
   2. Landscaping
   3. Site Paths and Paving
   4. Outbuildings
   5. Fences and Site Walls

B. Building Exterior and Structural Systems
   1. Roofing
   2. Exterior Walls, Including Exterior Cellar Walls and Floor
   3. Exterior Woodwork
   4. Exterior Windows, Doors, Porches

C. Building Interior and Structural Systems
   1. Cellar
   2. First Floor
   3. Second Floor
   4. Attic

D. Mechanical and Electrical Systems
   1. Heating, Ventilating, and Air-Conditioning System
   2. Plumbing System
   3. Electrical System
   4. Other Systems

During the field survey, access to remote areas of the house, including roofs and chimneys, will probably require a ladder. Inside, rather than have the building-conservation consultant make an extensive room-by-room survey of interior finishes, request a walk-through of the house interior to assist in locating exterior leaks (the cyclical maintenance plan can address interior finishes

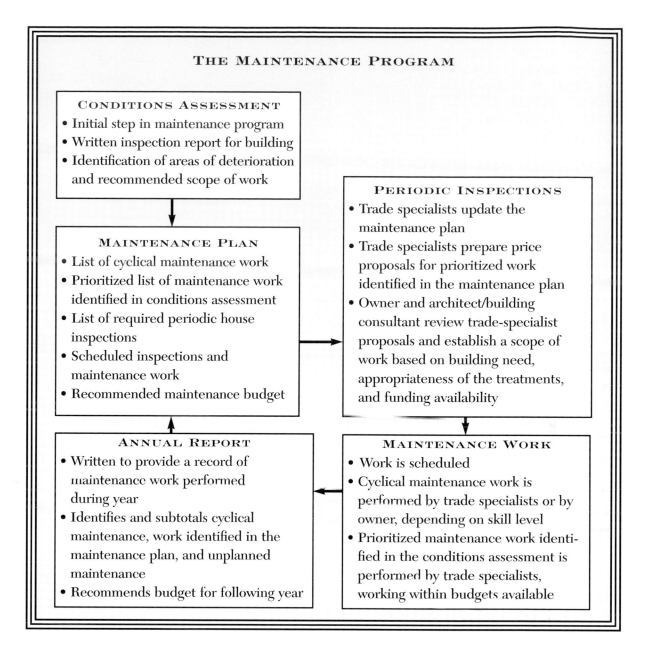

THE MAINTENANCE PROGRAM

CONDITIONS ASSESSMENT
- Initial step in maintenance program
- Written inspection report for building
- Identification of areas of deterioration and recommended scope of work

MAINTENANCE PLAN
- List of cyclical maintenance work
- Prioritized list of maintenance work identified in conditions assessment
- List of required periodic house inspections
- Scheduled inspections and maintenance work
- Recommended maintenance budget

PERIODIC INSPECTIONS
- Trade specialists update the maintenance plan
- Trade specialists prepare price proposals for prioritized work identified in the maintenance plan
- Owner and architect/building consultant review trade-specialist proposals and establish a scope of work based on building need, appropriateness of the treatments, and funding availability

ANNUAL REPORT
- Written to provide a record of maintenance work performed during year
- Identifies and subtotals cyclical maintenance, work identified in the maintenance plan, and unplanned maintenance
- Recommends budget for following year

MAINTENANCE WORK
- Work is scheduled
- Cyclical maintenance work is performed by trade specialists or by owner, depending on skill level
- Prioritized maintenance work identified in the conditions assessment is performed by trade specialists, working within budgets available

in general). Although most building-conservation consultants are not expert in the assessment of existing heating, plumbing, and electrical systems, the consultant can contribute broad observations regarding the systems. A detailed survey of the mechanical and electrical systems can then be conducted by reputable contractors who specialize in each trade.

MAINTENANCE PLAN
The maintenance plan is the primary written planning document of the maintenance program. With a written maintenance plan in place, the maintenance program can continue uninterrupted following a change in management personnel or even property ownership. The maintenance plan should be in an outline format, easily read as a list of activities to be completed. For a sophisticated maintenance-management program, the maintenance plan is the first section of a maintenance manual, which would also include extensive building, equipment, and cleaning-program data, supply sources, vendors, maintenance contractors, and information on conservation of specific historic building materials.

A written maintenance plan is vital to a successful maintenance program. To be effective, the maintenance plan must be simple and specific. Unrealistically frequent inspections and overreliance on professional consultants will make the maintenance plan unworkable. It is helpful to divide the maintenance needs among several categories.

CYCLICAL MAINTENANCE

Cyclical maintenance consists of regular preventive maintenance completed on a periodic basis to ensure the continuing performance of building components and assemblies. It includes cleaning gutters and downspouts, replacing filters on air handlers, testing storm drains, and trimming foliage in contact with the house. Most cyclical maintenance can be completed as part of required periodic inspections (see below). For example, air filters can be changed at the same time the boiler is serviced and heating system is inspected. Gutters and downspouts can be cleaned as part of the roof inspection, if the roof is inspected annually.

PRIORITIZED MAINTENANCE WORK

All nonroutine work identified in the conditions assessment should be prioritized in the maintenance plan. This might include work to ensure life safety of inhabitants (such as repairing faulty wiring, locks on doors), repair of water leaks, structural repairs, building-security work, electrical repairs, mechanical-system repairs, long-term envelope preservation work, and restoration of finishes. The initial prioritized list of maintenance work is a preliminary draft list, to be measured against the maintenance budget. High-priority items may be planned in full if the budget allows, or a repair may be made and the major maintenance component deferred, or the first phase of a multipart work item may be planned. For example, if the conditions assessment recommends replacement of the existing wooden shingle roof, but your maintenance budget does not allow for this major expense, you could repair areas of active water leakage and defer the larger project until funding can be put in place. Or, if the roof is made up of many small sections, you may replace the worst sections in the first year and the remainder of the roof in phases over a few years.

Storm damage, severe winters, and unexpected failures of mechanical equipment wreak havoc on maintenance budgets. If possible, set aside a contingency fund for such situations; even so, as with any major repair, you may have to do the work in stages.

"Before" and "after" views of the 1900 reroofing of Lafayette's quarters (Gideon Gilpin House) at Brandywine Battlefield Park, Chadds Ford, Pennsylvania, provide a historical example of cyclical maintenance. A contemporary newspaper account reported that the shingles furnished by S. R. Dickey of Oxford, Pennsylvania, were "black oak pieces [cut] into the proper shape for reduction into the shingles of three feet each," apparently matching the size of existing shingles, which were also made by Dickey some twenty years earlier.

PERIODIC INSPECTIONS

Because buildings deteriorate over time, the condition of the building at the time of the conditions assessment is a baseline for the maintenance program, not a fixed scope of maintenance work. To remain current with changed conditions at the historic house, the maintenance plan should identify recommended periodic inspections for specific components of the building. These inspections should be conducted by historic trade specialists—contractors with experience in the assessment and restoration of historic building materials—who are also capable of completing periodic repair work. With the maintenance plan in hand, the trade specialist completes a survey and submits a brief inspection memorandum and cost proposal for completing identified repairs. The owner and the preservation consultant review the

This standing-seam metal roof was installed in 1976. Lack of cyclical gutter and downspout cleaning has resulted in deterioration of both the galvanized-steel built-in gutter and large portions of the bracketed wooden cornice.

Historic-roofing specialist William Dunleavy inspects a standing-seam metal roof at the Victorian Heely House in Washington Crossing, Pennsylvania. Periodic inspections of building systems by historic trade specialists update the maintenance plan.

SELECTING
❧ A BUILDING-CONSERVATION ❧
CONSULTANT

Except in the case of houses owned by experienced preservationists, the conditions assessment should be completed by a building-conservation consultant. The consultant must be impartial and must have an understanding of historical building techniques, architectural styles, and modern building-conservation techniques and materials. The individual may be a restoration architect or a preservation consultant who specializes in historic-building maintenance and building conservation. To locate a qualified professional in your geographic area, contact several sources for references. Sources to contact include restoration directories published by historical commissions, preservation conservancies, and historic-district commissions; state historic preservation agencies; historical museums and house museums in the area; and local chapters of the American Institute of Architects.

After contacting several organizations and historic-building owners for directory listings and recommendations, a short list of qualified and recommended firms and individuals should emerge. Most directories and commission lists do not recommend one firm over another, but historic-house museums that use consultants generally are willing to comment on the performance of those with whom they have worked. When you have developed a list of qualified consultants, invite each to visit the site and submit a written scope of services and fee proposal. Consulting firms generally do not charge for this preproposal site visit.

When a consulting firm prepares a conditions assessment report for a historic site, its purpose is not only to assist maintenance planning but also (and often primarily) to support a grant application to fund the work. Such reports generally are more detailed and provide more background material than is needed for the individual historic-house owner. The most productive and cost-effective use of the professional's time is to prepare the conditions assessment in outline format, in direct and telegraphic language, and this should be made clear to the preservation consultant prior to preparation of a scope of services and fee proposal.

In evaluating the consultants' proposals, look for one who is most qualified, experienced, fairly priced, and best suited to the scope of work required. Because your long-term goal is to establish an ongoing relationship with a consultant, it is important to select a firm or individual who is both experienced in conditions assessments and in assisting historic-house owners in major maintenance work. Firms that handle projects greater than $1 million are not likely to perform well in the numerous small assignments required for your maintenance program.

inspection memorandum and cost proposal and decide upon the scope of maintenance work, if any is required.

The maintenance plan should identify which inspections are required and the frequency of the inspections. A roof, for example, should be inspected annually, while stone masonry might be inspected every three years. Some inspections will be completed as part of annual system service. The heating system, for example, can be inspected as part of an annual cleaning and tune-up. Without overburdening the maintenance budget with inspections, have the following building components inspected regularly by trade specialists:

- Roofing: Depending on the age and type of roof, every one to three years
- Masonry: Depending on the condition of masonry and pointing, every two to four years
- Exterior woodwork: Depending on the extent and condition of exterior woodwork, every two to three years. This inspection should also include exterior paint.
- Mechanical system: Annually
- Electrical system: Depending on the use of the building and age of the system, every two to five years
- Security system: Depending on the age of the system and number of problems experienced, annually. Smoke detectors should be tested annually.

ANNUAL REPORT

At the end of each year, you should write an annual report, which need be no more formal than a list of maintenance activities completed during the year, backed up by trade-specialist inspection reports, invoices, proposals, receipts, and other maintenance documentation. The annual report breaks down maintenance costs by type, including a comparison of budgeted expenses versus actual expenses for each type of maintenance. The report should evaluate the success of the maintenance program during the previous year. Were gutters cleaned out regularly? Were filters changed in air handlers? Were periodic inspections undertaken and the findings of the inspections acted upon? Was the year's prioritized maintenance work completed? Were emergency repairs quickly and efficiently addressed? Was the preservation consultant's participation valuable and professional? Were any known maintenance problems not addressed? If so, have they been added to the next year's list? The report should also assess the quality and workmanship of completed repairs in order to avoid previous mistakes and build on previous successes. Contractor performance should be noted in terms of quality of work, responsiveness, and schedule.

Although compiling them may seem tedious, annual reports provide continuity in a maintenance program, ensuring that long-term prioritized work is not forgotten, and that cyclical maintenance continues each year. On the basis of the previous year's costs, along with scheduled work in the prioritized maintenance plan, the maintenance budget for the next year can be developed. Also, a change in the person responsible for managing the maintenance program is less burdensome if annual reports are available for the new person to gain an understanding of the maintenance program and history of the building.

BUDGETING AND SCHEDULING

For the historic house, the most successful maintenance program is one that preserves the historic resource and maintains the building's historical integrity, that allows the "aesthetic life" of the building to continue indefinitely—at minimal cost. There is a misconception among building owners that maintenance budgeting cannot be done without computers and a spreadsheet or database program. In fact, maintenance budgeting for the historic house can be as simple or

The vine growing on this house adds a picturesque quality but ultimately is destructive to the wooden roof. Leaves and other organic matter retain moisture and foster rot and insect infestations, while the tendrils and stems of the vines invade gaps between elements and literally pry them apart as the vines grow. This material should be removed as part of a cyclical maintenance program.

The maintenance plan is an invaluable tool in establishing the scope of restoration work when natural disaster strikes. For example, if 30 percent of a roof is destroyed by a hurricane, the maintenance plan can be utilized to identify the most cost-efficient means of repair. If the existing roofing is asphalt shingle, but the maintenance plan calls for a major roofing replacement in five years using the original standing-seam metal roofing, instead of patching with more asphalt shingles, an entire new standing-seam metal roof may be warranted.

complex as the owner chooses, and whether or not a computer is employed as a computing tool is of little consequence to the effectiveness of the effort.

The steps in budgeting are essentially three: 1) develop a list of maintenance tasks as described in the maintenance plan, 2) assign a cost to each maintenance task, and 3) assign a desired completion date (year) for the task. The sample maintenance plan given on page 36 provides a model for developing a maintenance budget.

From the list above, a maintenance budget is established for the year. Costs for cyclical maintenance work after the first year of the program are available from historical cost data and/or from new price quotations. Costs for prioritized maintenance tasks after the first year of the program will be available from the previous year's maintenance budget. In the first year, costs are obtained from either the maintenance plan or from contractor price proposals. Costs for annual inspection tasks are obtained from trade-specialist proposals, which means that the trade-specialist reports must be completed prior to development of the budget, unless a reasonably accurate allowance can be created on the basis of historical cost data (the average cost in previous years). The cost of unbudgeted repairs can only be estimated on the basis of historical average annual costs, as a budget allowance.

Projecting maintenance costs in the form of a five- or ten-year maintenance budget enables the historic-house owner to plan for anticipated future maintenance expenses and to budget (or borrow) to cover years with major projects. If a major budgeted maintenance project, such as the roof replacement in the fictional "Heritage Hall" maintenance budget on page 37, cannot be completed in its scheduled year for financial reasons, the budget must be modified to accommodate this change. The major maintenance project might be deferred (possibly increasing the cost of the project due to increased deterioration), phased, or an alternate system considered (such as a substitute material).[2]

EVALUATING ALTERNATE SYSTEMS

Maintenance decisions are made on the basis of cost, anticipated service life, and preservation of the historical integrity of the building. When historic wooden shutters are deteriorated, two options are available to the historic-house owner: to repair the shutters or to replace them with replicate wooden shutters. One would not, for example, replace them with mass-produced, home-improvement-store-variety plastic shutters. Thus, in this case, only the cost of repair versus duplication is considered because other solutions would compromise the historical integrity of the building and would be inappropriate since they would likely not be the same size or detail as the original shutters.

However, legitimate cost-based maintenance decisions do confront the historic-house owner. The decision to repair an aging boiler or to replace it with a new, high-efficiency boiler can be solely a cost-based maintenance decision.[3] The length of the "payback" period can be calculated by estimating the annual energy savings and reduced maintenance costs relative to the annual cost of the new equipment. More sophisticated methods of economic analysis are also available but have greater applicability to larger scale maintenance decisions than normally confront the historic-house owner. For example, a university facilities department deciding between restoring or replacing six hundred windows in a historic dormitory building is more likely to utilize detailed cost-analysis methods, which compare the total cost of each window option over the service life of the window system, than would a homeowner confronted with window deterioration.

Two frequently employed methods of analysis are the uniform-annual-cost method and the present-value method.[4] Both take into account the time value

BUDGET CATEGORY	EXAMPLES	FREQUENCY
CYCLICAL MAINTENANCE TASKS	Gutter and downspout cleaning	Spring and fall
	Grass mowing	Weekly during season
	Walks and steps sweeping	Weekly (as needed)
	Window cleaning	Annually
	Boiler service	Annually
	Interior house cleaning	Varies—daily, weekly, annually
PRIORITIZED MAINTENANCE TASKS	Roof replacement	Establish a date for complete roof replacement (this could be fifty years in the future for a very durable roofing material), as well as estimated periodic maintenance prior to replacement.
	Repoint chimney	If deteriorated, establish a date for partial or complete repointing of chimney.
	Paint exterior woodwork	Establish a date for repainting exterior woodwork. Expected service life is six to seven years.
	Repair rotted windowsills	Establish a date for repair of rotted windowsills.
	Repair rusted iron fence	Establish a date for repair of rusted iron fence.
	Replace bulkhead doors	Establish a date for replacement of bulkhead doors.
PERIODIC INSPECTION TASKS	Spot repointing	Current year
	Adjust door	As soon as possible
	Reset stone paver	Current year
	Replace cracked glass	As soon as possible
	Replace fallen slates	As soon as possible
	Resolder broken flashing seams	Current year
UNBUDGETED REPAIRS	Broken glass	Emergency repair
	Repair storm damage	As soon as possible
	Replace smoke detector	Emergency repair
	Remove graffiti	As soon as possible
	Replace plumbing valve	Emergency repair
	Repair damaged plaster from plumbing leak	As soon as possible
	Improvement projects	As budget allows (for example, higher efficiency lamps)

HERITAGE HALL FIVE-YEAR MAINTENANCE BUDGET

	Service Life/ Frequency	Annual No. Occurrence	Cost per Occurrence	Annual Costs—Five years				
				Yr. 1	Yr. 2	Yr. 3	Yr. 4	Yr. 5
CYCLICAL MAINTENANCE TASKS								
Grass mowing	wkly.	26	$80	$2,080	$2,080	$2,080	$2,080	$2,080
Window cleaning	annly.	1	400	400	400	400	400	400
Gutter cleaning	twice yrly.	2	150	300	300	300	300	300
PRIORITIZED MAINTENANCE TASKS								
Roof repair/replacement	25 yrs.	N/A	N/A	$400	$400	$400	$26,000	$0
Repoint chimney	40 yrs.	N/A	N/A	0	0	3,000	0	0
Paint exterior woodwork	7 yrs.	N/A	N/A	200	12,000	0	0	0
Repair rotted sills	N/A	N/A	N/A	1,500	0	0	0	0
PERIODIC INSPECTION TASKS								
Adjust door	N/A	N/A	N/A	$50	$0	$0	$0	$0
Replace fallen slates	annly.	varies	varies	200	-	-	-	-
Resolder broken flashing seams	N/A	N/A	N/A	150	-	-	-	-
Annual inspections allowance	annly.	varies	800	N/A	800	800	800	800
UNBUDGETED REPAIRS								
Repair broken glass	N/A	N/A	$40	$40	-	-	-	-
Repair storm-damaged shutters	N/A	N/A	700	700	-	-	-	-
Annual unbudgeted repairs allow.	annly.	varies	1,200	-	1,200	1,200	1,200	1,200
TOTAL COST (Current dollars)				$6,020	$17,180	$8,180	$30,780	$4,780

Sample Analysis Using Uniform-Annual-Cost Method

The following example compares two hypothetical boiler options. This example is for illustration purposes only, to show varying initial costs, operating costs, and service lives, and does not represent expected costs for actual oil- and gas-fired-boiler options.

The comparison is made by converting the costs to a uniform annual cost, based on a 10 percent discount rate for money. The initial cost is converted to a uniform annual payment by multiplying the cost by the factor A/P for the service life of the system (taken from a table of Present and Future Value Factors for 10 Percent Discount Rate, available from cost guides such as those published by R. S. Means and listed in Further Reading; this factor will also be a feature on a financial calculator). Annual operating costs are not discounted for comparison purposes.

In this example, inspired by an R. S. Means model, an oil-fired boiler in a large historic house has failed. Two options are considered: 1) replacing the existing unit with a new oil-fired boiler, and 2) upgrading to a high-efficiency gas-boiler system. Option one includes replacing the existing oil-fired boiler and relining an existing chimney. Option two includes new high-efficiency gas-fired boilers, which are side-vented. The oil-fired option is less expensive initially ($16,000 versus $26,000), but has a shorter service life (fifteen years versus twenty years). Despite the lower annual operating costs of Option two, Option one is cheaper when the initial cost, operating cost, and service life are all taken into consideration. Option one has a uniform annual cost of $4,679 per year compared to $4,918 for Option two.

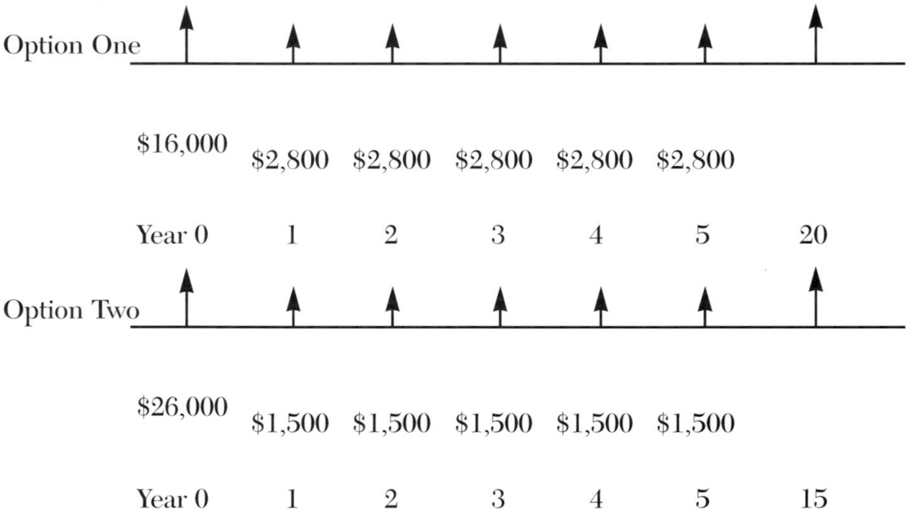

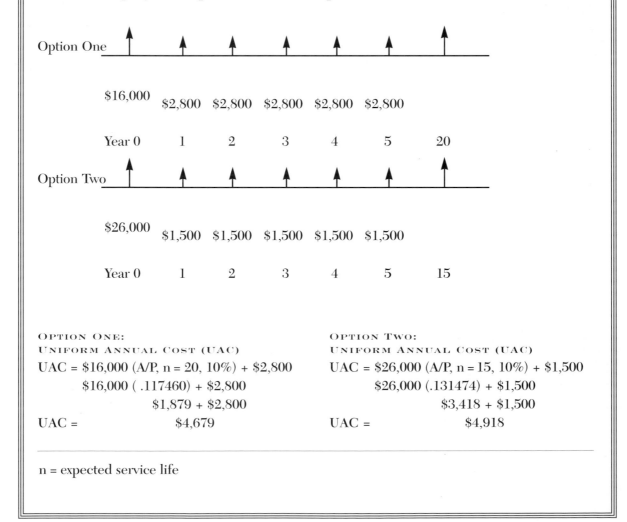

Option One:
Uniform Annual Cost (UAC)

UAC = $16,000 (A/P, n = 20, 10%) + $2,800
$16,000 (.117460) + $2,800
$1,879 + $2,800
UAC = $4,679

Option Two:
Uniform Annual Cost (UAC)

UAC = $26,000 (A/P, n = 15, 10%) + $1,500
$26,000 (.131474) + $1,500
$3,418 + $1,500
UAC = $4,918

---

n = expected service life

of money. In the uniform-annual-cost method, present and future costs are expressed as equivalent recurring cash flows. This method is typically used to compare options with differing service lives. Major maintenance costs, such as a replacement roof, are converted to annual cash flows, as are projected maintenance costs over the life of the roof. This method allows comparison of the equivalent annual cost of, for example, a terne-coated stainless-steel roof with a high initial cost and low future maintenance costs, with that of a membrane roof that has both a lower initial cost and shorter service life.

The second method, the present-value method, also requires projections of current and future costs. Future costs are converted to present costs by means of a discount factor, which for a business is equal to the anticipated return on any investment, or for a historic-house owner, the rate of borrowing money. The total present value of each option is then compared, and the lesser cost option selected.

Historic-house maintenance requires a planned maintenance program to achieve the goal of long-term preservation of the historic resource. Nowhere is the old adage "A stitch in time . . ." more applicable than to the early repair of a water leak in a historic building. Maintenance planning is self-rewarding: managed maintenance costs less than unprogrammed maintenance. Whether the initial step is a conditions assessment by a preservation consultant or writing a checklist of cyclical maintenance items, the key to increasing the effectiveness of maintenance spending is to begin planning today.

ACKNOWLEDGMENTS

The author would like to thank Barry Schnoll, architectural conservator, for his contribution to this chapter, and Hugh C. Miller, FAIA, for his comments and maintenance-cycle diagram, which provided the basis for the Sample Maintenance Plan.

Notes

1. "Cold and rational economics" is intended as a simplification. A historic house's service life has been extended because of its value as a historic resource, and that value affects economic decisions. For instance, the replacement of deteriorated historic windows with vinyl replacement windows might in the short run cost less than replicating the deteriorated sashes and restoring the wooden frames, but would reduce the value of the property—and often neighboring properties as well—in a district of historic houses. This economic rationale of appropriate preservation of historic houses is central to justifying historic district zoning.

2. The hypothetical "Heritage Hall" maintenance budget is included to present a format for budgeting and scheduling maintenance. It is not, however, intended to represent the full scope of a maintenance budget for any individual historic house. Interior cleaning and routine mechanical-system maintenance, for example, are not listed as part of cyclical maintenance.

3. If the existing boiler is frequently broken, thereby threatening the building with loss of heat and potential water damage, the decision is more than simply cost based.

4. Numerous books are available on life-cycle costing. See Further Reading.

STRUCTURAL SYSTEMS

ROBERT SILMAN

WHAT IS THE STRUCTURAL SYSTEM?

We generally say that the structural system for a building is composed of its framework and foundation. However, defining the structural system for a house is not as clear-cut as for other building types, skyscrapers, for example. In the latter case we can say that the framework is made up of the steel or reinforced concrete members such as slabs, beams, girders, and columns, and the foundations are the footings, piles and pile caps, grade beams, and walls. In a house, the framework that provides the support may serve a dual function—for example, wooden stud-bearing walls also serve as partitions and weather barriers. This chapter will deal with the structural aspects of these systems of framework and foundations.

WHY CARE FOR YOUR HOUSE'S STRUCTURAL SYSTEM?

The answer to the question above seems too obvious. If neglected, the house could become unlivable or, at worst, unsafe. Many owners are reluctant to think about structural care. For one thing, a person generally cannot see the structure of the house, which is usually concealed behind finishes such as plaster or flooring, and an owner would much prefer to spend money on visible improvements or decorative items. Second, there is the "out of sight, out of mind" syndrome at work: it is easy to ignore unseen potential structural problems. And third, many homeowners do not understand or are afraid of structural systems and therefore avoid dealing with them. This chapter will explain the necessity of good structural maintenance, describing typical systems and their common problems. Never has the adage that An Ounce of Prevention Is Worth a Pound of Cure been more applicable than in structural maintenance. The costs of removing and replacing historic finishes are often many times that of the actual structural repair.

UNDERSTANDING STRUCTURAL SYSTEMS

It would be impossible to describe here all the many possible styles and types of structures. Below are given some of the more common types and how to identify them.

The first structural distinction to look for is whether the walls of a house are solid and load-bearing. In this category are stone, brick, and adobe walls as well as solid-log walls (as in log cabins). These structures have dual-purpose walls—they both support the roof and floors and keep out the weather or serve as room partitions. In general, these walls have far more structural capacity than is required for support. They must still be maintained, however, to avoid eventual degradation. Especially critical are areas and material above window and door openings, where the structural system has been interrupted. These are generally supported by *lintels*, horizontal beams that bear on the jambs along each side. Often these lintels are of wood or steel, and if the opening is not *flashed* (waterproofed with sheet metal or a flexible membrane) properly or not flashed at all, water can attack and damage these beams. They should be carefully inspected. In masonry walls, lintels are sometimes made of large, single-piece stones. Such stones make poor beams because they are weak in tension (one side of a beam is always in tension), a state of stress that causes the beam to pull apart, and

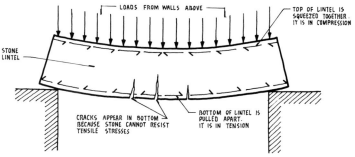

Stone is weak in tension, and the bottom of a simply supported beam is in a constant state of tension (see arrows), which can pull the bottom fibers of a beam apart. If tension forces exceed the capacity of stone to resist, cracks develop. The top of the beam is in compression (see arrows), which tends to push fibers together, but since stone resists compression forces well, it does not fail.

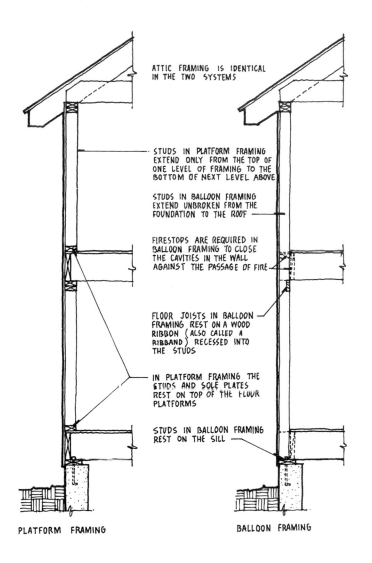

ATTIC FRAMING IS IDENTICAL
IN THE TWO SYSTEMS

STUDS IN PLATFORM FRAMING
EXTEND ONLY FROM THE TOP OF
ONE LEVEL OF FRAMING TO THE
BOTTOM OF NEXT LEVEL ABOVE

STUDS IN BALLOON FRAMING
EXTEND UNBROKEN FROM THE
FOUNDATION TO THE ROOF

FIRESTOPS ARE REQUIRED IN
BALLOON FRAMING TO CLOSE
THE CAVITIES IN THE WALL
AGAINST THE PASSAGE OF FIRE

FLOOR JOISTS IN BALLOON
FRAMING REST ON A WOOD
RIBBON (ALSO CALLED A
RIBBAND) RECESSED INTO
THE STUDS

IN PLATFORM FRAMING THE
STUDS AND SOLE PLATES
REST ON TOP OF THE FLOOR
PLATFORMS

STUDS IN BALLOON FRAMING
REST ON THE SILL

PLATFORM FRAMING

BALLOON FRAMING

In balloon framing, the studs are one piece continuous from foundation to roof, with the joists supported by a ribbon or ledger. In the platform frame, the studs are only one story high, and they are supported on the top of the platform of the floor below.

they should be checked for the presence of cracks. Openings in masonry walls are commonly spanned by *true arches* made of stone or brick segments called *voussoirs* and a stabilizing *keystone* at the central uppermost point of the arch. If the joints in the masonry have eroded or if there has been any settlement or if the buttressing action of the wall at the side of the arch is inadequate, the arch may show signs of failure such as cracking or displacement of stones or bricks. Arches often have very little rise, resulting in extremely high horizontal thrust forces that can push out a wall, particularly if the window or door opening is adjacent to the corner of a house.

A second type of load-bearing wall is not solid but is composed of closely spaced vertical wooden members called *studs*. These are generally spaced no more than twenty-four inches apart and they form a structure called either a *balloon frame* or a *platform frame*. The former was developed in the middle of the nineteenth century in the United States, where two events of the Industrial Revolution combined to make it possible—the commercial sawmill (water or steam powered) and the nail-making machine. The balloon frame uses many small studs (nominally two by four or two by six inches), is connected with many nails, and can be erected by relatively unskilled labor since it requires few, if any, complicated joints or saw cuts and the individual pieces are lightweight. The corresponding floor beams, called *joists,* are supported on the ledger strips and are also nailed to the sides of the studs. The platform frame, a later variation on the balloon frame, is made of similarly close-spaced wooden studs in the walls but each story is built independently on the platform created by the floor structure of the story below. Studs are only one story high, with sill and cap plates; floor and roof joists bear directly on the cap plate. The platform frame allows for green lumber to shrink uniformly in the plane of the floor, thus avoiding a gap caused by large drying shrinkage where the floor joists would meet the studs in the balloon-frame house. Lateral bracing of platform-frame stud walls is usually achieved by means of a sheathing nailed directly to the studs, but let-in diagonal bracing (inset into studs that are notched) can also be found in houses sheathed with boards rather than plywood.

The last type of timber structure is the *heavy-timber frame,* found commonly in houses built before 1870 and even in many houses after that date. This type of framing is derived from barn structures of Northern Europe and North America, where heavy timbers (often nominally eight by eight inches or more) are fastened together with complicated joints such as mortise and tenon, timber pegs, and shiplaps. Metal fasteners are usually few and far between. Between heavy beams run floor joists or *roof purlins* (beams that usually are parallel to the ridge and eave of the house) that are covered with plank floors and plank or batten roofs. Exterior walls are laterally braced by means of diagonal *knee braces,* between posts and beams, or occasionally with full-height *X-braces.* More closely spaced studs or joists may be used to fasten finish materials such as lath and plaster or wooden siding or paneling, but these often do not serve a major structural function.

Timber roofs generally are pitched and take many configurations. The *gable* roof, with slopes in both directions, is the most common. At the ridge in

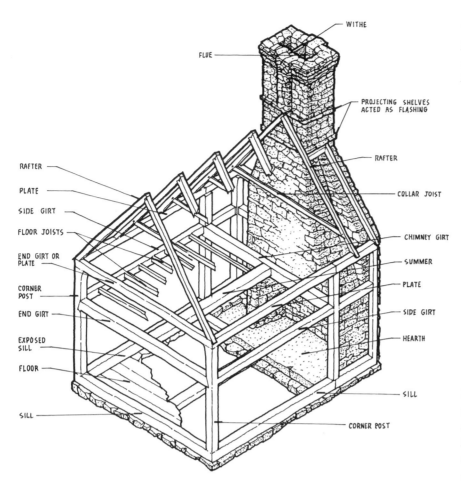

WITHE

FLUE

PROJECTING SHELVES ACTED AS FLASHING

RAFTER

RAFTER

PLATE

COLLAR JOIST

SIDE GIRT

FLOOR JOISTS

CHIMNEY GIRT

END GIRT OR PLATE

SUMMER

CORNER POST

PLATE

END GIRT

SIDE GIRT

EXPOSED SILL

HEARTH

FLOOR

SILL

SILL

CORNER POST

Considerable carpentry skills are required to make proper joints for heavy-timber frames. Large timbers are used for beams, girts, and posts; smaller members are used for rafters and floor joists.

In the drawing below, the thrust from the rafters pushing out on the knee wall cannot be resisted by the attic floor because the rafters bear at a higher level on the top of a knee wall that has no resistance to the lateral thrust forces.

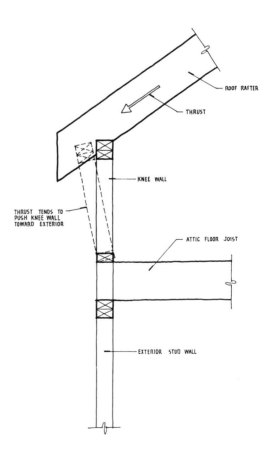

ROOF RAFTER

THRUST

KNEE WALL

THRUST TENDS TO PUSH KNEE WALL TOWARD EXTERIOR

ATTIC FLOOR JOIST

EXTERIOR STUD WALL

most timber-framed houses, the rafters butt either directly against each other or against a small ridge board. The ridge provides no vertical support, only horizontal support created by an equal and opposite thrust. It is important that this equal and opposite force be maintained. In gable roofs, a considerable horizontal thrust can develop at the bottom or eave of the sloping rafter. This is conventionally resisted by nailing the attic floor joists to the rafters and thus countering the thrust by creating a tie across the bottom of the roof.

Problems with gable roofs occur when the design simplicity has been violated, disrupting the concept of equal and opposite force. Often subsequent alterations, particularly the installation of dormers, destroy this equilibrium. The most common culprits are rafter ends that do not bear (carry weight) at a level even with the attic floor, but rather much higher. Here the outward thrust is resisted only by the stiffness of the wooden stud wall projecting above the attic floor, which is often woefully inadequate. Collar beams or *ties*, usually in the upper third of the rafter, do not provide much tying or tensile resistance; rather, they act more like compression struts to prevent the roof from sagging inward.

Shed roofs, sloping in one direction only, do have vertical support at both top and bottom ends of each rafter and therefore are not subjected to the same horizontal thrusts as gable roofs. In some gable and shed roofs, the rafters span from side to side rather than from top to bottom. Although this eliminates any tendency for thrust, it can compromise the effective strength and stiffness of the rafters if they are canted to have their short face parallel with the slope of the roof, rather than being installed vertically. In heavy-timber frames, the ridge is usually a heavy beam capable of providing vertical support to rafters or purlins and thus eliminating horizontal thrust in those members.

Floors in balloon- and platform-framed houses are made of closely spaced joists covered with nominal sheathing (about an inch thick), sometimes tongue and grooved, or, in more modern houses, with plywood. The sheathing, or *sub-floor,* is usually nailed to the joists, and often the nail holes have enlarged over time, causing the floorboards to squeak. In heavy-timber frames, if the floor or roof beams are spaced closely enough, say eight feet maximum, then often there are no such purlins or joists: heavy two- or three-inch planking is used to span and form the floor surface.

Beginning near the turn of the twentieth century, the use of steel and cast iron found its way into large-house construction. Primary floor systems made of steel beams (first rolled commercially as I-beams in 1893), or their earlier wrought-iron counterparts, are generally connected to each other using clip angles and steel bolts. Supporting columns may be round or square cast-iron members with molded *bearing seats* (projections to support ends of beams) and often with integrally cast decorative trim. In modern steel frames, the columns are rolled-steel H-sections. Floors may be of timber joists, or terra-cotta tile or brick arches topped with concrete slabs, or cast-in-place rein-forced-concrete slabs formed around and encasing the beams. Generally, steel frames were originally designed by an architect or engineer and thus have capacity to resist normal residential loading with little problem.

In rare instances one will find a house frame made of reinforced-concrete slabs, beams, girders, and columns. This is an unusual choice for single-family homes because concrete is inherently weak in tension and must be reinforced with steel rods placed strategically in areas where tension stresses may occur. Producing a concrete frame is very labor-intensive as it requires the building of a complete set of forms into which the concrete is poured but which are later removed and discarded.

CLUES TO STRUCTURAL PROBLEMS

The most significant indicator of a serious possible structural problem is a crack. Cracks indicate movement of some kind. Many movements in a house are normal and of no structural consequence. These often occur due to changes in temperature and humidity, which concurrently cause building materials to expand and contract. These cracks are generally described as "hairline," and they are simply a cosmetic nuisance. Often, attempts to patch these cracks fail and the cracks open again during the next cycle of tempera-ture or humidity change. The structure has simply formed permanent reliev-ing joints; the house owner probably will have to accept these and not worry that they are a symptom of structural damage. (Even then, masonry cracks may need to be sealed or pointed to prevent water damage; see pages 75–76.)

What type of cracks indicate potential structural damage? Stepped cracks in a brick or stone wall, chimney, or foundation wall indicate a differential set-tlement of the soil or foundation support. Soils can settle many years after a house is built due to changes in subsurface conditions. Most of these are caused by flowing underground water that carries away fine soil particles, caus-ing the larger stones or particles to readjust. Frost heave (an upthrust of earth caused by freezing of moist soil) can also cause settlement if there is insuffi-cient depth of embedment of the bottom of the footing and the soil is a fine-grained one susceptible to heave. In a house built on fill that contains organic materials, or built on wooden sills, the organic supports may eventually rot out and collapse. And finally, in houses originally built on a compressible soil such as organic silt, soft clay, peat, or marshland, the settlement may continue for many years.

Another significant indicator is a straight-line crack across a plaster ceiling in the middle of a room perpendicular to the direction of span of the floor joists above. This indicates that the joists have deflected or sagged to such an

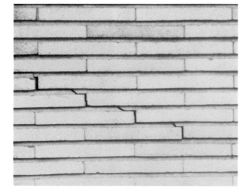

The stepped cracks in this brick wall indicate settlement of the building's foundations. The left side is settling downward with respect to the right side, causing the wall to crack in the stepped pattern as shown.

extent that the plaster cannot maintain its integrity and must crack to relieve the high stress. Similarly, horizontal cracks in basement walls near their mid-height indicate a weak foundation wall.

Vertical cracks in plaster or other walls should be investigated. Those occurring near corners of walls indicate separation of walls at an intersection. This may result from an improper attachment of timber, insufficient *keying* of masonry, or differential movements between different parts of the house. Vertical cracks often appear at locations where previous alterations have occurred (such as where door or window openings have been filled in) and the joint between the materials has not been made sufficiently strong to bridge without cracking.

Cracks in houses with concrete slabs, beams, or walls are common. Many of these cracks form just after the concrete is poured and are related to shrinkage forces in the newly cured material. Another common category of cracks is caused by thermal movement—expansion and contraction with changes of temperature. Both types of crack can be difficult to patch permanently because the concrete structure must relieve pent-up stresses, and the cracks indicate natural locations to do that. Both types are generally small cracks and, although they may be cosmetically unpleasant, they usually cause little harm to the structure. If water is allowed to penetrate into these small cracks, however, and particularly if the water freezes, the cracks may expand and become more serious.

It is very important to keep water out of concrete structures. Concrete, by itself, is not waterproof; it requires a protective covering or coating. If water comes into constant contact with reinforcing bars or structural-steel beams, causing them to corrode, the resulting very high *jacking* (prying-apart) forces against the surrounding concrete will cause it to crack or *spall* (chip) due to the by-product of oxide expansion. If the concrete has been made with cinder aggregate (a residue of coal-burning power plants), as was common from about 1910 to 1935 in many urban areas, water may react adversely with the unburned sulfur to form a weak solution of sulfuric acid, which further accelerates corrosion of steel and deterioration of the concrete matrix. Cracks from these latter causes are very serious and usually require immediate repair, which includes the chipping back of concrete to expose the damaged reinforcing, repair or replacement of this reinforcing, and, finally, repairs to the concrete itself.

The second major category of potential danger signals is that of observable movement. Deflected (sagging) floors or roofs are the most common. There is a difference between the *strength* and the *stiffness* of a structural member. While the former may be adequate, often the latter is not. Older houses were often designed using a minimum of materials, resulting in floor joists or beams that are not stiff enough for their spans. Over a period of time they may sag in the middle, causing the floor/ceiling sandwich to deflect. Roofs also often show signs of sagging as it was common to use undersized rafters or purlins in construction. Another type of movement is where one side of a room or a building is lower than another— there is a pronounced slope to the floors and the doors and window frames may be *racked* (misshapen so that the sides remain vertical but are no longer at right angles to the top and bottom). One cause of this could be differential soil settlement. Another common cause is inadequately sized girders in the basement that have deflected, causing the structure of the house above to move downward. Deterioration on one portion of a house, such as rotted sills, also can result in sloping floors.

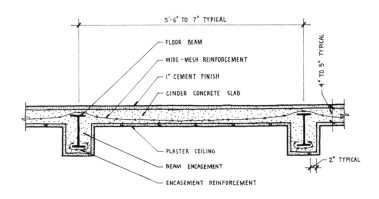

A concrete floor slab is formed and cast between and around structural-steel beams. The slab is reinforced with wire mesh draped over the tops of the beams and sagging downward at the midspan between them.

Another clue that structural damage might be impending is the presence of water or staining inside the house. Roof leaks are the most common, but water can also penetrate around windows and doors; at gutters, drains, and downspouts; at projecting decorative elements such as cornices, water tables, bay windows, dormers, and railings; and at foundations through the walls, window wells, joints between basement floors and walls, or up through the floor itself. A further source may be condensation resulting from moisture-laden air coming into contact with a surface cool enough to cause a change from water vapor to liquid water, at the so-called dew point. Mold or mildew is a sign of excessive moisture from either leaking water or from condensation.

And finally, an owner of a historic house must be on guard against attack to wooden members by animals or fungi. Chewing rodents such as squirrels or rats can make holes in wood, as can nesting birds. Insects like termites, carpenter ants, bees, or powder-post beetles may leave signs of their work, such as wood dust, termite tunnels, and pinholes in the sides of members. Mold and fungus can appear in many forms, usually as discoloration, and are often accompanied by odor. Wooden members in contact with or in close proximity to the ground should be checked carefully; these include sills, floor joists in shallow crawl spaces, and posts going down into the earth. Many of these symptoms cause the wood to become soft and spongy when probed with a sharply pointed awl or ice pick.

How to Avoid Structural Problems

Maintenance

Many structural deficiencies can be avoided or prevented. The most important defense is proper maintenance. Among maintenance issues, the single most significant is keeping water and moisture out. Clearly the roof, walls, windows, doors, foundations, drains, and other structural elements must be kept functional or altered to perform properly. Roofs should be checked by a skilled roofing contractor or consultant at least once every three years. Caulking and flashing around windows and doors must be maintained. Roof drains, including gutters and downspouts, must work properly, particularly the outflow directed away from the house into site drains or dry wells. The grade adjacent to the house must be sloped away from the foundation walls. This is particularly important in houses without gutters, where roof water pours down directly along the foundation line. In these cases it is often necessary to install a layer of relatively impervious clay several inches below the top of the ground to prevent water from seeping into the soil near the foundation. And finally, site water that runs along the surface of the ground from hillsides should be diverted before it reaches the house by means of swales, ditches, or underground interceptor-curtain drains (see page 48).

To prevent condensation, you must ensure that the air does not contain high levels of water vapor. Adequate ventilation will help dry out potentially damp areas; mechanical fans can be used to good advantage. In roof and attic areas, air should be allowed to enter through vent holes or strips at the lower part of the roof near the eaves and exit near the top at the ridge through a ridge vent, gable-end vent, or dome-type exhaust vent. In older houses, often no provision was made for venting roofs, crawl spaces, or other areas prone to dampness or condensation. It can be difficult to install vents of adequate size without changing the visual appearance of the historic building, and a good deal of planning may be needed for the design of a proper ventilation system. Houses that have been retrofitted with insulation and particularly with vapor barriers can experience dramatic increases in the moisture content of the air and in resulting condensation. Houses whose roofs

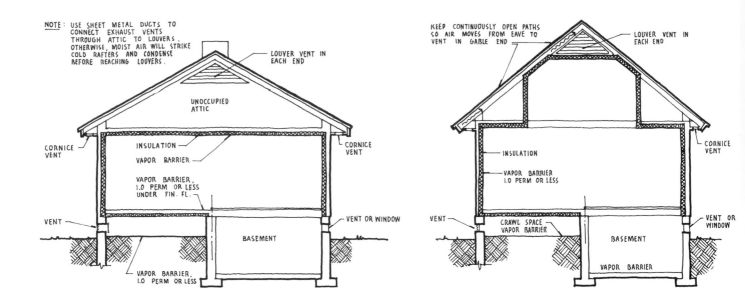

have been rebuilt also often show increased problems with condensation if the original roof "breathed" whereas the new one has been built more tightly to modern standards.

If an existing roof or floor is *understructured,* that is, it does not possess sufficient strength or stiffness to carry the loads imposed on it, you can offset the problem in several ways. Remove snow or heavy debris from roofs before it reaches a predetermined depth by shoveling it off or by using snow-melting equipment. Either can be a very dangerous activity on a sloping roof, so take great care if you choose to do this yourself. Inside the house, limit the load on floors that are not adequately designed. Place only lightweight furniture on the affected area, not heavy bookcases or storage trunks, and do not allow large numbers of people to congregate there. If the floor in a historic house is used in a way that is different from its originally intended purpose (e.g., if it is now a museum with public occupancy), the structural capacity of the floor members should be reviewed by a structural engineer.

ESTABLISHING A MONITORING PROGRAM

Regular maintenance to prevent serious structural damage should go hand in hand with a monitoring program to determine whether existing cracks or deflections are active or have stabilized and will go no further. The simplest of monitoring efforts is to use an ordinary tape measure or ruler to determine whether changes have occurred since the beginning of the program. It is important to establish fixed reference points to measure from, and it is vital to maintain extreme accuracy. Ideally, the same person should perform the measurement each time and should record the results in a logbook. To measure deflection, stretch a string tightly between two points and read the measurement at the lowest point of the structure. For a large, wide crack, draw two parallel lines, one on each side of the crack, and record the distance between the lines.

Often movements are too small to be recorded with a tape or a ruler that measures only to the nearest sixteenth of an inch. In this case, crack widths can be monitored using a commercially available transparent plastic card with a series of line widths printed on it. The card is laid over the crack until the width of the line matches the width of the crack. This simple optical comparator is quite efficient and inexpensive, but it does involve a certain amount of judgment. More sophisticated and permanent devices to record crack movement can be installed. The most basic of these is a two-piece plastic crack monitor costing less than fifteen dollars, which is glued to each side of

In timber-framed buildings, crawl spaces and basements are vented with grilles or windows. Attics are vented with cornices or eave vents that draw in outside air and end-gable louver or ridge vents that permit hot air to escape.

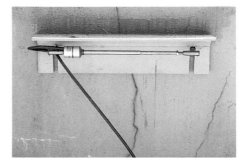

This crack in a concrete parapet at Frank Lloyd Wright's Fallingwater in Mill Run, Pennsylvania, is being monitored continuously and remotely with an electronic crack monitor. Data from crack monitors and tilt meters is fed into a portable computer that can be addressed remotely by modem. Readings are taken and information is downloaded on a scheduled basis.

the crack. A scale to read movement directly is printed on the plastic and it can be recorded on a regular basis. For difficult-to-reach cracks or for very sophisticated applications, electronic crack monitors can be glued across the cracks with a wire extending to a console. This type of crack monitor can be read on a regular basis or can be connected to a personal computer that will automatically read it at prescribed intervals. Data is stored in the computer and can be printed out upon demand or can be accessed remotely through a modem. The tilt or lean of a structural component can also be recorded, either visually or electronically, using a tiltmeter.

In a sophisticated measuring program, it is desirable to record the temperature and humidity as well as movement in order to correlate these movement changes to atmospheric conditions. Moisture in building materials can be monitored using a handheld meter or with permanently installed humidity gauges; the latter can be recorded and remotely accessed if desired.

Periodically review the history of any cracks or deflections. When was the area last painted? Was the crack patched at that time and has it reopened since then? Does a door bind rather than close easily, and has this condition changed recently? Are some cracks clearly newly formed, never before observed? If your monitoring and review program uncovers ongoing movement, seek professional advice immediately.

Prevent damage from insect infestation or fungal growth through periodic inspections and, if necessary, chemical treatment by a professional trained in this field. In most areas there are reliable exterminating contractors who can identify active infestation and can provide services to treat the soil and the building. If you wish an independent opinion prior to hiring an exterminator, some wood pathologists specialize in identification and treatment specifications for insects and fungi.

WHERE TO FIND HELP

The most important aspect of finding help is to be sure that the problem is correctly assessed and evaluated. If you are not able to diagnose the cause properly, seek professional help. The first reaction of many homeowners is to call a building contractor or repair service. This may or may not work out well depending upon the firm's specific experience. You may want to consider retaining a specialist in historic preservation, such as an architect, engineer, or conservator with known experience in dealing with problems similar to those at hand (see page 33). While this may seem to be an unnecessary expense initially, hiring a design professional can save money in the long run: by avoiding costly false starts, by having the work properly supervised, and by remaining true to principles of historic preservation.

Local preservation organizations usually maintain directories of qualified firms of architects, engineers, conservators, and contractors. Personal referrals are of course very valuable. Whatever the source, carefully check the firm's references. If possible, also visit sites where work has been conducted.

STRUCTURAL REPAIRS

Anyone making repairs to a historic house should conform to the recognized principles of preservation—minimizing disturbance to original fabric, minimizing intervention and ensuring that interventions are reversible, and differentiating clearly between original structural members and newly installed ones. Very often the requirements of the repair program, for example reinforcing the existing structure, involve a serious intervention, often of irreversible character, so it must be given a great deal of careful consideration before any action is taken. The potential remedies given below are intended as guidelines only. *Always* consult a structural engineer to make sure that any planned repair or reinforcement will be adequate to do the job.

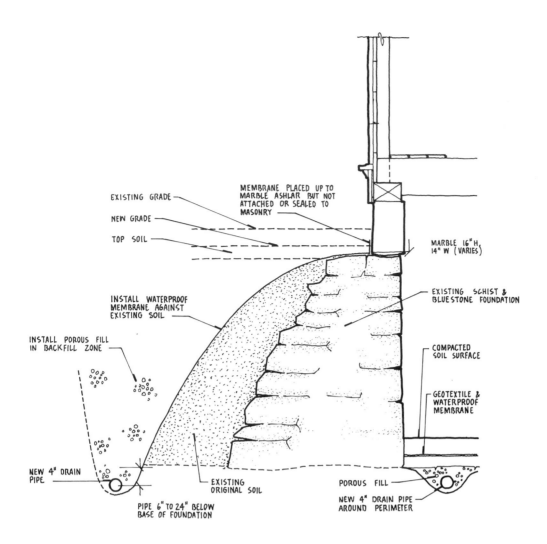

EXISTING GRADE

MEMBRANE PLACED UP TO MARBLE ASHLAR BUT NOT ATTACHED OR SEALED TO MASONRY

NEW GRADE

TOP SOIL

MARBLE 16" H, 14" W (VARIES)

INSTALL WATERPROOF MEMBRANE AGAINST EXISTING SOIL

EXISTING SCHIST & BLUESTONE FOUNDATION

INSTALL POROUS FILL IN BACKFILL ZONE

COMPACTED SOIL SURFACE

GEOTEXTILE & WATERPROOF MEMBRANE

NEW 4" DRAIN PIPE

EXISTING ORIGINAL SOIL

POROUS FILL

NEW 4" DRAIN PIPE AROUND PERIMETER

PIPE 6" TO 24" BELOW BASE OF FOUNDATION

If basement walls are bowing inward, first make sure that there is not a significant amount of water in the earth fill outside the wall. If not, and it is desired to reduce the lateral load on the wall, excavate the existing earth for the full depth of the wall and for a distance away from the wall equal to the depth, then fill the void with a lightweight aggregate manufactured from expanded clay or shale, a product used in the concrete industry. It weighs only half as much as earth, is free-draining, and is inert. Since the lateral pressure is a direct function of the weight of the backfill, the force pushing on the wall can be reduced by as much as 50 percent.

If groundwater flows are large, as from surface runoffs down a hillside, then you could place a curtain drain a short distance away from the basement wall. This is composed of a trench about two feet wide excavated to about the same depth as the basement or cellar floor. A perforated plastic pipe, usually four inches in diameter, is laid in the bottom of the trench, which is then carefully backfilled with crushed stone or gravel. If the surrounding soils contain fine particles such as silt, you may first line the trench with a geotextile fabric that inhibits the ingress of soil but permits water to flow through it. The perforated pipe is connected to a dry well, storm drain, or open-to-the-air outlet. If the curtain-drain solution is not indicated, but it is still possible to excavate along the outside wall, then you may wish to place a nonwoven geotextile drainage mat along the foundation wall, with a footing drain of four-inch perforated pipe laid in the bottom of the trench and backfill placed similar to the curtain drain. If excavation is not possible, there are commercially available a number of foundation waterproofing systems that inject material such as bentonite clay slurry through holes drilled into the ground alongside the founda-

Water flowing toward a stone foundation wall can be intercepted by a trench excavated to the same depth as the wall, lined with porous geotextile fabric on the side of the trench away from the wall and impervious membrane next to the wall, filled with porous crushed stone with a perforated drainpipe at the bottom connected to a positive outlet.

The rotted end of this timber beam is being reinforced by inserting a steel tee into a slot cut into the bottom of the beam. Missing portions of the beam are then replaced with epoxy paste and the steel tee is bonded to the remaining sound wood.

Wood epoxy resin adhesive is being pumped into holes drilled into the beam in order to bond the steel tee.

tion walls; the success of these systems varies widely (see page 78). And finally, if it is not possible to work on the outside of the house, water problems can sometimes be successfully dealt with from the inside by installing sump pits with pumps or underfloor French drains (perforated pipe surrounded by gravel and flowing into the sump or out to grade) or applying proprietary waterproofing compounds to the inside surfaces of walls, floors, and joints.

If all work must be confined to the inside of the house, walls can be buttressed or otherwise structurally strengthened in various ways. Additional supporting members can be added side by side with existing ones in a technique called *sistering;* however, it is often difficult to install the new members in one piece and still achieve sufficient bearing at each end of the supports. Furthermore, the existing members are usually deflected significantly whereas the new members are level: this causes a dilemma because the profile of the ceiling will have to change to accommodate the new straight joists or beams. An alternate approach is to reduce the span of existing members by introducing new girders or columns somewhere along the length of the span, ideally near the center. These new

members will most probably be in a plane below the existing ones, dramatically altering the appearance of the building. This may be perfectly suitable in unoccupied basements.

The myriad of potential reinforcing techniques include bolting steel plates to wooden members *(flitch plates),* screwing and gluing plywood sheathing to wooden joists *(stressed skin),* welding steel plates or tees to existing steel beams, and bonding fiberglass or carbon fiber to existing wood or concrete *(composite construction).* In exceptional cases, where an existing structural member is significantly undersized and understrength, the member may be replaced with a substitute of much higher strength that maintains an existing architectural profile or dimension. The classic example is to substitute a steel beam for a wooden one. Other wood substitutes include glue-laminated timber, laminated veneer and strand lumber, aluminum, steel cables or rods, steel pipes or tubes, and reinforced concrete, including precast lintels.

Wooden members deteriorated due to rot or insect infestation may be restored by drilling many small, closely spaced holes into the spongy wood and injecting an epoxy resin. At the same time, fiberglass rods or steel plates or tees may be inserted into holes or slots and bonded with epoxy, creating a new, reinforced composite member. This technique, called Wood Epoxy Repair (WER), can be used to advantage when you wish to keep the existing profiles of structural members intact. WER is also useful in repairing nonstructural items such as windows, trim, and railings.

Carefully evaluate cracks in masonry before making any repairs. If it seems likely that the crack is due to thermal movement and is a relieving joint, then patching it with mortar makes very little sense because it is likely that the crack will reopen at the same location. In such cases the mortar should be raked out and a backer rod and sealant (whose color matches the mortar) installed, carefully following the manufacturer's recommendations.

If the crack has stabilized, then it can be filled with a patching mortar. In selecting a mortar for pointing or patching, be careful to match not only the color and texture of the existing mortar, but also the strength and elasticity of the historic original. High-strength mortars will crack more readily due to thermal stresses (older buildings did not have control joints; modern ones should have them every thirty feet as recommended by the Brick Institute of America) or due to slight differential movements from settlement or load. (See Exterior Masonry for details.)

For cracks in structural concrete and, in rare cases, in masonry, repairs can be made with an epoxy-filler repair system designed to restore the full strength of the base material. Because so many epoxy products are available, it is often a good idea to call the manufacturer for technical advice on proper viscosity, surface preparation, temperature, pot life, installation, and cleanup. Generally, holes are drilled along the length of the crack at a spacing compatible with the viscosity of the epoxy, which is then injected from a pump, cartridge, or squeeze bottle. Be sure to follow the manufacturer's recommended safety precautions when using epoxies.

So many possibilities and factors contribute to the assessment of structural problems that it is not possible to establish formulas for dealing with every situation. The most important factor is making the proper diagnosis with the participation of all parties—the homeowner, the design professional, and, if possible, the contractor. In reaching a correct solution, due consideration must be given to the principles of historic preservation. However, it may be necessary to compromise some of these to achieve the required solution. The best advice to the owner of a historic house is to maintain the building properly to forestall structural damage, or, at worst, to address structural problems at an early stage before they escalate into major repair projects.

ROOFS

JOHN R. VOLZ

Roofs are not a very glamorous topic. Certainly one does not immediately think of the roof when a particular historic building is mentioned. Nevertheless, a roof and its drainage system are a building's primary defense against water—whether it be in the form of rain, snow, sleet, or ice— and thus are one of the building's most essential elements.

Roofs serve other important functions as well. In the Southwest, the mass of many historic roofs provides insulation against solar heat gain during hot days while heating the interior during cold nights through a property known as *thermal lag*. Essentially, heat is absorbed by the roof during the day, but the mass of the roof is thick enough to prevent the heat from entering the interior of the building until the evening hours when outside temperatures drop. At night, the roof mass is warmer than the surrounding air, and it radiates heat until the mass comes to equilibrium with the outside temperatures. At daybreak, the cycle begins again. As outside temperatures climb, the roof is cool, protecting the interior.

In southern climates, the roofs are designed to improve the building occupants' comfort by providing shade with porches and large overhangs and to mitigate the effects of heat and high humidity through ventilation. Typically, large attics with vents or dormers provide an environmental buffer between the interior and exterior of the building. In the days before central air-conditioning, the ceiling of the central stair hall often opened onto a windowed monitor at the apex of the roof. When the windows of the monitor were opened, hot air exhausted through the monitor, creating a chimney effect that moved air through the house.

Historically, roofs also served as a primary water-collection device and, as such, were critical to the survival of the building's inhabitants. Rainwater was collected by the gutters and piped through the downspouts to cisterns. Most systems had a valve that allowed the roof water to bypass the cistern. Normally the homeowner would allow the rain to wash the roof, gutters, and downspouts for a few minutes before directing clean water to the cistern.

Roofs are not only a primary functional element of a building but also a primary design element. The surface area of a roof compared to the surface area of the wall is often a large percentage of the total visual image of the building. Thus, the roofing material and its color, texture, and pattern are important character-generating elements. The roof's shape (gable, hip, mansard, gambrel, etc.) and pitch also contribute substantially to the style and character of a building. Other features, such as dormers, monitors, belvederes, widow's walks, turrets, chimneys, and even roof vents, interrupt the plane of the roof, adding visual interest. Eaves and overhangs provide a visual transition from lower roof surface to vertical wall surface and can be set off with

Roofs often define the architectural character of a house. The monitor, or lantern, at the top of this roof is not only ornamental, but it also brings light into the house and provides ventilation.

brackets, consoles, moldings, verge boards, and other elements. Roof edges are frequently embellished with decorative caps, finials, cresting, weather vanes, snow guards, snow boards, and railings. Even functional elements such as gutters have various profiles and add definition to the roof edge, as do leaders, downspouts, boots, and splashes associated with the gutters. In the Southwest and elsewhere, for example, many houses feature roofs concealed behind parapet walls. These roofs are drained by spouts or canales, whose pattern and decorative appearance are a significant design element of the building.

Each of the elements mentioned above contributes substantially to the appearance, function, and overall character of a roof. When performing maintenance on the roof, therefore, it is important that each element be treated in a manner that will ensure its preservation. If it becomes necessary to replace an element, the design and material of the replacement should match the visual characteristics of the original material as closely as possible. In assessing the roof of a historic house, it is also important to know which elements and materials are significant and which are not, and what significant elements, if any, are missing. A local archive or library may provide historic photographs or other information that will assist in making this evaluation.

Roof maintenance is generally a process that needs to be performed by experienced professionals. Problems of access, height, slope, and slippery roof surfaces are safety conditions with which most homeowners are not equipped to deal. Also, the techniques of repair often require specialized tools and replacement parts if the repair is to be done correctly. Yet it is important that the homeowner understand the mechanisms of deterioration and the needs of the roof and drainage system in order to be able to work with the roofing professional to keep the roof in optimum condition.

INSPECTIONS AND THE MOST COMMON MAINTENANCE NEEDS OF ROOFS

Dirt from the air, leaves, and other matter from adjacent trees tend to collect on roof surfaces. Wind and rain deposit the dirt and organic matter in valleys, gutters, and on flat portions of the roof, inhibiting the flow of rainwater as it tries to drain. Typically this matter collects in low spots or at the tops of the downspouts, creating a dam that prevents rainwater from draining from the gutter. In

The patterned polychromed slate, the cresting, the bell-cast mansard roof form, the decorative dormers, and the projecting bays contribute to the architectural character of this 1880s house.

extreme cases, the gutter fills to capacity, forcing rainwater to flow over the edges of the gutters. When this occurs, the water may flow over the flashings at the edge of the roof and into the structure of the eave, wetting the wood and eventually causing rot in the structure. Vines growing on a building can block a gutter, creating a similar problem. Also, the vines can grow under the roofing, dislodging the roofing material as the diameter of the vine increases with maturity.

Other problems can occur when a roof is not properly maintained. Often the weight of collected water and wet debris causes gutters to sag or deform. When this occurs, joints in the gutters open, allowing water and debris to leak onto the *fascia*, the flat horizontal board below the edge of the roof to which the gutter is attached. This type of leak initially causes staining on the fascia; over time, the constant wetting causes paint to peel and allows rot to deteriorate the fascia. Additionally, organic matter in gutters tends to retain moisture and decompose, creating mild acids that contribute to the corrosion of metal gutters and flashings. If not corrected, the corrosion will eventually create holes, which leads to staining, paint failure, and, eventually, wood rot. Large collections of organic matter also can become the home to insects, such as wood ants, creating another type of building deterioration.

The eclectic architectural forms of late Victorian houses required roofs that were geometrically complex and featured the use of many types of materials.

It is important to conduct periodic inspections to ascertain the conditions of the roofing materials, flashings, and drainage components. Casual inspections can be performed from the ground with the assistance of binoculars. Each surface of the roof should be viewed systematically for problem spots. Inspections during a rain will also show where drainage systems are working and not working. Record the location of any suspicious conditions on a sketch plan of the roof so they can be investigated in more detail.

Begin with a general overview of the roof, looking for gross defects, such as cracked, broken, missing, or eroded shingles, or obvious maintenance problems, such as collections of leaves in the valleys, noting any concerns on the roof plan. Starting at the roof edges, either top or bottom, check joints in materials for leaks. Telltale signs of leaks include streaking on or staining of materials, corrosion of metals, peeling paint, and rotted wood. Peeling paint at a specific spot on the *soffit* (underside) of an eave is a sure indication that the roof and/or gutter is leaking. Similarly, paint peeling from the fascia of the eave under a gutter suggests that the gutter may be leaking. If there are stains on the gutter adjacent to a joint, it is probable that the metal joint has opened and is leaking.

Next, survey the flashings at dormers and chimneys, checking to see if any are displaced, bent, or missing, or if sealants on the top edge of the flashings are deteriorated (cracked and/or separated from adjacent materials). Also, check the surface of flashings and other metal elements to determine if they are corroding. Rusting metal indicates that the protective coating has worn off and that new protective coatings are needed. If not applied in a timely fashion, the material will corrode until it fails.

While looking at the roof, study the tops of the chimneys. Are there shifting or missing bricks? Is the mortar flush with the face of the brick, or is it deeply recessed? If it is deeply recessed, are there small piles of sand on the roof surface? If the answer to any of these questions is yes, then the chimney needs repair and repointing.

Check roof accessories such as cresting, lightning-protection systems, railings, finials, and ridge caps, to name a few, for condition as well. If these items are leaning, sagging, deformed, discolored, or corroded, it is probable that they need repair. More important, their connections to the roof may be deteriorated and leaking. Because these roof accessories are part of the architectural character of the roof, they should be repaired if at all possible, not removed.

After surveying the exterior, check the interior of the house for evidence of leaks. Typically, water stains will appear as brown irregular circles on ceilings and walls or as long irregular streaks that taper on the walls as they approach the floor. The location of the stains can assist in locating the leak. For example, if the stain is above a fireplace, it is probable that the chimney flashings are leaking. On the other hand, water can enter the roof system at one point and travel downward for some distance along the roof rafters or deck before it drops onto a ceiling below. In such cases, it will be necessary to trace the leak in the attic. Typically, wood decking and structure will have dark stains or will be rotting at the location of leaks. (One does need to ascertain if stains are from a current leak or an old problem since corrected.) Also, if water is leaking into the attic at one location, running down the structure, and dripping in another location, stains on the structure should be apparent and should indicate the precise entry location.

An inspection of the attic is a good idea in any case. Try to survey the attic's roof structure for leakage during a rain, when the exact locations of leaks generally can be pinpointed. Then compare the interior leak locations with the conditions documented on the exterior to assist in defining the specific location and cause for the leak.

After the survey is complete, prepare a list of maintenance needs and establish priorities for maintenance and repair (see Establishing a Maintenance

PRODUCT	SUBSTITUTE FOR	CONSIDERATIONS
Fiber Cement	Slate Wooden Shingles Asbestos Cement	Colors often fade Surface-applied colors less durable than integral color Lighter weight than slate, cement, and clay tile Heavier weight than wood and metal More fireproof than wood Not all are suitable for all climates Some are susceptible to water absorption and leaching of cement ingredients Limited shingle sizes, thicknesses, and patterns Underlayment required
Concrete	Wooden Shingles Clay Tile Slate	Colors often fade Heavier weight than clay tile, wood, metal, asphalt, and fiber cement Lighter weight than slate More fireproof than wood Limited shingle sizes, thicknesses, and patterns Underlayment and battens usually required
Clay Tile	Wooden Shingles Slate	Colors do not fade Lighter weight than slate and some concrete Heavier weight than wood, metal, asphalt, and fiber cement More fireproof than wood Limited shingle sizes, thicknesses, and patterns Underlayment and battens usually required
Metal	Clay Tile Wooden Shingles Slate	Coatings subject to damage Subject to impact damage Lightest weight Underlayment required Limited shingle sizes, thicknesses, and patterns
Asphalt Shingles	Wooden Shingles Slate	Colors do not fade Lighter weight than most wood, slate, clay tile, fiber cement, and concrete tile More fireproof than wood Limited shingle sizes, thicknesses, and patterns; least acceptable visually Underlayment required Cheapest product Fifteen-to-forty-year warranties
Composite	Slate	Lighter weight than slate, clay tile, fiber cement, and concrete tile One shingle size, thickness, and pattern Underlayment required

Program). Leaks and severely deteriorated materials should receive immediate attention, while deteriorating conditions that are not causing immediate damage to structure and finishes should be addressed as soon as possible.

Because the roofs of historic buildings are unique and often have unusual features or elements, it is important that those who work on them respect and value those materials and elements that are essential to the historic character of the roof. Roofers and craftsmen should have previous experience with the specific roof material needing repair. Generally, it is a good practice to seek estimates for repairs from at least three roofing contractors. Require each to submit a written list of no fewer than five recent projects in which the same roof materials were repaired or installed by the workers who will be working on this job. Ask for references and check them all.

When working with original roofing materials, avoid simply replacing them, unless the material is deteriorated beyond repair. Keeping original materials preserves a piece of history, as well as the character and integrity of the building. If it is necessary to remove and replace some or all of the original roofing materials, those materials that are in good condition should be salvaged and reinstalled. As much as possible, group the salvaged original items and reinstall them in a single location on a principal facade. Replacement elements should match the original as closely as possible in material, shape, dimension, thickness, color, profile, sheen, finish, exposure, and texture. If matching replacement elements cannot be found, patch those original elements in good condition with the original materials removed from an inconspicuous spot on the roof, inserting suitable replacement elements in the inconspicuous spot. When replacement materials do not match the originals exactly and not enough of the original elements remain to cover the roof area completely, distribute the replacement materials among the original materials as required to produce a uniform appearance.

Although matching replacement roofing materials usually exist, local building codes or the cost of historic roofing may prohibit use of the historic material. When the use of substitute materials is necessary, the new roofing material should match the original material as closely as possible in scale, tex-

The ends of this board-and-batten roof have curled, creating a separation at the eave through which water can enter. Gaps in the roof have collected sufficient debris to allow the growth of small trees.

The shed-roof portion of this house retains its original nineteenth-century standing-seam roof. The recently installed wall flashing is not in keeping with the historic detailing or craftsmanship and detracts from the appearance of the building.

Concrete roof tile appeared in the 1920s. It was first used to simulate wooden shingles at Colonial Williamsburg. The moss and lichens growing on the shingles need to be removed.

ture, color, dimension, thickness, and overall character. In selecting a substitute material, a visual compromise will be necessary, but with care the degree of compromise can be minimized. Fortunately, there is a growing industry dedicated to producing "look-alike" roofing materials. Many of these products are only slightly less expensive than the real material, so be sure to compare prices. Also, because many of the substitute materials weigh more than historic roofing materials, the cost of reinforcing the roof structure must be factored in with the cost of the substitute material itself. Suggested types of substitute materials are outlined on page 55.

As repairs are made, try to match historic installation details as closely as possible. The color gradation of slates or tiles, the pattern of slates or shingles, the exposure of shingles or slates, and the design of valleys, hips, and edges have great impact on the appearance of the roof. Of similar importance is the retention and repair of roof accessories such as cresting, lightning rods, and finials. When it is necessary to correct defects in the original roof design, the modifications (expansion joints, new flashings, crickets, larger gutters and downspouts, etc.) should be made as inconspicuously as possible. These kinds of design changes are best made by an architect or roof consultant familiar with historic roofs.

When the roofing is removed, inspect the structural support elements covered by the roofing (sheathing, battens, nailers, rafters, etc.) and roofing felts, if present, and repair or replace as needed. When making repairs, take care to use the proper fasteners and flashings. The size and length of nails or other fasteners should be sufficient to anchor the roofing securely to the deck. Both fasteners and flashings should be fabricated from a noncorrosive material that is appropriate for the specific type of roofing being repaired. Hot-dipped galvanized-steel nails are generally appropriate for asphalt shingles, whereas copper or stainless steel is often used for cement, tile, or slate. It is also critical to ensure that dissimilar metals—of flashings, fasteners, accessories, or metal shingles—are isolated from one another to prevent electrolysis, which causes corrosion of the metals. For example, water washing off a copper roof onto an aluminum sash will cause the sash to corrode.

Avoid the temptation to smear on roofing tar, caulk, or other visible coatings. These types of repair are not only unsightly but also are only temporary fixes. When applied over certain metals, they can cause excessive corrosion and necessitate complete replacement in the future. Generally, it is much better to repair metals by soldering the defective element. Pieces of sheet metal or roofing felt can be used over or under shingles and tiles until suitable replacements can be installed.

Installation techniques for roofing materials should comply with the material manufacturer's written instructions and local building codes. This is particularly important in areas where high winds or earthquakes are a consideration. Communities in such areas often have special requirements for anchoring metal roofs, shingles, and tiles in a manner that will reduce the potential for the roofing to leave the roof surface.

Some older roofing materials, such as cement shingles, roofing felts, and roofing cement, contain asbestos. In many

Original roofs may survive in attics of later additions. Here, a projecting comb ridge is preserved in this fragment of a mid-nineteenth-century wooden-shingle roof.

cases, asbestos-containing roofing materials should be left in situ, undisturbed if possible. If repairs are needed and the materials must be disturbed or removed, the work must be performed by specially trained contractors. Laws governing these materials vary from state to state, so homeowners who suspect that their roofing materials contain asbestos should contact their city and state health departments for information on applicable procedures, names of licensed contractors who can test and remove the hazardous materials if appropriate, and legal disposal sites.

Be sure that the roof remains watertight at all times. If it is necessary to remove roofing elements during repairs, install heavy plastic, tarps, or roofing felt over the repair area and integrate it securely with the edges of the remaining roofing to prevent water from leaking into the structure. It may be necessary to underlay plywood or other material to support the protective covering. Too often temporary protection fails due to the weight of water ponding upon it or from wind that dislodges it.

TYPICAL TYPES OF DETERIORATION AND METHODS OF REPAIR FOR SPECIFIC ROOFING MATERIALS

CLAY, CONCRETE, OR METAL TILE

Roofing tiles can be damaged from the impact of hail, tree branches, or roofers walking on them to make repairs. Once deformed, cracked, or broken, the damaged tile will allow water to enter the roof structure, affecting nailers, fasteners, and, possibly, the structure itself. The damaged tile also can slip or be lifted by a high wind, causing impact damage to tiles below. In cold climates, ice may build up under tiles and cause breakage during the freeze-thaw cycle.

Often the structure itself can contribute to roof leakage. If it is underdesigned, the weight of a tile roof may cause sagging or deflection, which may cause gaps between individual tiles, creating possible leaks. If unchecked, water and rot will destroy the structural integrity of the wood, causing tiles to become loose and, in extreme cases, the roof structure to collapse.

Failure of fasteners is one of the most common problems with tile roofs. Wooden pegs, such as those used in the seventeenth and eighteenth centuries, rot. Iron or steel nails are corroded by tannic acid from wooden battens and sheathing or by electrolysis if used with a shingle or flashing of dissimilar metal. If the installer did not use a fastener of sufficient length to penetrate the sheathing or batten, or if he missed the batten or sheathing when nailing, the tile is not adequately secured to the roof structure.

Materials and manufacturing techniques affect the durability of tiles. The clay or concrete used in tiles determines their color, strength, and chemical stability. The fabrication process also affects the density, porosity, and durability of glazes and other finishes. If a ceramic tile is underfired, it may be too weak to withstand the freeze-thaw cycle, or it may be too porous and subject to damage from water. Similarly, if glazes are not well adhered, they tend to flake from the body of the tile, exposing its interior to damage from water.

Tiles fabricated from painted galvanized (zinc) iron or steel frequently corrode when the paint coating is not maintained. Corrosion becomes particularly acute where the protective galvanized coating is damaged at seams or where the shingle is nailed to the deck during installation. Unpainted galvanized metal shingles will also begin to rust when the protective galvanized coating erodes due to weathering, exposing the steel underneath. To prevent corrosion the shingles must be painted with a rust-inhibiting paint.

Most tile roofing is designed to shed water, not to provide a waterproof roofing. As a result, tile roofing usually has an underlayment of *roofing felts* that provide a secondary water barrier. Over time, these felts may become brittle and crack, allowing water to enter the roof structure even when the tiles themselves are in good condition. Roofing felts generally last between thirty and fifty years. Usually the felts are checked when there is a leak and there are no other obvious problems. If the felts are found to be defective, then they must be replaced. While the tile is off the roof, the deck should be inspected and repaired as needed. Use of a waterproof underlayment is a wise investment, and a variety of products are available. Most common are reinforced rubberized asphalt products.

To protect fragile roof tiles from damage by foot traffic, roofers often use ladders hooked onto the ridge or wood planks secured to the deck to support and evenly distribute their weight while making repairs. If the tiles are too fragile to allow these methods of access, it may be necessary to remove several rows of them to provide safe access to the problem areas. Tiles should be removed carefully by cutting the fasteners holding the tiles in place with a slate ripper or hacksaw blade inserted under the tile. As the tiles are loosened and lifted, they should be numbered sequentially, removed, and carefully stored until they can be reinstalled.

If only one or two tiles are being replaced, it may not be possible to nail them to the structure as done originally because adjacent original tiles will cover the nail holes. The replacement tile can be secured in place by one of several methods. A tab of double-thickness copper stripping (or of other compatible metal if repairing a metal shingle) can be nailed to the sheathing below the tile and bent over the bottom edge of the tile after it is slipped into place; a slate hook, or *tingle,* can be used in the same way. When using these replacement methods for clay or cement tiles, it is a good idea to supplement the fastener with a daub of roofing mastic or adhesive applied to the bottom surface of the tile.

If more extensive tile removal is required due to failure of fasteners, extensive breakage, or failure of the underlayment, original tiles in good condition should be salvaged and numbered on a diagram so they can be reinstalled in their original location if practical. Even if the tiles will not be reinstalled in their original locations, it is important to document the placement of the tiles by type, size, and color. Also, the location of specialty pieces such as ridge or vent tiles or closure pieces should be documented to facilitate reinstallation and to allow an accurate restoration of the roof. Documentation is something that the homeowner should require the contractor to do. Many contractors will not want to do this and will charge more. At a minimum, the homeowner and/or the contractor should take detailed photographs of the roof before any tiles are removed. The photographs can be used for a visual comparison of the roof before and after repairs.

Once the roof deck is exposed, it should be inspected for deterioration and repairs made as needed. The deck should then be covered with new roofing felt or a heavier duty waterproof underlayment, such as rubber roofing membrane, to protect it during reroofing and to provide an extra measure of protection once the tiles are reinstalled. Since valleys, ridges, and the edges of the roof are particularly vulnerable to leaks, a double layer of felt or a single layer of the waterproof underlayment at these areas is advisable.

Damaged or deformed metal tiles, particularly those made from copper, can be repaired. An experienced sheet-metal worker can literally beat the metal back into its original profile using *sand beds,* leather bags filled with sand, and special tools. Holes and cracks can be repaired with solder or strips of new metal soldered to the back of the tile. Although this is a laborious process, it is usually more economical than reproducing the metal tile.

Finding matching replacements for clay or concrete tile can be difficult. Often the name of the manufacturer and model number of the original tile are stamped on its back or edge. When supplied with this information, along with photographs of the tile and samples, today's roof-tile manufacturers often can provide suitable replacements. Several of these companies have been in business since the turn of the century and are still producing many of the older tile shapes. Unfortunately, not all of the historic tile shapes are in production, and the colors of new tiles may not match the historic tiles. It may be necessary to custom fabricate replacement tiles to match original colors, profiles, or special shapes.

A good source for used tiles is a tile-locating firm. These firms maintain a national network and are generally successful in finding matching tile. Local building-salvage companies stock materials that were used in the area and may have what is needed. Unlike the manufacturers of new tile, these firms do not provide material warranties for the products supplied.

SLATE

Slate is one of the most attractive and durable roofing materials. Although used in Jamestown, Virginia, as early as 1625, slate roofs were most popular in this country during the late nineteenth and early twentieth centuries. United States slates come in a variety of colors: gray, blue-black, black, various shades of green, deep purple, red, and mottled varieties. Depending upon their composition, they are classified as *fading* or *unfading*, according to their color stability, and have various durabilities.

Mineral impurities in the slate, primarily calcite and iron sulfides, affect how it weathers. Over time, these impurities react to form gypsum. Since the gypsum molecule is larger in volume than the molecules of calcite or iron sulfide, its formation creates stress in the slate, which results eventually in *delamination*, or cracking of naturally occurring faults in the slate. Initially, the gypsum appears on the surface of the slate as a white haze. As the chemical reaction continues, larger quantities of gypsum leach to both the top and bottom surfaces of the slate. Concurrently, the slate loses strength and toughness and absorbs more water, accelerating deterioration and becoming more susceptible to breakage and cracking. Generally, dense slates with low porosity or low calcite content tend to weather slowly. Conversely, slates with high calcite content or high porosity tend to weather more rapidly.

Installation details also affect the durability of slate. Roofs with steep pitch shed water more effectively than those with lower pitches and, as a result, provide less opportunity for water to be drawn under slates by wind or capillary action. The drier the slate remains, the less opportunity there is for chemical weathering. Generally, slate should not be used on roofs with a *slope* of less than 4:12. The slope of the roof is the amount of rise per unit of horizontal width. A 4:12 slope means that the roof rises four inches in height for every twelve inches in horizontal width. One roof, for instance a gambrel roof, may have several slopes. For slopes of 4:12 to 8:12, the slates should lap under the second slate course above by four inches. For slopes of 8:12 to 20:12, a three-inch minimum lap is needed. For slopes over 20:12, a two-inch lap is required.

Improper nailing and lapping of slate will cause early failure. Nails that are driven too tightly will crack the slate, and nails that are not driven tightly enough will puncture the slate above. Exposed nails provide a point of entry for water. Ferrous nails rust and, when severely

A hailstorm damaged these copper shingles.

To repair the roof, the copper elements were numbered, removed, and taken to a sheet-metal shop. Dents were removed from each element by hand using a sand bed (leather bags filled with sand) and specially shaped wooden blocks.

The underside of this roof shows how early tile roofs were installed: with pegs projecting through tile shingle and hooked onto the top edge of the shingle lath.

corroded, will allow the slate to slip from the roof. When slates are laid so that they lap the joints in the course below by less than three inches, water can seep through the joints and nail holes into the structure. This condition not only creates leaks, but it also provides moisture necessary for chemical weathering.

Slate deterioration can also be caused by several forms of mechanical damage. Once chemical weathering has begun, thermal expansion and the action of frost can accelerate delamination. Strong winds can lift and drop slates if they are not properly nailed, causing them to break or crack. The impact of tree limbs or workers walking on the slate can cause breakage or slippage of the slate.

Damaged slates can be removed by cutting or pulling the nails with a slate ripper. If the slate is tightly wedged, it may need to be punched with a slate hammer and pulled from its position with the sharp point of the hammer inserted into the hole. A replacement slate that matches the old slate is slid into place and held in position by one nail inserted through the vertical joint between the slates in the course above and about one inch below the bottom exposed edge of the slate two courses above. A piece of copper flashing, measuring approximately three inches wide by eight inches long, is inserted under the joint between the two slates above and over the new nail hole to prevent water from entering the hole. In climates where snow and ice do not accumulate on roofs, a copper strip can be nailed to the deck just above the top of the slate in the course below. After the replacement slate is slid into position, the end of the strip can be folded over the bottom edge of the slate to hold it into position.

Slates should not be repaired with mastics or sealants because these materials become brittle with age and fail, allowing water to enter. They are also unattractive and make future repairs more difficult.

Replacement of individual and small groups of slates is a viable repair procedure. If more than 20 percent of the slates on a roof or portion of a roof are deteriorated, however, it probably makes more sense economically to replace the entire roof. This is particularly the case when the slate exhibits advanced chemical weathering and is at the end of its service life.

If it is necessary to completely reroof or to acquire matching new slate for repairs, the new slate should match the color, texture, thickness, and dimension of the original slate as closely as possible. Additionally, the replacement slate should be sound and resistant to chemical weathering. Slate meeting the S-1 grade as defined by the American Society of Testing Materials is of the highest quality, with high strength, low absorption, and high chemical stability. Unfortunately, many slates that were used historically do not meet the rigorous standards of the S-1 grade. Also, many slate suppliers misrepresent their slate as S-1 when it does not meet all of the testing requirements. If a substantial amount of slate is required, it is best to have representative examples of the new slate tested by a reputable testing agency to ensure that the material is as represented.

Gypsum is leaching through the surface of this late nineteenth-century slate and causing delamination of the surface. The replacement slate is held in place with a metal strip.

Often, deteriorated flashings and roof accessories are the true cause of leakage rather than the slate. When this occurs, slates adjacent to the flashings must be removed and stored during replacement of the flashings.

While exposed, the deck should be inspected for rot. Have deteriorated wood replaced with new wood of similar dimension as the original. It may be necessary to *shim* (level) the new material since modern wood is thinner than old milled wood. The replacement material should be firmly secured to the roof structure with corrosion-resistant nails. At hips, valleys, and intersections with vertical elements, consider installation of a self-adhering waterproof membrane in lieu of the more traditional felt since it will provide a more durable layer of protection against leaks. Use of a heavier waterproof underlayment is almost always advisable if the homeowner can afford the cost. As a percentage of the total cost of a slate or concrete- or clay-tile roof, the cost of underlayment is small.

The repaired or replacement flashings should be installed over a rosin-sized slip sheet that has been placed on the self-adhering waterproof membrane. New flashings should be fabricated from an appropriate weight or gauge of corrosion-resistant material, such as copper or terne-coated stainless steel, that is visually and galvanically compatible with the old flashings. Dissimilar metals should not be used or must be isolated from one another since the more electronegative metal will corrode rapidly due to galvanic action. Once the new flashings are in place, the salvaged slate can be reinstalled, restoring the roof to full service.

WOOD

Wooden shingle roofs were the most common residential roof type until the early twentieth century. The shingles lasted from fifteen to thirty years, depending upon the quality of wood, environmental conditions, and level of maintenance. Until the advent of sawmills, shingles were hand split from logs and tapered and dressed smooth with a drawknife. Shingle-making machines were developed by the nineteenth century and, after the turn of the century, sawn shingles became common. Early shingles were made from the rot-resistant heartwood of local trees. Today, western red-cedar heartwood is considered the best shingle material because of its high natural rot resistance and ready availability. Redwood, white cedar, white oak, and cypress are also used for shingles but are less common.

Forms of wooden-shingle deterioration include erosion, buckling (called *curling* and *cupping*), cracking (or *checking*), and decay. Corrosion of nails can also result in roof failure. Physical erosion of wooden shingles occurs from exposure to weather. Over time, ultraviolet sunlight breaks down wood fibers, turning them gray in color. The freeze-thaw action loosens the deteriorated fibers. Rain softens the fibers and washes away the loose ones. All exposed surfaces, including the space between shingles, are subject to erosion; thus, thicker wooden shingles normally outlast thinner shingles.

Checking is a separation of the wood fibers, along the grain and across the growth rings. There are two types of checking. *Weather checking* occurs on *flat-grain* shingles, which are cut from wood in a manner that places the growth rings of the tree parallel to the face of the shingle. When a flat-grain shingle has been exposed to the weather for some time, swelling and shrinkage from moisture fluctuations create stress in the *rays*, or dense tissue that radiates from the center of the log to the bark, perpendicular to the growth rings. Over time, the stress causes small cracks at the rays. As the wood erodes, the cracks widen. Eventually, the stress is relieved by complete separation of the wood fibers. Since wide flat-grain shingles are especially susceptible to this type of cracking, it is best to use shingles that are less than six inches in width.

Weather checking is accelerated in shingles that are wet when installed. Stress will be created in the rays as the shingle dries and the wood shrinks. If the shingle is held tight by two nails, the stress will be relieved by cracking, often over the gap or joint in the course below.

Wind checks are caused by natural damage to the growth rings of the living tree. Wind checks might also be called *seam checks*. They are radial cracks, often overgrown by callous tissue, caused by wind, lightning, frost, or other action that damages the cambium layer and creates bark inclusions. Wind-damaged wood appears as light streaks ending in a wrinkled-looking grain; bark inclusions appear as dark streaks along the grain. Both types of damage create weakness along the grain (growth rings) of the wood and may cause cracks in *vertical-* or *edge-grain* areas of shingles, which are cut from wood with the growth rings perpendicular to the face of the shingle and parallel to the shingle's sides.

Curling and *cupping* are caused by the swelling and shrinking of the wood in the direction of the growth rings as it absorbs and loses moisture. The exposed end of the shingle curl shrinks while the underside of the shingle remains wet and swollen. The shrinkage of surface causes the end to lift and curl as the shingle dries. Cupping occurs as the curved rings are shrinking and trying to straighten out. Both curling and cupping are more typical in flat-grain shingles because the growth rings parallel with the shingle's surface slow down the movement of moisture through the thickness of the shingle.

Wood decay (rot) is caused by fungi that use wood as food. Typically, these decay-causing plants attack the outer wood of a tree, or *sapwood,* which lacks the natural fungal-resistant chemicals found in heartwood. Once decay starts, it will spread to adjacent shingles and support structure unless the affected shingles are removed quickly. If left unchecked, the decay will destroy the structural integrity of the wood.

Fungi must have moisture, in addition to air and food, to thrive. Decay is encouraged by conditions that do not allow the shingles to dry. Wooden roofs that are in shade or that have collections of leaves on them are candidates for problems. Similarly, wooden roofs with interlaced felts, solid decks, or occupied spaces directly below will be more subject to decay than those without felts and those on shingle lath with a ventilated attic below. Most older (and historic) wooden-shingle roofs were installed without felts. The shingles were nailed or pegged to wooden lath, which was spaced according to the exposure of the shingle. The underside of the shingle was largely exposed to the attic, allowing it to dry rapidly. Modern installations on plywood and/or with felts interlaced between shingles slow the evaporation of water, allowing the moisture content of the shingle to remain at a level that encourages rot-fungus growth. Algae, mosses, or lichens growing on shingles are a sign that the moisture levels of the roof are high enough to support rot fungi.

In maintaining a wooden-shingle roof, the most important thing that can be done is to keep the roof clean and dry. Both the shingle surfaces and the keyways between shingles should be hand-brushed or power-washed periodically to remove moss, lichens, and accumulations of debris. Take care not to erode the surface of the shingles or to drive water under the roof. Diluted bleach solutions and other chemicals can be applied to the wood to remove and inhibit the growth of mildew and algae, as well as moss and lichens. Because many of these materials are corrosive and/or toxic to plants, animals, and humans, carefully follow the manufacturer's written instructions for mixing, application, setting time, rinsing, and safety precautions. Treated shingles will need to be recoated periodically (according to the manufacturer's recommendation) to maintain the effectiveness of the treatment.

Once the roof is clean, trim adjacent trees to reduce shade on the roof and possibly increase air circulation, which facilitates drying. Prune limbs in direct contact with the roof surface to reduce collections of organic matter and prevent physical abrasion of the shingles from rubbing.

Severely damaged or loose shingles identified by the maintenance inspection must be removed carefully to avoid damage to adjacent shingles. A thin tab of galvanized stripping, or *babbie,* can be nailed to the shingles below the replacement shingle and bent over the bottom edge of the new shingle after it is slipped into place.

New shingles used for repairs should match the size, shape, thickness, finish, and wood species of the existing shingles. The replacement shingles should have vertical grain, even if the remaining historic shingles have flat grain, with minimum of sapwood and defects. The visual difference between flat and vertical grain is minimal, particularly from the ground, after the shingles have weathered. Shingles labeled "no. 1 grade" should be 100 percent clear heartwood, with 100 percent vertical grain. Use of lower grade material is not cost effective; however, if using a lower grade of wooden shingles is unavoidable, trim sapwood and defects from the edges. To reduce cracking, the shingles ideally should be no wider than six inches and no narrower than four inches. Most existing wooden-shingle roofs will not be original material.

If large areas of shingles must be replaced, those in the center of the patch should be hand-nailed with hot-dipped galvanized shingle or box nails of appropriate gauge for the shingle size. This requires a maximum of two nails per shingle, placed not more than three-quarters of an inch from each edge. Nails should be hand-driven so the head is close to the wood but does not crush it. Place nails at least an inch higher than the butt line of the course above so that nailheads are protected from weather. The space between shingles should be one-eighth to three-eighths of an inch to allow for swelling of shingles; they will buckle if there is not enough room. The joints between shingles at succeeding courses (sidelap) should be offset by no less than one and one-half inches and should not be in line for at least three courses. The exposed portion of the shingle should match the existing (original) shingles in dimension and shape. The shingles at the top of the patch, adjacent to the existing ones, will need to be secured with babbies. The visual contrast between the existing and new shingles can be reduced by spraying a mixture of one pound of baking soda and one gallon of water on the new shingles. With a few hours of exposure to the sun, the new shingles should turn gray.

On roofs where more than 20 percent of the shingles are deteriorated, consider the option of total replacement. When replacing shingle roofs, be aware of local building codes, which must be followed. In some jurisdictions, wooden-shingle roofs are not allowed. If confronted with this situation, the homeowner may apply for a variance, citing the historic qualities of the building. Often building officials will allow use of pressure-treated, fire-resistant wooden shingles. Assess the life expectancy of the wood and the treatment before installing fire-resistant shingles. If this approach is unsuccessful, consider using an appropriate substitute roofing material (see table on page 55).

METAL

The use of metal roofing in the United States during the eighteenth century was limited to roof surfaces that were not suitable for wood, tile, or slate shingles, as well as for gutters, flashings, conductor heads, and downspouts. Early on, imported copper or lead was used for roofing sheets that were joined with either flat or standing seams. By the 1840s, United States production of copper had risen significantly. In the early years, it was used mostly on public buildings due to its high cost. As local production increased, the price of copper dropped and its use increased. Copper's resistance to corrosion and its malleability made it a popular roofing material. It was used for flat- and standing-seam roofs, pressed into decorative shingles and crestings, and made into weather vanes, finials, hips, and other decorative elements. Similarly, by the mid-nineteenth century, United States production of lead increased sufficiently to satisfy the demand for roofing materials.

Sheet iron was produced in this country shortly after the Revolution. Corrugated iron was available by the 1830s and, by the 1850s, galvanized iron was a very popular roofing metal. Galvanized iron and steel were used for machine-pressed shingles, flashings, roof crestings, and finials. Roof ornament was often made from wrought or cast iron.

Tinplate iron was also imported for roofing from the late eighteenth into the late nineteenth century. It was used for joined-panel roofs, machine-pressed-shingle roofs, and flashings, valleys, ridges, hips, gutters, downspouts, and dormers. After rolling mills were established in this country, tinplate roofing became one of the most common roofing materials. *Terne* plate, which is an iron plate dipped in an alloy of lead and tin, also was popular in the nineteenth century and is often confused with tinplate. Zinc came into use in the 1820s but was never widely used.

Metal roofing deteriorates from chemical action by corroding, pitting, erosion, and streaking. Sources of chemical attack include air pollution; acid rain; acids from plant materials growing on roof elements; alkalis from lime mortars or portland cement that wash down the roof from masonry chimneys, walls, and parapets; or tannic acids from wooden sheathing under the metal or from red-cedar or oak shingles. Corrosion also can occur from *galvanic action,* when two dissimilar metals, such as iron and copper, are in contact with each other or with an electrolyte such as water. Ferrous metals (iron and steel) rust unless they are painted or plated with tin, terne, or zinc. The metal will corrode if the coatings are not maintained. Corrosion becomes particularly acute at seams, where the metal is bent, or where the metal is nailed to the deck during installation.

Metal roofing can deteriorate by metal fatigue caused by expansion and contraction of the metal in response to thermal changes. Typically this type of deterioration is found at joints, bends, or protrusions in the sheathing below. Lead is subject to *creep,* a condition where the metal sags in the direction of flow due to the force of gravity. Roofing elements of large size and thin gauge are more susceptible to fatigue than elements fabricated of small sheets and thicker gauges. The proper size and gauge depend upon the type of metal. Metal manufacturers and trade associations have guides for selection of proper gauges for specific uses. (See also Preservation Resouces at the back of the book.)

Metal roofs can be damaged by the impact of hail, workers walking upon them, or structural movement of the building. Hail often creates depressions in the metal. If struck with enough force, the metal can crack. More typically, the impact damages the protective coating on ferrous metals, allowing rust to form. Similarly, workers walking on a metal roof can crack soldered seams or bend standing seams, causing joints to open. The weight of ladders used to gain access to the roof can cause gutters and edge flashings to bend or deform, stressing joints and causing them to open. If used on a metal roof surface, the feet of a ladder can permanently deform or tear the metal if the roof surface is not protected. Buildings respond to expansive soils or inadequate foundations by shifting or settling. Such movement will stress flashings and metal roof systems, causing seams to open or the metal to deform.

It is at roof edges or where they interface with gutters and flashings or other elements such as cresting that movement from expansion and contraction is greatest. Often joints at these locations are created by lapping metal over metal. If the length of the lap is insufficient, or if the lap is sloped contrary to the flow of water, a leak will occur. The movement of lapped metal can damage paint or galvanized coatings, precipitating corrosion. Anchors through the metal may become loose, creating a leak; or may tend to resist movement caused by thermal expansion, tearing the metal; or, if they are not compatible with the roofing, may create corrosion from electrolysis.

Generally, however, metal roofs will last indefinitely, if properly installed and maintained. As with other roofs, the secret is to keep the roof surface as clean and dry as possible. Also, coatings on ferrous-metal roofs must be maintained to prevent corrosion.

Needed repairs should be made by experienced sheet-metal mechanics. Holes, tears, open joints, and other defects should be repaired with solder whenever possible. It is difficult to solder weathered ferrous metals, but good mechanics often can effect lasting repairs with careful preparation of the surface and use of proper materials, adequate heat, and patience.

Corrosion on ferrous metals, if not too severe, can be arrested by the application of a rust-inhibiting coating. First the corroded surface should be cleaned to bright metal with a wire brush or fine-grit sandpaper; then the surface should be inspected to ensure that the corrosion has not created holes through which water can enter. Immediately afterward, metallic dust should be removed and the metal coated.

Avoid using mastics, particularly on ferrous metals. Over time, the mastics will react with the metal, causing corrosion. They also crack and tend to retain moisture, which will accelerate corrosion. Mastics are hard to remove and make it difficult later to make long-lasting repairs with solder.

In some cases it may be necessary to replace portions of the roof that are too deteriorated to repair. The extent of replacement will depend upon the type of metal and its overall condition, the type of seams, and the capability of local craftsmen. When the replacement is made, it is important that the underlayment is also replaced properly. Flat- and standing-seam roofs should have a rosin-sized slip sheet between the metal and the underlayment. Terne metal roofing, however, should *not* be placed over roofing felt or other waterproof underlayments; rather, it should be back-primed with a rust-inhibiting paint before it is laid. Corrosion-resistant metals, such as copper and terne-coated stainless steel, can be laid over roofing felts covered by rosin-sized paper.

Within the past ten to fifteen years, a variety of proprietary metal-roof-coating systems have been developed. These systems are designed as retrofit roof systems for prefabricated metal buildings whose roofs have failed. The materials and quality of each vary, but these systems offer the potential for extending the life of historic metal roofs when no other means of repair is available. The successful application of these systems requires the proper preparation of the metal surface. Loose or otherwise defective coatings must be removed. Corroded areas must be cleaned properly and primed with a rust-inhibiting primer provided by the manufacturer. The coating is then sprayed onto the roof surface in multiple applications. Joints and other elements that are subject to movement are reinforced by embedding a woven matting into the wet coating. The final coat is often colored. Typically, application must be made by an applicator approved by the manufacturer in order to receive a five-to-ten-year warranty, generally renewable by the cleaning of the roof surface and application of a new top layer of coating.

While these systems offer great potential, they have limitations. If the existing metal roof surface is not properly prepared, the new coating may not adhere properly, creating bubbles where water can collect if the surface of the coating becomes damaged. If the roof metal is ferrous, such a condition will create a serious corrosion problem. In certain climates, condensation may tend to form under the coating, creating adhesion problems and potential corrosion problems if the roofing is ferrous. Most of these coatings are not designed to be submerged in water for any length of time; thus, they cannot be used in gutters or on surfaces where water collects. Application of the coating must be monitored to ensure that scuppers and downspouts are not clogged.

Top: This new standing-seam roof was not designed properly for the slope of the roof when it was installed. When it began leaking, comparison in cost was made between repair by traditional sheet-metal techniques and repair with a proprietary coating system. The proprietary coating system was substantially cheaper and the manufacturer offered a renewable warranty. This photograph shows the installation of reinforcing stripping on all of the joints.

Above: Pictured here is the completed installation. The coating application has performed well for more than five years.

Composition Roofs of Asphalt or Asbestos Cement

Asphalt-based roofing materials were available as early as the 1880s. These early products consisted of fiber mats impregnated with bituminous compounds. After 1900, asbestos-cement roofing, made by mixing asbestos fibers and portland cement and then pressing the mixture into shingles, was available. By the 1920s, these materials were established as low-cost and fire-resistant alternatives to traditional roofing materials.

Both types of roofing were available in a variety of decorative interlocking patterns— square, rectangular, hexagonal, and diamond shapes—and multiple colors. Asphalt-shingle manufacturers advertised the benefits of their products, which included double-locked tabs to prevent curling, cupping, or wind uplift; increased headlap to prevent blowing rain or snow from reaching roof boards; quality materials, including slate and stone granules to provide fire- and time-resisting endurance; and improved aesthetics from the variety of colors available and tilelike shadow tones of the patterned shingles. The asbestos-cement-shingle manufacturers made similar claims.

As with any roofing material, asphalt-shingle roofs should be kept clean. Accumulations of dirt and organic matter will collect under the unsealed edges of the tabs, causing the edges to curl and eventually crack. Foot traffic on the roof surface should be minimized because it can break shingles, particularly as they age and become brittle.

Missing shingle tabs are an obvious damage signal for an asphalt-shingle roof. Windstorms often cause a few tabs to loosen and/or break away. If damage to asphalt shingles is not too severe, they can be repaired. Loose tabs can be readhered by carefully lifting the tab, removing debris from under it, applying roofing cement to the layer below, and embedding the tab in the cement.

Individual damaged shingles can be replaced in a similar manner. The tabs of the shingle course above must be gently separated and lifted. The damaged shingle is removed and replaced with a new, matching shingle, which is nailed to the deck over new felt. The edges of the new shingle should be embedded in roof cement. The tabs of the shingles above are then bent back to their original position and embedded in roof cement. In making such repairs, it is important to ensure that the tabs of the shingle course above are not damaged by the repair process. If they crack or break, it may be that the shingles are too brittle to allow repair.

A pattern of missing tabs in combination with other forms of deterioration is a sign that the roofing needs to be replaced. Bare spots indicate that the mineral granules that protect the asphalt liner from sun degradation are washing off. A random pattern of small, circular spots signals that the shingles have been damaged by hail. Extensive granule loss indicates that the liner is becoming brittle and is nearing the end of its useful life. Curled, cracked, or swollen shingles also indicate advanced deterioration.

In some situations, it may be necessary to replace the shingles on one side of the roof but not the other. Shingles on the sunny side of a roof, for example, often deteriorate more rapidly than those on the shady side.

Lumpy or uneven shingles should be removed before reshingling. Less severely deteriorated shingles may be left in place and new shingles installed directly over them. As always, consult local building-code officials to determine what is allowed in your area. Some building codes allow two layers of asphalt shingles on a roof; others allow up to three.

Repair or replacement asphalt shingles must meet local building-code requirements for fire and wind resistance. Generally, shingles should meet the testing requirements of ASTM 3462 for fiberglass-mat shingles. To reduce the potential for damage from condensation, attic spaces over which the shingles are applied should be adequately ventilated. Improper or limited attic ventilation can lead to shingle blistering and premature failure. Many shingle manufacturers will not provide a warranty for shingles installed over an unventilated attic.

Handling asbestos-cement roofing materials requires special care since they contain varying amounts of asbestos (see pages 57–58). Deterioration of asbestos-cement-shingle roofs generally is limited to corrosion of fasteners, fading and erosion of the surface, and breakage from thermal shock and impact damage. Corrosion of fasteners allows the shingles to slip or drop from the roof, often breaking as they do so. If the fasteners are universally corroded, the shingles should be removed and reinstalled with corrosion-resistant fasteners. If the deterioration is isolated, the affected shingles should be reset using the same techniques described previously in the slate-repair section of this chapter.

The severity of fading and erosion of the surface of asbestos-cement shingles is related to the manufacturing process, the quality of the materials, and the type of environmental exposure the shingle is subject to. If the shingles are physically sound but need cosmetic restoration, they can be cleaned with a low-pressure water wash and painted with an acrylic-latex coating. The selection of the coating should be based upon test samples that demonstrate the coating will achieve the same color, gloss, and general character of the original finish as closely as is possible. Once painted, the coating will need to be renewed every three to five years. If the deterioration goes beyond the cosmetic, the shingles probably should be replaced.

Broken shingles can be replaced as described in the slate section of this chapter. The greatest challenge will be finding a suitable replacement shingle. If the original shingle can be removed without additional damage and the broken piece is retrievable, it may be possible to glue the pieces together using an epoxy adhesive. Voids at the fracture can be filled with epoxy filler and acrylic-latex paint can be used to restore the finish appearance. If the repair is successful, the shingle can be reinstalled with a piece of metal flashing under it to provide adequate protection. If gluing is not an option, a suitable replacement may be available from current manufacturers of cement shingles, or it may be possible to job-fabricate an acceptable replacement from a cement-sheet product.

Until they leak, roofs generally are taken for granted. A leak may be considered a distress signal, indicating that the roof or one of its auxiliary systems needs immediate maintenance. The consequences of ignoring the signal for an extended period of time can have major financial implications. Periodic roof inspections can identify potential problems and allow timely repair before damage occurs. Keeping the roof, gutters, and downspouts clean will do much to lengthen the life of the roof.

Roofs of historic homes are unique and require a special commitment on the part of owners to ensure that those architectural qualities that make them distinctive are maintained and preserved. Caring for a historic roof requires sensitivity to its design and to the materials from which it is crafted. This entails learning about the materials and the historic-installation techniques that create the roof's character and allow it to function well.

When repairs are required, it is essential to employ craftsmen who are used to working on historic buildings and who have experience in making repairs to the type of roofing to be repaired. An experienced craftsman and a knowledgeable homeowner, working as a team, will ensure sensitive roof preservation.

EXTERIOR MASONRY

RICHARD PIEPER

Masonry is an important character-defining element for historic buildings. The texture and patterns of brickwork, ornament in stone and terra cotta, and the color and configuration of mortar joints reflect the technology and styles of the past. Much more advance planning is required for successful masonry repairs to historic structures than is normally necessary for the maintenance of contemporary masonry buildings.

Masonry may easily be neglected. Stone, brick, and concrete are generally among the most durable of materials, and masonry problems are not always as apparent as leaks from a failing roof or flaking paint on rotting wood. Masonry deterioration is frequently neglected until significant repair is required. As with other building deterioration problems, however, expensive repairs can be avoided with judicious periodic maintenance.

Except for major deterioration problems caused by poor original design, or the use of a failure-prone material, a well-constructed masonry wall can stand for hundreds of years if it is protected from moisture damage. Ironically, well-intentioned but inappropriate repairs can often cause more problems than they solve. Many historic masonry buildings have been irreversibly damaged by cleaning techniques such as sandblasting or the use of harsh chemicals. Others have been unsuccessfully coated with water repellents or treated with consolidants in a vain effort to "preserve" them.

The key to successful maintenance of historic masonry is understanding the materials and methods of original construction and carefully evaluating the cause of deterioration. The selection of appropriate maintenance procedures, use of skilled laborers, and timely scheduling of the work are other factors that contribute to the sound preservation of historic masonry.

The texture and patterns of stone masonry are important features of this house in New York State.

IDENTIFYING MASONRY MATERIALS

Brick in historic buildings varies greatly in appearance and durability. Through much of the nineteenth century, locally made "common" bricks were used for construction of the faces of masonry walls. Somewhat irregular in size and appearance, these bricks required larger (typically three-eighths of an inch) mortar joints to accommodate their unevenness. Pressed bricks and, later, extruded bricks were much more consistent in size and appearance and were generally used with much narrower "buttered" mortar joints. As the brick industry centralized and developed in the late nineteenth and early twentieth centuries, bricks were usually more carefully fired than earlier common bricks and thus are not as prone to having the outer surface break off *(spall)* from moisture or frost.

Stones used in walls and foundations vary greatly in durability and appearance. Much of the granite used in buildings is relatively impervious to water and suffers little damage from water infiltration or wind erosion. Conversely, most brown sandstones (brownstones) commonly in use in the nineteenth century are very prone to failure. A common mode of deterioration is *exfoliation,* the leafing away of large layers of stone. Sandstones deteriorate differently depending on the orientation of their layers, or *strata,* in the completed wall. Because stone is frequently used as an exterior veneer on brick-wall construction, sandstone is often *face bedded,* with its strata parallel to the face of the wall. Stone laid in this fashion is much more likely to experience extensive delamination of the stone's face than is stone that is *quarry bedded,* with its strata laid horizontally. Limestones and marbles are not generally subject to such dramatic failure but are sensitive to acid rain and may deteriorate quickly in polluted environments. Some coarse-grained crystalline limestones are prone to *sugaring,* or disaggregation, in polluted and moist environments. It is interesting that marbles and limestones may deteriorate most dramatically in areas sheltered from rain. *Sulfate skins* may form in such areas when airborne pollutants are deposited by condensation and not removed by rainwater.

Cast stone is not stone at all but concrete formed in molds, employing decorative aggregates, tinting compounds, and tooling to imitate natural stone. With developments in the portland cement and concrete industry at the end of the nineteenth century, cast stone became widely accepted as an economical substitute for natural stone. Good cast stone can look deceptively natural to the layperson and may be difficult to identify as such. Correct identification is crucial to establishing appropriate repairs, however, as the nature of deterioration of stone and cast stone can be radically different.

Surface induration (crust formation) of porous stones like brownstone occurs when soluble binder within the stone dissolves and redeposits through repeated wetting and drying. Damage may not be apparent until the stone is sounded.

Terra cotta is a fired clay product, like brick, but is generally fabricated in larger ornamental shapes, and may be fired with a decorative glaze. Glazes were frequently specified to imitate stone, and terra cotta was sometimes used for elaborate ornament where cut stone would have been prohibitively expensive. Terra cotta can deteriorate through failure of its surface glaze, exposing the softer porous clay body underneath to moisture damage. Because most terra-cotta units are hollow, with only a thin (one to one-half inch) clay wall on the front, blocks are sensitive to mechanical damage, and pieces on corners or adjacent to doorways can easily be damaged. Serious damage may also result when water collects in the voids within terra-cotta units and freezes, cracking them. Terra cotta may also exhibit severe cracking when rigid mortars and improper installation methods do not allow for thermal expansion.

"Cast stone," precast concrete with exposed decorative aggregate, was frequently used for ornamental masonry elements early in the twentieth century.

Even when you have correctly identified the material and system of construction of a masonry wall, the correct historic appearance of a masonry building may not be immediately apparent. Although it is common desire to strip paint from exterior brickwork, much early brickwork was intended to be painted and should not be exposed, for reasons both of durability and of historical accuracy. Similarly, irregular rubble stonework often received a coat of stucco, sometimes scored to resemble finer stonework. Exposing the stone gives a radically altered appearance to the building and is inappropriate. When original appearance is in doubt, additional historical and physical evidence must be evaluated before masonry repairs are undertaken.

EVALUATING MASONRY PROBLEMS

WHERE TO LOOK

Not surprisingly, masonry problems are more likely to occur in areas that are heavily exposed to moisture or significant temperature fluctuation. Parapets, chimneys, balustrades, windowsills, stairways, and foundations are more likely to require maintenance than are vertical walls, which are relatively sheltered from rainwater.

Masonry problems are often caused by inappropriately detailed or poorly maintained drainage at the roof and the foundation. Foundations and lower walls frequently suffer the most serious deterioration. Leaking walls in basements or ground floors may often be attributed to rainwater runoff from the roof that is not adequately directed away from the base of the building. Small concrete splash blocks that are commonly placed beneath downspouts are usually insufficient to shed water away from the foundation. Foundation masonry problems sometimes manifest themselves as open joints or missing

Water infiltration and frost often cause serious deterioration of mortar and stone in exposed landings and stairways.

mortar at the very bottom of the wall where moisture is highest, but water can also wick up in porous masonry to cause damage high above ground level. This *rising damp* may cause a line of masonry damage several feet above ground level at the point where water in the masonry evaporates, leaving masonry above and below this point relatively unaffected.

Many historic buildings lack a dampproof layer at the top of the foundation to prevent water from rising into upper wall masonry, and, where ground water levels are high or roof drainage collects, damage from rising damp often results. The wicking of water into porous masonry may also be a serious problem when landscape changes have allowed soil levels to rise above the top of the foundation. Soil resting against porous brickwork may cause spalling brick and joint erosion on exterior surfaces, and can result in serious damage to interior wall finishes.

Leakage from downspouts and built-in gutters frequently causes leaching of mortar on corners where downspouts are mounted or on tops of walls. Masonry damage associated with roofing problems can go unnoticed until serious damage has resulted, especially if it is concealed in an attic or closet. *Copings,* which cap the walls rising above a roof, are difficult to inspect and maintain. Water will seep through open coping joints, leading to upper wall deterioration. Left unattended, leakage from a drainage system or through coping joints can require major reconstruction of the top courses of a masonry wall. Masonry copings themselves often deteriorate and may require replacement as well.

Chimneys are among the masonry features that require the most frequent maintenance, but they are usually neglected because of their location. Timely maintenance of a chimney top is extremely important because of its susceptibility to water damage. This usually requires repointing of coping joints and may involve replacement of a stone coping or mortar cap over the brickwork, or possibly reconstruction of several top courses of the masonry. Leaks resulting from poorly detailed or deteriorated roof flashing can cause masonry problems where the chimney pierces the roof. This is often a serious problem when the chimney is located at the eave or on a slope rather than at the peak of the roof. Snow or ice that collects against the chimney can also cause leakage. Recurrent chimney flashing problems may require construction of a *cricket,* or deflector, to direct water away from the chimney. Chimneys are also subject to deterioration from pollutants in flue gases. Leaning or bending of a chimney is sometimes attributed to expansion from sulfate impurities in mortar.

WHAT TO LOOK FOR

MORTAR EROSION AND MORTAR DETERIORATION

Mortar serves several functions—its primary purposes are to join the irregular surfaces of the masonry units and to keep water out of the masonry. Some weathering of mortar surfaces is normal, but serious erosion of the face of the mortar joint on a parapet, near a gutter, or behind a downspout is a sure indication that water is running over the face of the wall or penetrating behind the face of the masonry. Mortar that is moist or crumbling also indicates a moisture problem. In severe cases of water infiltration, mortar may become *spent*, and lose all strength and cohesion, allowing masonry to be easily disassembled by hand and necessitating reconstruction.

EFFLORESCENCE AND SUBFLORESCENCE

Efflorescence is the recrystallization of soluble salts from within the masonry on the surface of the masonry. Efflorescence is frequently found in attics on the inside surface of gable-end walls where coping joints are open or on

eave walls where gutter overflow or gutter leakage is a problem. Efflorescence on the inside of foundation walls indicates that exterior foundation surfaces are inadequately protected against water infiltration. *Subflorescence* is similar recrystallization of soluble salts *beneath* the surface of the masonry. Subflorescence often occurs in conjunction with efflorescence and may seriously damage masonry units by causing the surface to spall or flake away.

The salts that may effloresce are numerous—on upper wall surfaces efflorescence is often calcium sulfate formed by the effect of acid rain on mortar or limestone. On foundations and steps, sodium chloride from deicing salts may be found. Nitrates often appear where pigeon roosting has been a problem. Phosphates can be introduced in masonry by fertilization of plantings near the foundation. The improper use of paint removers and alkaline masonry cleaners can form sodium and potassium salts within the masonry as well. Severe and recurrent efflorescence sometimes indicates the presence of an improper mortar mixture used in original construction. Whatever the salt, efflorescence is a certain sign that moisture is entering a wall. Severe efflorescence often indicates that the cementing components of the mortar are being damaged by being dissolved, altered, and recrystallized.

STAINING AND BIOLOGICAL GROWTH

Soiling of exterior masonry surfaces does not necessarily signal significant masonry problems. Rust staining on stone surfaces, however, may reflect deterioration of iron cramps or anchors within the wall and indicate that open joints are admitting water into the wall. Moss or algae on masonry surfaces are more likely to be present on the shaded side of buildings but may also reflect drainage problems from gutters and downspouts. Biological growth not only is an indication of harmful moisture levels, but it also serves to hold water in the

Wicking of moisture frequently causes stucco failure at the base of brick walls. Installation of impermeable stucco repairs hinders evaporation and often causes damage to brick and stucco at higher levels on the wall.

Leachate deposits on exterior stone surfaces are evidence of recurrent water leakage into the core of the masonry wall, and may signal serious masonry damage.

Cast-concrete copings are deteriorating at this Frank Lloyd Wright–designed house in Buffalo, New York.

Efflorescence and subflorescence on interior surfaces beneath leaking parapets or copings can result in significant damage to brickwork.

masonry and, over time, can accelerate damage to masonry surfaces. Despite their picturesque appearance or historic appropriateness, most ivies and climbing plants harm masonry surfaces by growing within open joints, attaching to masonry surfaces, and fostering moist wall conditions. Climbing or creeping plants growing directly on masonry surfaces without removable trellises generally should be avoided.

SPALLING AND EXFOLIATION

Spalling of brick and exfoliation of stone often reflect elevated levels of moisture in masonry but may also be caused by defects in the original masonry units. An underfired brick may spall while an adjacent brick remains sound under the same moisture conditions. A high concentration of spalled brick in one location, such as a parapet or wall base, usually reflects a moisture problem that must be corrected. In winter, high moisture content in masonry may lead to *frost spalling*, the fracturing of brick or stone due to the freezing of water in porous masonry. Some building stones may be prone to failure and may deteriorate even in the absence of a specific moisture condition requiring correction. Even stone from the same quarry varies in composition and it is not unusual to see one stone exfoliating in an otherwise sound masonry wall. Stone spalls may also be caused by *oxide jacking*, pressure from expansion of rusting iron or steel anchors. An experienced eye is often required to establish the cause of masonry unit failure and to determine what repairs are necessary.

CRACKS, SHIFTS, AND BULGES

It may seem obvious that a crack in a masonry wall indicates a problem that requires correction. Yet cracking may reflect previous settlement or shifting that is now stable and requires no action other than grouting or repointing to keep out moisture. Frequently, cracking is caused by deterioration of structural steel or steel reinforcement embedded in the masonry. Cracking of brick at the heads of windows, for instance, is often caused by deterioration of steel window lintels and requires replacement of the lintel with galvanized steel. Similar cracking is often found at the corners of masonry-clad, steel-frame buildings where structural steel is rusting. Diagonal cracks below windowsills, on the other hand, generally indicate uneven foundation settlement. If such cracking is not alarmingly sudden or large, a structural engineer may choose to apply *tell tales* to monitor the crack before recommending repair. Cracks due to stable ground settlement often need only be sealed, or *pointed*, to prevent the entry of water.

Slight bulging or shifting out of plane in a portion of a masonry wall often indicates that the brick or stone masonry surface veneer is separating from the rest of the wall masonry. This may be because water is entering at a crack or joint, dissolving mortar, rusting ties, or freezing and moving brick or stone outward. A slight shift in a piece of stone veneer accompanied by mortar staining or rust staining from a joint is often the first evidence of water entry into a wall. Visible cracks or bulges generally should be inspected by an architect or structural engineer.

APPROPRIATE MASONRY MAINTENANCE

MASONRY CLEANING

Cleaning is often the first "improvement" specified for a masonry wall and usually the least important requirement for proper maintenance. Generally, cleaning is an aesthetic concern rather than a maintenance requirement, although it can be important in cases where significant contamination with sulfates or other salts is causing recurrent damage. Cleaning may also be necessary as a part of a larger repair project that involves repointing or replacement of damaged wall sections. Because cleaning may actually damage the historic masonry through inappropriate procedures or selection of a harsh cleaning method, take particular care in the selection of an appropriate cleaning technique. In most cases, a contractor's recommendations should *not* be relied upon exclusively but balanced with a knowledge of the risks inherent in the various cleaning options.

Numerous methods are used for cleaning masonry. Selection of an appropriate method depends on the nature of the masonry surface to be cleaned and the nature of the soiling to be removed. It is always wisest to choose the gentlest means possible for cleaning and to keep in mind that the goal of cleaning should be not a "like new" appearance but one that exhibits a certain patina of age.

Some masonry surfaces, especially limestone, can be cleaned successfully with water alone. A gentle water misting is applied to masonry from a drip hose or row of spray heads for a period of time (several hours to a day) to soften the dirt, and the wall is then sprayed clean with a medium-pressure water spray. While this system may seem foolproof, if any open cracks are present it may introduce large amounts of water into exterior walls, causing interior staining or plaster damage. Large amounts of soluble salts in "hard" water may also cause a problem with this technique. In addition, the method cannot be used when there is a risk of frost damage or freezing. Considerable time for drying of the wall must be allowed, so the technique is most appropriate for use in late spring or summer.

Some sandstones, especially those with clay-rich or calcareous binders, may deteriorate dramatically in areas exposed to frequent wetting and drying.

Specifications for cleaning historic masonry often call for use of *nonionic* detergents to avoid introducing harmful chemicals into masonry, as might happen with a phosphate detergent. Many proprietary nonionic detergents specifically formulated for use in masonry cleaning are available.

Frequently the quickest cleaning results come from the use of alkaline or acidic chemical cleaners, and not surprisingly these are often preferred by masonry contractors. Acidic cleaners (usually hydrofluoric and orthophosphoric acid) are inappropriate for use on *calcareous* stones, such as limestone or marble, as they may significantly dissolve the surface of the stone. Acidic cleaners are often used for cleaning brickwork or *siliceous* stones, such as granites and most sandstones. They may be very successful if carefully used, especially with granites, with little alteration of the appearance of the stone. If an overly high concentration of cleaner is used, or if it is allowed to remain on the wall too long before rinsing, the cleaner can "burn" the stone, leaving a light film of insoluble silica on the surface. This is most likely to be noticeable with brickwork or darker stones. Alteration of iron-bearing minerals and subsequent iron staining can also be a problem. Acidic cleaners can also irreversibly damage the surface of brick or terra cotta, dissolving portions of the fire skin and reducing its durability against weathering.

Alkaline cleaners (usually potassium or sodium hydroxide) are generally used on limestone and marble. While they will not burn masonry as acid may, they are difficult to rinse off and may cause subsequent efflorescence problems. Alkaline cleaners are generally followed with a mild acetic-acid application to assure neutralization and assist in rinsing. Alkaline compounds can form insoluble iron stains if iron is present in the stone being cleaned.

The use of air abrasives (sandblasting and wet-grit blasting) to clean masonry facades has caused major irreversible damage to numerous historic buildings. Sandblasting can damage or remove the protective fire skin of brick and terra cotta, leaving the more vulnerable interior exposed to the elements. Bricks damaged by sandblasting can never be repaired satisfactorily, and may spall or flake continually, even if painted. Damage to some stone and precast concrete is less extensive, but the pitting and softening of features that result may still be extremely disfiguring and accelerate future deterioration. Less damage may result from air-abrasive cleaning that uses ground walnut shells,

Chemical cleaning methods must be tested and carefully evaluated to avoid damage to historic masonry surfaces.

corncobs, or plastic beads, but this technique can be extremely expensive. In recent years, microabrasive cleaning techniques, generally using very fine aluminum-oxide abrasive grit and low pressures, have been introduced for masonry cleaning. Often these systems utilize vacuum enclosures to reduce ambient dust from cleaning operations. Microabrasive cleaning, unlike traditional sandblasting, may be an appropriate and useful cleaning method, especially where stone must be chemically consolidated before cleaning or where aqueous methods would mobilize salts in the masonry.

It is always important to test masonry cleaning methods in an inconspicuous location prior to commencing overall work. Choose a spot or spots that reflect a range of typical soiling patterns. Vary cleaner concentration (one part cleaner to three parts water, one to five, etc.) and the period of time that the cleaner is allowed to remain on the masonry before being rinsed off. Make a sketch locating individual tests to assist in evaluating them after the masonry has dried. Remember that more than one cleaning system may be appropriate and that sometimes using several gentler methods in sequence will give more satisfactory results than one application of a stronger concentration.

REPOINTING

Sometimes incorrectly called "tuck-pointing," *repointing* is the raking and refilling of the outer face of mortar joints. Repointing is a basic periodic maintenance task for masonry buildings. Properly done, and undertaken when needed, repointing can prevent moisture infiltration and extend the life of a masonry wall indefinitely. Often, however, overall repointing is neither necessary nor sufficient to halt water infiltration and is undertaken needlessly. Generally, water does not leak through the vertical surface of a masonry wall. Wind-driven rain may wet the wall, but the water will later evaporate without causing damage. Most interior damage on wall surfaces can be traced to coping leakage, roof flashing or gutter failure, or leakage around window frames. Even a cracked joint may not warrant immediate repointing unless it is in an area subject to water infiltration. Unless mortar failure is obvious and serious, the decision to repoint must be made with careful deliberation.

Improper repointing can be disfiguring and unsightly. It can alter the appearance of a building immeasurably and irreversibly and accelerate future deterioration. Careful selection of materials and methods prior to repointing is extremely important.

Mortars vary greatly in appearance and composition. The three major components in most contemporary mortars are cement, lime, and sand. These components can be varied in proportion to produce mortars of strikingly different qualities. Variations in the sand itself, in the coloration of cement, and, when they are used, in tinting pigments also dramatically affect the appearance of the mortar.

Until the last quarter of the nineteenth century, most mortars in the United States were composed solely of lime and sand. The discovery of limestones, which, when burned, produced a "hydraulic" lime that would harden underwater, gave increased early strength and flexibility of use to lime mortars. The development of the portland cement industry in this country at the end of the nineteenth century led to dramatically increased use of cements in mortars. Cement-rich mortars are harder and, just as important, less permeable to water than lime mortars. Impermeable mortars force moisture in the wall to evaporate through the brick rather than through mortar joints. The use of cement-rich mortars to repoint early brickwork can in this way cause brick to deteriorate through spalling at the edges or by subflorescence of salts in the brick.

It is important, therefore, that repointing mortar be mixed from individual components and that premixed bagged mortars not be used. If possible, a formulation for repointing mortar should be prepared by an architectural conservator based on an analysis of the original mortar and an acid-washed sample of the mortar aggregate. When this is not feasible, the mason should prepare several mortar samples, varying the sand, cement color, and pigmentation (if required), basing the samples on a standard mortar formulation. For early (pre-1900) brick masonry, a Type O mortar (about one part cement, two parts lime, and eight parts sand) is usually appropriate; for later brick and stone, an N mortar (one part cement, one part lime, six parts sand) may be satisfactory. White portland cement, rather than typical gray or light gray cement, is almost always preferable for matching nineteenth-century mortars. Dry mortar samples should be matched with a clean broken sample of the original pointing mortar (which may be different from the mortar used to bed the masonry). Remember that when joints weather, much of the appearance of the joint is contributed by sand that remains on the mortar surface, so matching the original aggregate is very important. In general, bagged mason's sand, which is unlikely to be from a local source, should not be used. Local sand and gravel pits may have an appropriate aggregate that matches the original. Generally, several grade sizes may be available. *Mason's sand* is often finer and more uniform in size than the historic aggregate. *Concrete sand* generally has a wider range of particle sizes, including some small pebbles, and may be useful for matching nineteenth-century mortars.

Even if appropriate mortar is used, considerable damage can be done by careless *raking*, or removal of mortar from mortar joints. The use of hand-held circular grinders to open joints can cause extensive damage, especially when fine joints are widened or when the cutting of vertical joints damages the brick above and below the joint. It is much safer to use hand tools or, if necessary, fine pneumatic chisels that have been adapted from the stone-carving industry. Joints generally should be raked to the depth of mortar deterioration. To assure proper mortar adhesion, rake to a depth not less than two and one-half times the width of the joint (about one inch deep for a three-eighths-inch joint). Many authorities recommend repointing in multiple *lifts*, or layers, so that mortar is less likely to shrink or crack upon curing.

New joints should be tooled with a metal joint tool to match the original joint appearance. Joints that are struck flush, sloped with a weather joint, or tooled with a recessed grapevine joint are common. More specialized jointing, like *tuck-pointing*, in which a thin line of tinted mortar is applied over bedding mortar, is also found. Repairs tooled with a standard contemporary concave joint may not match adjacent historic profiles. Often, after mortar has set but not completely cured, it is possible to "weather" it slightly by brushing and lightly spraying with water to expose more of the sand. New repointing will almost always be lighter than adjacent original mortar, which has soiled. The difference will be less noticeable if the masonry has been cleaned, but even expertly done spot repointing will be visible for several years until the mortar weathers. It is often advisable to repoint all of a particular feature or area so that repairs are less visually obtrusive.

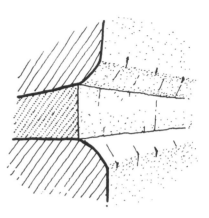

Deterioration of the arris, *or edges of masonry units, can sometimes cause an apparent widening of masonry joints that are repointed.*

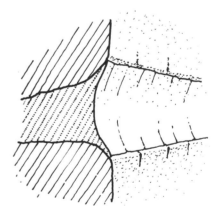

CAULK AND SEALANTS

Frequently, caulking or sealants are inappropriately used for sealing joints when mortar should be used. In general, the use of such sealants should be restricted to joints of horizontal or slightly sloped surfaces that are exposed to moisture. Sealants are also appropriate for use where wood or metal abuts a masonry surface, such as around window frames. Sealants are often used on copings and exterior stair tread joints. It is good practice to point the joint up to within an inch of the surface, then apply backer rod and sealant. Temporarily taping over the masonry units on either side of the joint will ensure a neat finish. Always use a backer rod and a primer, if required by the sealant system, to ensure that the sealant will hold. Urethane sealants last much longer than common butyl or latex caulks for masonry applications, and come in a variety of colors.

REPAIR AND REPLACEMENT OF DETERIORATED STONE AND BRICK

It may be necessary to replace or repair seriously deteriorated individual bricks or stones to ensure that the wall remains watertight and adjacent masonry is not affected. The replacement of individual bricks is delicate work but can be done successfully by a skilled mason if matching bricks can be found. Specialty bricks, such as hand-molded bricks, are still made by a handful of manufacturers but generally only for larger custom orders. Brick can sometimes be "borrowed" from a hidden location on the building being repaired. Damaged brick can also in some cases be turned back for front. When using new or salvaged brick, remember that once the brick is installed, even minor differences in appearance are magnified. If adjacent masonry is not threatened with damage due to water infiltration, it is often preferable to leave a slightly damaged brick in place. Large-scale replacement or refacing goes beyond maintenance and requires the assistance and supervision of an architect or architectural conservator, although small repairs can be undertaken by skilled masons without professional direction. Common repair methods include:

COMPOSITE REPAIR

When the surface of a stone has failed, or a stone has been chipped or a corner broken, a mortarlike cementitious composite may be sculpted in place to replicate the missing piece. Composite repairs are often made with tinted mortar or with mixes specifically marketed for this application. The color of completed composite repairs can vary dramatically with small changes in the pigment content or amount of water used in mixing. For this reason, preformulated mixes may be easier to work with than site-prepared mortar and can ensure a more consistent match if a standard color matches the work at hand. Custom colors usually require bulk purchases. Satisfactory repairs can sometimes be made using a Type N mortar and mortar-tinting compounds. One problem with composite repairs is that, as the patch weathers, the aggregate becomes more visible. A dark composite patch with a light sand aggregate may lighten considerably as it weathers, so that it no longer matches the stone. Patches to lighter stone are generally more successful. Besides the difficulty of achieving color matches, composite repairs tend to fail over time, cracking or falling off. Failure is more likely in high-moisture areas such as copings or windowsills. Large composite patches and those applied in areas where failure could be dangerous should always be anchored with an armature secured to the stone. Nylon- or stainless-steel-threaded rods epoxied into holes drilled in sound substrate are often used for this purpose.

RETOOLING

When the stone deterioration or flaking stone is quite shallow and does not afford sufficient depth for a composite repair, the surface of the stone may sometimes be retooled satisfactorily to resemble adjacent original surfaces. This technique generally works best on relatively plain flat surfaces. Extensive retooling of moldings or decorative features can alter profiles significantly and is seldom warranted.

DUTCHMEN

A *dutchman* is a stone patch set into a larger stone to replace a damaged portion. Dutchmen were sometimes used in original construction when a small defect occurred in an otherwise perfect piece. Dutchmen can be very successful for repairs in fine-grained homogeneous stone. Stones with strong pat-

A dutchman installed in this masonry wall has cracked because structural movement was not corrected.

terns, such as variegated granite or marbles, are difficult to repair successfully in this manner. A dutchman provides a very durable repair, but is expensive, and thus is usually reserved for prominent locations or high-moisture areas where a composite repair might fail quickly.

FOUNDATION WATERPROOFING

Foundations of historic homes were seldom waterproofed adequately. In locations with poor site drainage, or where roof drainage is not directed adequately away from the base of the wall, water seepage, efflorescence, and mortar failure will occur on the interior of basement walls. Coatings, paints, or waterproofing applied to interior wall surfaces cannot stop water from infiltrating into the exterior of foundation masonry. The wall remains wet, and the coatings will eventually flake off, taking a portion of the stone and mortar with them. Exterior soil injections are usually not completely successful at halting water penetration.

Often the worst deterioration can be mitigated simply by installing pipes above or below the grade to route roof drainage from downspouts away from the base of the wall. If this is not adequate, and the basement houses finished space, consideration should be given to waterproofing the exterior of the foundation wall. This is a major undertaking, and usually an expensive one, and generally should not be undertaken without the supervision of an architect or engineer. Most excavation adjacent to historic buildings will also require archaeological investigation. Careful excavation adjacent to the foundation is required around the perimeter of the building, exposing the foundation wall to its base, or *footing*. The exposed exterior wall surface is waterproofed with an applied coating or membrane, which may be plastic, cementitious, asphaltic, or even clay based. If the wall surface is very uneven, it may be necessary to render or stucco it to provide a base for the coating. Usually a perforated-pipe *footing drain* is also installed, which drains water adjacent to the foundation to a dry well or to the grade. Keep in mind that following waterproofing, efflorescence will actually increase for a period of time as the wall dries, a process that may take a year or more. (See also Structural Systems.)

INAPPROPRIATE TREATMENTS

Beware of quick fixes! There are no wonder products that can be brushed or sprayed on that will substitute for the recommended treatments in this section. "Waterproofing" applications are almost always unnecessary if other repairs are properly done. Most masonry does not need water repellents for protection.

Some "waterproofing" treatments can cause considerable damage by preventing the escape of water vapor from damp masonry when moisture has penetrated it due to flashing or joint defects. Cementitious coatings are frequently applied to exposed party walls or parapets where bricks are spalling, but in many cases, the coatings themselves spall off, taking a portion of the deteriorated brick with them, further damaging the wall.

SCHEDULING AND CONTRACTOR SELECTION

Plan carefully before proceeding with any masonry work. Poor repairs are not easily corrected and can do permanent damage. Give careful consideration to scheduling and selection of an appropriate contractor before any work is done (see Establishing a Maintenance Program).

Most repairs to historic masonry are beyond the skill of a maintenance person or jack-of-all-trades and should be performed by a skilled mason. Select a mason who has previous experience with historic structures and be sure to request references. It is usually advisable to visit one or more referenced projects and examine the completed work. Is new work a reasonable match to adjacent historic masonry? Was stone or brick damaged by joint raking? Did the mason use a matching mortar? Is there evidence of overcleaning? If previous work shows adequate skill, be sure that the same mechanic or crew that completed that work will also be working on your building. Remember that the skill of the helper doing preparatory work, like joint raking, is as important as that of the mason.

While it is often useful to obtain more than one bid for required work, without detailed specifications a meaningful comparison of bids may be difficult. If costs vary widely for the same scope of work, there is cause for concern, and it may be advisable to seek the assistance of a conservator or preservation architect. It is unreasonable to expect sensitive work from an unrealistically low bid.

Scheduling of work is extremely important. Repointing or aqueous cleaning should be done when there is no danger of freezing. It is prudent to restrict work to seasons when night temperatures will not fall below 40 degrees Fahrenheit, unless heated enclosures are provided for work areas. Freezing of wet mortar damages it and dramatically reduces its durability, while wet porous stone and brick are susceptible to damage from frost spalling.

Resist the temptation to proceed with work immediately if conditions appear or seem to worsen in late fall or winter. Masonry damage is seldom of such urgency that remedial work cannot be delayed until spring. Use inclement weather to plan carefully for necessary repairs, refining the scope of work and reviewing the methods and materials to be used. Remember that the work you undertake may be in place for hundreds of years. Take the time to plan to ensure that repairs are done properly

EXTERIOR WOODWORK

JOHN LEEKE

ARCHITECTURAL CHARACTER AND PRACTICAL PERFORMANCE

Much of the architectural character of a wooden building is provided by decorative features such as siding and trim. This exterior woodwork also provides the practical function of protecting the interior structure of the building from weather and deterioration. It is important to keep both decoration and function in mind as you maintain the exterior woodwork of your historic house.

All of the exterior parts of a building work together, forming an enveloping skin that keeps out wind, water, and sun. Imagine a raindrop falling from the sky and splashing on the ridge of the roof. It flows down the slope of the roof, drips over the eaves and down the side of the building, and runs off across the lawn. Its path defines the *weather envelope*. This envelope can even be thought of as wrapping underneath the building, forming a total *environmental envelope*.

The weather envelope is formed of many individual elements that work together in systems. On the wall, each wooden shingle overlaps another, forming a system of siding that effectively sheds water. At the eave of the roof, a gutter catches water and pours it into the rest of the drainage system, which might include downspouts and underground drainage lines. Each element and system performs a specific function that contributes to the protection of the building.

When an individual element fails, an entire system may fail. For example, the function of the gutter is to protect the side of the house from the deterioration caused by excessive water. If a wooden gutter rots out and falls off, water pours down the side of the building, bypassing the entire drainage system. The result is accelerated deterioration of the woodwork all across the side of the house. Each and every element is important and must be maintained so it can perform its function.

This homeowner has been making spot repairs to shingles, clapboards, and moldings over a period of a few years. This approach is cost-efficient and saves as much historic material as possible.

Exterior elements come in an astonishing variety of shapes, sizes, and materials. Wooden shingles are small, thin, and flat. Hollow porch columns are built with *staves*, like those of a barrel, and range up to forty-five feet tall. Gutters, really just large wooden moldings, can be thirty feet long. A round wooden turning can cap a four-inch stairway newel post or reach for the sky as a spire atop a three-story tower.

Most wooden exteriors are integrated with elements of other materials. Sheet-metal flashings and downspouts twist and wind in convoluted forms. Paint is a thin film that itself is made up of several layers. Panels of terra cotta, brick masonry, or stucco are sometimes used along with wood to form the weather envelope. The maintenance and repair of each type of material require very different techniques and skills. On a typical restoration project each type of work is performed by a separate trade. First, framing carpenters repair structural members. Then masons restore brick and stucco. Sheet-metal workers fabricate flashings, finish woodworkers cut and fit trim, and, finally, the painters show up. This disconnected procedure sometimes produces poorly designed and loosely assembled exterior details that fail before they should.

To ensure long-term performance, the various materials and methods must be "woven" into a "fabric" that forms an effective weather envelope. For example, metal flashing must be interleaved with wooden shingles where a wall meets a roof; wooden joints beveled so water will drain out; and primer, caulk, and paint properly layered. To do this work efficiently, two or more trades may be needed at the same time. Workers with knowledge and skills in more than one trade or a tightly knit crew of workers with a wide range of skills are crucial to effective exterior maintenance and repairs.

COMPREHENSIVE CONDITION SURVEY

To maintain exterior woodwork successfully, you must understand its condition. More than just identifying general conditions, however, you will also need to focus on problem areas and understand the root causes. Only with this knowledge can you then specify effective treatments. For example, if peeling paint on the side of a building is scraped off and recoated, and nothing is done to fix the leaking gutter above that caused the peeling paint, the leak will continue, exposing the wood to excessive moisture and eventual wood decay.

Before deciding what to do about any specific problems, conduct a comprehensive condition survey of the whole building. The purpose of the survey is to assess the broad needs of the entire building and to locate problem areas. At this initial stage, it is more important to gain a comprehensive impression of conditions than to find every case of deterioration. A survey that locates only 60 to 80 percent of the cases of deterioration may still be considered effective if it locates all of the wider problem areas.

Begin with a quick walk around the building. Consider the building's surroundings, including the landscaping, bodies of water, and even other buildings that could affect the "microclimate" around the building. Then view exterior surfaces of the building in more detail, facade by facade, including the roof. From the ground, stand back and use binoculars to view the details of upper stories. Consider each element separately and along with neighboring elements and systems. The vantage from an upper story or roof of a neighboring building may be helpful. Look for the following conditions:

- Trees and shrubbery near the building that may be trapping moisture in building parts
- Vertical streaks of gray or brown stains that indicate water flowing from behind gutters and other woodwork
- Cracks in foundation walls that indicate structural movement

Because the sun shines less on eastern and northern facades than on western and southern ones, the former are often damp. Check for the following signs of high moisture and decayed wood:

- Black spotty mildew, green algae, or mold
- Paint peeling down to bare wood, indicating high moisture
- Sunken surfaces, indicating decayed wood beneath

While full sun on western and southern facades helps prevent surface decay, the drying heat of the sun can shrink wide boards, causing loose and open joints. Water enters the joints, causing decay deep within walls. Surface weathering and deterioration are likely on wood not protected with paint. Look for the following conditions:

- Loose and open joints between elements
- Misalignment of woodwork, indicating structural movement beneath
- Fuzzy gray fibers on surfaces of bare wood
- Weather checks, especially on horizontal surfaces

Record your findings in simple but accurate pencil sketches of each facade. Fancy architectural drawings are not required. Further notes can be taken on separate sheets of paper and keyed to the sketches.

Analyze the results of the survey. Look for patterns of deterioration, such as a vertical strip of peeling paint beneath a leaking gutter. Structural shifting can cause clusters of loose and open woodwork joints along the lines of movement. Look for similar patterns on other facades. For example, if a pattern of loose joints and decay shows up along the headers of third-story windows of one facade, give close scrutiny to this same location on other facades, where the pattern may continue. Locate problem areas and begin to speculate on principal causes of deterioration, such as excessive moisture or structural movement. These problem areas will require more detailed assessment and investigation.

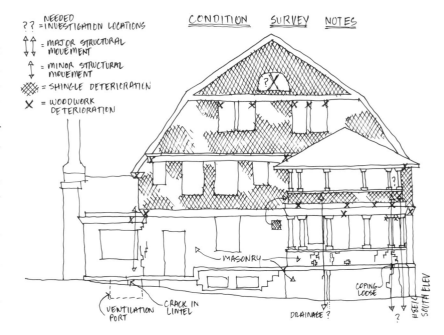

DETAILED ASSESSMENT AND INVESTIGATION

The purpose of assessment and investigation is to determine the importance of the elements in the problem areas and the root causes of significant deterioration. Assessment must be done close up (at arm's length), making access to upper stories and towers important. Ladders and cherry pickers provide the short-term access needed most efficiently. Scaffolding usually makes economic sense only if assessment is to be done immediately prior to a facade repair project that would require scaffolding.

Begin by describing the materials and methods of construction for each element and system in the problem area. Note which elements and systems are significant historic material and which are modern replacements. Then determine and note the condition of each element and whether or not it is performing its function. Focus in on elements in fair or poor condition for further investigation.

Once you have identified all apparent damage, it is critical to investigate causes. Moisture and movement are the two principal causes of damage to buildings. Following the path of moisture and movement back to their sources will lead you to the all-important root causes of damage and deterioration. For example, if the paint on a wooden gutter is peeling down to bare wood, indicating excessive moisture and possible wood decay, an electronic moisture meter can be used to determine the amount and extent of the damage. Where moisture is greatest, probe along the gutter with an ice pick to determine if decay has softened the wood and, if so, how much. If dark vertical water stains are visible on the *fascia*, or frieze board behind the gutter, it may be overflowing or leaking. Follow the water flow down to the lower section of the wall. There may be paint peeling to bare wood, verifying the path of the water. If the clapboards at the base of the wall are deteriorated, they may not be protecting the structural elements within the wall. Use an electronic moisture meter to measure the moisture content within the wall. If the moisture content is high (above 15 to 20 percent), remove a few clapboards to determine if the sill is actually decayed and, if so, to what extent. Assessment and investigation may have to be done over a period of time to gather information on intermittent conditions or ones that appear only during certain seasons. Inspections during rainstorms or in the middle of the winter can be especially revealing. The cause and effect of each deterioration can be tracked down using this and a wide variety of other investigative methods and techniques, as outlined below.

This sketch maps out woodwork and masonry deterioration. Weathering is a cause of woodwork deterioration over the entire facade. The deterioration is concentrated in areas where structural movement has opened up joints in the woodwork and allowed water to enter, causing damage.

The loose and open joint in this crown molding was caused by a leak in the flashing above the joint. Nails holding the molding in place rusted out. Rainwater now penetrates the joint, soaking directly into the end grain and causing limited decay.

Ice buildup in this leaking wooden gutter is literally ripping the gutter apart. Routine gutter cleaning would have prevented the decay that weakened the gutter and caused the resulting leak.

SURFACE WEATHERING

When bare wood is left exposed over the long term, the surface weathers away. Wood is formed of tan or brown *lignin,* a natural polymer that holds together the wood's gray cellulose fibers. Ultraviolet rays in sunshine break down the lignin, exposing and loosening the gray cellulose fibers. You can recognize this condition in the characteristic gray and fuzzy surface of weathered wood. As the fibers are washed away by rain and wind, the surface wears down at the rate of about one-quarter inch to one-half inch per century.

Flat-grain wood can develop *weather checks* (see also page 62). When a fresh wood surface is left exposed to the weather, very tiny cracks are formed by the expansion and shrinkage due to moisture changes. The sun shines into these cracks and weathers away their sides, making the cracks wider. Moisture flows into the cracks, increasing expansion and shrinkage and lengthening them. After several years or a few decades weather checks can grow up to one-quarter of an inch wide, three-quarters of an inch deep, and four to six inches long. Weather checks are most commonly found in horizontal surfaces such as porch-deck boards, the tops of balustrade railings, and on windowsills. To limit surface weathering, protect wood from sunlight and moisture, usually with coatings of paint or stain.

FUNGAL DECAY

Decay or rot is caused by fungal organisms that consume wood when it does not have a chance to dry out and is damp over the long term. One type of fungus that attacks wood is called *cubic brown rot.* It eats the cellulose fibers of the wood, robbing the wood of its strength and leaving the brown lignin in characteristic dark brown cubic shapes. To limit fungal decay, wood must be kept dry. Wood can be kept dry by coating it (such as with paint or stain), by installing drainage systems (gutters, downspouts), and by sealing open joints with caulking or by rebuilding to close the joint

INSECT ATTACK

Several types of insects damage wood. Termites build tunnels of mud from the ground up into a structure, where they eat the wood. Carpenter ants carve galleries out of wood in which to nest, leaving the *frass,* or sawdust, in piles that are sometimes found along the foundation of the house. Both termites and ants leave a thin shell of wood at the outer surface of where they've been, making visual inspection for damage difficult. Tapping on the surface of decayed wood makes a hollow "thud" compared with the higher pitched "ring" of sound wood. An ice pick can be used to probe for weak wood. Because these insects favor damp, softened wood, keeping wood dry helps limit their activity.

PHYSICAL DAMAGE

The wear and tear of foot traffic on a door's threshold or tree branches brushing against a building will slowly wear down wooden surfaces. Catastrophic events such as storms can break and blow tree branches against buildings, damaging woodwork and breaking the weather envelope. Limit subsequent damage by inspecting exteriors after storms and making necessary repairs.

JOINTS BETWEEN ELEMENTS

Even if wooden elements are not deteriorating, wood expands and shrinks across the width of a board as it absorbs and releases moisture to the air. This movement results in loose and open joints between wooden elements, causing a break in the weather envelope. Structural movement beneath the finish woodwork can also break open joints between elements.

To keep water out of the woodwork, builders have flashed joints with a wide variety of materials, including thin strips of wood, birch bark, tar paper, and sheet metal. Sheets of these materials behind the joint catch penetrating water and guide it back to the outer surface of the woodwork. If joints open wide enough to expose the flashing to the weather, it will deteriorate. Usually the surrounding woodwork must be removed in order to replace or renew flashing.

Flexible caulks and sealants are also used to close joints. They allow some movement while maintaining a seal. Caulks and sealants fail by losing their flexibility over time and by losing adherence to the sides of the joints. Usually, caulks and sealants can be renewed by raking out the old material, cleaning the sides of the joints, and applying new sealant.

Fungal decay has eaten away the interior of these three-inch-thick porch-column staves leaving an outer shell of sound wood. Holes were drilled to dry out the wood and were then filled with a treatment of epoxy consolidant to stabilize the decayed wood.

TREATMENTS

Once conditions are understood, treatments can be developed to repair damage and to address root causes so deterioration does not reoccur. *Treatments* is a broad term that covers all of the specific materials, procedures, and techniques used to repair and maintain the woodwork. Treatments should leave the woodwork in a condition that will resist weathering, help the element perform its intended function, and be easily maintainable in the future.

PREVENTIVE TREATMENTS

Preventive maintenance anticipates deterioration and improves conditions before substantial woodwork damage is done. The basic goals of routine woodwork maintenance and repairs are to keep the wood dry and allow for movement. Painting and caulking are the most common and effective preventive treatments for wooden exteriors. Routine spot-paint maintenance and recaulking of open joints help to maintain the weather envelope that protects the wood beneath.

When damage does occur, making limited repairs that are physically and visually compatible with the surrounding area of an element is a priority when that element contributes to the historic character of the building. For example, large classically styled fluted columns across the front portico of a southern plantation house would be considered a significant contribution to the architectural character of the building. Frequently, the bottom six to twelve inches of the columns will be decayed, with a few open joints running up the shaft of the column. A common treatment for this condition is to pull out the columns and put in new ones, but effective alternatives exist that can preserve much of the original column. The joints can be stabilized with dowels and the decayed bottoms treated by replacing short sections with new wood or filling with epoxy consolidants. Often these treatments cost much less than complete replacement.

Sometimes, however, an element is so deteriorated it is not economical or practical to preserve it, and a replacement is needed. The new element should match the old in material and design, based on surviving ones elsewhere on the building or other clues such as paint shadows of missing moldings.

A short section of molding is custom shaped to match an existing molding. The sheet-metal pattern aids accuracy in matching the profile.

The new cap on this rooftop railing (left) has decayed in just six years due to its laminated construction.

Whether parts are preserved or replaced, they should be treated with methods that ensure a long life with low maintenance. Keep in mind the following guidelines:

- Select appropriate materials. Species of wood such as redwood or cypress resist decay where moisture cannot be avoided as in wood gutters. White oak used for door thresholds resists decay and holds up to abrasion.
- Ventilate hollow spaces. Stave-built columns, built-up pedestals, and enclosed cornices require upper and lower openings to promote air movement that carries moisture away.
- Eliminate joints when possible. Joints are obvious entry points for moisture. Building up parts by tacking on moldings or by gluing up several laminations of thin wood increases the number of joints and the possibility of joint failure. The use of solid wood in the making of parts reduces the possibility of joint failure.
- Drain horizontal surfaces. Balustrade cap rails and windowsills will shed water if they are pitched for proper drainage.
- Protect individual parts. Backpriming or painting all surfaces of a part before installation ensures moisture will not penetrate. Trims and cuts during installation should be coated as well.
- Seal joints between parts. Flexible caulks and sealants allow for wood movement and keep water out of the joints.

ORGANIZING LONG-TERM MAINTENANCE AND REPAIR PROJECTS

Bring together a team to help you plan exterior woodwork maintenance and repair. Your team should include an architect or consultant for independent advice and the tradespeople or contractors who will do the work. If you depend only on yourself or on one contractor to plan a project, you limit the possibilities for effective problem solving.

For conditions surveys, assessments, and investigations, consult a professional with an understanding of both earlier building technologies and the modern field of construction. An independent and objective view is necessary.

Team members will often suggest very different solutions to your problems, which is good because it provides you with choices. Architects or consultants serve mainly to provide these alternatives. The practical experience of the tradespeople on the team is valuable. If they help develop solutions and participate in decisions, their performance on the job will be much more effective than if they are just told what to do.

Historic-house restoration and preservation work is significantly different from the modern practice of woodworking and carpentry. Seek workers who have plenty of experience on buildings similar to yours. Begin by checking with your local and state historic preservation organizations. If you cannot find workers with old-house experience, consider bringing in a preservation specialist to train a local crew in the needed methods, skills, and techniques.

STRATEGIES FOR REPAIR

Mounting a major corrective maintenance project makes sense if you have a complete and thorough plan in place and significant funding is available to carry out all necessary treatments for upgrading conditions. This might include repairing some parts in place; removing, preserving, and reinstalling other parts; or fabricating new wooden parts. This type of project often extends to other parts of the building, including windows and doors, gutters and drainage, and roofing. Sometimes this extensive work is spread out over two to five seasons, proceeding facade by facade around the building. (See also Establishing a Maintenance Program.)

If you have a limited but regular and continuing supply of resources (time and money), you can develop a strategy to stabilize the current conditions with regular preventive maintenance and slowly upgrade problem areas. Upgrading poor and fair conditions on an incremental basis allows you to learn continually and become more effective as you go. Setting priorities and planning effectively are very important with this strategy.

If resources are extremely limited, deal only with poor conditions that have the highest priority. Temporarily protect critically damaged systems, such as roofs with holes, and elements of historic significance, such as carved panels, from further deterioration. (See also Roofs.)

Before this molding is nailed in place, sealant is applied at the edges of the muting surfaces. This provides an effective seal against rainwater. Note that the lower edge is not sealed, allowing any water that does get in the joint to readily drain out.

CONTINUING MAINTENANCE

Whenever exterior woodwork is done, schedule a round of minor touch-up repairs for the next season. This follow-up work is needed because, no matter how well the work is done, the woodwork will inevitably expand and shrink, causing some joints to open up and a few areas of paint to peel. If these minor repairs are not taken care of, they will become trouble spots in the future.

A program of routine continuing maintenance will do the most to preserve your historic house. Simple seasonal cleaning of the exterior to remove leaves, mold, and mildew will help prevent significant deterioration. Spot-painting and joint-caulking maintenance will keep woodwork dry and free of decay at minimum cost. Control these activities with a written schedule and keep a log or journal of everything that is done to the building.

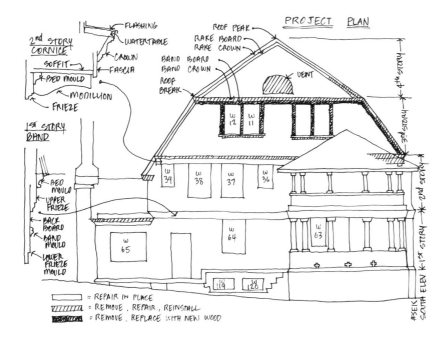

Even a rough sketch can provide practical guidance for a corrective maintenance project. Here all exterior woodwork parts are named and procedures clearly indicated. This helps avoid confusion as building parts are removed for various treatments and eventually reinstalled.

Wooden Windows

Charles E. Fisher

We interact with windows on a daily basis. They provide our visual link to the outside. Without leaving the house, we can see if it is raining, where the children are playing, and if the grass needs cutting. We usually welcome the sunlight inside; we utilize curtains and shades to control the light and provide privacy; and many of us still open and close the sash, depending on the weather. Builders trimmed windows both on the inside and out, usually with decorative moldings in keeping with the architectural style of the building. They recognized the importance of windows and framed the opening almost as if it were a large picture frame. We have further embellished the window with practical, yet decorative features, such as shutters, shades, and, particularly, curtains. In all, windows are one of the most important parts of the historic house and deserving of ongoing care and maintenance.

Whether highly ornate or simply detailed, windows are an important part of the historic character of a building.

Historically, houses had windows for a variety of reasons. Prior to the advent of central heating and air-conditioning and inexpensive electric lighting in the early twentieth century, windows allowed sunlight in to illuminate the inside of homes naturally, and they let breezes flow through the house during warm weather and kept cold air out during the winter months.

Other than exterior doors, windows are the only common architectural feature that contributes to both the interior and exterior appearance of homes. The desire for aesthetic symmetry and balance has had as much influence on the placement of windows as the practical functions they serve. Yet the varying function of windows can dictate appearance and, at times, disrupt balance on the outside of a building; for example, windows located on stair landings between floor levels or, in later construction, over kitchen sinks can appear to be haphazardly placed from the exterior.

While windows contribute to both the design and practical functioning of a home, their maintenance and retention are particularly important in terms of historic preservation. First, windows make up as much as 20 to 30 percent of the exterior walls of a house, representing a significant amount of historic material. Taking into consideration a corresponding interior function along the outer walls, one can understand the importance of their preservation.

Most windows found in older homes have not deteriorated to the point where they need replacement. Peeling paint, cracked glazing putty, and cold drafts of air during the winter are all conditions that are routinely addressed through scheduled maintenance. Properly maintained, windows can last for hundreds of years.

Although windows will tolerate periods of neglect, next to gutters and downspouts they are probably the most important feature of a home that requires regular care to avoid decay or loss. Keeping the window properly painted and caulked, the glass cleaned, the glazing compound securing the glass sound and weathertight, and the sash in a condition that is easy to open and close are the principal goals of window maintenance. This chapter will address these goals, along with ways to improve the performance of existing windows.

WINDOWS OF THE PAST

Early windows in the English colonies were of a casement design with wide wooden *muntins* separating small panes of glass. Because of the high cost of imported glass, casement windows were usually small in size and few in number, particularly in northern climates where the small size of windows was also attributed to the cold weather. Two types of window glass were available, both of which were handblown. In the colonial period and early years of our new nation, the highest quality and most expensive glass was *crown glass*, which was handblown into a flat disk, then cut into small panes. More free of imperfections than the alternative *cylinder glass*, crown glass was most often found in affluent homes. Cylinder glass was by far the most prevalent glass used in windows through the nineteenth century. Also known as *broad glass*, it was formed when a long cylinder was created, then split along its length so that it could be rolled into a flat sheet for cutting into small panes. By the latter part of the nineteenth century, cylinder glass could be made in very long lengths, using mechanical means.

Today, most historic houses have *double-hung* windows, yet this design did not appear until the mid-eighteenth century. The double-hung window has two sash—an upper and a lower sash—set into a window frame. The upper and lower sash are separated by a small wooden strip on the window frame, known as the *parting bead*. Both sash slide up and down and usually are counterbalanced with *sash weights*, which are concealed from view in the frame.

The forerunner of the double-hung assembly was the single-hung window, which appeared in the colonies at the turn of the eighteenth century. The single-hung window had an upper and lower sash, but only the lower sash slid vertically and it was not counterbalanced. Instead, it was commonly supported in the open position by a pin inserted through holes in the frame and sash; the upper sash did not move. Since it did not need a hollow area within the sides of the window frame to conceal the sash weights, the single-hung window utilized a simple frame placed against the wall frame or masonry opening. Pullies were also not needed. By the late eighteenth century, single-hung and double-hung windows had replaced the casement design as the prevalent window styles. While the double-hung window was a distinct improvement over the single-hung window, the latter was cheaper to make and remained in use in less expensive dwellings and in utilitarian buildings, such as carriage houses and car garages, until World War II.

By the early nineteenth century, large sheets of glass had become less expensive. It was also established that, by increasing the depth of the muntin (and thus the thickness of the sash), the width of the muntin could be narrowed

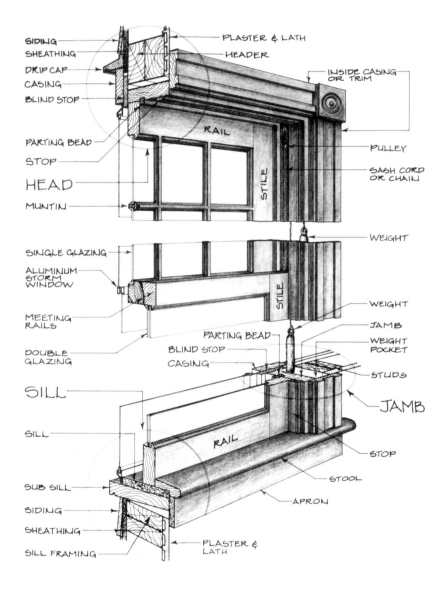

Anatomy of a double-hung window

significantly without sacrificing any strength in the sash. This led to both the windows and the glass panes becoming larger and muntins becoming narrower in width. With this development, the general operation and appearance of the double-hung window was largely set for the next hundred years. As glass increased in availability and dimensions after the Civil War, individual panes became even larger. Sash were soon appearing with only a single pane of glass. Throughout the nineteenth and the first half of the twentieth century, stylistic changes—such as whether the top of the window was flat, segmented, or round—affected the appearance of the window.

By the last half of the nineteenth and into the twentieth century, windows changed in appearance mostly in terms of the use of muntin divisions. An Arts and Crafts residential window made shortly before World War I might have three or four *lights* (glass panes) in the upper sash, all set vertically, but only a single light in the lower sash, which provided for an unobstructed view from the inside. During the Colonial Revival era, sash with lights set in multiple rows in both the upper and lower sash were common, often employing a wider muntin that recalled an eighteenth-century appearance.

Many of the features associated with modern windows have historic ties. Although insulating (thermal) glass was not commonly available until the 1970s, some sash made as early as the 1840s had two layers of glass with a dead-air space in between. Various forms of weatherstripping were used even in the colonial period, although the common felt weatherstripping was a product of the post–Civil War industrial era. While sash are counterbalanced in a variety of ways today, even our modern window industry would acknowledge that the sash pullies-and-weight system that appeared in the eighteenth century remains the most durable.

WHY WINDOW PROBLEMS OCCUR

Very few components of historic windows ever break or wear out. Window glass obviously breaks when struck by force, but glass essentially is a very durable product. Sash cords, which connect the sash to counterbalanced weights, do wear out with use and through time, representing the weak link in the traditional wooden window.

Functionally, the operability of window sash—the ability to raise and lower them—may eventually be impeded in several ways. Careless painting, which can include painting the window shut, is probably the most common impediment. Accumulated paint layers can also make it harder to raise and lower windows unless certain maintenance steps are undertaken. Broken sash cords naturally will affect the operation of windows, as will faulty sash locks or weatherstripping and broken or worn parting beads. All of these problems can easily be corrected with simple maintenance work.

Peeling or cracked paint and loose or cracked putty and caulk are problems that will occur over time, even when good maintenance practices are followed. Although these problems may at first seem minor, failure to reestablish a sound paint surface and weathertight glazing and caulk around the window frame will eventually lead to deterioration of wooden joints and decay of the wood. This deterioration occurs as a result of moisture penetration and entrapment. While routine maintenance can prevent such problems, once such deterioration and decay occur they can be expensive and time-consuming to correct properly. Fortunately, older windows traditionally were made of more decay-resistant wood than they are today, helping to account for their high survival rate, despite occasional deferred maintenance.

Less frequent are window problems associated with termite infestation; racking of the window frame as a result of wall settlement; and physical abuse from window air-conditioning units. Usually such damage in a house is not widespread but rather confined to a few windows.

Window Maintenance

Keeping Windows Clean

To most of us, cleaning windows means simply cleaning the glass and occasionally dusting the frames, but this is not always enough. In some geographic locations and in rooms with high humidity, such as kitchens and baths, condensation forming on windows may be a seasonal condition. Condensation will usually occur on the inside of the glass and may puddle or pond along horizontal surfaces as it runs off the glass. With air-conditioning, the condensation may occur on the outside. In either case, horizontal surfaces of the sash and sill should be wiped to remove excess moisture. Failure to do so will lead eventually to wood rot of the muntin and sash joints. In the short term, it can lead to mildew with resulting dark stains. Where mildew is present on surfaces that are not to be repainted, clean with a gentle (5 percent) solution of bleach in water.

Keeping windows clean is especially important today because of our knowledge of health risks associated with lead paint. Since the majority of paint made before 1970 contained lead, you should assume that there is lead present in the paint on your windows. Even where repainting has occurred recently, the lead paint underneath can be chipped or exposed, especially along the sides of the window when sash are raised and lowered along a friction surface.

It may be appropriate, in some cases, to remove the paint completely. If not, each homeowner can take certain measures to control lead hazards. The friction surfaces of the window, particularly along the jamb where the sash slides and along the painted edges of the sash, generate paint dust for which wet cleaning is needed. Unless you have a HEPA (High Particle Air Filter) vacuum, using your household vacuum is not effective since it creates considerable dust in discharging air. Windows that are in relatively good condition, with paint intact, should be cleaned regularly using a trisodium phosphate (TSP) solution. TSP is available in powdered form at your local hardware store. Clean the sill and apron on a weekly basis during seasons when the windows are opened and closed. Clean both the inside and outside portions of the sill. Additional steps for managing the risk from lead paint are discussed as we go through various maintenance procedures. See also page 19.

The Sticking Window

Most older houses will have one or more of the sash stuck shut, especially with upper sash, where lack of use or measures to reduce air infiltration, such as caulking, prevent their opening. Never use screwdrivers and a thick pry bar to open a stuck sash on historic windows because of the damage or disfigurement to wood that inevitably occurs. By taking a little time and the right tools, most stuck sash can be opened easily without damage. The first step is to use a razor knife to cut any paint film between the sash and the frame, taking care not to gouge the wood with the sharp edge. This will keep the paint from chipping, producing an irregular paint surface and creating chips that may contain lead. Utilizing a putty knife three inches or wider, insert the blade between the sash and the wood stop along the frame, working it along the entire side. Repeat this step along the other side, at the meeting rail if necessary, and at the head or sill, depending on whether you are working with the upper or lower sash. Place a large block of wood along the rail and stile, tapping it with a rubber hammer as you move along the edge of the sash. If there still is resistance, repeat the entire procedure. At this point, you should be able to open the window. By taking your time and not trying to pry open the window, you can avoid unnecessary damage. Rubbing a little wax or silicone along the jamb should also make the window easier to open and close. Be sure to clean surfaces as previously described.

The small panel along the jamb allows access to the sash weights. The panel cover has been removed to show the cylindrical weight.

Right: The wooden stop on the room side needs to be carefully detached in order to remove the sash.

To provide a weather seal, glazing compound is worked by hand into a long strip; seated against the glass and wood; and then beveled using a putty knife.

BROKEN SASH CORD

Most double-hung sash are connected to large cylindrical metal weights on both the left and right sides, utilizing either a sash cord (rope) or metal sash chain. The cord or chain is fastened to the top of the sash stiles and protrudes out of the top of the sash; it is set through a metal pulley at the top of the frame and connected to the metal weight concealed in the frame. When the cord breaks, the weight becomes disconnected, affecting opening and closing of the sash. Replacing sash cords takes some time, since the sash usually need to be removed from the frame.

First, examine the window frames at the jambs (pulley stiles) to see if metal weatherstripping is present. If there is no weatherstripping, look for a small access panel near the bottom of both jambs. Gently remove this cover to gain access to the sash weight. If no access cover exists and you have interior shutters with wall pockets, check the inside casing for an access panel. If none exists here, the inside casing trim will need to be removed to get to the sash weight.

Many historic windows have had weatherstripping added. If metal weatherstripping exists in the jambs, it may have a raised *kerf* (ridge). This will need to be removed to get access to both to the weight pocket and the sash.

By carefully removing the weatherstripping as you remove the sash, the weatherstripping most likely can be reused.

To reduce any lead dust, first mist the stop with a TSP water solution, then, using a knife blade, break the paint seal on the wood stops holding the lower sash in place. Employing patience, a wide-blade putty knife, small flat pry bar, and block of wood, carefully remove the stops at the bottom, sides, and top of the window. Then, lift the lower sash up off the sill and toward you, removing the other sash cord if it is still secured to the sash. The upper (outer) sash can be removed at this time by removing the parting bead. This strip of wood is seated in a groove in the jamb and is usually pressure fitted. After cutting any paint film, pry the strip out carefully, starting at the bottom. If finishing nails are present, these wood strips can be gradually worked loose. If it splits, replacement pieces should be available at most millworks and lumber yards, although they may vary in size from those currently in your window. It is important that the new parting bead be the same width. Since the bead is a friction surface, remove the paint or, if necessary, replace it. If integral weatherstripping exists, slide the upper sash down and remove the nails from the weatherstripping along the upper jamb. With the sash lowered, disconnect any sash cord or chain still connected and gently lower the weight to the bottom of the pocket.

While all the sash are out is a good time to clean the pulleys by removing and soaking them in paint remover, then applying a lubricant. It is also good practice to remove the paint from the friction surface on both edges of the sash stiles by wet scraping and limited chemical stripping. Then feather the paint edge using a sponge sanding block. Paint on the friction surfaces of the jamb can be removed using similar methods.

Feed one end of the new sash cord through the loosened pulley and tie a small weight behind it, allowing it to fall to the bottom of the weight pocket. Then attach the cord to the sash weight. Establish the appropriate length of the cord, or chain, making sure that the sash weight will not hit the bottom of the pocket when the sash is closed. Then secure the cord to the sash and reinstall it. Secure the pulleys and any existing weatherstripping. If the integral weatherstripping is being reused, make sure any paint has been removed before reattaching. If sash chains exist instead of sash cords, they can be chemically cleaned before reusing. If the chains are worn excessively or have other defects, they should be replaced.

While reattaching sash weights takes some time and involves a learning process with the first one you do, the end result of the work accomplishes numerous tasks. The pulleys are reconditioned, lead paint hazards reduced, and the sash operates smoothly. If the interior sash is still very tight, the interior stop can be set back slightly from its original location before repainting.

Broken Glass

Broken glass is an annoyance and takes time to fix. If older glass is present in the sash, there may be a distinct change in the visual quality of a replacement piece. Old glass has varying optical qualities, which we usually fail to notice until after new glass has been used to replace a broken pane. If appearance is an issue, you can either investigate some of the reproduction glass available or simply borrow glass from a less visibly prominent window with similar size glass to use as needed with selective replacement on other sash.

Replacing a pane properly takes time because of the number of steps involved. First the broken glass and glazing compound have to be removed. Sometimes the old glazing compound is so deteriorated that it comes out easily, but in most cases it will test your patience. A number of techniques can be used. First, water mist the paint on the inside and use a razor knife to cut the paint film. Then cover the opening on the inside. Certain paint removal gels will soften the old glazing compound enough so that it can be removed. A heat gun can also be used, but take care to protect adjacent unbroken glass using a nonasbestos heat shield. Heat shields are available at most hardware stores, since they are commonly used in copper plumbing repair. Once the glazing compound is removed, extract the glazing points—small metal pieces that help to secure the glass. Then remove any broken glass and scrape the old putty from the glazing channel, or *rabbet*. Take care not to gouge the wood when removing the old putty.

To install the replacement glass (which is cut slightly smaller than the opening), first clean the glazing rabbet, and then apply either a mixture of linseed oil and turpentine or a good paint primer for wood. This will provide for a more effective bond between the glazing compound and the wood. After this dries, apply a thin layer of glazing compound to the back of the glazing channel, around all four sides, then press the replacement glass up against the compound and secure it with several glazing points. This "back putty" helps seal the glass and prevents it from rattling; it is set between the inside edge of the glass and the back of the rabbet. Add a final seal of compound and bevel around the edge of the glass. The compound should not protrude past the edge of the muntin, as this will be noticeable from the inside. Excess compound can be removed easily at this point. The glazing compound will take time to set, so painting will come later.

When the compound or putty has set, use a muntin or sash brush and apply a high quality exterior paint so that it extends onto the glass approximately one-eighth inch. When scraping off excess paint, be sure not to remove this one-eighth-inch paint line as it acts as a weather seal. An inexpensive plastic drywall knife (one-eighth-inch thick or more) can be used as a straight edge—set on an angle against the glazing compound—when scraping off excess paint with a razor blade, taking care not to scratch the glass.

PAINTING AND CAULKING

Perhaps more than any other part of a house, the window requires particular attention in painting. Whether you are painting the windows yourself or having a contractor do it, you should ensure that these steps are followed:

SURFACE PREPARATION

Removing paint without gouging the wood with scrapers or using chemical strippers in a manner so as not to raise the wood grain or cause excessive "fuzzing" necessitates both patience and some skill. When dealing with older paints, always take proper safety measures against the probable presence of lead paint. In many cases, it is not necessary to remove all the paint if it is in generally good condition; however, feather paint edges where paint has chipped or flaked off. Where the paint is in fair condition, remove old paint from the jamb, pulley stiles and stops, and the sash, both to achieve better paint adherence and also to lessen health risks from lead paint.

Be sure that you are ready to paint (at least within a few days) once all unpainted surfaces have been sanded and cleaned. Sunlight damages an exposed wood surface very quickly and causes poor paint adhesion with premature paint failure. Over the long term, sunlight will cause exposed wood to take on a gray color. Where gray coloration has occurred, sand down to a natural wood color. Before painting, clean with a TSP water solution, which, unlike household soap, does not leave a soapy film. Most important, buy the best quality paint from a major manufacturer, making sure that it is compatible with existing paint. You get what you pay for in paint quality and performance. When hiring a contractor, insist on this, since contractors often will use a cheaper grade "contractor's paint."

PAINTING

Follow the paint manufacturer's recommendations. Do not paint when the sun is directly shining on the wood. Apply paint coats as instructed, remembering that top-quality paint and proper painting methods and preparation will provide for an extended life of both the paint job and your windows. Too often, a poor paint job leads to an owner's frustrations and the decision to replace the windows unnecessarily. Since wooden sills are usually the first area to exhibit paint failure, more frequent painting of the sill may be necessary.

CAULKING

Windows need to be caulked to keep out the weather (both wind and rain). A good bead of caulk should be run where the window joins with the wood siding or masonry. Caulk also needs to be maintained where the sill and the jambs meet. This is an important junction, since water seepage at this joint will lead to time-consuming repairs later on.

INSIDE FINISHES

The inside surfaces of the window need less frequent refinishing. Areas that need to be maintained, however, are the intersections of the muntins, where cracks in the finish film can occur, and horizontal surfaces on the muntins and at the meeting rail and sill. In these areas, condensation can seep through, causing the finish to fail and flake and lead to more serious damage from moisture, such as wood rot.

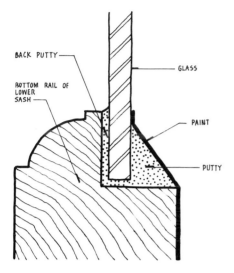

When applying paint to the sash and the glazing compound, the paint film should extend beyond the putty onto the glass by one-eighth of an inch in order to provide an effective seal.

IMPROVING THE PERFORMANCE OF EXISTING WINDOWS

Too often, windows are replaced unnecessarily, resulting in a significant loss of historic fabric and changing the architectural character of a building. A number of measures can be taken, however, to improve the performance of your historic windows without spending the money to replace them.

WINDOW SCREENS

If many or all of your windows lack insect screens, a procedure common in the first half of the century, and still practical and inexpensive today, was to install half screens on the room side of the opening. Half screens can be made by any local millwork shop and consist of a slender wooden frame that is channeled on the side edges so that it will slide on a simple bead or track fastened to the interior window stop. To permit ease of removal for window cleaning, one channel is cut deeper and several band springs are attached. This allows the screen to pop in and out of the opening as needed. This simple solution keeps the window appearance unaltered on the outside. The screens are usually intended for the lower sash; when not in use they can be raised to the upper half, providing a clear view out the lower sash.

WEATHERSTRIPPING

Where existing weatherstripping is deficient or lacking altogether, the addition of new weatherstripping is the single most cost-effective way to improve the energy performance of your windows. There are many different types of window weatherstripping. Some are surface mounted and easily installed, while others require removal of the sash and minor cutting in order to install integral or interlocking seals.

STORM WINDOWS

Storm windows have been used since the nineteenth century as a means to improve the energy performance of windows. Placed on the outside, storm windows cover the entire opening and, in combination with the historic windows, can provide better energy performance than most modern windows, which utilize insulating glass (two separated sheets of glass set within the sash). An exterior storm covering the entire opening can also provide significant protection from the weather to your historic windows. If old or historic storm windows exist, consider continuing to use them. A triple-track exterior storm window custom painted to match the color of the historic windows is the least expensive approach for new storms; however, many people object to the visual impact of the protruding metal track for the storm and screen panels, preferring to use a wooden frame or single-track aluminum frame with removable screen and storm panels rather than sliding units. The storm panel in these units can be removed from the room side and a screen inserted seasonally. This system eliminates having to climb an outside ladder each fall and spring.

Storm panels can also be installed on the room side of the window. Some storm systems are designed to set within the opening, and others are attached on the facing of the window trim, utilizing a magnetic seal or Velcro strips. Interior storm windows usually have to be removed to gain access to the sash. This is essential for maintenance and removal of condensation, which may occasionally collect between the storm and the historic sash. There are available, however, some good simple-frame interior storm windows that are self storing.

WHAT TO DO WITH SEVERELY DETERIORATED WINDOWS

Most windows are repairable, although a severely deteriorated window may cost as much to repair as to replace with a good quality window. Expe-

Historic windows should be repaired and maintained whenever possible. Shutters should be mounted on appropriate hardware and not affixed flat against the wall.

rienced contractors utilize a combination of *epoxy* (a modern wood consolidant and filler) and *dutchman* (splicing in new wood) repairs where sills, frame, or sash joints are rotted. Avoid contractors who simply want to cover the frame over with aluminum sheeting (called *panning*). Sometimes historic sash or frames are deteriorated to the point that replacement is appropriate. Many companies custom-make replacement sash to match the muntin profiles, glass-light division, and appearance of the historic sash. Avoid applied or fake muntins if the new sash is to have dual glazing. More successful alternatives are available. Replacement sash can be installed in existing sound wooden frames with little or no alteration, using a variety of installation methods. Considering the expense of replacement and the loss of the historic material, however, repair rather than replacement of historic windows is always the best preservation approach.

If you believe that one or more of your sash need replacement, be sure to contact either an architect or contractor with considerable experience in working on historic buildings, and always ask for references. Either your local historic district commission or your state historic preservation agency may be able to recommend an experienced contractor sensitive to the preservation needs of historic buildings. In nearly all cases, replacement windows will need to be custom made, carefully matching the historic unit.

If your windows are in fair to good condition for their age, proper maintenance is both cost-effective and manageable. Peeling paint, cracked glazing putty, and cold drafts of air during the winter are all conditions addressed through routine maintenance. Whether you do the work or employ an experienced contractor, the better the quality of work, the longer the windows will last. Given the quality of original construction with the availability of much better lumber in the past for use in millwork, and the importance of windows in the overall preservation of a building, good window maintenance makes good sense.

Exterior Paints and Other Finishes

Andrea M. Gilmore

The exterior surfaces of historic houses are painted for two primary reasons—to protect and preserve their exterior building fabric and to create color schemes appropriate for their architectural style. As an exterior finish, paint is a protective coating. It requires maintenance and renewal to ensure a house's long-term preservation. As a renewable coating, paint also enables the owner of a historic house to enhance the house's architectural style with original or appropriate period colors that can be applied for a relatively modest cost and are readily changeable within the house's eight-to-ten-year repainting schedule.

Overview of Exterior Architectural Paints

The history of exterior architectural paints falls into two broad categories: hand-mixed paints made and applied before the Civil War and the ready-mixed paints that flooded the market in the second half of the nineteenth century. Both the hand- and the ready-mixed paints were made with similar materials—pigments ground in oil (most commonly linseed oil) and turpentine (used as a thinner). Before 1860, a painter used a stone slab and muller to grind the pigments in oil for each paint color used. After the paint industry was mechanized, pigments were ground in a factory and could be bought fully prepared in sealed cans.

In the seventeenth and eighteenth centuries, the exteriors of American houses were minimally painted. In the country, often the trim boards were painted and the clapboards remained unpainted. The paint color most frequently found on these very early trim boards is dark red. In urban areas, both clapboards and trim were more likely to be painted in strong contrasting colors. The colors found on these early buildings are shades of brown, red, yellow, and orange.[1]

Toward the end of the eighteenth century and into the first half of the nineteenth, both the clapboards and trim continued to be painted with a limited palette of colors; however, they were joined with lighter shades of green, yellow, blue, and white. In his 1812 paint guide entitled *Directions for House and Ship Painting . . . ,* Hezekiah Reynolds provided recipes for ten colors of exterior paint—white, cream, straw, orange, pea green, parrot green, grass green, red, slate, and black.[2] Turn-of-the-century homeowners continued to paint their clapboards and trim contrasting colors, the trim typically painted a lighter color—often cream or white—than that of the clapboards.

During the early years of the nineteenth century, the appearance of American house exteriors was transformed by the abandonment of the boldly colored eighteenth-century paint schemes and the ubiquitous adoption of the white-clapboard and green-shutter paint scheme. Two contemporary accounts suggest how popular this paint scheme was. Charles Dickens, writing about Worcester, Massachusetts, in 1842, stated that "all the buildings looked as if they had been painted that morning . . . Every House is the whitest of white; every Venetian blind the greenest of green."[3] Samuel Sloan, a Victorian architect, elaborated further, stating, "On entering some of our villages, the only color which meets

Primer and finish coats are being applied to this nineteenth-century Stick Style house.

the eye is white. Everything is white; the houses, the fences, the stables, the dog kennels, and sometimes even the trees cannot escape, but get a coat of white wash."[4]

Since the mid-nineteenth century, white clapboards and green shutters have remained a very popular exterior paint scheme. This preference was not without its critics, however. In the same year that Dickens wrote about Worcester, Andrew Jackson Downing, in his book *Cottage Residences*, criticized this paint scheme as follows: "There is one colour . . . frequently employed by house painters, which we feel bound to protest against most heartily, as entirely unsuitable, and in bad taste. This is white, which is so universally applied to our wooden houses of every size and description. The glaring nature of this colour, which seen in contrast with the soft green foliage, renders it extremely unpleasant to an eye attuned to harmony and coloring, and nothing but its very great prevalence in the United States could render even men of some taste so heedless of its bad effect. . . . To render the effect still worse, our modern builders paint their venetian window shutters a bright green!"[5] Downing recommended that "drab" colors "harmonious" with the landscape be used for the exterior of houses. In *Cottage Residences*, Downing published one of the first color cards, which included three shades of gray paint and three shades of fawn-colored (cream/tan) paint. Other colors recommended by Downing included shades of rose, green, and blue. These "harmonious" colors were frequently used on Italianate and Gothic Revival houses built in the middle of the nineteenth century. They appeared less often on the earlier Federal and Greek Revival houses, which continued to be painted white with green shutters.

In the 1860s, the development of the ready-mixed paint industry led to the general availability of multiple paint colors (pigments ground in oil sealed in metal cans) for use on American house exteriors. Manufacturers' promotional materials contained color sample cards of their paints as well as recommendations and illustrations for how they could be combined on houses. The development of balloon-frame construction and the manufacture of dimensional lumber provided a welcoming market for the bold and varied colors of the ready-mixed paint industry. Building magazines and architectural pattern books also encouraged varied paint colors for their Victorian house designs. The *Scientific American Architects and Builders Edition* of December 1887 recommended the following treatment for a Stick Style house: "Great care should be exercised in painting the exterior. The colors selected should be a happy blending of light and dark shades. They should be graded from rich heavy grades at the bottom to the lighter tones at the gable peaks, preserving through the intermediate section, a consistent harmony. The roof may be of dark slate color. The trimmings may be colored with a combination of blue, black and Indian red. The body of the house may be varied to suit the above. It must be distinctly borne in mind that all buildings of the same class cannot be treated alike. Trees have a wonderful effect on colors used, and the main study of the painter and the owner should be that the salient points of form and detail be enhanced by the proper selection of the various colors."[6]

Bold, heavily pigmented paints appeared in the second half of the nineteenth century. The early nineteenth-century practice of painting trim a lighter color than the body was replaced with that of painting the trim a bold, contrasting color. For example, a dark red house often had a dark green trim. The landscape architect Frederick Law Olmsted chose these paint colors for Fairsted, his Federal-style home in Brookline, Massachusetts, which he remodeled in 1883. Neighboring architect Henry Hobson Richardson also used dark greens and reds extensively on his late nineteenth-century buildings. Other common late nineteenth-century paint colors for the body and trim of houses

A Victorian house before and after its early paint colors were restored. The house was transformed from a white house with green shutters to a house with a red body color, light brown trim and window sash, and dark green shutters.

included browns, grays, and dark yellows. The very bright colors—yellows, blues, and oranges—shown on Victorian color charts were used primarily to highlight architectural ornament rather than as body or trim colors.

As the nineteenth century closed, the bold and varied colors of America's Victorian architecture fell out of vogue. Classical Revival–style houses replaced Queen Anne and Stick Style residences. The Classical Revival houses borrowed the paint schemes of the late eighteenth- and early nineteenth-century houses. Popular body colors were blue, gray, and yellow. The wooden trim, including the window sash, was nearly always painted white and the window shutters dark green or black. For much of the twentieth century, the dominant practice has been to paint American houses light colors—many continuing the tradition of the Greek and Classical Revivals. In its extreme, this practice has even painted the grand nineteenth-century Stick Style and Queen Anne houses monochromatically—often white or tan.

With the renewed interest in Victorian architecture in the 1970s, the practice of integrating architectural style with paint color has reemerged. Nineteenth-century paint guides have been republished and numerous books and articles have been written describing how to choose paint colors for your house. In addition, the examination of architectural paints—removing paint samples from a building and identifying the original paint colors with microscopy—has enabled conservators to identify and place the actual paint colors used on historic buildings. Victorian houses, once characterized as the "white elephants" of the neighborhood, are being transformed into the "grandes dames" of architectural fashion. Italianate and Gothic Revival houses are appearing in soft tones of tan and rose, while Georgian and Federal-style houses are being painted with yellow, gray, and blue bodies and white trim.

Choosing paint colors for a historic house will always present a challenge to a homeowner. However, a wealth of information about appropriate period colors exists. Homeowners also have the option of hiring an architectural conservator to identify the original paint colors on your house or help you select paint colors. Once paint colors are chosen, it is a good idea to paint samples on the house before undertaking the full paint job. See also the section ahead on types of paint, which may affect your color selection.

MAINTAINING EXTERIOR PAINT ON A HISTORIC HOUSE

REPAINTING

Maintaining the exterior paint on a historic house is critical to ensuring its long-term preservation as well as enhancing its architectural style. By virtue of their age and the physical properties of their exterior paints, historic houses are prone to a variety of paint-related problems, including excessive paint buildup, surface cracking *(alligatoring)*, blistering, peeling, mildew growth, soiling, and staining. It is important that a house be repainted *before* its paint fails and allows moisture to penetrate to the substrate, causing the paint to deteriorate at an accelerated rate. Severely deteriorated paint requires costly surface preparation and jeopardizes the future performance of paint on the house.

With the exception of excessive paint buildup and alligatoring, moisture in the walls of a historic house is the primary cause of paint failure. Leaking roofs, deteriorated flashings, and leaking or missing gutters and downspouts are the most common sources for water entering exterior walls. Other possible sources of moisture in the walls include insulation installed without a proper vapor barrier, ice dams, blocked gutters, and trees and shrubs next to the exterior walls or overhanging the roof. *All* repairs to the exterior building fabric of a house required to make the walls watertight should be undertaken prior to, or in conjunction with, preparing the exterior surfaces for repainting. Failure to repair deteriorated exterior building fabric prior to repainting will cause a new paint job to fail prematurely.

The discussion of exterior paint maintenance that follows focuses on wood substrates. However, many of the procedures for surface preparation and painting described may also be used for exterior masonry surfaces. It is a general rule that acrylic paints perform better than alkyd paints on masonry. This is particularly true of masonry that tends to be chronically damp.

SURFACE PREPARATION

LEAD PAINT

Lead was used in the manufacture of exterior paints throughout the 1960s and is present on the exterior of most historic houses. Lead is a toxic substance and if ingested, particularly by small children, may cause physical and neurological damage. Thus, it is crucial that all paint-surface preparation be undertaken with the full understanding of the health risks involved and knowledge of the local and state regulations regarding the disturbance of lead-based paints. (See also page 19.)

The surface preparation of exterior painted surfaces presents several opportunities for lead exposure. Sanding paint surfaces creates lead dust, which can be ingested by pets or through hand-to-mouth contact by small children. Open windows provide a ready means for outdoor sanding to deposit lead dust on floors, carpets, and furniture where children and pets crawl and play. When sanding, shut all windows and enclose the area to limit the spread of the dust. Tools used for removing lead paint should be fitted with vacuum attachments to control airborne lead dust. Using a damp cloth, wipe up any lead dust created by sanding. It should not be vacuumed, except with a vacuum cleaner specifically designed for toxic materials. Household vacuum cleaners disperse the dust into the air. Similarly, collect scraped chips of flaking lead paint with drop cloths, and wipe away any residue immediately.

Removing lead-based paint with heat releases toxic lead gases. While these gases tend not to pose health risks to the inhabitant of a historic house, they do pose risks to the workers removing the paint. Homeowners or workers performing thermal paint removal, therefore, should be protected by OSHA-approved masks with organic vapor cartridges.

All lead paint removed from a historic house should be disposed of according to state and local regulations. Since these vary from state to state, homeowners should contact their state historic preservation agency or the state agency responsible for lead abatement to obtain the guidelines that apply for their area.

COMMON CORRECTIVE PREPARATIONS

The extent of surface preparation required to achieve a paintable surface varies considerably from building to building, depending upon how the existing paint has been applied and maintained. On most historic buildings, limited paint removal, combined with scraping and sanding, will create a suitable surface for repainting. Typically, levels of paint problems or failure vary on the different sides of a building, and the surface preparation undertaken should reflect this variability. Recommended surface preparations for common types of paint problems or failure are as follows:

Paint Buildup and *Alligatoring:* In most instances, alligatoring can be treated by scraping to a sound surface and lightly sanding the surface of the paint layer that is to receive the primer. Removing alligatored paint from carved or molded surfaces is more difficult than from flat surfaces and may require the use of specially shaped scrapers. If the alligatoring has penetrated the full depth of the paint layers and has caused the bond of the paint to the substrate to fail, the paint will have to be removed completely before repainting.

Blistering and Peeling: Sanding and scraping are also the best way to remove peeling paint. As with all surfaces that are sanded and scraped, take care not to damage the substrate. Wood surfaces can be gouged easily and excessive sanding will round the shapes of molding profiles.

Mildew: Remove mildew from exterior painted surfaces by washing them with a solution of one part bleach to one part water. A strong solution can be used since the surface is to be repainted. Apply the bleach solution to the painted surface with a soft-bristle brush and rinse off with low-pressure water. (A garden hose is fine for this type of rinsing.) Allow the surface to dry thoroughly before painting.

Since mildew growth is usually associated with moisture, preventing its recurrence requires that the source of the moisture be removed. This may in-

These nineteenth-century clapboards exhibit alligatored and peeling paint.

Paint failure caused by moisture generated rot in this wood.

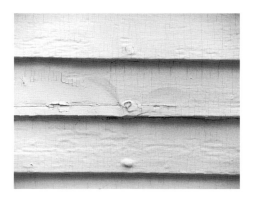

Lapped ends, handwrought nails, and years of paint buildup can be seen in these eighteenth-century clapboards. A heavy buildup of paint reveals unsuccessful efforts to remove the paint with a rotary disk sander. Rotary sanders cannot remove paint around rose-headed nails and will leave circular sanding marks on the clapboard surface.

Paint is being removed from these eighteenth-century clapboards with a solvent-based paint stripper.

A heat pad is being used to remove paint from a historic building. The deteriorated, pitted surface of the wood is the result of previous stripping with a rotary disk wire beater.

clude trimming trees and shrubs and repairing gutters and downspouts. Mildew-resistant paints may also help prevent the mildew from recurring.

Soiling is the term given to dirt that is deposited on a painted surface. It can include soot, cobwebs, bird excrement, and general airborne pollutants. Remove soiling from exterior paint with a nonionic detergent and water, applied with a bristle brush. Rinse the detergent with low-pressure water and allow the surfaces to dry thoroughly before repainting.

Staining usually is caused by moisture migrating though the substrate and depositing stains on the paint surface. For example, metals rust and redwood and red cedar bleed through the paint surface. In both instances, it is important to reduce the source of moisture behind the paint surface as much as possible. Remove rust from metal surfaces and coat with a rust-inhibiting primer. Countersink exposed nailheads and fill with a high quality wood filler. Back prime red cedar and redwood clapboards and then coat with a stain-blocking primer.

PAINT REMOVAL

If the condition of the paint on a historic house requires that the paint be removed before repainting, the task of surface preparation becomes far more difficult and costly. There are three general methods for removing paint from a building—mechanical, chemical, and thermal.

Mechanical means of paint removal include hand-sanding and scraping, which are practical for removing small areas of paint from a house, but not for its entire stripping. Sanding machines speed up the process considerably and can produce satisfactory results if used by an experienced operator. Use only orbital and disk sanders, not rotary sanders, which leave circular sanding patterns on the wood substrate.

Abrasive blasting, another mechanical method of paint removal, should be used only for the preparation of metal surfaces, *never* on wood or masonry surfaces. Abrasive blasting disfigures wood surfaces, pitting clapboards and obscuring molded detail. It removes the fired surface of brick, leaving it pitted and more water absorbent than before.

The two principal types of chemical paint strippers are *caustic* and *solvent*. Caustic strippers, either sodium, potassium-hydroxide, or carbonate based, can be applied to a painted surface by brush, or removable elements can be immersed in the stripper. Caustic strippers are not recommended for wood substrates because they may cause the surface of the wood to darken and individual wood fibers to separate. They also are prone to depositing salts in wood and masonry materials. In wood, the salts cause paint-adhesion problems; on the masonry materials, they cause efflorescence.

Like caustic strippers, solvents can be either applied by brush or used to dip removable architectural elements. They soften the paint binder so that the paint can be scraped off with a metal tool and the remaining wood surface lightly sanded and wiped with mineral spirits to remove the wax residue. Solvent-based strippers are efficient but pose health risks. Most contain methylene chloride, which is a carcinogen.

Exterior paint can also be removed by heat. Heat coils and hot-air guns produce satisfactory results and, if used carefully, do not pose a fire threat to the historic house. Open-flame torches are a fire hazard and should not be used to remove paint. Their heat may cause materials inside a wall to smolder for hours before bursting into flame.

CHOOSING AN EXTERIOR PAINT

OIL-BASED PAINTS

Exterior oil-based paints manufactured today share few physical properties with the eighteenth-, nineteenth-, and early twentieth-century paints found on historic houses. Until the 1960s, the majority of exterior paints were manufactured with linseed oil and lead white (lead carbonate), the latter used as a coloring pigment as well as a drying agent and frequently supplied to a painter as a lead-and-linseed-oil paste. As Morgan Phillips writes in his "Survey of Paint Technology," "A painter could easily work with the white lead paste, color pigments ground in oil, extra oil, turpentine, and driers to formulate and tint paints for every application, interior and exterior, matte and glossy."[7]

In the late 1960s, concerns regarding the toxicity of white lead resulted in its elimination from the manufacture of housepaints. In most exterior paints, white lead has been replaced with titanium dioxide and the traditional linseed-oil binder has been replaced by synthetic alkyd resins. Linseed oil is still used in the manufacture of exterior housepaints, but its slow-drying properties make it less popular than the alkyd-resin paints.

Alkyd resins are made by the direct chemical combination of the fatty acids of drying oils with acids and alcohols. These modern resins are fast-drying (twenty-four hours between paint applications) and more durable than linseed-oil paints. They are, however, more impermeable and therefore not as suitable for use on aged building fabric covered with old, brittle, and more permeable linseed-oil-based paint.

A difficulty encountered in evaluating the performance properties of modern alkyd-resin paints is that the ever-changing VOC (volatile organic compounds) regulations, which vary from state to state, have led to their frequent reformulation. Traditional formulations for alkyd resins include toxic, air-polluting solvents. Each time the use of one of these solvents is banned or the percentage that can be used in a paint is reduced, the paint formula has to be adjusted. Consequently, many paints currently for sale have not been time tested on historic buildings.

ACRYLIC-EMULSION (LATEX) PAINTS

Modern acrylic-emulsion paints consist of minute particles of polymer suspended in water. They form a paint film by the evaporation of the water and the coalescing of the polymer particles. Acrylic-emulsion paints are popular because of their ease of application and cleanup. In recent years, paint companies have devoted their major research efforts toward the improvement of acrylic-emulsion paints because they do not contain toxic, air-polluting solvents.

Acrylic-emulsion paints also are subject to less yellowing than traditional linseed-oil or alkyd-resin paints. These are not well suited, however, for use as primers on aged wood or deteriorated paint surfaces. Unlike an oil binder, which penetrates the wood or paint surface, the water binder causes the acrylic-emulsion paint film to form on top of the substrate. This creates a weak bond between the paint and the substrate that ultimately results in paint failure. In recent years, a number of historic buildings have been stripped of their historic paint and primed with an acrylic-emulsion paint, only to have the paint fail because of the inadequate bond of the primer to the aged wood substrate. The condition worsens over time, as the weight of succeeding layers of paint pulls the paint away from the substrate.

There is no hard-and-fast rule for choosing a type of paint for the exterior of a historic house. The technical consulting services of most major paint companies presently recommend that a historic house be primed with an alkyd-resin oil primer and finished with an acrylic emulsion. The alkyd-resin primer penetrates the aged wood or paint substrate and creates the strong bond over which the alkyd emulsion is applied.

Although the acrylic-emulsion paint is often considered a more desirable finish coat because it is subject to less discoloration and is a more permeable surface coating than the alkyd-resin paint, from the perspective of a historic house, this is not necessarily the case. Historic linseed-oil paints definitely discolored. Further, permeability of the finish coat may be desirable if the exterior walls of the house tend to be damp. Personal experience has found that alkyd-resin paints for both primer and finish coat perform well and replicate the appearance of the historic lead-based linseed-oil paints better than the acrylic-emulsion paints. Also, the use of acrylic emulsion implies a long-term commitment because an acrylic-emulsion finish coat cannot be painted over later with alkyd resin.

Regardless of the combination of paints ultimately selected, two basic rules should be followed. First, the primer should be an alkyd-resin paint; second, both the primer and finish paints should be from the same manufacturer and meet the manufacturer's compatibility requirements.

SUITABLE CONDITIONS FOR EXTERIOR PAINTING

The satisfactory performance of a paint job depends upon the application of the paint under suitable environmental conditions. The performance of an exterior paint job will be adversely affected if the temperature is too hot or too cold; if the surfaces to be painted are too wet, due to either high humidity or rain; or if the paint is applied on a windy day to a house located in an area of airborne pollutants.

Paint manufacturers publish temperature requirements for their paints. As a general rule, it is recommended that they not be applied when the temperature is below 40 degrees Fahrenheit (or predicted to go below 40 degrees Fahrenheit within twenty-four hours after the application of the paint) or above 90 degrees Fahrenheit. Low temperatures may cause emulsion paints to coalesce improperly and will slow the drying times of alkyd-resin paints. Temperatures over 90 degrees Fahrenheit may cause the solvents in alkyd-resin paints to blister.[8]

Applying a coat of paint to a wet substrate will create a weakened bond between the new paint and the substrate. This will result in paint blistering and peeling. In extreme conditions, if the paint is an impermeable alkyd, the blisters may fill with water that is unable to evaporate through the paint film.

Painting in high winds may also cause the solvents in alkyd-resin paints to dry too quickly. In addition, airborne dirt and pollutants may be trapped on the surface of a wet paint film, which may create an irregular paint surface that is aesthetically unacceptable and may jeopardize the bond of the next paint layer applied.

A final consideration is the timing of the application of the primer and finish coats of paint. Historic linseed-oil-based paints require two to four weeks between the application of the primer and finish coats, allowing a relatively flexible painting schedule. Modern alkyd-resin and emulsion paints should have their primer and finish coats applied within forty-eight hours, as the primers, which are always intended to be covered with subsequent coats, are not designed to weather between coats.

METHODS OF PAINT APPLICATION

Historic paints were traditionally applied with natural-bristle (hog's hair) brushes. Used with oil paints, bristle brushes hold paint well and allow easy paint application. In his article "Painting Techniques: Surface Preparation and Application," Brian Powell describes the advantages of the natural bristle: "The *natural bristle* fiber tapers a bit from root to tip and has small barbs that project from the tiny grooves along its length, thus promoting the holding of paint. The fiber's end is not blunt but rather fractures into many small divisions known as flag. As the bristle wears, new flag develops. These characteristics allow a smooth, even distribution of paint unavailable from other common fibers."[9]

Natural-bristle brushes, however, do not perform well with acrylic-emulsion paints. Their water binder softens the bristles and the brushes lose their flexibility and shape. Therefore, acrylic-emulsion paints should be applied with a synthetic fiber brush.

In applying either oil- or acrylic-based paints, brushes have the advantage of working the paint into the surface being painted. This is a particularly important factor when applying a primer, since it improves the bond of the primer to the substrate.

Another method for applying paint to a historic house is by spraying. There are two types of spray equipment—air and airless spray. Most contractors today use airless sprayers, which apply the paint by pressure that atomizes the paint and propels it onto the wood surface. Spraying has the advantage of being much faster than brush painting; however, it creates a weaker bond of paint to substrate than brushing. This is especially true if an acrylic-emulsion paint is used. Also, to perform well, spray painting requires that the surface be well prepared and clean, which is not always consistent with the "quick and inexpensive" paint jobs associated with spray painting.

A combination of spraying and brushing may work well on large buildings where one or two paint colors are used. The paint is applied to the surface with a spray and then brushed in. Supervision is required, however, to ensure that contractors do not omit the step of brushing on the paint.

CHOOSING A PAINT CONTRACTOR

Prior to talking to prospective painting contractors, a homeowner should prepare a scope of work for the painting project so that the work bid by each contractor is comparable. All scope-of-work outlines should include plans for identifying and then removing or protecting nearby items—such as plantings and sidewalks—during the painting contract. Window shutters and miscellaneous hardware should be labeled, removed, and stored for reinstallation at the completion of the contract.

Two critical areas for mutual understanding are the level of surface preparation sought and how the paint is to be applied. It is also important to identify for potential paint contractors the number of paint coats you intend to have applied to your house. Spot priming (of only those portions of the wood surface that are exposed) and full priming are two different paint jobs, determined by the extent and level of paint failure. Specify to prospective paint contractors the commercial brand and types of paints you want to use on your historic house, as well as the number of colors. Contractors are also often wedded to paint brands and types. Most are fond of acrylic-emulsion paints because of their ease of application and cleanup. Homeowners, however, should remember that there are several different painting systems, with good performance records, to choose from and that they should at least discuss options with potential paint contractors. One choice that should not be negotiable, however, is the alkyd-resin-based primer on bare wood or aged paint.

With a written scope of work in hand, a homeowner is ready to solicit bids from potential contractors. Ask all those who bid for the work to state in writing any changes they would make to the written scope if they were to receive the contract.

There are no standard rules for selecting paint contractors. Word of mouth often is the means by which names are passed around. Local historical societies and state and local historic commissions also often maintain lists of painting contractors. Whatever the source of the paint contractor, it is important to check references (a minimum of three for each contractor) and to inspect their completed paint projects. Paint jobs of very different quality can look equally good soon after they are completed. Ideally, therefore, completed paint proj-

Notes

1. Roger Moss, Paint in America *(Washington, D.C.: National Trust, 1994), 23–24.*

2. Ibid., 38.

3. Charles Dickens, American Notes for General Circulation *(London, 1874), 81.*

4. Samuel Sloan, The Model Architect *(1852; reprint, Mineola, N.Y.: Dover Publications, 1980), 77–78.*

5. Andrew Jackson Downing, Cottage Residences *(1842; reprint, Mineola, N.Y.: Dover Publications, 1981), 13–14.*

6. Scientific American Architects and Builders Edition (December 1887): 64.

7. Moss, Paint in America, *245.*

8. Ibid., 236.

9. Ibid., 219.

ects for inspection should have been weathering for three to five years, since this will give you a better idea of the job's long-term performance.

ROUTINE MAINTENANCE FOR EXTERIOR PAINTS

Once a historic house has been repainted, its annual maintenance schedule should include the painted exterior. (See also Establishing a Maintenance Program.) Within the first one to two years of completing a major repainting, the contractor should be willing to come back to do touch-up painting. After that it becomes the homeowner's responsibility to hire a painter or to do it personally. In either case, it is always important to make sure that the surfaces to be painted are prepared well and that the paint used for touch-ups is the same as was used for the original painting. At the completion of a painting contract, have the contractor prepare one unopened gallon of each color of paint used, to be reserved for touch-up painting. This is particularly important if custom-colored paints are part of the color scheme.

Touch-up painting is important for two reasons: it maintains protective coverage for the exterior building fabric and it prolongs the life span of a paint job. A long-term preservation goal for historic houses is to minimize the buildup of paint on their exterior surfaces, so that stretching the interval between major repaintings without jeopardizing the preservation of the exterior building fabric is an important maintenance practice. Excessive paint buildup covers over architectural detail and contributes to paint failure.

In urban areas where there is likely to be much airborne dirt deposited on the painted exterior surfaces, maintenance of the exterior paint might also include periodic washing. This washing should be done with a non-ionic detergent, bristle brushes, and low-pressure water. As part of the surface preparation, be sure to wash heavily soiled surfaces before doing any touch-up painting.

Routine maintenance should also include cleaning the gutters and downspouts, repairing leaking roofs and flashings, and trimming trees that shade the house. Failure to perform these tasks will adversely affect the performance of the exterior paints.

PLASTER

DAVID FLAHARTY

Plaster-restoration specialists are indeed fortunate that many of the material and procedural dilemmas facing other trades do not apply to them. Caring for interior plaster finishes, whether of a plain or ornamental nature, has not changed significantly since the early structures were built, nor did it need to. From time to time, a substitute material may be considered but, in general, plaster then is plaster now. Georgian ceilings, the several nineteenth-century revivals, and pre-Depression urban theaters provide excellent modes for contemporary practitioners, whose work looks to the past rather than to the present and beyond. With properly observed maintenance procedures and schedules, homeowners and house-museum managers can defer restoration long into the future. Key to this process is an understanding of plaster's makeup as well as the causes of plaster failure and the procedures that should be undertaken to repair the damage when it occurs.

PLASTERING MATERIALS

Historically, interior plaster walls and ceilings were composed of mixtures consisting of lime as the binder, a sharp sand filler, and reinforcing strands of animal hair mixed together with clean water. Lime was produced by heating natural limestone to high temperatures in kilns, thereby calcining the rock and releasing its carbonic acid while simultaneously evaporating its moisture. The resulting quicklime was later hydrated, or *slaked*, in an earthen pit or a mixing box to generate lime putty. The most effective sand filler was of an angular nature, thoroughly washed, accurately graded, and bone-dry. Sand from the sea was less satisfactory because of its rounded grain shape and its salt content. The animal hair, a slaughterhouse by-product that, like sand, was washed and dried, acted as the early equivalent of today's fiberglass, strengthening the plaster mix beyond the cohesive ability of the lime.

These ingredients, in differing proportions, were used for base-coat plastering; finish-coat work frequently substituted fine-grained white materials such as marble dust for the "coarse stuff" substrata. In the late nineteenth century, a crystalline limestone called *gypsum* was introduced to hasten the set time and curing rates of the finished plasters.

Plaster of Paris, obtained by gentle calcination of gypsum, sets rapidly and within a few hours acquires its full strength. It is very soluble in water rendering it unfit for exterior use but invaluable for running cornice profiles and casting ornaments in flexible gelatin molds. Because gypsum expands as it sets, it is ideal for repair work, and, because it sets rather than air dries, lime putty and gypsum mixes considerably decrease plastering cure times, allowing the subsequent trades to begin work sooner.

The Old Merchant's House, c. 1832, in New York City, boasts robust Greek Revival plasterwork. The matching ceiling medallions in the double parlors are unquestionably the finest designs to survive from the American classical period.

The builders of this mid-eighteenth-century house installed the baseboard molding first, then applied paling, a mud-and-horsehair plaster, to the masonry wall. Lime was used for the finish plaster. Also shown are the hacking marks that prepared the wall for a subsequent layer of plaster.

Traditional plastering techniques have changed little over the years. Below left, the plasterers apply scratch coats to wooden lath and scarify the planes; below right, flat planes are established by brown coating to plaster screeds; bottom left, a cornice profile is run in place; bottom right, a finish coat of gypsum and lime is applied and troweled smooth.

LATHING

To establish the planes of plaster walls and ceilings, wooden, metal, or gypsum-board lath is fastened to interior framing. Until the twentieth century, the most common lathing material was wood, either hand-split or sawn into suitable lengths. The strips were nailed at right angles to studs and joists, leaving a gap between each lath. The first coat of plaster was pressed onto the lath through the spaces so as to form stabilizing *keys*. Modern metal-lath design introduced much more keying than did wooden lath. Gypsum-board lath, often called *Rocklath*, was nailed directly to the framing as a substitute for the first coat of plaster, reducing the amount of moisture in the building.

Plaster was often applied to masonry substrata either directly or onto lath fastened to furring strips that held the plaster away from the brick or stone. This was important on exterior walls because moisture entering the rooms through the masonry damaged the plaster surfaces.

HISTORICAL TECHNIQUES

The best plastering consists of three coats of material: a *scratch coat*, so called because it forms a mechanical bond with the lath and is *scarified*, or scratched while still soft to form a rough surface; a *brown coat*, which is applied to the scratched planes and leveled to wooden or plaster strips called *screeds*, used as a thickness guide to achieve uniformly flat surfaces; and, finally, a *finish coat* of gypsum and lime troweled smooth.

Riven, or sawn, lath was wet before the scratch-coat application because dry lath would absorb moisture from the mix, resulting in dryouts and soft, ineffective, or broken keying. It was important to apply the plaster carefully so as to form substantial keys. Scratch-coat thickness was usually three-eighths of an inch.

The brown mortar, a somewhat poorer mix, was applied to the scratch coat while it was still damp but after it had set. This base-coat plaster was then floated against preinstalled wooden grounds around doors and windows and screeds formed on large wall or ceiling planes. Grounds were set to permit plaster thicknesses to be three-quarters to seven-eighths of an inch.

If the base coats had dried before the finish coat was applied, they were remoistened and abraded with an *angle plane* to remove loose grains of sand that would mix with the finish coat. This coat was generally smoothed and polished with a steel trowel.

ORNAMENTAL PLASTER

When a ceiling plan specified *plain-run* or *enriched cornices*, the molding was applied before the finish-coat plaster was troweled onto the base coats. This allowed the plasterer to correct any irregularities in the wall or ceiling planes where they met the cornice. To form a cornice, a sheet-metal template representing the full-size molding section was cut, filed, sanded smooth, and nailed to a *stock and slipper*. A handle/brace reinforced the wooden "horse," so called because, in traditional ornamental plaster shops, templates for over-large bench-run entablatures with fully developed cornice, frieze, and architrave moldings were drawn by mules. High-gauge (or rich-mix) plaster screeds were applied to the brown-coat walls and ceilings, and the walls below the cornice line were fitted with *running strips* (much like the sawn wooden lath) nailed and wadded to snapped chalk lines. The lubricated slipper was pushed along this track behind hand-troweled gypsum and lime, producing the cornice molding.

Because it was not cost-effective to produce a large cornice profile made entirely of plaster and lime, a slightly smaller *muffle blade* was attached to the mounted template, and the resulting profile was run on the wall or ceiling using the less expensive brown mortar reinforced by nails with heads protruding into the path of the template. With this muffle run complete, a thin coat of plaster and lime was applied to the muffled section, and the template, minus the muffle blade, was passed over the new mix several times until the profile was perfected. The stock and slipper of the running template prevented the cornice molding from penetrating into the miters. Following the runs, therefore, mitering was accomplished by hand using *miter rods* or run on a bench, then set, and hand-tooled at the miter and butt joints.

Large cornices could also be blocked and lathed rather than muffle run, again reducing the quantity of gypsum and lime required. Off-site cast enrichments were later applied to plain-run profile depressions cut into the metal blades using plaster as an adhesive. As with the cornice ornaments, plain-run or enriched ceiling medallions were turned on-site with a separate template and applied in layers according to the needs of the design. Regardless of application method, the action in each case had to be the same: a smooth finish could be achieved only if the template followed the identical path with each pass over the hardening plaster.

WHY PLASTER FAILS

Early plaster walls and ceilings are remarkably durable provided that they are not subjected to any number or combination of deleterious effects. When compromised, lime plaster on wooden lath becomes the weakest ingredient in period structures. The following cause-and-effect checklist will allow you to diagnose and attempt to cure failing plaster.

FAULTY WORKMANSHIP

The bedrock of plaster substrata is the riven, or sawn, wooden lath. To be effective, it must have been wet immediately prior to scratch-coat application and it must have been spaced so that adequate keying was formed between the laths. In addition, the laths measuring one-quarter inch by one and one-quarter inches by four feet should have been staggered in groups of eight or ten so that all lathing did not terminate at a common stud or joist.

If the lathing was not properly applied or if the scratch-coat mixture was composed of too much aggregate to be held together with the lime-and-hair binder, a poor mix with inadequate keying was the result. Such conditions can often be evaluated easily in attics without floors. Broken keys can simply be picked up or vacuumed with a heavy-duty "shop-vac" and the remaining keys counted and tested for condition. The effectiveness of the base-coat mix can be determined by attempting to crush a key manually. A poor mix will crumble, indicating that the ceiling is in danger of collapsing as keys continue to break. Walls are similarly jeopardized under these conditions but with less gravitational effect.

Over time, humidity causes wooden lath to expand and contract, especially against exterior masonry walls where condensation is a factor in winter months. As keys

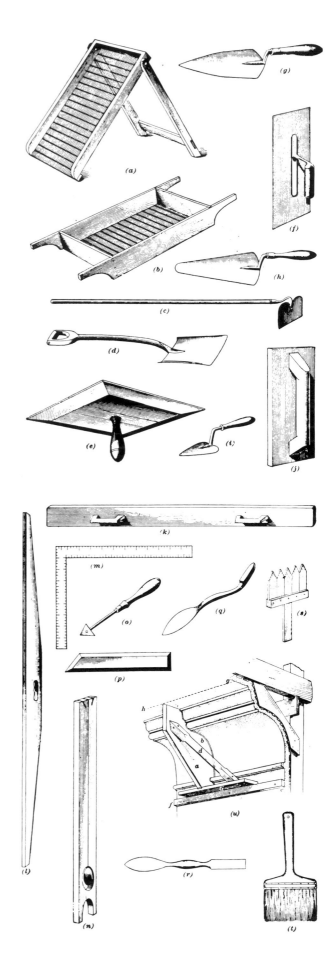

*Many of these traditional plastering tools
are still used today: (a) screen to separate
coarse sand from fine sand; (b) lime screen
to remove unslaked particles of lime; (c) hoe;
(d) shovel; (e) hawk to hold small amounts
of plaster; (f) angle float to apply finishes
to inside angles; (g), (h), (i) assorted trowels
to apply base coats and finish coat;
(j) padded float to level off humps and
fill in hollows caused by other tools;
(k) two-handled float or "darby" to float
larger surfaces; (l) simple straightedge;
(m) square to test the trueness of angles;
(n) plumb to check verticality of plastered
surfaces; (o), (p), (q), (r) jointing and
mitering tools to pick out angles in
decorative moldings; (s) comb made of
sharpened lath pieces to scratch the base
coat of plaster; (t) brush to dampen plaster
surfaces while they are worked smooth;
(u) template made of wood and metal
to cut a required outline for a fancy mold.*

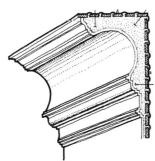

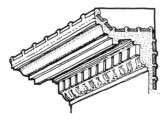

*The cornice section at top was muffle run
against wooden lath using brown mortar
and finished with gypsum and lime. The
cornice above was blocked out using wooden
lath to reduce the amount of finish plaster
required to produce the moldings.*

break, a ceiling can crack and sag, pulling the tapered-cut nails free from studs and joists. Finally, the bond between the plaster plane and the framing fails, and the ceiling collapses. Heavily ornamented ceilings are of particular concern because the supporting structure is usually identical over the entire ceiling field up to the cornice line, regardless of the increased load from the ornamentation.

STRUCTURAL OVERLOADING
Undersized structural members can cause plaster failure. If the building's frame is inadequate or if adaptive reuse or later alterations cause added weight to the building, plaster is often an early barometer of problems to come. For example, if a cedar-shake roof is replaced with slate, additional loads are placed on rafters and purlins, which bear on wall plates and studs. Load-bearing interior walls that have been sized incorrectly, in combination with faulty lathing, poor base-coat mixes, rusting lath nails, and structural movement, cause stress cracks, usually observed moving diagonally upward from the corners of windows and doors.

WATER INTRUSION
Humidity fluctuations, while often harmful to interior plaster, are by no means as dangerous as a leaking roof or a plumbing failure. Inadequate roof, gutter, or downspout maintenance causes framing and lathing to expand rapidly, breaking base-coat keys. Wet interior masonry walls transmit salts to plaster, especially when gypsum and/or lime was applied directly to the brick or stone surface. Excess water splashing at the foundation will eventually wick up, damaging the plaster at the baseboard and above. And early plumbing, often introduced to update an even earlier structure, never fails to leak.

Easily spotted evidence of water intrusion includes staining on walls and ceilings caused when wooden members are wet directly adjacent to interior plaster. Efflorescence, which can cause paint-bond failure at the least and complete disintegration of the plaster at worst, appears as dry yellow "bubbles" on a plaster entablature. Unfortunately, the site of visible water damage is frequently not an indication of intrusion immediately above or behind; water entering a building at one location may travel a substantial distance before appearing on the plaster surface elsewhere.

Plumbing may fail due to faulty workmanship, deteriorating materials and joints, or simply improper use. If, for example, a filling bathtub or sink is left unattended, the resulting overflow will damage plaster walls and ceilings sooner or later following the event. Whether from plumbing problems or leaking roofs, water intrusion in a building, if left unchecked, will eventually result in plaster failure at the base-coat/lath interface regardless of whether the lathing is wood, metal, or gypsum board. Keys will break between wooden laths; metal lath will rust eventually, rotting the material; and plaster will delaminate as Rocklath disintegrates.

VIBRATION
In combination or by itself, from whatever source, vibration causes plaster to separate from its anchors. In urban centers, heavy vehicular traffic and nearby blasting for construction shake a building perceptibly. In an extreme example, cannon salutes at Arlington National Cemetery caused plaster failure following water intrusion at Arlington House. Not much can be done to alleviate this type of damage, particularly at sites near train tracks or subway lines.

STRUCTURAL SETTLING
Period structures with plaster walls and ceilings move as a result of several factors, including gravity, seasonal moisture fluctuations, construction

irregularities, improper material applications, alterations to adjacent structures, and adaptive-reuse decisions. In general, if plaster on lath remains as built, without the intrusion of foreign materials, it will survive nicely. But if the plaster moves against the lath or the lath moves against the framing, keys will break and plaster will fail. If the Leaning Tower of Pisa had been made of wood rather than stone, its interior plaster would have fallen long ago.

INADEQUATE CURING

Plaster cures properly within a temperature range from 55 to 70 degrees Fahrenheit. Under conditions above that, especially with low humidity, historic plaster may have dried before it set, requiring affected walls and ceilings to be rewet to set the plaster. Conditions below that, particularly at the frost level, would have required demolition and replastering. Reduced air circulation causes rotting conditions to plaster and wooden lath. The speed at which gypsum sets was often regulated in the field using a retarding agent with the plaster and lime. Exceeding the recommended quantities of this material slowed the set beyond useful limits and sometimes prohibited setting altogether. Plaster that didn't set didn't cure.

INSENSITIVE ADAPTIVE REUSE

Early architectural plans are often found to be impractical as the needs of new occupants differ from those of the original owners. And as electrical, plumbing, and HVAC services have developed to today's degree of sophistication, plaster walls and ceilings inevitably must be penetrated to accommodate new equipment. These conversions can be accomplished successfully by good designers and skillful tradespeople; most often, however, poor conversions result in damage to the building. Activities to restore rooms to their original grandeur frequently reveal the extent of prior damage that may have been invisible before the work began.

For example, the need to divide, say, a large formal double parlor into smaller rooms may have resulted in damage to walls and ceilings, especially to plain-run or enriched cornices. The sensitive procedure would be to frame stud walls, leaving the moldings uninterrupted by *coping* (shaping) the cornice profile where walls meet ceilings. That is seldom done because it is difficult and labor-intensive; most often, the cornice is simply chopped out to receive studs and drywall. When the partition walls come down, the wreckage of the original cornice appears.

Early lighting fixtures originally descended from hooks or eyes attached to the central ceiling joist and were lit by candles or whale-oil fonts. In the nineteenth century, gas service was introduced by removing floorboards in chambers above parlors and running pipes to ceiling centers; later, electrical wiring was installed similarly. During these conversions, ornamental-plaster ceiling medallions often sustained damage. Modern fixtures sometimes even appear off-center within the medallions because new electrical boxes were attached to the side of the joist rather than on-center.

Added plumbing, either for running water or for steam heating, fortunately was often left exposed. Because pipes were installed so as to be unobtrusive at sides or corners of rooms, however, the plumbers usually drilled holes directly through cornices, often at the miters, leading to efflorescence when the connections failed.

HVAC ductwork calls for supply-and-return grilles, often through walls and ceilings but through floors as well. No interior plane is left undisturbed for the installation of these services. It is frequently unavoidable to box in the ductwork, and, as with radiator plumbing, cornices may be severely interrupted to provide the homeowner with heating and air-conditioning comforts.

To run a cornice profile in place, a "horsed-up" template blade is passed along a one-quarter-inch running strip over hand-troweled masses of gypsum and lime. The sheet-metal blade is nailed to a wooden stock and slipper. Note the modern expanded metal lath on the ceiling.

PLASTER REPAIRS

Plasterwork, particularly ornamental plaster, is clearly part of the permanent house architecture. The building may be significant because of its occupants, location, and history as well as its date and architectural style. Therefore, to remove, add to, or update its plasterwork involves philosophical and aesthetic considerations in addition to practical and physical concerns.

Faced with the need to repair historic walls and ceilings, the homeowner or house-museum manager is confronted with many questions or dilemmas: Is the evident damage the result of faulty routine maintenance or due to a onetime act of badly planned adaptive reuse? What procedures are required to correct the failure? What are the potential hazards to original material in correcting the damage or decay, and how can they be avoided? Under what circumstances can the homeowner act as a do-it-yourselfer, and at what point must professionals be called in? The following sections provide broad guidelines for assessing damage and choosing the appropriate method of repair.

HAIRLINE CRACKS

It is difficult to imagine a historic house that has survived without hairline or map cracks visible on walls and ceilings. Before attempting to cover or fill cracks, ascertain the cause of the damage with the help of a plasterer or architectural conservator. If cracks appear merely because of aging or if they appear because wooden lath expands and contracts with fluctuations in humidity, they can be either *canvased* or filled using a gypsum and/or lime patch.

Acrylic adhesives are injected into drilled holes in each wooden lath, thereby reattaching the scratch coat to the lath and forming a monolithic ceiling plane.

Canvas is applied using wheat paste and is, therefore, not an irreversible technique. Canvas provides a suitable ground for decorative painting and wallpapering. A similar treatment is fiberglass mat, adhered using what manufacturers describe as a *saturant*. Paint is often used as a saturant, creating a paint bond to the plaster. Fiberglass mat is not as fine as canvas and results in a rough texture. Both canvas and fiberglass sheets are difficult for the layperson to apply since the entire planes of walls and ceilings must be covered to achieve a successful result. Thereafter, surfaces may be painted or papered.

While large cracks and holes in walls or ceiling fields require the skill of a professional plasterer, a handy homeowner should be able to fill hairline cracks using a ready-mixed taping compound or a rich mix of plaster and lime putty. Trowel the all-purpose joint compound into the cracks, where it will shrink as it air dries, requiring subsequent coats in advance of sanding with successively finer grit paper.

Gypsum and lime mixes cure to become hard rather than simply losing their moisture, and they swell as they set. To patch small areas, estimate the required quantity of plaster, then put half that amount of hydrated lime on a mortarboard covered with polyethylene sheeting to prevent absorption of wet materials. Another suitable mortarboard is a plastic-laminate cutout from a countertop sink. Trowel the lime into a ring and pour into it a volume of water that, with the addition of plaster of Paris or *gauging* plaster, will equal the quantity of lime.

When the dry plaster is saturated with water, mix parts of it with the lime until the "gauge" is smooth and thoroughly blended. Mixed plaster sets rapidly; therefore, do not mix the entire quantity at once. Trowel the material into the cracks and follow the same steps for the ready-mixed joint compound.

The same effect may be achieved using hydrated or slaked lime only. The plaster base coats will absorb moisture from the lime, causing them to dry rapidly. Plaster of Paris or gauging plaster by itself does not handle well for patching because, by the time it has set sufficiently to become thick enough for application with hawk and trowel, it is only seconds from setting too hard to apply.

SUBSTANTIAL CRACKS AND SMALL HOLES

Cracks in the plaster fields due to structural movement require a different approach, as well as professional input. First, the cause of the structural activity must be identified and repaired by an architectural conservator, contractor, or engineer. After the movement has been stabilized, the plasterer goes to work. The cracks are *chamfered*, or V-grooved, and treated with a colorless or pigmented polyvinyl acetate (PVA) bonding agent. Thereafter, plaster and lime are gauged, applied, and troweled smooth. Holes in the plaster field are generally demolished to their perimeters to remove loose or delaminated material but not the wooden lath. Metal lath sections are fastened to the wood structure, the wood is wet, and a PVA bonding agent is applied to the old plaster. Larger holes require base-coat mixes representing scratch and brown coats, which are cut back so as to accommodate the finish coat of plaster and lime polished smooth and flush with adjacent material.

Purists may be uncomfortable with the application of expanded metal lath over period wooden lath; however, metal lath is a favorable recent development that provides significantly increased keying when used with moistened original lath and framing and contemporary plaster base coats with bonding agents.

DELAMINATION

As with many plaster problems, repair of delaminated coats can be adequately achieved by the homeowner if square footage is very small and on plain cornice or flat walls and ceilings. Provided that lath and framing are secure and that moisture is prevented from entering walls and ceilings from behind or above, you can replaster using traditional materials for brown and finish coats, followed by an application of PVA bonding agent according to manufacturer's instructions.

RESTORATION USING ACRYLIC ADHESIVES

Early techniques to accomplish reattachment of ceilings to lath/joist structures used bonding agents and gypsum and wire mesh applied to the laths in each joist bay. The action of this system bonded the reinforced gypsum to the original keys at the spaces between the laths only, and it introduced a great deal of additional weight to the framing. Today, ceilings decorated with ornamental plaster and/or paint finishes in danger of failure due to inadequate keying may be reattached to lath and joists by a system of *rekeying* using injected acrylic materials.

The process calls for holes three-sixteenths of an inch in diameter to be drilled, two or three each into every lath, between each joist over the ceiling field. The holes penetrate the lath only, not the plaster scratch coat; sawdust is removed with the shop-vac. A prewetting solution of water, alcohol, and acrylic adhesive is injected into the holes using spray equipment. Acrylic adhesive mixtures are then injected under pressure into the holes, causing them to travel along the interface between the scratch coat and the underside of wooden lath, forming a bond that hardens into a monolithic plane over the ceiling field. During the injection process, excess liquid must be cleaned away frequently to avoid migration to the ornamented plane through cracks in the ceiling.

The laths must be firmly attached to the joists following acrylic injection, which can be done in several ways, depending on site conditions. A product called *cornerite* is often screwed to the sides of the joists and plastered to the wooden lath using an acrylic-modified gypsum. Mechanical systems can also be used either alone or in combination with the cornerite. It is neces-

Ornamental plaster ceiling medallions originated in period stylebooks and trade catalogues. This example is from Minard Lafever's 1835 Beauties of Modern Architecture.

Rubber-mold tooling replicates period plaster enrichments with fingerprint-detail fidelity. This polysulfide mold was made in two pieces to achieve the penetrations in the original design.

sary to identify the attachment problem and exercise creativity in devising a suitable solution.

Walls may be similarly treated, but, without access to the laths behind the plaster, injection must be accomplished from the front. In either case, the skills and experience essential to acrylic reattachment of plaster elements are not normally possessed by the homeowner, and professional plasterers are needed.

CEILING MEDALLION REPAIR OR REPLACEMENT

With a few exceptions, ornamental plaster medallions are installed on ceiling planes, framed, and lathed on-center using the same methods as for the cornice line. Thus, keys are damaged on period ceilings, and medallions are often partially or altogether lost because of the added weight on center substrata.

A matching replacement medallion, say for a Greek Revival identical double parlor, can be made using running, molding, casting, and installation operations that are identical to those from the 1830s. Since one medallion always falls before the other, ornamental plasterers are often engaged in replications based on original models. If the model medallion has sustained damage during conversions from gas to electrical service, conjectural decisions will have to be reached to complete the missing units. Because modern codes require that access to the electrical box be maintained rather than restricted, additional creative judgments may be necessary.

Homeowners or house-museum managers frequently observe "ghost" markings on the ceiling of an ornamented parlor, meaning that a central ceiling medallion existed prior to substrate failure. To reconstruct a mystery medallion, you can borrow designs from other rooms in the house or from other houses in the neighborhood. Another option is to research trade catalogues and period stylebooks to match the existing cornice ornament in the room with plates depicting appropriate medallions, being careful not to exceed existing ghost dimensions. Local historical societies, museum curators, or restoration architects may also provide advice in choosing the most historically appropriate medallion.

"Ghost" markings indicate that ornamentation existed on this wall plane. The bellflowers had been set using plaster as an adhesive. The design composition was established by drawing a grid on the wall with chalk lines.

CORNICE REPAIR OR REPLACEMENT

While ceiling medallions succumb to gravity and lighting-service adaptations, plain-run or enriched cornices are damaged by plumbing installations, adaptive-reuse projects, and water intrusion, particularly at exterior walls. As with flat-wall plaster, small cracks and holes may be filled with gypsum and lime and tooled with a straightedge or miter rod. Paint-bond failure and mild efflorescence can be repaired by gently removing the loose material, then bonding with a PVA material, filling, sanding, and repainting. Damage of a more radical nature, including severe water damage, stud-wall interruptions, and fallen or missing cornice sections, present greater challenges and are best undertaken by an ornamental plasterer.

Again, many of the replacement procedures follow long-established practice, with some exceptions. In period structures with ornamented entablatures, plaster enrichments were attached to plain-run moldings using plaster as an adhesive. The cast was soaked in water until it was supersaturated, plaster the consistency of pancake batter was slathered onto the back of the cast, and the cast was pressed into place, butting tightly against its neighbor, and excess adhesive removed immediately with a brush. Today, the back surface of a replacement cornice section is coated instead with PVA bonding agent, removing the need to soak the cast and allowing the painting contractor to begin work sooner. The bonding agent forms a barrier film that rewets on contact with the plaster adhesive but prevents the dry cast from drawing moisture from the mix.

Precast cornice moldings are sometimes produced to replicate damaged ornamental entablatures if many linear feet are required to complete the restoration. Such precast units simplify installation of the various cast enrichments, but they restrict the spacing of the casts to replicate the original dimensions, particularly if they were idiosyncratic from wall to wall. Restorations are often less difficult if the moldings are produced in two pieces, say, cornice and architrave, or jointed within a major cove molding to be hidden later by a cast enrichment.

Regardless of the restorative procedures, check that complete finishing operations, such as pointing casts and removing superfluous plaster adhesive, are carried out by the plasterer. Failure to do so will cause additional work by the painting contractor before painting, glazing, or gilding.

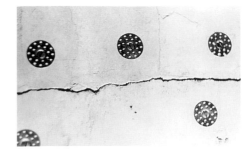

Flat-head wood screws and plaster washers were used to reattach loose ceiling plaster to the wooden lath in a late eighteenth-century house in Massachusetts. After the crack is covered with fiberglass mesh tape, both the taped crack and the plaster washers will be skim coated with a patching material.

MAJOR CEILING FAILURE

Three-coat plastering on ceilings is very heavy, and, when keys break, from whatever cause, large sections of ceiling planes succumb to gravity and fall to the floor. Areas adjacent to the failure should be examined for soundness by a plasterer and reinforced using *plaster washers* and galvanized deck screws around the perimeters. Plaster washers are applied using a screw gun or a cordless drill and drawn up snug as they penetrate the plaster, lath, and joists. Plaster washers one inch in diameter may, however, be countersunk using a one-and-one-quarter-inch *spade bit,* which also forms a pilot hole for the screw. Such a procedure is effective on ceilings of three-coat work; it is less successful on scratch-and-finish two-coat systems.

With the perimeter of the area secure, remaining loose plaster and broken keys are removed, leaving wooden lath in place. Galvanized-metal lath may be fastened to renailed wet lath, and plastering may proceed after a PVA bonding agent has been applied to the old plaster at the perimeter. The finish coat of gypsum and lime should be troweled smooth and flush with original work, at the same time covering the screw heads and plaster washers.

Some existing wooden lath may have to be replaced due to its condition and the thickness of the period plaster. Laths should be carefully cut around the perimeter of the hole and removed and lath nails pulled or driven flush with the joists. Ceiling joists are fitted with a vapor barrier or painted to avoid absorption of water from the scratch coat, resulting in parallel dryouts. Metal lath is then cut and fastened to the joists, bonding agent applied to original plaster around the perimeter, and three-coat work begins.

Yet another approach to plastering a major hole in a wall or ceiling is to stabilize the perimeter with plaster washers and remove the wooden lath, then cut three-eighths-inch gypsum board or Rocklath to fit the irregular opening and screw it to the studs and joists. The gypsum board acts as the scratch coat to which brown and finish coats are then applied, thereby obviating the need to form a barrier against the framing. The original thickness of the wall or ceiling plane can be achieved with something just under one-half the moisture being introduced into the room. In addition, since no sand is required in the scratch coat, the resulting patch is lighter in weight.

FINDING AND EVALUATING PLASTERING CONTRACTORS

Once an engineer or architectural conservator has identified the plaster damage or deterioration, the historic-property owner or house-museum manager must locate an experienced, reputable restoration contractor before proceeding further. A wide disparity of skills exists within the trade today, due in part to the introduction of gypsum board as a substitute for traditional plastering. As drywall became popular after World War II, plasterers saw the demand for their services decline. Plastering techniques were forgotten because they were less often passed down within shops and families. However, flat- and ornamental-plaster shops have seen a resurgence in demands for their services in the last decade, particularly as more historic buildings are rehabilitated.

Many professional preservation organizations can provide references for restoration contractors suitable for your particular needs. Local plasterers' unions will also be able to identify contractors with experience in the flat and ornamental trades. Architects with preservation and restoration project experience may recommend contractors with whom they have had satisfactory past experiences. Museums with period rooms often engage craftspeople to assemble the backgrounds for the display of antique furniture and decorative arts. Finally, historical societies, whether national, state, or municipally organized, may have funded projects that repaired or restored interior plaster.

Prospective contractors should be invited to visit the job site to see and define the scope of work; written proposals, including prices from all bidders, are essential for comparison. References should be provided and investigated. An outside consultant may be engaged, or an informal adviser designated, to aid in evaluating the experience and the proposals of the bidders. To get the total picture, the homeowner should visit a completed project with the contractor present to answer questions that inevitably arise.

Finally, when possible, visit the bidder's shop to see ornamental work under way, preferably on a normal working day. In some cases, ornamental- and flat-plastering bidders allow visitors while working on a job site. Some ornamental plasterers simply do not have shops. They prefer to cast on-site, as was the general practice while building the splendid 1920s theaters in New York City and around the country.

Restorative techniques and materials are at once sophisticated and banal. As with general building projects, cost reductions may be achieved by a team approach in which preparatory and cleanup operations are completed by the homeowner, with the actual plasterwork accomplished by a plastering contractor. Ultimately, the most successful restorations are conducted by dedicated, skilled, and enthusiastic practitioners with abundant experience in the American architectural arena.

WALLPAPERS

T. K. McClintock

Original wallpapers contribute immeasurably to the identity and historic integrity of a room. The surfaces they enhance may be larger than those covered by any other material that visibly distinguishes the historic-house interior. Because of their inherent fragility, the exposure to which they are subjected over time, and the fluctuations in taste that result in their replacement, the survival of historic wallpapers in a condition that reflects the large place they held in an original furnishing scheme is becoming increasingly rare.

THE APPEAL OF HISTORIC WALLPAPERS

The study of historic wallpaper has blossomed over the last decade. International associations sponsor regular conferences and publications. At least one museum is devoted solely to the subject, and specialized curatorial departments exist in many others. Illustrated scholarly publications document the history of wallpaper design, production, and use. Wallpapers are also featured at auctions and offered by specialized galleries. These currents reflect a maturing appreciation of original historic wallpapers and an awareness that important pattern and scenic designs originally produced in hundreds or thousands of impressions may now survive only by the handful or as singular examples becoming, in that regard, rare graphic works.

Many fine examples of early wallpapers survive in their original domestic installations; others were remounted in later structures and period rooms or survive as samples in institutional and manufacturers' reference collections. Many later wallpapers of interest, beauty, and appropriateness can be found in homes, institutions, and commercial facilities. Such papers, though not technically historic, may be of high quality or unusual design and are also deserving of attention and care, as replacing or replicating them might otherwise be difficult or costly.

Historic wallpapers hold as much interest for the story they tell as for their appearance. They reflect the economics of taste, the rapid international currency of design, the influence of industrial changes and trade, national allegiances, technical developments, and, finally, the cherished place they held in a home to have survived changes in fashion.

After pasting the reverse, a length of conserved French scenic wallpaper, c. 1830, is positioned during remounting. The wallpaper was removed for cleaning and repair of both the paper itself and the plaster walls behind it.

HISTORY OF AVAILABILITY AND PRODUCTION

Like other graphic works, printed wallpapers evolved from simple hand-colored relief prints into complex exercises in design, production, and application. As early as the sixteenth century, paper sheets were produced specifically to cover walls; Albrecht Dürer produced a print that would form a composite image when multiple sheets were placed upon a wall. The designs were meant to be pleasing in and of themselves, but it was also reported to be less expensive to apply a simple wallpaper than a finish coat of plaster. Wallpapers were used in place of or to simulate other decorative materials that were more expensive or locally unavailable, such as woodwork, stone, textiles, or wall paintings. The enormous popularity of wallpapers generated a need by manufacturers for materials, which, in the first quarter of the nineteenth century, served in part as the catalyst for the development of a commercially viable machine to make paper; before then, rolls of paper had to be assembled from overlapping handmade sheets before they could be printed upon.

The American market was served by English imports until after the Revolution, when native manufacturers began to produce simple patterns and commemorative designs. Imports from France and, later in the century, from England met more grandiose needs. By the late eighteenth and early nineteenth centuries, wallpaper designs maximized the peculiar advantages of the materials and methods used in their production. According to Véronique de Bruignac, curator at the Musée des Art Décoratifs in Paris, wallpapers "took up and [were] integrated into the architectural vocabulary of the house"; they had become brilliant, refined, preferred. French and English manufacturers in particular sent their products to retailers and individuals all over the world.

Of particular interest are the scenic or panoramic wallpapers produced in France in the first quarter of the nineteenth century. They were considered technical tours de force; their printing necessitated the registration of more than a thousand relief printing blocks and the coordination of several hundred colors. The designs represented all subjects of contemporary interest in a period of great discovery—mythology, history, current events, leisurely pleasures, and the fauna, foliage, landscapes, and peoples of distant lands. The didactic quality of scenic wallpapers was intentional; they hold interest as much for their social documentation as for their decorative contribution. The handful of specialized firms exported a good portion of their production to the young United States, where they were considered a cherished component of the decorative scheme of the sophisticated household.

A taste arose as well for designs from China, which were produced with other fine-art and decorative works as an export commodity. Though hand-painted, wallpaper sets with virtually identical designs are found in far-flung locations. The compositions evolved toward the categorical—figures in landscape, occupations or seasonal activities, birds, rocks and flora—but their popularity was such that simulations were even produced by European manufacturers. The Chinese export papers introduced Asian aesthetics to New England and Europe well before it was possible to gain exposure to the sophisticated imagery and handling found in scroll paintings, whose principles of design the wallpapers mirrored with genuine fidelity.

The availability of designs proliferated with the introduction of machine printing, as did the use of poor quality papers made from wood pulp and other inferior fiber stock. Pattern papers continued to be used simply as decorative wall coverings, where they lent a cosmopolitan flair that often belied their presence in homes far from the sophisticated centers of taste. In 1880 the American art critic Clarence Cook wrote a pamphlet entitled "What Shall We Do with Our Walls?" which, not coincidentally, was published by a wallpaper manufacturer. Cook's pamphlet reflected the contemporary mania for papering just about every available surface. Reactions to this profusion of patterns were simultaneous and contradictory. The English Aesthetic movement encouraged the production of high quality designs exhibiting simplicity and an expression of truth to materials, while exhaustion probably helped to stimulate an appreciation of the simple painted or plastered wall. Wallpapers continue to be produced in abundance, sometimes to simulate more fashionable surfaces or to reproduce historical precedents, and sometimes to reflect popular currents of design.

ORIGINAL METHODS OF MOUNTING WALLPAPERS

In American homes, wallpapers were mounted to plaster or wooden wall surfaces using a vegetable paste. After the late nineteenth century, linings of blank paper were often mounted to the walls beforehand to provide a more uniform working surface. Linings of fabric were less usual, except in cases where the wallpapers were transferred from another location or were displayed on a wooden strainer or frame to which the edges were secured with tacks or an adhesive. Wallpaper was also adhered directly over an older paper, which served, in effect, as a lining for reinforcement. The pattern of the underlying paper may remain legible in the case of a design being printed with a pronounced three dimensionality or when pigments or binders have bled through or corroded the overlying paper. The edges of rolls were originally overlapped to minimize separation; later, the rolls were butted to achieve a seamless appearance.

Additional designs often accompany a prominent pattern or scenic side papers. Borders vary in width, pattern, richness of materials, and location; more pronounced designs may be found below a chair rail, on wainscoting, or on the ceiling. Patches were often applied to scenic or Chinese wallpapers to accommodate an awkward transition in space, such as around a fireplace, or to disguise earlier damage.

COMPROMISES IN CONDITION AND APPEARANCE

While many features of condition are shared by fine-art and historic works on paper in general, much deterioration arises from wallpapers being mounted to the walls of a room. It is critical, therefore, that the building envelope, structure, and systems relative to the walls be sound. It is especially important to identify potential sources of water penetration that could damage the wallpaper or plaster mounting surface. See relevant chapters on how to examine the roof, gutters, siding, windows, foundation, and plumbing or hot-water heating systems for signs of leaks. The location of the room, prevailing weather patterns, and vegetation surrounding the house can also have deleterious effects.

It may be evident from damage to the wallpaper itself that plaster is separated from the laths, has gaping cracks, or is dislodged; gentle hand pressure exerted over the entire surface will reveal the extent. Cracks often indicate an accommodation of the disparate structural components, particularly in corners, that is not necessarily compromising to the security of either the walls or the wallpaper.

Ascertain the thoroughness of attachment of the wallpaper to the plaster. If there is a lining of fabric or paper, it may be revealed at a tear edge or behind a loose section. A lining provides reinforcement to the wallpaper as it expands and contracts in response to the inevitable changes in temperature and relative humidity. It also serves as a helpful layer to which loose edges can be readhered. Linings can be of poor quality, however, lacking in strength or a potential source of staining by transfer. Separations, tears, and areas of loss in the paper can be very compromising to its security or appearance, particularly if they are accompanied by major distortion. The relative thickness and flexibility of the wallpaper will largely determine how easily repairs can be made. It is also of interest to be aware of the roll widths, whether the seams overlap, and the size of the design repeat.

Changes in appearance are inevitable. There may be discoloration from exposure, particularly when paper of inferior quality was used (most common around the turn of the century), including overall or selective fading of the colors. Staining also arises from contact with acidic wooden surfaces or corrosive metal tacks, water damage in the form of tidemarks, mold, and microorganism

Original French scenic wallpaper, c. 1830, mounted, after conservation treatment, with reproductions of the original border, dado, and side paper. The reproductions were produced from surviving fragments and historic photographs.

activity. Surface coatings of natural or synthetic resin, glue, or starch may have been applied to saturate the colors or to protect the surface, but they almost invariably discolor or develop a pattern of cracking or loss. Soiling from airborne grime is deposited in characteristic patterns, with more on the exterior walls and surfaces near the ceiling. Particularly harmful or disfiguring are cleavage of the design layer and loss from abrasion, which reveal the underlying paper surface, and ill-advised repair efforts (however well intentioned), especially the use of synthetic adhesives (white-glue emulsions) for readhesion of loose pieces and overpaint to disguise staining or loss in the design.

Compromises in condition and appearance should be identified, recorded, and prioritized. Measure the surfaces and prepare simple elevation drawings on which the aspects of condition can be schematized and notes recorded. Overall and detailed color photographs are valuable for future comparison and if a professional conservator has to be consulted.

TREATING DAMAGED WALLPAPER

CONSULTING A PROFESSIONAL CONSERVATOR

The deterioration of this English wallpaper, c. 1780, is a result of the physical and chemical instability of the wooden-plank mounting surface and the corrosive green pigment used in the printing.

For whatever value the distinction bears, wallpapers are considered a decorative art—singular examples are elevated to the distinction of fine art—with all of the attendant responsibilities for their preservation. Priorities for care can be more clearly appreciated following a thorough examination. A need for repairs to the building structure may be obvious and first-aid preservation measures simple to execute, such as securing draping separations with plastic tacks or moving furniture to prevent abrasion. It is undoubtedly more difficult to determine what improvements could be safely attempted by individuals who have clear objectives and some dexterity with the relevant repair materials yet who lack professional conservation training. If the project seems at all complex or if the wallpaper is of recognized importance either independently or in the context of the historic house, consult a paper conservator. A professional experienced in the particular specialty of wallpaper conservation can determine whether responsible compromises exist, what place there is for conservation of the original painted surfaces and plaster, or the advisability of using reproduction wallpapers in conjunction with or in place of conservation. For example, repairs that remove or reduce stains may be appropriate for a fine-art print or drawing on paper, but it may be considered less critical for a historical or decorative work whose legibility is not particularly threatened by the same type of damage. The treatment of historic wallpaper is approached not simply as large paper artifacts that happen to fill the walls, but as central components to an integrated architectural statement. The appearance and priority of wallpapers as a specific material relative to others, such as woodwork, painted surfaces, textiles, and furnishings, will vary with the circumstances of the historic house or private home.

Wallpaper conservation projects range from simple treatments by a single paper conservator to more complex projects for which more specialized experience is recommended—to place the room in context, to develop accurate budgets, and to have available adequate resources of studio space, equipment, and trained personnel. Conservators have the expertise to evaluate condition, formulate treatment objectives and priorities, and interweave procedures designed to improve the condition and appearance of historic wallpapers. They are able to guide the homeowner through the decision-making process and to explain what results may be expected, as well as what may influence a need to change treatment procedures or objectives. A written examination and condition report with treatment recommendations is the cornerstone of a shared responsibility to proceed with treatment. It is a document for which a fee should be expected if the project is extensive or complex.

Whether repairs can be made best, and perhaps most economically, on-site or by removing the wallpaper for treatment in a conservation studio may be difficult to ascertain if the project is more than basic. Overall removal using moisture, steam, or solvents is very difficult and may be practically impossible, particularly if the wallpaper is weak and well adhered directly to a plaster or wooden surface (versus being mounted with a fabric lining on a strainer). Despite these caveats, removal may be preferred specifically to gain access to walls in need of repair, to manage uniform overall reattachment, to address consolidation, or to attend to pronounced staining or large networks of tears and loss.

Assistance in locating and selecting a conservator may be available through a local or state museum or historical society. The Foundation of the American Institute for Conservation in Washington, D.C., also operates a national conservation-services referral system.

TREATMENT PRIORITIES AND OPTIONS

Marked improvements can be made with wallpaper remaining on the walls, and most treatments take place under those circumstances. Taking the first step of correcting the underlying condition(s) that caused the problem is generally attended by an improvement in appearance. Enormous good can be achieved even if every possible improvement can't be realized because of a lack of human or financial resources.

An appreciation of the distinctive characteristics of paper and design mediums is essential to understanding how the wallpaper might respond and why certain procedures and materials have been developed for use in conservation. Paper is essentially a matrix that is formed by distributing fibers that are suspended in water onto a porous screen and drying the sheet in conjunction with some pressure or tension. Linen or cotton rags were the original source of fibers for hand papermaking in Europe and America while bast fibers were most commonly used in Asia. With a larger demand for fiber stock than could be met, created in part by the development of the papermaking machine, it became necessary to use other plant fibers, notably processed wood pulp. The strength of a paper sheet is measured in the simplest terms by its ability to resist folds or tears. That strength depends on the quality of pulp used in production (the length of the fibers and their resistance to embrittlement with age and exposure), the use of adhesives as internal or surface sizing agents (for tear resistance and to restrict the absorption of printed design mediums), the method of sheet formation (by which evenly distributed fibers bond physically and chemically with each other in a sheet of more or less uniform density and thickness), and finally, on the environment to which it is exposed.

Wallpaper stock is usually prepared by the printer with a ground layer to create a uniform surface for printing that is smooth and opaque but not absorbent (essentially it contains a higher concentration of pigment to binder). The design mediums are applied in several stages by assorted relief and planographic printing methods. They consist of coloring agents, pigments or dyes of more or less colorfastness, in a binder, an adhesive diluted in water or solvents with various working qualities, including some resistance to resolubility.

What results is a lamination of materials that may be quite fragile after years of exposure and that is extraordinarily sensitive to water. And because the adhesives that are most stable and reversible from a conservation standpoint are water based, it is critical that they be used judiciously and in the appropriate sequence.

Some of the procedures used by conservators may be undertaken by the nonprofessional—provided that he or she follows some basic guidelines, is familiar with the materials to be used and has practiced on expendable papers, and appreciates his or her capabilities and limitations. Improvements that a nonprofessional can make, preferably after specific recommendation by a paper conservator, include surface cleaning, tear repair, and filling of losses. More advanced procedures that a technician may undertake might include limited stain reduction, overpaint removal, and inpainting.

In any procedure that is undertaken, only stable materials and reversible techniques that are included in the conservation literature and catalogues should be used. Carefully test the treatment beforehand in unobtrusive areas and document the results in writing and by photography. Proceed slowly, and pause regularly to evaluate the desirability of the resulting changes. Whether the work is done by a nonprofessional, a technician, or an experienced conservator, it is of paramount importance that treatment be guided by respect for the integrity of the artifact. It is far better to do less and minimize further damage than to risk causing unwarranted changes in character or irretrievable damage.

BASIC TREATMENT PROCEDURES

Removal of surface grime is the first priority, because it may be largely responsible for a discolored appearance and because it might otherwise become lodged in the paper fibers during subsequent procedures. Loose grime or cobwebs can be removed with a soft brush or vacuum cleaner on low suction. A vacuum is particularly helpful in removing loose plaster debris that can fall behind a draping piece of wallpaper and form a ridge or bulge. A permeable material should be held against the wall surface or wrapped over the nozzle to prevent pieces from being dislodged and lost (plastic window screening or cheesecloth work well). Wiping with a sponge made from open-cell vulcanized rubber (used by fire-recovery cleaners) will remove more entrenched grime, but caution is necessary. Fragile paper and printing surfaces may be susceptible to abrasion or disruption. This is particularly true of flocked wallpapers because the colored fibers become brittle with age. More aggressive removal of entrenched grime may be possible with the controlled use of assorted rubber or vinyl erasers (abrasive or solvent-imbibed erasers are not recommended); however, pay careful attention to the effect on the surface (which may include limited burnishing). It may be that only one portion or color can be safely cleaned more than the others and you will have to evaluate the acceptability of that potential imbalance in appearance. Surface cleaning also may reveal previously shrouded disfigurements, such as abrasion or fading of the design, or earlier staining.

In addition to discoloring, a surface coating of varnish, glue, or starch may become powdery or develop a widespread pattern of cracks. Only the most gentle surface-cleaning method should be used if these fragile conditions exist. Reduction or removal of a discolored or embrittled surface coating usually involves organic solvents and, often, removal of the paper from the walls; these procedures should be left to experienced conservators.

Wallpaper can be torn or separated from the walls in ways that require a variety of techniques for mending or reattachment. It is critical to be aware of the response of paper when it comes into contact with any moisture, such as that contained in even a viscous adhesive. The paper can expand in size, and discolored deterioration products within it can be made soluble and cause staining. Therefore, the use of adhesives must be limited and controlled. Wheat-starch paste (which has to be cooked and has a limited shelf life) and various cellulose ethers (such as methylcellulose) are favored by paper conservators for their working characteristics, stability, and reversibility. Methylcellulose may be most appropriate for use by the nonprofessional. It is readily available from conservation suppliers, easy to prepare, and has a long shelf life. Its gellike quality is both appropriate to the task and makes for relatively easy use.

This American block-printed design, c. 1800, benefited markedly from careful surface cleaning with erasers after removal from the plaster wall.

It is generally safer to leave untouched areas that are separated but otherwise supported around the edges like a bubble or drumhead. Otherwise, an incision would have to be made. Also, spreading an appropriately uniform adhesive layer is difficult, and, because there is more surface area of wallpaper than of wall surface to which it would be adhered, staining and expansion become distinct possibilities. Similarly, creases from settling of the structure are frequently best left alone because their reattachment to a flat surface may shatter the paper.

It is important, however, to secure lifting edges at tears, losses, and areas of detachment or separation at margins, seams, or overlays. If unattended, they can become worse and/or generate disfiguring planar distortion or *cockling*, or become a repository for grime. A simple first-aid measure is to hold the wallpaper in place with noncorrosive thumbtacks or pushpins until more long-lived procedures can be undertaken. A small piece of paper can be helpful as a buffer between the tack and the wallpaper, and both can be painted to be less conspicuous.

If the torn wallpaper is flexible enough to allow some manipulation, adhesion of paper strips behind tear edges promotes a more secure attachment to the plaster and less likelihood of staining. The strips can also bridge tears with large gaps caused by contraction of the edges or cracking of the plaster. While the use of a long-fibered Japanese paper is preferable, a good-quality, acid-free, hand- or machine-made printing or drawing paper with a smooth surface (available from better art-supply stores) can be suitable; the printing or drawing paper can also be used to fill areas of loss. Mending strips can be applied in several pieces, but they should underlap the edges by at least a quarter of an inch if possible. They are pasted with an adhesive that is viscous enough to minimize penetration and positioned on a rigid piece of clear plastic (like Mylar). Slip the strip and support all the way under one edge, push the strip off with tweezers, and pull it partially under the other edge, bridging the tear. Apply gentle pressure with a paper towel through the wallpaper and allow the strips to dry in contact with the plaster surface. After slipping a piece of Mylar under the tear to protect the adjacent paper surfaces, apply adhesive to the reverse of the tear edges with a brush or with the support plastic that has been thinly smeared. Gently press the tear edges against the strips and dry them. To promote adhesion and minimize the risk of staining, a hair dryer or small tacking iron (with a non-stick interleaf such as silicone paper) can be used for drying. Tear edges can also be adhered directly to a plaster surface if the wallpaper is too brittle to manipulate.

Large losses can be filled with archival-quality papers that are similar in texture and thickness to the original. They can be toned beforehand to match the background color of the surrounding wallpaper using watercolor or acrylics. Trace the contours of the loss on clear plastic, which serves as a template to cut the fill paper, adding a margin of a quarter of an inch for pasting and discrepancies of size. Paste the piece overall on the back (it will expand slightly in size), then position it under the edges of the loss, press to the wall surface, and allow to dry. Adhere the tear edges as described previously.

ADVANCED PROCEDURES

Elaborate procedures of stain reduction, overpaint removal, and inpainting should be undertaken only by a professional conservator or by technicians following a conservator's project specifications. Procedures are described both to discourage the well-meaning nonprofessional from trying them without forethought as to the damage that can be caused and to prompt some consideration about what skills might be expected of personnel who could serve as technicians on a project.

The local repair here uses wheat-starch paste applied behind a separated seam and secured with a tacking iron. The wallpaper is from the Jeremiah Lee Mansion, 1768, Marblehead, Massachusetts.

LOCAL REPAIRS

The hard edge of staining in the form of tidemarks may be reduced with moisture poultices and heat. A thick blotting paper is cut into strips wider than the "fingers" of the stain. A narrow line of water is painted onto the strip, which is then pressed against the discolored edge of the stain with a permeable interleaf (a nonwoven polyester such as Hollytex or Reemay) to prevent the blotting paper from adhering to the paper surface. When a warm tacking iron is pressed against the surface, the discoloration matter in the wallpaper should be drawn into the blotter. The process may need to be repeated; however, the wallpaper may be able to tolerate only limited direct contact (if any). The moisture in the blotter has to be limited carefully as well; otherwise, discoloration products in the paper or the wall surface may be made soluble and generate new staining. Considerable experience is required to determine the threshold of tolerance of the wallpaper. A professional conservator should be able to ascertain whether the desired improvements will be possible and whether the procedure can be undertaken without being unduly time-consuming.

Before and after: photographs from another impression served as guidelines for the inpainting of this block-printed French scenic design, c. 1830. The wallpaper had suffered from cleavage, loss, and abrasion at tear edges.

It is common to find that damage from loss, abrasion, or staining was disguised in the past simply by painting over the affected areas. Because this overpainting is often clumsy in execution and may cover considerably more of an area than is affected by the damage, the appearance can be disfiguring and compromising to the integrity of the historic wallpaper. Its reduction or removal may be possible with the controlled, local use of moisture or organic solvents on absorbent swabs. Extreme caution has to be exercised; components may develop within aged paper that are prone to cause staining if made soluble, and overpaint may contain coloring matter that is quick to bleed into the wallpaper.

The lavish presence of overpaint may offend our sensibilities, but it may not be so compromising when considering the pattern of a wallpaper in a room that is densely textured with furnishings. It is important to distinguish overpainting from *inpainting*, a procedure used by conservators to make losses in a design less distracting. The intention may be to produce a general background tone or to replicate faithfully the color and design, but the work is confined strictly to the areas of loss and documented with photographs so that no confusion will exist about what is original. It is undertaken with restraint by professionals familiar with the techniques that can best match the surrounding surfaces, and using only the most stable mediums, generally watercolor and pastels. While inpainting is reversible when it is undertaken on a fill (because the fill paper can be removed), it may be only partially reversible when applied to an original paper surface. The appropriateness of inpainting should be evaluated carefully for that reason, and because it is time-consuming and lends the (false) impression of contributing more to the restored appearance of a wallpaper than all of the conservation procedures directed at its underlying condition.

A professional conservator should be able to tailor the use of treatment procedures, such as those described above, as well as others that are more creative, to the particular condition and context of the wallpaper and to the budget available for conservation. Even if a project has to be limited in scope, the conservation purpose, balance, and craftsmanship that are brought to it need not be.

REMOVING WALLPAPER FOR TREATMENT

In some cases, local procedures may not address major elements of damage, for which full or partial removal of rolls or sections may be a viable course of treatment. While more treatment options are available with the wallpaper removed from the walls, expectations for improvements in appearance are also raised. An overall project may grow larger in scope and expense. Removal of historic wallpaper also entails marked risks. Despite tests that led one to believe otherwise, it may not come off safely, or it may take considerably more time than was estimated. It may reveal additional conditions that must be incorporated into an already developed treatment strategy. The most significant risk is that removal may cause more new damage to the paper than is acceptable. Sections of historic wallpaper are awkward to handle, particularly when the extensive use of moisture is necessary, which is more often the case than not. The prospect of such an extensive treatment scenario should raise important questions about the specialized experience of the conservator and about the legitimate expectations of the client.

If the wallpaper has maintained its strength or if the plaster surface has become crumblike, it may be possible to remove the paper dry using the variety of spatulas that paper conservators have tailored to the task. More frequently, the adhesive will have to be swelled, weakened, or made soluble with moisture in the form of steam or water. Nonaqueous adhesives used in later repairs may be made sufficiently reversible with heat or an appropriate organic solvent. As with all conservation procedures, the response of the original paper, design mediums, and mounting adhesives to the materials and techniques to be used during treatment have to be gauged beforehand. The wallpaper is removed in the largest sections that are safe to handle, although these may be separated later at tears or roll overlaps to facilitate the treatment procedures that follow.

Controlled exposure to water in the conservation studio is essential for cleaning, removing of old adhesives, relaxing of planar distortions, and restoring paper strength on a microstructural level. Prolonged exposure of historic wallpapers to moisture may not be possible, however, because of the potential solubility or fragility of the design mediums or staining of the paper. In those instances, the conservator must exercise particular finesse in the use of adhesives to consolidate earlier linings or to build up new layers of reinforcement before remounting. Progressions of overall exposure to water may include facing with moistened absorbent papers, placement on a saturated bed of blotters, the use of a suction table, or partial or complete immersion of the wallpaper. As a corollary procedure, it may be possible to undertake limited stain reduction with bleaching agents that are rinsed out with the same techniques. The response of the paper and design mediums, the extent of cleaning desired, the size of the sections, and the procedures to be used beforehand and afterward influence the selection of a specific washing method.

Steam is being used to remove a French pattern wallpaper, c. 1820, for studio treatment. Removal is a particularly delicate procedure that should be undertaken only by experienced professional conservators.

Consolidation of a design layer that exhibits *cleavage*, or poor attachment to the paper surface, is the most challenging condition to address. Regrettably, no adhesive available completely satisfies the conservation criteria for efficacy, stability, and reversibility and leaves the design unaltered in appearance. Local cleavage can be attended by slipping any one of several natural and synthetic adhesives under the lifting flake. Marked improvement has also been made by passing an adhesive such as gelatin through the surface while the wallpaper is on a suction table. However, cleavage may remain a feature that will need periodic attention after remounting.

Filling areas of loss with paper similar to the original is directed at reducing discrepancies in level, texture, and color. If those discrepancies are insignificant in appearance or location, or if the project budget is constrained, a uniformly toned lining paper can serve as a background in place of individual fills. This option is not only less time-consuming, it also is visually evident, which serves to highlight the original material.

It can be seen from this sequence of procedures that overall treatment of historic wallpaper may necessitate the wallpaper's virtual disassembly and reassembly. In the process, a paper lining is often adhered to the reverse for reinforcement (generally using long-fibered Japanese *kozo* papers and wheat-starch paste). A final interleaving layer of cotton or linen fabric is now customary if the wallpaper is to be mounted to plaster walls, although it was an infrequent original addition historically. Linings provide additional reinforcement during changes in temperature and humidity or if the plaster surface is disrupted. They also facilitate removal of the wallpaper in the future. The fabric and paper interleaves may be applied to the wall before the wallpaper is remounted, or the wallpaper and linings may be joined in the studio if the sections need more structural integrity for remounting.

The majority of historic wallpapers were mounted directly onto plaster, and the lively undulation of original surfaces is a desirable feature to maintain in the repair of walls. Remounting the wallpaper as panels is recommended if that was the original format. It is also an option if physical or environmental insecurities make a surface unsuitable for reattachment. Several traditions of construction and design have evolved specifically to incorporate panels, such as the paper-covered lattice core panels used in Japan, or fabric-covered strainers used in European interiors, or the honeycomb panel, variations of which remain as viable options for remounting. An appropriate selection would depend on the condition of the wallpaper, cost, section configurations, and environmental and structural conditions. Because the depth of surrounding moldings often cannot accommodate the additional thickness of new mounting panels, their use is rare.

The number of side papers, dados, borders, and columns included in a design scheme makes the careful organization of remounting essential. Slight dimensional changes may have to be accommodated and new elements, such as reproductions or conserved or repainted woodwork, harmonized. The wallpapers should appear as much as possible as if they had never been removed and undergone extensive repair: horizon lines should be level, vertical elements plumb, design elements registered, edges true against moldings, and overlapping seams discreet.

REPRODUCTION WALLPAPERS

It is recommended that one first explore all avenues for the conservation of original historic wallpapers and exercise some patience with their evolved appearance before resorting to their replacement with reproduction wallpapers. The use of reproductions can be very appropriate, however, when original accessory wallpapers are missing, when conservation simply cannot breathe life back into an original pattern wallpaper that is compromised in condition and appearance, or when the cost of a conservation project is disproportionate to the value of the wallpaper. Many historic houses have successfully blended conserved and reproduced wallpapers within the same interior. It is worthwhile to research original wall treatments, examine suppliers' catalogues and samples, prepare a diagram of the room with the coordinated selections, and to pin up large samples before committing to the purchase and mounting of reproduction wallpapers.

The better reproduction wallpapers tend to be those that are characteristic of their historical period. A faithful reproduction is distinguished by artwork that has not homogenized the original design, a color scheme that accurately reflects what research has revealed, and a quality of printing that simulates the textures of the original. Producers are capable of replicating the original printing mediums and methods using mineral pigments in a glue binder and relief printing with woodblocks on rolls made from joined sheets of paper. It is most common, however, to find designs that are printed using synthetic mediums and silkscreens onto machine-made paper of varying qualities. Many firms produce excellent simulations with these methods. If too many shortcuts are taken, for instance using a reduced number of separations, or colors and mediums that appear synthetic on the commercially popular paper stocks, the results can look lifeless when compared with the very textured originals. More care, but not necessarily more expense, may be required to locate printers and manufacturers whose productions resonate with authenticity.

To ensure long life, reproduction wallpapers should be mounted with overlapping seams using archival adhesives (such as methylcellulose or cooked and strained wheat-starch paste) onto walls prepared with linings of archival paper (long-fibered heavyweight Japanese paper is preferable) and cotton fabric. While it is recommended that original historic wallpapers always be mounted by or in consultation with an experienced paper conservator, some paper hangers are qualified and experienced in the handling of valuable reproduction wallpapers. Such a person should be able to provide references, present photographs of other projects, and knowledgeably discuss patterns of application and methods of mounting.

PRESERVATION OF HISTORIC WALLPAPERS

It is worth reiterating that maintenance of the building envelope and structure, as well as the plumbing and heating systems within the walls and floors, is critical to the health of historic wallpapers. While the optimum environment for paper artifacts is frequently identified as 65 to 70 degrees Fahrenheit at 50 percent relative humidity, it is even more important that extreme fluctuations of temperature and relative humidity be tempered. (See also *Caring for Your Collections* for further guidance on maintaining a safe environment.) The use of humidifiers in winter and dehumidifiers in summer may be effective. To prevent fading of colors and weakening of the paper, minimize exposure to sunlight by closing draperies or shutters when the room is not in use and covering the windows with ultraviolet-light-filtering acrylic sheets. Keep forced-air heating systems and fireplaces clean to minimize the deposit of airborne grime on the walls. It is particularly important that abrasion to the wallpaper be minimized by the thoughtful positioning of furniture and by the careful handling of draperies.

It is often true that the same standards that are applied to the conservation of smaller works on paper can also be applied to the conservation of historic wallpapers. Identifying the characteristic features that contribute to the condition and appearance of historic wallpapers, and examining the various options for their treatment, are critical to their connoisseurship. From there one can develop an understanding of what constitutes the integrity of the artifact, what elasticity there may be for tolerable compromises, and where painstaking efforts have to be focused.

INTERIOR PAINTS AND OTHER FINISHES

JEFFREY GREENE

Detail of restored stenciled patterns at the Hackley House in Muskegon, Michigan

When you walk into a historic house, the collected ideas of architects and builders, as well as those living and those who have lived there, resonate around you. Historic-house owners are challenged to understand not only their own idea of a home, but also that of the people who created and lived in the house they now occupy. What painting materials were available to them? What did they think was beautiful and practical to put on their walls and ceilings? And how do the present owners begin to integrate their needs with the traces of the past homes that they have inherited? A practical guide for the maintenance of historic finishes is necessary to fulfill the responsibility of stewardship for those who own a historic house.

In any interior space, paint is not usually considered one of the building systems, such as plumbing or the exterior envelope. Paint is often thought of as an impermanent material. Perhaps this misconception has to do with the fickle changes in decorating tastes and styles and the ease with which paint is renewed. For this reason, paint is often taken for granted, not usually noticed unless it is specialty paint, unusually colored, or beginning to deteriorate. However, considering paint as a building system composed of substrata, primer, and finish coat, and understanding what paint is made of, how it functions both technically and aesthetically, and the tools and techniques for application will give the homeowner some valuable insight into how to treat this aspect of the historic home. Historic paint can last a very long time if properly applied and maintained, and restored paint should retain its beauty for many generations.

Caring for historic paint that may be failing need not be complicated. A general understanding of the underlying properties of paint and some clarification of the confusing nomenclature of the trade can quickly demystify the process. What is that stuff on the walls after all? What is the difference between distemper paint and latex? What should be done with "fancy work," the decorative techniques of painting once fashionable and now in need of repair? How do I maintain my existing paint surfaces? Which cleaners should be used and which avoided? What is causing my paint to fail? Should I repaint and if so with what? The mission of this chapter is to answer these questions, to assist in efforts to conserve what already exists, and to restore what may have been thought lost. It is a practical guide to the identification, restoration, and conservation of historical and contemporary interior paint, both decorative and plain.

WHY CONSERVE?

A tangible history lies in the layers of paint on our walls, and attempts to restore and conserve historic paint, instead of erasing this history, reveal it. The importance of historic paints lies in their subtle optical and textural qualities. Glue distemper, for example, has a muted flatness that gives its color a unique and striking depth.

Historical paint interiors were often designed with complete attention to decorating all surfaces, as can be seen in this description of the English painter Frederic Leighton's study in the 1870s: "The walls of the studio were a dull Egyptian red; around the base were luminous Oriental tiles; the door and the woodwork were dense black. The frieze was cast in brown plaster of the Parthenon series. At the end of the room was a wide semi-circular recess roofed with a gilded semi-dome."[1]

We appreciate the detailed craft that was once the norm. Historic painted surfaces should be durable, but with uninformed treatment they can easily be damaged irreparably or lost, despite the best of intentions. Decorative painting may be covered over or touched up with a distracting color, or harmed by certain cleaners or the wrong protective coating. All paints may look like color on the wall, but they have extremely important differences that absolutely require careful, informed handling for cleaning and repair. Further, all repair work should be done with the understanding that, instead of making "like new," the conservator's task is to maintain a physical, living connection to a space's past. Rather than eliminating signs of wear, restoration should reflect the spirit of a place.

The prevailing preservation philosophy, as embodied in both the Secretary of the Interior's standards for historic restoration work and in the American Institute for Conservation's code of ethics, calls for treatments that use minimal intervention, maintain the integrity of original historic fabric, and can be reversed. These standards will also guide our approach to this topic.

HISTORIC VERSUS CONTEMPORARY PAINTS: A QUICK OVERVIEW

In essence, paint is little more than pigment and a binder. The varieties of paints differ in the composition and interaction of these two primary elements and, to a lesser degree, other constituent components. Over time, a large and specialized vocabulary evolved to describe different types of paint and their properties and uses. In the following section we will describe the differences between historic and contemporary paint.

Paint technology developed very slowly, with minimal changes until the beginning and middle of this century. Originally, painters used a *muller*, a sort of flattened stone, to grind their pigments on a slab. The invention of the paint can at the end of the last century allowed for the manufacture of standardized paint as opposed to the individual painter mixing ingredients at each jobsite. Paint technology was revolutionized by the introduction of synthetic materials in the 1930s and 1940s. By the end of World War II, the practice of making one's own paint was largely obsolete, although it was considered a necessary skill for painters to be able to mix their own colors until the advent of universal colorants and computerized color matching in the 1970s and 1980s.

Old paints were intended to last indefinitely. (Ironically, paints containing toxic lead, now illegal in most states, are still the most durable product for many surfaces. See page 19 for guidelines on handling lead-based paint.) One would think that modern technology would develop longer-lasting paints, but, even with many specialized modern coatings, general housepaint produced today has an inherent obsolescence factor. Modern paint is intended to last only three to seven years. The most fundamental differences between historic and modern paints have to do with the durability and subtle optical qualities of the former, which cannot be reproduced with synthetic materials; the gloss, texture, and coloration of paint made from historic materials can only be approximated today.

UNDERSTANDING PAINT

PAINT AS A SYSTEM: PIGMENT, BINDER, AND SOLVENT

Paint is a mixture of different substances designed to produce a liquid that will change into a solid. The needs of the user, the surface to be covered, and the flexibility and resistance to light and moisture determine the type of paint used. All paints consist of a *pigment*, or colorant, combined with a *vehicle*, composed of *binder*, which holds the paint together and adheres it to the surface, and *solvent*, in which the paint ingredients are dissolved or carried. Other ingredients in paint, called *additives*, perform a variety of important functions. Examples of these include carriers (dilutants), emulsifiers, extenders, wetting agents, driers, freeze-thaw stabilizers, pigment-suspension aids, fillers, and preservatives. The combinations of these ingredients determine the qualities of the paint.

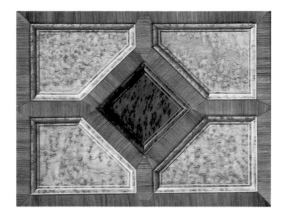

This panel demonstrates how paint, glazes, and specialized tools can be used to imitate natural wood grain.

Pigments are the dried powders that determine the color and opacity of the paint. In traditional paints, pigments have been extracted from mineral, animal, and vegetable sources. A knowledge of when various pigments were in common use is often helpful in dating a paint layer. This information is most readily obtained from a professional consultant.

Many of the most common pigments come directly from the earth and take their names from their original sources, as in raw sienna, raw umber, and English red. The ranges of many of these natural earth colors were expanded by burning or calcimining the raw earth to produce entirely different hues, such as burnt umber, burnt sienna, or lampblack. Other pigments came from animal and vegetable sources, such as indigo, carmine, and madder, among others. All pigments are graded or considered in terms of lightfastness and permanence. The inorganic mineral and earth pigments tend to be more permanent than the vegetable and animal pigments. As a rule, strong, bright colors, particularly red, blue, and yellow, are more prone to fading and color shifts than earth tones and light-tint colors.

The vehicle, consisting of the binder and solvent, creates the flow and cohesion properties of a paint. Solvents (water and turpentine are common examples) are carriers that help liquefy the paint, and some of these solvents are lost as paint dries. Binders remain part of the paint as it dries, holding the pigment together and, in many cases, to the surface. As a rule, solvents and binders determine the reversibility, shrinkage, and elasticity of a paint. Often a paint's name is taken from its binder, as in casein, oil, or acrylic paints.

Paint composition (the type and proportion of the pigment, solvent, and binder) is manipulated to vary its characteristics, depending upon the intended use. For example, the addition of more oil or other binder makes a glossier and more durable paint. A paint with a high percentage of pigments and *fillers* (additives that alter the consistency and sheen of paint) will tend to be flatter and more opaque, providing better coverage.

CURING

Paint's composition also determines how it adheres to the *substrate,* or surface to which it is applied. Paint can adhere to substrates in three ways: mechanically, according to the tooth, texture, or porosity of the surface and paint; adhesively; and chemically, although a chemical bond formed between the paint and the surface is rare. All of these ways of adhering in turn affect the way the paint is dried, or *cured,* the process by which the liquid is solidified and a film is produced. There are four categories of curing:

In *solvent loss,* the paint's coating is formed by the removal of the solvent by evaporation, leaving the binder or resin with the pigments on the surface in a cohesive film. The solvents can either be aqueous or otherwise, and the binder can be either natural or synthetic. Two very different examples of this type of paint are glue distempers, where water is the vehicle/solvent, and shellac, where alcohol is the vehicle/solvent. In solvent-loss paints, the solidification of a vehicle can be reversed by reapplication of the solvent.

Curing by *coalescence* applies predominantly to emulsion-type paints. In these colloidal systems, globules or particles of one liquid, such as resin or pigment dispersions, are suspended in another liquid prior to drying. Examples include acrylic, polyvinyl acetate, and latex paints. This system applies mostly to modern paints (post-1930s). Earlier, emulsions were relatively uncommon; they consisted of such systems as oleocasein (casein and oil), ammonia stain (shellac and water), and egg-oil emulsion.

Curing by *cross-linking* requires the reaction of the binder with a catalyst. The traditional example is linseed oil, which reacts with oxygen in the air over a long period of time. Modern examples are two-component epoxies in which one component reacts with another via a third chemical catalyst. Another modern example is water-cured urethanes, which rely on moisture in the atmosphere as a catalyst for curing.

Curing by *crystallization* occurs either through the chemical reaction between the substrate and the paint or through a petrification of the paint itself and applies to several distinctly different types of paints, each of which goes through a chemical reaction upon drying. In some cases, a chemical bond is formed with the substrate. One well-known example of this process is *fresco*, in which pigments mixed in limewater and applied to the wet plaster become carbonized together. In the case of *Keim waterglass* (potassium silicate), the paint petrifies with the masonry substrate. In other cases, such as that of cementitious paint, the binder chemically bonds itself and the pigments to create a continuous film.

IDENTIFICATION OF PAINTS AND THEIR SUBSTRATES

Accurately classifying the type of paint and substrate is a crucial beginning step in dealing with older paint. The substrate is often a common building material such as wood, plaster, masonry, metal, or modern Sheetrock. Substrates can also include leather, fabric, glass, or paper. A primer coat is used for sealing an untreated surface so that it can be followed by other coats of paint. It is intended to saturate into various substrates. It is important to consider the porosity of the substrate and the absorption of the backing when choosing primer and paint systems.

Understanding how various types of paint systems work in relation to the substrate is important in order to understand how to treat or conserve these finishes. A working knowledge of the particular properties of paint will be useful toward this end. The following explanation of terms aids in identifying types of paint and substrates, their common uses, and potential problems in conservation and restoration.

Paints can be categorized variously as those that need water to carry them (aqueous) and those that use vehicles or solvents other than water (nonaqueous or solvent-borne). Other categories of paints include cementitious paints and unusual combination systems such as those used in decorative painting. Following is a comparison of the properties of historic and modern paints for the purposes of paint identification.

These bottles contain dry pigments in powder form, which are further pulverized using a glass muller on a stone or glass surface. These same tools are used to grind and mix the pigment with its vehicle, whether oil or otherwise.

WATERBORNE SYSTEMS

TRADITIONAL WATERBORNE PAINTS

In general, historic water-based paints are characterized by a matte finish. They do not yellow with age, but they do become brittle and they may support bacterial or fungal growth.

Whitewash is a general term used to describe a mixture of lime (calcium oxide), whiting (chalk, crushed limestone, or calcium carbonate), water, and pigment. Whitewash solidifies through weak crystallization of the lime component, and this crystallization was often enhanced by addition of glue or casein. Whitewash is made by hand and is not commercially available, although some very unsatisfactory synthetic substitutes are marketed as whitewash. The synthetics can become brittle and do not bind well over time. True whitewash was a very common early utilitarian finish used on plaster, wood, masonry, and other porous surfaces. It was renewed frequently, often by washing off the old finish with water and a brush, followed by repainting.

Calcimine is a general term used for glue distemper mixed with casein paint. This paint is very similar to whitewash, with a high ratio of pigment and filler to binder. It was both mixed by hand and commercially manufactured in powdered and liquid form. Its binders were stronger than those of whitewash, but still much weaker than the binders in most modern paints. It is also susceptible to microorganisms and resoluble in the presence of moisture. This has proven problematic in many historic homes, where calcimine was painted over, causing incurable peeling. Calcimine should not be painted over unless a special primer is used (see page 137).

Casein is a milk protein used as a paint binder, an adhesive, and a paper coating. Early forms were made with farmer cheese, and casein later became commercially available in both powdered and liquid form. It was suitable for both porous and relatively nonporous substrates, including plaster, masonry, and wood. Casein is insoluble in typical organic solvents and resistant to solvent-based paint strippers. Hybrids of casein paint, such as oleocasein (casein with oil), were also used.

Milk paint is a form of casein that declined in the fifteenth century with the advent of oils but was reintroduced in France during the eighteenth century. It was known as lime-casein, although it did not always contain lime. Recipes circulating in America in the 1800s called for milk to be used in a mixture for outdoor paints, with beer to be substituted for the indoor-paint mixture. It is still commercially available in a dry powdered form. Although milk paint is flat, the colors have a rich velvety quality.

Glue distemper is one of the most common binders for traditional paint. The glue is made from animal parts, including skin, bones, and cartilage. Traditionally, it was painted on while warm, which required the painter to mix his paint on a daily basis. Its vehicle is water. Straight glue *size* (without pigment) was often used to seal plaster before finish painting with oil or distemper. Distemper binder will not yellow with age but is susceptible to microorganisms and damage from moisture.

Gouache and other forms of watercolor are paints made from plant gums and glues such as gum arabic, or gum senegal. Dextrin is the gum now used commercially. In the Southwest, paints were made from cactus juice and used on adobe. Historically, gouache was often incorrectly referred to as distemper or tempera paint.

MODERN WATERBORNE PAINTS

Emulsions, or *latex paints,* were introduced in 1948. The original formulations used chlorinated rubber, hence the name latex rubber paint. These were unique because they contained pigments suspended (emulsified) in a water base. *Latex* is a general term that covers many different kinds of paint. The more technical name, *waterborne polymer emulsions,* is a better way to describe these paints, which include acrylics, polyvinyl acetate, and styrene butadiene. With these paints, the molecules of binder and pigment are suspended evenly between the molecules of water, creating a stable paint with uniform texture that dries by forming a film rather than through solvent evaporation. Unpigmented acrylic may be used as an adhesive or additive consolidant for plaster and paint. Because latex paints are waterproof, nontoxic, and very stable, they have largely replaced traditional distemper paints.

NONAQUEOUS SOLVENT-BORNE SYSTEMS

Solvent-based paints depend on substances other than water to transport their components. The solvents could include mineral spirits, turpentine, alcohol, acetone, toluene, or a variety of combinations of other solvents. Older nonaqueous paints include traditional oil paint (linseed, walnut, or other natural oils), enamels, resins, and varnish. The newer nonaqueous paints include lacquers, epoxies, urethanes, and solvent acrylics. Unfortunately, there is much confusion in the nomenclature because virtually all nonaqueous solvent-borne systems are referred to as oil paint.

TRADITIONAL NONAQUEOUS SOLVENT-BORNE PAINTS

Traditional *oil paint* was made with linseed oil (which is derived from the flax seed) and pigments. Occasionally walnut oil or other, cheaper oils were used. It also contains turpentine or some other solvent to reduce its viscosity. As oil paint dries, some turpentine is lost, causing oxidation to occur much more slowly. Ingredients such as lead siccatives and cobalt driers were added to speed the drying process. The pigments used also affected the drying time of the paint, its opacity, and its other characteristics. The glossiness of the dried paint is related to the amount of pigment, oil, and turpentine present. Traditional oil paint was a very versatile and durable material. It could be used to cover virtually every substrate. Resins were added to oil paints to strengthen them. Before the early twentieth century, painters made their own paint or modified store-bought paint to suit their specific decorating needs.

Oil paint becomes brittle with age, and it can be attacked by alkalis in lime plaster. Lime plaster should always be thoroughly cured before applying oil paint. The oil binder has a tendency to yellow with age.

TRADITIONAL RESINS AND VARNISH PAINTS

These types of paints were originally derived from plant and tree gums and resins such as copal and balsam. *Rosin,* used in varnishes, is the residue left after making a turpentine distillation of pine balsam. It was usually used in low-grade varnishes due to its tendency to yellow and become brittle with age. Early resins were also made from waxes, coal, and pine tars (pitch) mixed with drying oils. Most of the resin paints remain soluble and are therefore reversible.

Shellac (the resin secreted by a scale insect, dissolved in alcohol) was used as a clear coating and in combination with pigments or dyes to create paints and varnishes. Shellac was often used to seal new plaster as well as knots in wood and other absorbent or staining surfaces, in preparation for finishing with oil paint. Also a historic woodwork covering, shellac tends to darken and become brittle with age. Modern shellac is graded by color and *cut;* the cut refers to the amount of lac flakes to alcohol. Shellac colors represent the refinement of the solution, ranging from bleached white to natural orange and dark brown.

Japan paint was an early type of varnish paint commonly used for coach and sign painting.

Like the term *latex,* *enamel* is another now-generic term whose specific meaning has been lost. When we refer to historic enamels, we are talking about a high-gloss paint made with traditional oils cooked with melted hard resins. This reaction product is then thinned with more oil and afterward liquefied by the addition of a solvent. Unpigmented, it is used as a varnish, and pigmented it is called enamel and often used on trim, doors, and in kitchens. It is a very durable finish, though prone to embrittlement with age. Natural resins such as those formerly used in enamels were replaced by *alkyds* (or *alkids*) in 1928. These paints dry faster and resist weather damage, but they will peel when applied over older oil paint. Alkyds were subsequently replaced by synthetic resins such as epoxy, urethane, or acrylic-urethane resins. Their drying process is complex, but they can be very flexible and durable.

A small selection of the brushes used by painters historically and still in use today.

MODERN SOLVENT-BORNE PAINTS

There exist too many modern specialized solvent systems to list them all here, but a couple that came into existence in the 1920s are relevant in the context of this chapter. The following list consists of modern solvent systems that have had a great impact upon paint technology or that are especially helpful to conservators.

Introduced in 1928, *alkyd resins* were the first synthetic paints. The development of an emulsified oil as a substitute for the traditional linseed-oil-based paint was a milestone in paint technology. The new synthetics dried faster, were more durable, and were lower in cost. They were combined with traditional oils and resins to create long, medium, and short-polymered oil alkyds. Alkyds combine the best characteristics of both oils and resins.

Lacquer was also first introduced in the 1920s. In its clear, unpigmented state, it was used as a substitute for shellac on wood because it could be sprayed and dried quickly. The pigmented versions were used on all manner of objects and equipment due to their durability. The original synthetic material had a nitrocellulose base.

Solvent acrylics are worth noting in this section because of their usefulness in conserving historic paint. This material is little more than a plastic or acrylic resin dissolved in an appropriate solvent such as toluene, acetone, or mineral spirits. These paints dry as the solvent evaporates, leaving behind the acrylic film. These same solvents can be used easily to reverse or redissolve the film. Contemporary conservators often use solvent-based acrylics as consolidants, adhesives, and varnishes. As a consolidant, the material is often used to reinforce or replace a weakened binder in a traditional paint system. Mixed with pigments, the material is often used as a reversible inpainting or touch-up medium. In its clear state it is often used as a reversible isolating or final varnish.

UNUSUAL PAINT SYSTEMS

The following uncommon paint types are sometimes combinations of systems discussed above (deco paint), or unique systems unto themselves (encaustic).

Traditional *wax encaustic* is applied while hot and dries from cooling and partial loss of solvents. The binder is beeswax, which is extremely permanent. Wax was often mixed with oil, resins, turpentines, and other solvents to create a myriad of hybrid systems. Encaustic paints are soluble in organic solvents and can be melted by heat. These systems were predominantly used for artistic and decorative painting.

Cementitious paints use portland or other types of cement, silica, and plaster as binders. This paint is characterized by curing through crystallization. Cement is very resistant to weathering and consists of silicates, aluminates, or alumino-ferrates. It is used mostly on masonry, brick, stone, or plaster. In modern times these paints have been modified with acrylics and other polymers, but in historic homes, a great range of obscure materials and techniques combining plaster, cement, and paint were used. These included polishing and waxing pigmented plaster to create stucco lustro. Cementitious aggregates were used in paint binders to create textured paint, which could be manipulated into an endless variety of patterns and textures and then stained or glazed with thin, transparent oil or distemper paint.

Keim is a potassium-silicate-based paint of European origin, developed as a lightfast, outdoor paint for extreme temperature fluctuations. It was designed as a kind of synthetic fresco paint and may be used on masonry without primer as it penetrates and binds with the substrate. It is very resistant to bacterial and algal growth, and its inorganic components make it nearly inflammable.

Fresco is a term loosely used. *Buono*, or true, fresco refers to painting with pigments on wet lime plaster. *Fresco secco* refers to painting with almost any medium on dry plaster. In American historical references, the term *frescoing* usually refers to any pictorial or decorative painting on a wall.

Decorative painting, which will be discussed below, often combines any or all of the above techniques to create its desired effects.

Restoring and Maintaining Historic Paints

When working with historic surfaces, important decisions must be made. For instance, if the four walls surrounding you are covered with numerous layers of paint, which is the best layer to restore? Is there a particular surface that deserves your attention more than the others? A combination of professional help and diligent historical research is often required to answer such questions adequately. Professionals can provide help with paint analysis and production history. This information can be added to research of home and local historical documents and photographs to form a more complete picture of what kind of surfaces lie underneath, and what is special about them.

As described above, historic paints are chemically different from paints produced today. They were in most cases designed to last as long as possible rather than to be redone. However, historic paints also have inherent flaws, such as pigment aging, binder breakdown, and loss of adhesion. These problems may also stem from external causes: excessive light and water or accumulation of surface dirt and accretions can lead to mildew, microorganism growth, and efflorescence (mineral salts in the substrate). Paint composition and incorrect application can cause trouble, as can chemical or mechanical incompatibility between paint layers. Cleaning and repair processes are often different for plain and decorative paint. Once a paint is identified, a plan to restore it can be put into action. The next step is to determine which methods of cleaning, consolidation, and/or repainting are appropriate for the type of paint.

Paint Analysis

Methods for determining original colors, type of paint, and decorative patterns can run the gamut from simple cleaning and solvency testing to sophisticated laboratory analysis for medium and pigment identification. Some cases require professional care, particularly with specialty paint or when original paint colors are obscured. A conservator can analyze paint samples, test cleaning methods, and provide special tools for paint removal in difficult areas. Researching any available documentation is crucial; anything relating to the construction methods, dates of construction, and names of original client or architect will aid a conservator. Old black-and-white photographs are valuable tools for determining whether decorative painting such as stenciling or graining exists, although they cannot be relied on to evaluate the accuracy of color values.

Methods available to homeowners include the crater method, which uses a low-power microscope to examine "craters" made by cutting through layers of paint and polishing with a wet abrasive. This is a preliminary, on-site method to determine likely areas from which to carry out more extensive examinations. Good samples are often found in drops of paint on door hinges or places where paint has a thick accumulation. Samples should include the substrate to orient the mapping of the layers.

In a lab, many different techniques can be used for paint identification, including chromology, X-ray diffraction, X-ray fluorescence, electron-beam microprobe, energy dispersion, infrared spectroscopy, or gas. Samples subjected to these tests are often mounted in order to make them easier to examine. Color matching is achieved through the use of Munsell or Plochere color charts, books of color chips that are matched against the cleaned samples. Specialty paints and decorative work often require the application of different solvents and neutralizers to the surface in order to remove the paint one layer at a time. Simple manual tools such as surgical scalpels are often used to remove paint layer by layer. Layer-by-layer removal allows the creation of an exposure window, through which it is possible to view any decorative work present.

IDENTIFYING COMMON PAINT FAILURES

Paint failure, while often related to simple age, is also an index of the condition of the paint's particular environment. Paint failure can clue the homeowner in on serious structural difficulties such as leakage. It can also occur as a result of improper preparation of the substrate, application of layers of paint that do not adhere to one another, and exposure to extreme environmental conditions such as continuously high humidity, maritime climates, and architectural features that shed or trap water on a surface. The following sections present common paint failures and possible solutions.

Peeling and *blistering* can be caused by chemical incompatibility between layers of paint or trapped moisture. After diagnosing and remedying the cause, these areas should be scraped and sanded before repainting.

Checking, or *crazing*, also known as cracked or *alligatored* paint, results from age and embrittlement of inflexible or overly thick layers of paint that cannot respond to changes in the substrate from temperature fluctuation. It can also be caused by layering incompatible paints. The damaged layers can be removed for repainting by wire brush, sandpaper, or scraping.

Staining is due to both internal paint weakness and external causes such as pollutants, mildew, or oxidation of metal supports. Stained paint may be cleaned if the source is external, and it must be removed if internal. Sealers may also be applied to the surface to prevent external staining and directly to the offending substrate to prevent internal staining.

Wrinkled paint is caused by the application of a top layer before the bottom is dry, extreme temperature when paint is applied, or too much paint applied at one time. Wrinkled paint can be redissolved and smoothed. If repainting, wrinkled paint should be removed.

Chalking is caused by internal paint failure such as binder breakdown due to aging. Chalked paint should be dusted and lightly washed with detergent and then rinsed with water. It is next primed with an oil or alkyd primer, allowed to dry, and then repainted.

REMEDIES FOR PAINT FAILURE

CLEANING

Cleaning begins with vacuuming or brushing off the surface and then spot testing it for reactions to washing with detergent and water. Spot tests should be conducted on small, out-of-the-way areas. Some of the best detergents to start with are Ivory, Dirtex, or TSP-free soap. Kodak Triton-X, a soft-washing soap used in film development, is another gentle cleaner. Mineral spirits can be used for heavy layers of grease. If the area is neither damaged nor cleaned by the spot test, you might want to spot test a stronger cleanser. If the test damages the surface, you may need the services of a professional conservator. For cleaning, conservators may use aqueous or nonaqueous solvent-based cleaning products, as well as dry mechanical methods (such as brush removal), solvent gels, and enzyme solutions.

CONSOLIDATION

Consolidation, or reattachment, consists of the reintroduction of binders or adhesives into paint film. Consolidation can be used to cure both powdering and peeling or flaking conditions. Successful consolidation must readhere the paint to the substrate, provide cohesion between paint layers, and adhere itself to the surrounding paint. Consolidation techniques must accomplish the above without discoloring, producing extra gloss, collecting dust, or making the surface vulnerable to bacterial or fungal growth. Some common consolidants are water, gelatin, starches, vegetable gums, cellulose ethers, and solvent-soluble synthetic resins. These components are often used alone or in combination, depending upon the demands of the job. The expertise of a paint conservator is required for consolidation.

With most architectural paint, the consolidants are applied directly to the face of the paint. Reversible isolating varnishes can be used for this purpose. One could also use selective inpainting to match sheen and color. When dealing with fine-art murals or special, hard-to-replace decorative paint, consolidants can be introduced by injection to the rear of the paint failure or through capillary action, usually with a syringe. Another technique applied to fine art and some special painting involves the application of facing paper or tissue to hold paint flakes in place. One common technique for reattachment of fine-art oil paint is the use of wax and a hot tacking iron to reform flaking paint, consolidating and readhering it simultaneously.

Paint samples are commonly examined through a microscope to identify the various layers of paint.

REPAINTING

After any consolidation procedures are carried out, it must be determined whether any repainting or inpainting is required. This judgment should be based on the existing condition of the decoration and whether any intervention would enhance or detract from the original intention.

Replication of historic paint requires sensitive color matching that is almost impossible to achieve by eye due to the alterations of time and the inevitable layering of paint. Some conservators re-create historical paints with original materials, but the instability and inconsistency of these paints may lead to later discoloration. Other conservators approximate historical paints with inventive use of modern paint materials. A varied approach, depending on the needs of the project, is best. Conservators' work should always be reversible and as accurate as possible.

PREPARING HISTORIC SUBSTRATES FOR REPAINTING

Some finishes, such as protective coatings and overpainting, may, where needed, be removed before repainting. As in cleaning, a small area should be tested to determine the solubility of outer layers before attempting to remove them. Solvents such as mineral spirits or denatured alcohol are used to remove protective coatings, although stronger solvents are sometimes required, rendering the task significantly more hazardous. Necessary precautions such as wearing protective clothing, gloves, and respirators must be taken.

If many layers of paint are to be removed, heat guns and heat plates are recommended, removing from the thickest areas of paint application first. Paint is scraped off as it begins to bubble and liquefy. Elaborately molded areas require special scraping tools and the expertise of a paint conservator. If heat is used to remove paint, do so first in thickly painted areas by holding the heat source over the area until the paint lifts, and then begin scraping. Cleaned areas may scorch later, so use caution. After scraping, sandpaper or solvents may be used after the surface has cooled. Because heating paint may release toxic fumes, work should be done in a well-ventilated area and an inhaler mask with vapor cartridges should be worn.

Be extremely cautious of heat removal as it can cause cracked glass, scorching, or even fire. In general, heat should be very carefully used, and treated areas should be checked regularly for forty-eight hours following use. Remember to work in a clean area with a fire extinguisher and water nearby and not to use heat on or near window glass. Do not use heat-removal methods on lead-based paint as it will cause the release of harmful pollutants. Also, heat is not effective on shellac, varnish, or casein paint.

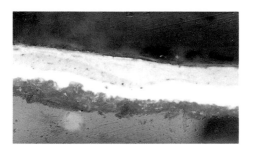

This informative paint sample reveals many layers of historic paint.

Chemical strippers are based on either organic solvents or lye. Commercial firms use lye-based chemical strippers. No-rinse strippers are useful on ceilings, and, while water-rinse strippers will raise the grain of wood and loosen glue and veneer, they are less caustic than no-rinse strippers. During

With the stencil template in place, an artisan uses a stencil or stippling brush to achieve one stage in the application of a stenciled design.

application, cover the paint surface with cloths or plastic to keep it from drying out before scraping. Wallpaper steamers are sometimes used to help lift off the paint with a stripper. After applying, a small area should be tested to see if the paint comes up completely before attempting removal. Second coats of stripper may be applied to stubborn areas and to woods that are open-pored.

Solvent strippers are noxious and should be used with extreme care. Wear a respirator mask and cartridges, as well as gloves and protective clothing. Ventilate the area well during and after removal as chemical solvents contain carcinogens and toxins. Be aware that some chemicals are flammable, so keep an extinguisher nearby. Always dispose of waste as directed by the environmental authorities in your region.

An alternate stripping method is to sand by hand. A power sander can damage wood and is not recommended. Air abrasives are safe but difficult to handle effectively.

Historic Paints Requiring Special Preparation

In most cases, layers of paint must be removed in order to get to the substrate. However, older paint can be used as a substrate if it is in good condition (i.e., it is smooth and free of the problems mentioned above, such as cracking). Before painting in damaged areas, conservators will apply a sealer over older paint to protect the older undamaged surface. Certain paints, such as glue distempers, almost always require professional attention. The following is a list of other paints that either require special treatment for successful overpainting or should not be painted over.

When painting over old oil paint, an oil or latex primer should be used and allowed to dry thoroughly before the next coating.

Calcimine paint should be removed before repainting or treated with a specially formulated primer that will bind with other paints. Trisodium phosphate and hot water can remove calcimine paint when scrubbed with a bristle brush. If calcimine is under other layers of paint, it can be removed using steam, heat, or chemical methods. If you do not want to remove it, the surface should be completely cleaned and sealed with an alcohol-thinned, pigmented shellac or primer as described above.

Casein or milk paint must be removed with ammonia and fine steel wool (take precautions such as gloves and a respirator mask when working with ammonia). The ammonia may need to soak on the paint surface for a few minutes before it will penetrate it.

Preparing Historic Nonpaint Substrates

A primer should be used over lime and gypsum plaster. If the plaster is old, it should be pH-tested and cleaned before applying oil paint. If salt deposits appear on the plaster after wetting, brush them off before painting the dry plaster. Paint on plaster may be removed with gentle stripping or chemical solvents. Over time, too much oil paint on plaster can pull the plaster apart as a result of the paint's shrinkage.

Before repainting wood, wash with detergent and rinse with water or mineral spirits. If the wood needs roughing, use sandpaper or a deglosser. If paint is cracking, scrape it off with the grain of the wood (be aware of possible lead-paint dangers and take necessary precautions). Caustic removers may damage wood and deposit salts that will cause adhesion problems later. They may also soften the wood. If caustic removers are used, neutralize the wood with an acid wash afterward and then test its pH level (generally, 6.5–8 is an appropriate level) before repainting. As mentioned earlier, sand- or grit-blasting methods of paint removal will damage wood and are not recommended.

An exposure window was created through layers of paint to reveal the original finish at the Hackley House.

Sheetrock and concrete should be sealed with a primer before painting. On old concrete, either latex or oil paint may be used as a primer if the concrete is clean and dry. If concrete is stained with oil from molding or dirt from weathering, it can be washed first with ammonia water and then water rinsed and allowed to dry. Brick and stone may require cleaning with a wire brush and water wash. Latex is the best primer for sealing chronically damp places on masonry.

TREATING SPECIALTY PAINT

In the case of specialty painting, the emphasis should be on retention rather than removal for repainting. While most historical painting, such as applying a single color to a surface, was done with rough, rectangular-bristle brushes (for distemper paints) and finer circular-bristle brushes called rounds (for oils), decorative painting was done with a variety of specialized tools made of bristles and quills, among other materials. Commonly used tools for fancy work included overgrainers, quill striping pencils, combs, floggers, dusters, and stipplers. There are innumerable ways to use paint decoratively, including the use of textured paints, pictorial painting (murals), and other faux techniques. Common types of decorative work are listed below.

- *Stenciling* was popular from the seventeenth through the twentieth century and refers to painting a pattern from a template.
- *Sponging* or *mottling* creates an uneven paint texture by blotting the wet paint with a sponge.
- *Glazing* is the application of a pigmented transparent paint over an opaque surface to create a greater depth of color.
- *Graining* is the painted imitation of wood, often found on doors. This effect is achieved by layering different color paints, creating an irregular and stippled surface.
- *Gilding* is the use of metallic powder or leaf to simulate metal. The surface is prepared with a special mixture and then gold leaf is applied and smoothed with a particular brush. It is then burnished and shellacked.
- *Marbleizing* is usually done on baseboards and fireplace mantels in imitation of marble stone. The veins of paint are applied, with a feather or thin brush, on a tinted glaze over a base coat.

CLEANING SPECIALTY PAINT

Begin by testing a weak cleaning solution on a small, hidden patch of the paint. Dust the surface well first, then apply the cleaning solution, and rinse several times. If the paint comes off with water, use mineral spirits. If it does not appear to come off with water, then try a slightly stronger detergent. Test the entire area carefully as different colors may respond differently to the cleaning solution. Dry-cleaning methods are often necessary for cleaning specialty paint. A professional's services may be needed if colors respond to the cleaner differently, or if the paint comes off with both water and mineral spirits.

Gilding in particular must be cleaned by a conservator, as the patina is easily damaged by conventional cleaning solutions. Metal leaf (a kind of gilding) and bronze paint will discolor if not sealed properly and must be repaired by a professional. Deteriorating protective finishes on gilding, metal leaf, and bronze paint should also be removed professionally to avoid damage to the underlying layers.

REPLICATION OF SPECIALTY PAINT

The first task with replication is to determine the makeup of the original paint, through its appearance, document research, or by testing small patches with different solvents. If you cannot determine the type of paint, consult a profes-

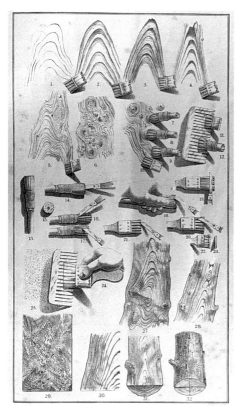

This illustration from a nineteenth-century artisan's book on decorative techniques shows some of the tools used in the various stages of creating a grained surface.

In the studio a gilder burnishers gold leaf that has been applied to a molded plaster ornament.

sional conservator. The next step is to determine and match the color and/or pattern of the original. Matches for specialty painting may be particularly tricky. Again, the services of a specialist are invaluable for re-creating both color and certain decorative techniques. The following details replication techniques for specific paints.

Gilding requires the services of a professional. It begins with the application of glue, chalk, and gilder's clay (bole) to a clean, dry surface. A base is then applied, made of either an alcohol and water mixture or an unpigmented oil base called gold *size*. Leaves of gold are painstakingly applied, smoothed, and polished with special tools. The gilding is finally sealed with a protective finish.

Stencil patterns may be re-created using a variety of materials. Once colors and patterns have been determined, patterns are traced and cut out of a stencil material such as acetate. Usually, different stencils are used for different colors to maintain clear distinction among them. Stencils are positioned with measuring tools and held firmly in place while paint is applied. Japan or other oil paints are applied with a brush, and each color must be completely dry before another color is applied. The final step is to apply a clear, protective coating.

Glazing involves the application of a base coat such as latex, which is allowed to completely dry before a glaze is applied. A glaze is traditionally a mix of pigment, varnish, linseed oil, and either turpentine or mineral spirits. Often textured immediately after application, glazing can be a two-person job. A thin glaze can be textured with a sponge dipped first in mineral spirits and then in the glaze. Texturing can also be achieved by dabbing the wet glaze with cheesecloth or a sponge, dragging over it with a dry brush, or stippling with a dry brush. Once the glaze is dry, a protective coating is applied.

Marbleizing begins with a coat of "ground," or base coat, color that matches the main color of the stone to be imitated. When dry, a second coat of the same color is applied with a sponge or other tools. While this coat is still wet, veins are painted on with a thin brush or feather dipped in darker paint and run irregularly over the surface. Further effects may be added by blending with crumpled newspaper, cheesecloth, or a sponge. Once dry, the application of a protective coating is the final step.

Graining is created by many methods, all involving the layering of differently colored coats of paint. The base coat is applied and sanded, then glazed with a darker color. While wet, this darker glaze is stippled and broken up in an irregular wavy pattern by various tools such as a stiff brush. Other effects can be added, such as painted-on veins or knots formed by blotting. The final step is a protective coating.

Clearly, a wide range of traditional paints and finishes are available to enhance historic buildings. As with any conservation activity, caution, observation, and restraint should be exercised in both preparation for and execution of work upon these historic finishes. If the finishes in your house should require attention, first devote time to researching the finishes and the options for their conservation. The more information you have about paint surfaces and traditional techniques, the better you will appreciate the beauty of historic paints and finishes and understand the problems that may be affecting them.

Any conservation work should be well considered and reversible. The materials and techniques used should be sympathetic to the historic fabric. Most important, you as owner should understand what your limitations are and when to ask for expert advice. Conservators and historic-paint specialists are available for consultation and can often be located through regional museums or state historic preservation offices. The cost of consulting a professional is minimal when one considers the enrichment of interior spaces provided by the conservation of historic paints and finishes.

Note

1. *Shapes That Pass* (1928), 176–77.

Interior Woodwork

James Boorstein

When European settlers arrived in America, the forests seemed unlimited, and there were few permanent dwellings. Early housing consisted of caves, cliff dwellings, huts, and wigwams. Today vast areas of the forest have given way to hundreds of millions of permanent structures. Wood has been used for a building's skeletal structure, skin, roof, floors, walls, furnishings, and as decoration. No other raw material has been used for so many parts of our homes and lives. Styles of architecture and decoration continually change but the material itself remains basically the same.

Many species of hardwood and softwood are used to fabricate interior architectural elements. The wood is sawn from tree trunks in different ways to produce desired structural and visual characteristics depending on its intended use. The visually wild, quarter-sawn grain of oak is in strong contrast to the same tree's stable and uniform rift-sawn boards. (See illustration on page 154.) Within most species of wood, there can be a wide range of properties, appearance, and color. The quality of the material combined with the skill and style of human work can provide a final product worthy of protecting.

Almost every American building has interior wooden elements and trim; they are what we see and touch each day. Paneling, or *wainscoting* as it was more commonly called, has appeared in American homes since the 1600s. Some historians believe it was used as insulation in the cold, damp interiors; others believe paneling was more important as a decorative element.

The earliest paneling, usually from floor to ceiling, was created by installing a succession of vertical boards, generally with a bead or chamfer on one or both vertical edges. This vertical board style was later used in secondary and informal locations, such as kitchens, pantries, or service halls. Formal styles were characterized by a series of flat or raised rectilinear panels framed by vertical and horizontal members. As life in the New World grew less precarious, decoration became increasingly important. Paneling tended to be lower, often only to the height of the chair rail, perhaps to open the wall area for other decorative treatments.

The most common wooden horizontal trim was *baseboard*, which originally formed the base for wainscoting and provided a seal between the wall and floor. Chair rails protected formal wainscoting from chair backs. Later they were used without wainscoting to serve as a visual delineation and to protect wall finishes. Picture rails and cornices form the uppermost band of horizontal trim and, along with ceiling molding, were made of either wood or plaster.

Fireplace mantels can be the most elaborate wooden element in a room or be so simple as to go unnoticed. Individual wooden mantelpieces often include many woodworking techniques, from millwork to carving.

Stairs can be a significant visual element in a historic house. They are a complicated hybrid of diverse parts: flooring, baseboard handrail, decorative spindles, and applied ornament. Stairs are load bearing, with their own self-contained, concealed, wooden structural system. Freestanding wooden columns are also frequently both decorative and load bearing.

In the 1950s and 1960s, architectural elements were frequently painted white for a clean, "modern" look. Removing the paint thoroughly and safely is painstaking work. The goal is to avoid scratching or damaging the woodwork, leaving only the richness of the natural wood.

In addition to fixed decorative elements, the moving parts of buildings—doors, windows, and interior shutters—often were and continue to be made of wood. These parts are framed by an element called *casing*. Casing surrounds the moving elements on two, three, or four sides, forming a visual transition. Casings hide the rough area at the juncture between the structure of the building and the moving elements. In contrast, built-in cabinetry and window seats function more like furniture than architecture and are rarely surrounded by casing.

Wood as a material is remarkably tough and versatile; it has no single enemy. Protected, woodwork can easily last for centuries. Interior woodwork has no finite life span the way paint, roofs, or plumbing do. Deterioration of woodwork is generally caused by poor building design, faulty construction, failure of another building component, and/or a lack of maintenance. When a building as a whole is cared for, the woodwork is also protected. Caring for wood consists of an awareness of materials and conditions, ongoing maintenance, and a stable environment.

HARMFUL FORCES

PEOPLE

People can be a considerable hazard to architectural woodwork. Teenagers with posters, tape, candles, and darts; young children prying off loose pieces of molding; and overzealous or untrained cleaning people can all cause surprising damage. Careless mopping near woodwork, for example, can cause discoloration, which is difficult and expensive to correct.

Cleaning services or housekeepers, often with no training or direction, frequently become the sole caretakers for room upon room of historic woodwork. Everyone needs to be shown what to do, what not to do, which products to use and how to use them, how often certain areas need to be cleaned, and which areas should never be touched. Instruction from a knowledgeable person is essential.

Awareness and sensitivity are important. Demonstrate each step, even how to wring out a cloth so that it is damp, not wet. Review cleaning work the first day, and again after several weeks.

Workers in the trades pose a threat to woodwork, especially to unprotected wooden floors and wainscoting. Unnecessary damage is done by carelessly carrying ladders through houses, painting without covering woodwork, and thoughtlessly opening walls to gain access to hidden pipes. Window washers often fail to wipe up excess water. Exterminators can be sloppy, and electricians find it easier to mount new fixtures on woodwork. Telephone, cable, and security-system installers with staple guns and tight schedules all pose a threat.

To offset these hazards, seek out sensitive and thoughtful workers when possible, and always take the time to review the work that will be done. If you cannot be present, it is advisable to have someone supervising work in sensitive areas. When favorite fragile vases are being taken off the mantel and put away in preparation for work, the mantel itself should also be protected. Protection is an investment; it is the best insurance and, done routinely, can prevent damage.

WATER

Water, beyond the confines of pipes and fixtures, is usually a result of other

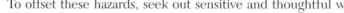

problems: fire, roof leaks, inadequate grout, tub or sink overflow, leaking pipes, or even an open window during a summer rain. Humidity is a daily problem. It is the same water but suspended in air, invisible, like water in a sponge.

Relative humidity (RH) is the ratio of the amount of moisture in the air relative to the maximum amount of moisture the air can hold at a given temperature. As temperature increases, the amount of moisture that air can hold also increases, and the RH goes down. A decrease in temperature causes an increase in relative humidity.

Wood is an organic, hygroscopic (water-absorbing) material. It actually moves in an attempt to maintain equilibrium with its surroundings, physically taking in water as the air becomes more saturated and later shrinking when the water is given off to drier air. Humidity and wood have a relationship like that of too many calories to the waistline: the expansion and contraction in wood is primarily in width (across the grain). All properly constructed wooden elements allow this normal movement. Improper changes or repairs restrict this movement and, over time, can have problematic consequences.

A safe range for woodwork is between 40 and 60 percent RH, which is also a healthy range for people. Above 70 percent can be dangerous; wood will swell and can buckle. Repeated expansion can compress wood fibers, leaving permanent gaps. High moisture levels are also inviting to damaging organisms. Low humidity, below 30 percent, can cause serious shrinking and resultant cracking. Veneered woodwork is most susceptible to humidity extremes. High humidity softens the glue, diminishing veneer's resistance to swelling and blistering. Low humidity can cause glue to become dry and brittle.

A simple sling psychrometer is the most basic and accurate way to measure RH. Small, inexpensive battery-powered thermohygrometers are also available. Both can easily record highs and lows in a particular area or room. With a few minutes each day or week a monitoring program can uncover problem areas and seasonal variation. Every year, the accuracy of measuring devices, especially inexpensive ones, must be calibrated in a laboratory or against another, more accurate device.

Microclimates exist in many rooms, and one should attempt to learn where they are. The driest air is often near radiators or areas of intense sunlight. Frequent large shifts in RH, such as those caused by direct sunlight followed by blasts of cool moist air, can be very damaging to adjacent woodwork. High humidity inside and cold temperatures outside can cause condensation, which deteriorates finishes and leads to other water-related problems. Prevention is not necessarily expensive, but it requires attention.

In many parts of the country, having a humidifier or dehumidifier is necessary to maintain a safe and stable humidity level. If RH readings indicate a dangerous range, either purchase one or more small units or consult an engineer who has experience with climate control in homes, not just museums or office buildings, for which the problems, concerns, and issues are not the same. Once the equipment is in place, whether built-in or portable, it must be used and maintained properly to provide any benefit.

LIGHT

All light is damaging. Natural and artificial light change organic material. The effect of light on woodwork is most visible as fading, or even complete bleaching, of color. Light woods often darken while dark and colored woods fade. Sunlight also breaks down finishes, causing them to yellow and darken. Light can quickly bleach stains and dyes of all color.

Ultraviolet (UV) light, primarily from sunlight, is the most damaging. All glass offers some protection against UV, but significant protection is achieved only with UV filtering films. Indirect light, which bounces off white walls, is significantly less damaging.

Infrared radiation (IR) is heat and poses the same threat as other forms of heat. Infrared rays refracting through a cut-glass window or dangling prism can focus enough heat to leave burn marks on woodwork.

Visible light is measured in footcandles with a *luxmeter.* The recommended level for wooden objects is 20 to 40 footcandles. Colored textiles and paper art are far more vulnerable and require even lower levels. The effects of light are cumulative: three hours of bright light (not direct exposure) at 50 footcandles is the same as a ten-hour day of a dim 15 footcandles. Closing shutters or curtains routinely during the brightest times of day or when rooms are not in use is an effective method of reducing long-term light damage. Scrim shades reduce light levels in actively used rooms.

TEMPERATURE

Temperature affects woodwork less than it affects humans. Most homes in the United States have equipment to alter the interior temperature; the resulting comfort provided to humans also benefits woodwork. Temperature affects woodwork primarily because it affects RH. The hotter it is, the lower the RH. Rapid temperature changes, from opening shutters at midday, for example, can cause a significant and rapid increase in heat and therefore a drop in RH. This small but abrupt change can seriously degrade woodwork and finishes if it occurs frequently. Quickly heating a room or a house for a few hours or a weekend is not a good idea; gradual temperature shifts are important in order to preserve fragile woodwork.

Even in well maintained houses, one can often observe the poor condition of woodwork near radiators; this is a function less of the heat than of frequent climate change. High temperatures increase the speed of chemical reactions, an aspect of degrading finishes. Inspect material directly near all hot equipment and windows. A healthy house for woodwork has a stable environment with temperature in the range of 68 degrees Fahrenheit and RH close to 50 percent.

FUNGAL GROWTH

Even though countless spores are always present in the air, if humidity and temperature are kept low, there will be no difficulties with mold, mildew, or rot. Light, dryness, and moving air are the enemies of such plant life. Fungal problems often make themselves apparent as discoloration, a softer than normal surface, and a dull rather than solid sound when the infected wood is tapped.

Dry rot, despite its name, needs moisture like all living organisms. It can produce its own water by a metabolic process. It can also live and spread in completely dry wood by importing water through long, veinlike cells from adjacent damp masonry. Dry rot is in the family of brown rot and leaves telltale brown rectangular-shaped bits of crumbling wood dust. It is most common in softwood but also can be found in hardwood.

White rot is more common in hardwood and can destroy paneling and trim. It leaves a fibrous, powdery, light-colored dust. Dry rot and white rot can grow almost anywhere. Cellar rot and most other rots require a very high moisture content in the wood itself, not just in the surrounding air, in order to grow.

Unlike rot, mold does not destroy wood; however, it can ruin a finish and cause unsightly stains that are difficult to remove. Mold and mildew are also important as indicators of a climate that is hospitable to otherwise unnoticeable organisms with greater appetites.

PESTS

Certain insects have voracious appetites for wood. Termites are most specifically feared because they eat structural building elements. Numerous less common bugs pose a threat to interior decorative elements.

It is difficult to detect the presence of insects in woodwork until damage is done. Occasionally the sound of bugs eating can be heard. More common clues are a hollow sound when woodwork is tapped, round or oval exit holes (about one-sixteenth to one-half inch in diameter), and the frass they leave behind. Frass accumulation on horizontal members, like the top edge of baseboard, and an occasional dead insect body may be the only signs of insect infestation. These signs will be noticed only through careful observation, often while cleaning.

Wood-eating bugs frequently enter a house in antique furniture. Bugs also enter buildings riding on firewood, cut flowers, and foodstuffs. Once bugs are found, one should determine the type and degree of infestation. An entomologist will be helpful with identification. Insect infestation generally calls for professional help—not necessarily the local exterminator, who may not have experience beyond ants and roaches. Certain conservators specialize in insect infestations of woodwork.

This Eastlake Victorian bedroom has been meticulously restored. The wooden elements—doorway with transom, fireplace, baseboard, chair rail, picture rail and window (hidden behind the drapery)—convey the authentic 1884 architectural feeling of the interior to us today.

Methods of extermination vary widely. Bug spray is not the solution; it can damage finishes and is not effective at eliminating insects living inside woodwork. Inquire about the toxicity of recommended treatments and follow precautions carefully. Most insects can reinfect an area, so exercise vigilance after treatment.

Gnawing rodents also damage woodwork. After you have determined how they entered, try to coax them out. Placing camphor or mothballs in the area may drive them away. Once they are gone, quickly and thoroughly seal the holes. If they cannot be driven out, rodents should be trapped, not poisoned, as dead meat in the walls can lead to other problems.

Pets can also be pests, especially when they claw on doors to get outside. Paneled doors can be seriously damaged in a short time by a persistent pet. In addition to training pets, immediately install temporary protection; acrylic or brass panels are effective.

DISASTERS

Most fires in historic buildings are directly related to building work; virtually all can be avoided with safe work practices. Every house should be inspected for safety. Workers should be diligent, cleaning up each day, unplugging equipment after use, and disposing of oily rags, which can and do spontaneously burst into flame.

Natural disasters are difficult to protect against. Often in the emotional crisis that follows a significant loss from fire or flood, usable material and valuable clues for accurate reproduction are lost in the effort to clean up quickly. Move slowly to determine what is damaged and to what extent. Water-damaged woodwork is often salvageable. Severely burned woodwork is usually destroyed, but lightly burned and smoke-blackened wood can often be resuscitated.

Restoration is frequently overlooked as an option because so many modern things are disposable. People automatically think, "That's ruined," or, "Can't

be fixed." Restoration utilizing original materials yields a significantly different result from that of careful reproduction with new materials. The cost of reproduction is frequently lower for several reasons. Rarely do prices for new work take into account the accurate matching of the historic materials: the wood species, the milling, the grain pattern and direction, the exact molding profiles and dimensions, the hardware, the finish, or the methods of construction. These details are only part of what makes the historic woodwork special. When reproduction work is thorough, it is usually more expensive than restoration. When funds are scarce, reproduction suffers, and cuts made in the early stages cannot be changed later. Restoration of existing woodwork, however, can be done in stages to accommodate funding.

Above: Much of the woodwork from the last century was very elaborate. Fluted columns, pilasters, and carved door casings exhibit a wealth of detail that can be dizzying. The first step in treating any wooden element should be stabilization to prevent further damage.

Below: Looking down on the top of this wooden capital reveals that it was made of four pieces of wood that have shrunk over time. In restoring it, thin wedges made of balsa wood were used to stabilize the gaps, while pine butterflies were inlaid to reduce future movement. After the ornament was restored, it was then reinstalled and painted.

ADDRESSING COMMON WOODWORK PROBLEMS

Neglect is usually bad, but it can be a savior of interior woodwork when no significantly harmful forces are at work. Woodwork that has been left alone, not reworked or "fixed up" over the decades, is often well preserved, though dirty. Most dirt does not damage woodwork. Overcleaning, on the other hand, causes problems. The protective finish can be worn away, allowing dirt to penetrate the wood itself.

Most problems with interior wooden elements—sticking doors, loose hardware, blanched finishes, woodwork pulled away from the wall, cracked panels, shutters that do not operate—have a cause. Understanding the cause before fixing the problem is the most effective and economical approach. Relieving symptoms can provide a temporary fix, but unless the underlying problem is resolved, the symptoms will return. The goal is to avoid symptom fixing and to learn a way of approaching and thinking about the problems to permit effective, economical, long-lasting solutions.

Usually, more than one possible solution exists. All solutions have different side effects or repercussions that must be considered. The common woodwork problem of a sticking door provides an example for considering the many possible ways to approach various other problems.

Sticky doors and other minor problems are frequently allowed to linger for years until a convenient moment when they are added to a list of items for a workperson to fix. A holiday, party, or pending home sale suddenly necessitates the repair of long-standing problems with great urgency. Handymen who may be good at opening clogged drains or changing hard to reach bulbs often have no experience at diagnosing or correcting recurring woodwork problems.

Uncertain of the cause of the problem, an inexperienced worker charged with fixing a sticking door often planes the leading edge. Soon the wooden edge clears but the metal lockset now rubs, quickly digging a grove into the doorjamb. Moving the lockset may necessitate moving the doorknob, which could require patching the face of the door. If the patching is done poorly or not at all, the doorknob and spindle will work loose, causing other totally unrelated problems to develop. This seemingly easy and quick "solution" has removed material from the door, compromising it forever without fixing the problem.

Fixing symptoms without understanding their cause is a significant problem in our houses. A door that has worked for years, through many seasonal cycles, does not suddenly grow, requiring trimming in order for it to fit into the doorway it has been married to for years. Doors, unlike waistlines, do not get larger, except for small seasonal shifts. It is necessary to look to the overall situation, not just the obvious symptom.

Noticing when a door begins to stick is an important key to learning what caused the problem. Is it as the weather changes? Was the room or door just painted? Perhaps the symptoms appeared after a visit by the locksmith, or following structural work on the floor below. Maybe movers jarred the casing or took the door down to move a couch, and something changed when it was rehung.

The problem is rarely with the leading edge of an old door; instead, the cause can usually be found on the hinge side or in the door jamb. It may simply be excess paint. The hinged edge is difficult to access and paint frequently accumulates there, causing the door to bind. Improperly installed screws can work loose over the years, making a door seem wider by forcing the leading edge to rub against the jamb. Often, simply tightening the screws will eliminate the problem. A skilled woodworker can perform many different adjustments on the hinge side of a door, shimming or remortising the hinges to adjust the hang, for example, leaving the original edge and shape of the door intact.

METHODS OF WORK

WOODWORK

Loose hardware damages woodwork, as moving metal quickly wears permanent scars into wood. Loose screws are the usual cause; tighten them. If they do not hold, shave several pieces from a wooden matchstick and put them into the screw hole. They reduce the size of the hole, allowing the screw to hold again. As needed, add more shaved wood, not glue. When mounting something new, drill a lead hole; this removes a bit of wood to prevent the screw from expanding and splitting the wood. A lead hole should also be drilled for all but the softest woods when nailing a piece of trim back on. Select a drill bit slightly smaller than the diameter of the nail. Protruding nails can usually be tapped lightly back into place. Use a metal nail set to prevent the hammer from hitting woodwork.

If the loose piece was glued originally, gluing it back in place is usually the right solution. Scrape away the old glue and check to be sure the piece fits properly. Clamps, weights, even low-tack tape can be used to hold small pieces in place. Apply a small amount of glue to both surfaces and gently push the piece into position. Remove the clamps or tape several hours later. Tape left on woodwork for weeks can lift the finish or leave a sticky residue.

Interior architectural woodwork glue joints rarely fail. If it becomes necessary to open them, they should almost always be cut apart, not dissolved as might be appropriate in furniture conservation work. (The scale of most interior architectural woodwork is too large for many of the techniques and attitudes of furniture conservation to be routinely applied.) Normal white and yellow glues (polyvinyl alcohol and aliphatic resin) are usually acceptable for repair. They can be dissolved, with difficulty, if necessary. Epoxies are not reversible and are rarely appropriate or required for the repair of interior woodwork.

Pieces of woodwork, trim, or hardware that come loose are important and vulnerable; they should be reinstalled immediately or labeled and stored. Placing the piece on a nearby countertop or in a drawer is an invitation for it to be lost, damaged, or thrown away. Label each piece with a paper tag (including where it is from) or mark on the back in pencil. Placing the piece in a resealable see-through plastic bag offers some physical protection and a visible reminder that repair is called for.

Fixing wooden panels with glue or nails is a common mistake. This happens when well-intentioned but inexperienced workers feel everything should be attached and secure. Panels in doors, shutters, wainscoting, and cabinetry are designed and built to float in their frames. They are not glued in place. This construction allows the wood to expand and contract without causing any harm to itself or the surrounding structure. Excess paint or finish can effectively bond the parts together, creating a time bomb of sorts that will begin to crack, warp, or buckle if the tension is not released.

FINISH

Time tends to darken and dull finishes, primarily by the accumulation of dirt and grime, which reduces the clarity of finish and affects the overall appearance of a room. Generally, the more transparent a finish is, the richer it appears, because it allows more of the figure of the wood to show through. Historic finishes are frequently removed in an effort to "brighten up" a room. There is not yet an established standard for valuing original architectural finishes as exists for antique furniture. The decision to remove historic finishes is sometimes based on the idea that conservation is more expensive than replacement, yet preserving an existing finish is often a more economical choice.

Rehabilitating existing finishes, allowing some imperfections to remain, preserves the character of a room, which is usually lost with new finish. More coats of compatible finish can be added to protect and enrich the appearance of the wood. If the finish is removed, it should be replaced by a finish that yields an appearance similar to the original.

In a stable environment, finished woodwork needs little more than an occasional dusting. Feather dusters, soft-bristled brushes, and clean, lint-free rags are good for dusting. Vacuums are excellent for getting dust out of recesses in woodwork without redistributing it around the room. Use a brush attachment that is in good condition or a small hand brush to sweep dust into the suction stream of the open hose end. All cleaning work should be done gently, taking care to avoid adding dents and scratches. Dirty woodwork should be dusted before cleaning so as not to push mud into the joints and grain.

Woodwork does not need the strength of typical household cleaning products. Aerosols (many contain silicones, which build up a gummy film) and polishes tend to trap dirt and usually are not appropriate. Abrasive cleaners should never be used. Mild nonsudsing soap (Murphy's Oil Soap or Original Finish Restoration Soap) diluted in water is good for cleaning finished woodwork as necessary. Use a sponge or rag that is damp, not dripping wet. Rinsing with a lot of water is not necessary; a rag moistened with clean water will remove the soap film. Standing water, even drops, should never be left on woodwork because it will leave a stain.

Deteriorated finishes offer very little protection or enhancement to woodwork. Depending on conditions, they can be gently cleaned with Original Finish Restoration Soap dissolved in solvent. Peeling, blistering, faded, dry, and alligatored finishes contain information about what has gone wrong over time. These characteristics tell of significant age, incorrect application of finishes, layers of incompatible finishes, or other problems. Some deteriorated finishes can be repaired or reamalgamated; otherwise, refinishing is required.

Investigation and analysis of finishes ranges from naked-eye observation to scanning electron microscopy. Regardless of the level of technology selected, one should learn what type of finish has been used. Simple solvent testing is the easiest way to determine this.

Testing should be done in inconspicuous areas, away from eye level. First clean a small area using mild soap on the corner of a moist rag. Then, using a cotton swab moistened with mineral spirits, gently rub back and forth. If sticky dirt accumulates on the swab, a layer of wax is probably present. If, after repeated swabbing, the dirt and wax stop accumulating on the swab at a clean hard surface, a varnish is probably indicated. Dampen a clean swab with alcohol and see if the hard finish dissolves with further rubbing. If it does, a shellac or alcohol-soluble spirit varnish is present. If not, it is probably an oil varnish or a modern finish. It is difficult to determine what is present with multiple layers of different finishes or when encountering "miracle" products that combine sealer, stain, and topcoat in one application.

Most traditional finishes are organic, made from plant and tree resins and even insect secretions. After World War I, synthetic resins were introduced as components of commercial products. Not until well after World War II did the chemical industry blossom, creating many of the products that are in use today. Polyurethanes, epoxies, and a number of water-based resins are newcomers relative to shellac, plant varnish, oils, and waxes, which have been used successfully for centuries. The strength of some modern finishes makes them the right choice for countertops or exterior woods; however, they do not have the richness of older finishes. Most polyurethanes scratch easily, have specific adhesion problems, and are difficult to touch up later.

A finish can last only as long as the surface it is applied to does. Loss of adhesion between layers is the most common cause of finishing problems. Substrates of wood or previous coatings must be well prepared and physically stable. Proper application following manufacturers' instruction is important for a long-lasting finish. Use the recommended thinner, primer, or sealer. Apply finish at moderate temperature and humidity, and always to a clean dry surface. Old wax must be removed and glossy surfaces sanded to ensure adhesion.

Rewaxing can inexpensively restore luster to the wood while preserving the original finish. Wax will work over almost any finish and, unlike oil, it can easily be removed in the future. Paste wax is best, dark for dark wood, neutral for light wood. Apply the wax with a cloth, using circular motions. A small amount of wax goes a long way and makes good results easier to achieve. Allow the wax to dry to a haze (five to twenty minutes); heat and humidity slow drying time. Then buff away as much wax as possible with clean dry rags. Wax collects dirt and builds up over time; periodically, it will need to be removed. Well-finished woodwork with a thin layer of wax, dusted regularly, may only need rewaxing every three to five years, with little appreciable buildup over time.

Early interior woodwork in the United States was more often painted than coated with clear finish. Painting has always been cheaper because lower grade wood could be used and less surface preparation was required. In the middle of the twentieth century, much of the woodwork that originally had a clear finish was painted over in an effort to achieve a bright, "modern" appearance. In the last twenty or thirty years, it has become fashionable to remove paint in order to expose woodwork that originally may not have been intended to be visible.

There are many methods of paint removal and a variety of good articles about how to use them, detailing which products are most effective and appropriate. Review the pros and cons, including potential damage to the historic wood, to the user's health, and to the safety of the building. Removing paint with heat is a common cause of restoration-related fires. New technology using gels and enzymes makes it increasingly possible to remove only some layers of paint and finish to expose a layer from one specific time in the past. This is a slow and delicate process, and it is rare that specific old layers can be revealed in their entirety.

Whatever the plan, it is useful to make a sample area of reasonable size to see if the old finish will really clean up well, or to see how a new finish will look before doing an entire room. A sample

Over the years, even built-in wooden elements, such as window casings, disappear. This cherry mahogany and ash window unit was saved using the existing casing as a pattern to reproduce the missing length. The carved brackets were copied from others found in the building.

Hardware is a crucial element in giving historic rooms an appropriate feeling. Casual observers may not consciously notice the difference between stock hardware and an original (or carefully made reproduction), but it significantly affects the overall experience of visiting a room.

Sometimes even old woodwork was not properly made. Here, the configuration of the carved mustache across the grain caused it to crack and fall off. After the final stages of paint removal, the original pieces were reattached, and the wood was refinished.

can also serve as a guide or specification for bidders. If the finish is to be changed significantly in a historic house, it is a good idea to save a sample of the original finish, exactly as it was found. This can be an eight-inch square on the far side of a chimney breast or other out-of-the-way location. Such sample areas allow interested future owners and scholars, with different priorities and perhaps more advanced technology, to have the opportunity to study the history of the house firsthand.

ROUTINE INSPECTION AND MAINTENANCE

Maintenance should be understood as ongoing and preventive care performed on a weekly, seasonal, or annual basis. Such care allows everything to last longer. Our society tends increasingly to ignore routine care, operating instead with the idea of replacing whatever is old or broken.

Maintenance is cheap and effective and, when practiced, drastically reduces the need for restoration work. By regularly repairing minor problems, one ensures that they will not expand over time, causing an entire area to dissolve into an ugly mess. Frequently, problem areas near radiators or doors begin as little problems. When they are not cared for over time, the area deteriorates, leaving replacement as the all-too-frequent choice.

Knowing about the architectural elements in one's home helps one to appreciate them and, in turn, care for them. Woodwork and its related parts provide many of the most significant stylistic clues for studying interiors. Molding profiles, panel styles, types of fasteners, hardware, finishes, and similar clues all provide valuable information in dating, restoring, and enjoying a home.

Often one begins to research and learn about a home only after damage has occurred. A careful look at one's woodwork once a year can be revealing. Knowing what it looks like on an ongoing basis will help in seeing what has changed and where problems may be developing.

Changes in surface appearance—worn or chipped finishes and woodwork, discoloration, missing or loose pieces of trim or hardware, new insect holes or frass, hollow-sounding woodwork, loose handrails, sticking doors, traces of water—are among the signs to look for. A spot with no finish left near a radiator may point to a leaking steam vent. Fix the steam vent and then

touch up the woodwork. Gently smooth out the bad spot with steel wool and brush or wipe on more finish. The next time the valve goes bad, the wood will be protected.

Cracks in woodwork should be monitored to see if they are becoming longer or wider. Existing architectural drawings are a good place to record information and to mark down changes in condition—such as areas of high RH or new repair work. Such documentation becomes a map that can be consulted over the years to provide factual, not emotional, information on changes and history.

Photographs, both details and overall shots of existing conditions, are easy to take and extremely useful to have for reference. Also, when wainscoting is down or the floor is open for repairs, a Polaroid or snapshot of what is hidden behind can be invaluable in the future. Labeling photographs with the date and a description of what the picture shows is critical. Though pictures are worth a thousand words, an unlabeled photo of an opened wall is usually unrecognizable a year later.

SEEKING OUTSIDE HELP

A professional survey can be very helpful in defining problems, especially when its scope is defined at the beginning. Comprehensive reports can be valuable; they can also be long and expensive without touching on important specifics.

Spending too much time and/or money at the beginning can take away from the actual work. Yet too little preparation, planning, or knowledge can cause delays, increase costs, lower the quality of work, and decrease one's satisfaction with the process. An owner's failure to define what work is needed, or even wanted, puts the proposal writer (sometimes an "estimator," not a restorer) in the position of determining what will be done in a home.

In speaking to the people who might do a survey, narrow down the issues that should be addressed. If cost is a problem, try to focus on the most important issues first (though these may not be entirely clear before the survey begins). The sticky door could be caused by a rotten post in the cellar, which in turn resulted from years of improper roof drainage. Be certain the survey will include recommendations for treatment, including alternatives.

If restoration specifications are made, review them to be sure they include specific information that will help the physical work to be completed satisfactorily. Far too often, specifications are closer to legal documents than descriptions of work. They tend to have extensive detail on new mechanical work and precious little about preservation or restoration of woodwork. Ask questions to understand the meaning of prices. A well-prepared proposal should include price breakdowns. Does the price to replicate woodwork include matching the profiles exactly? Will the grain and cut of the wood match or approximate the original? Will the color and finish stand out from the old work?

A price to remove the paint and restore woodwork may not be representative of the final costs. The relative age and condition of woodwork are difficult to ascertain when it is coated in paint. Woodwork that looks relatively uniform and solid may be cobbled together with extensive areas of nonwood patching. Tests and samples diminish this problem and give a more accurate sense of both the scope of work and its cost.

Repair estimates are usually "free"; surveys are not. A knowledgeable professional who spends a significant amount of time investigating your problem should be paid. Money not clearly paid for such services may yield a less thorough approach or be buried in other charges. Working relationships work best when things are open and clear from the beginning; everyone should benefit.

The saying that "No one does that work anymore" in the field of interior woodwork and finishing is a modern misconception. Finding knowledgeable, reliable, honest help simply requires effort. Check references. A single skilled individual may offer the lowest price, but on larger projects, companies with several employees can carry out the work at a quicker pace and often provide a more comprehensive and valuable service. It is a good idea to try any individual or contractor on a specific small project before diving into a large scope of work.

Employing firms or individuals experienced with old woodwork provides greater sensitivity and generally better results. Old houses have different requirements from those of newly constructed homes. The building materials are closer to antiques than the "disposable products" that make up the materials of late twentieth-century homes.

Buildings are complex and not replaceable like shelf products. Parts that have lasted one hundred years can usually last significantly longer if protected. Ideally, restoration work should retain as much original material as possible. Replacement parts should utilize traditional materials and should be reversible. Most successful approaches to restoration recognize and integrate the various possible techniques and methods.

Woodwork can withstand significant abuse over time—some of it miraculously translates into character. Houses last a long time physically, but their integrity can be destroyed by inappropriate work and/or the use of inappropriate materials. Owners should have a sensitive and informed relationship to their older homes, working with them, not against them.

ACKNOWLEDGMENTS
Thanks to M. Chaney, J. Ladd, K. Weinburg, J. Cenizoroz.

FLOORING AND FLOOR FINISHES

MARY HARDING SADLER AND W. CAMDEN WHITEHEAD

Like the walls of a room, the floor is a background: it should not furnish pattern, but set off whatever is placed upon it. The perspective effects dear to the modern floor-designer are the climax of extravagance. A floor should not only be, but appear to be, a perfectly level surface, without simulated bosses or concavities.

—Edith Wharton, *The Decoration of Houses* (1902)

Surely the most abused of the elements of any house, floors must support the often shifting loads of furnishings and of human traffic. They must absorb or resist more moisture and dirt than any other interior feature of a house. And, although American novelist Edith Wharton asserted that the floor should serve as a quiet background rather than as a feature on its own, the varied flooring found in significant American houses, particularly since 1902, suggests that Mrs. Wharton's advice has not always been heeded. From extravagant parquet floors, to marble terrazzo, to the vivid patterns found in resilient sheet and tile flooring, American flooring represents an ever-expanding range of materials. The discussion in this chapter will focus on the maintenance and protection of significant wood, ceramic, masonry, and resilient flooring.

Most early colonial American houses with flooring more sophisticated than tamped earth were originally constructed with so-called deal floors of plain pine planking. The very wealthy favored more elaborate pine floors constructed with splines or dowels joining the planks. Although terra-cotta or stone paving was occasionally found in kitchens or entry halls, floorings other than wood were not popularized in America until the mid-nineteenth century. After the Civil War, the availability of a broader range of materials, combined with the decorative intensity of the Victorian and Edwardian architectural styles, expanded ornamental treatment of floors in American houses. Imported and domestic ceramic and encaustic tiles enriched entry porches and vestibules; parquet flooring was popular in drawing and dining rooms, incorporating the varicolored hardwoods found in this country as well as exotic imported woods. In early twentieth-century kitchens and bathrooms there appeared so-called resilient floors, first linoleum, then asphalt tiles, followed by a wide range of vinyl-composition sheet and tile products. The choices in historic materials, colors, and sizes for replacement or reproduction flooring today are limited only by the homeowner's budget and imagination.

GENERAL MAINTENANCE AND REPAIR OF HISTORIC FLOORS

Most flooring problems can be attributed to one of four causes: persistent exposure to moisture (or significant changes in moisture levels), inadequate or inappropriate maintenance, use of incompatible floor finishes, and failure of the floor structure. Protection of historic or of any high-quality flooring dictates the following basic precautions:

- Removing water and dirt immediately
- Daily dusting or vacuuming
- Using appropriate floor-finish products according to manufacturer's directions
- Inspecting floor structure regularly for insect infestation or signs of rot and failure

The elegance of a black-and-white marble checkerboard floor is echoed in the coffered ceiling and other details of this American Renaissance gallery. The porosity of the marble requires regular maintenance, including the annual application of a surface sealer.

This stone flooring has held up well despite lack of maintenance. Weekly cleaning with clear water would be a simple, effective maintenance regimen that would reduce staining by plant materials and pollution. Removal of the existing stains might best be accomplished with a mild solution of a chemical cleanser manufactured for masonry cleaning, which should be tested in small, inconspicuous locations.

- Correcting structural problems
- Maintaining consistent levels of humidity

Regular care and maintenance of a historic or significant floor is a decidedly low-tech affair. The most effective measure the homeowner can employ in the preservation of high-quality flooring, whether wooden plank, parquet, marble, or ceramic, is daily removal of dirt and grime with a dust mop or vacuum. The dust mop can be treated with a spray product such as Endust for use on wooden, vinyl, linoleum, concrete, and many masonry surfaces. Do not treat dust mops when cleaning marble or terrazzo flooring, or on fabric or fiber mats or rugs.[1] Do place a mat at entry doors to catch dirt before it gets into the house, and regularly shake the mat out and clean beneath it. Placing rugs or runners in the areas of highest traffic further reduces the wear and tear on flooring and floor finishes.

Regular damp mopping (the mop should be thoroughly rung out, not dripping) with a solution of water and mild detergent, such as dishwashing liquid, is the second line of defense. Move furniture for protection prior to damp mopping. If you use a detergent solution, make certain that all traces of the detergent are removed by mopping with clear water.

The current fixation with replacing damaged elements or finishes with new, "maintenance-free" surfaces within homes is the greatest threat to historic flooring. The most fundamental preservation advice, codified as the Secretary of the Interior's Standards numbers 6 and 7, urges historic-property owners to "repair rather than replace" historic features, and, further, when cleaning or repairing, to use the "gentlest means possible." It is essential to the preservation of historic materials of all types that only compatible cleaning and finish products be used. Test the compatibility of the proposed product in an inconspicuous area, perhaps in a closet, and use all cleansers, coatings, or adhesives in accordance with the manufacturer's instructions.

Materials used to strip and renew floor finishes are often toxic and/or highly flammable. In many cases, they are best handled by professionals. Rags soaked in turpentine, wax, varnish, or shellac can ignite spontaneously. Do not leave these materials in a house (even during a lunch break!) unless stored in a closed, flameproof container.

We are sometimes unable to appreciate the inevitable signs of age and wear as valued evidence of a floor's ongoing history and use. The dents in a historic pine floor, the occasional crack in a marble or ceramic-tile floor, or the wear in an otherwise sound stone or wooden stair tread help reveal the story hidden within the walls of the house. Removal of these character-defining imperfections can result in a significant loss of historic material.

A significant sag in flooring, however, may indicate a serious structural problem (see Structural Systems), requiring analysis by a qualified engineer. Even minor problems, such as inadequate *bridging* between the floor joists, can also contribute to "bounce" in a wooden floor or cracking in stone or ceramic tile floors. Most bridging is wooden blocking nailed diagonally between floor joists. Prefabricated bridging of diagonal steel bracing can be installed in order to minimize floor-joist movement. Moisture damage can travel from roofing or clogged gutters and downspouts to framing and, ultimately, to flooring, where it causes staining and warping. Moisture attracts wood-boring insects like termites and powder-post beetles. Too much humidity in the air can also cause flooring problems and may need special attention.

Seek professional advice when preparing to seal or refinish flooring or whenever there are signs of structural damage or ongoing moisture infiltration. The following sections provide additional guidance in caring for specific flooring materials.

WOOD

Pine and oak have been the dominant woods used in flooring since the colonial period. In the Southeast and the mid-Atlantic states, the species of choice was the southern longleaf heart pine, a type of southern yellow pine, until the early twentieth century, when the beautiful graining of quarter-sawn oak became prized. Hemlock and white spruce floors were also found in the mid-

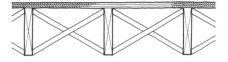

Diagram of bridging

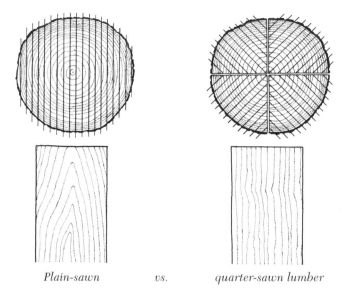

Plain-sawn   *vs.*   *quarter-sawn lumber*

Atlantic region. In New England white pine was more typical, and on the Gulf Coast cypress flooring was a regional favorite. The hardwoods sugar maple and black maple became popular for kitchen floors. Cherry, mahogany, and walnut, more richly colored hardwoods, were associated with the most formal settings. These woods are often seen in parquet borders.

Early wooden floors, sometimes called deal floors, were generally laid in planks six to ten inches in width and up to one and one-half inches thick. Until the late nineteenth century, subflooring was rare (except with parquet installations). The planks were laid directly on the joists. The graining in a floorboard is dependent not only on the species of lumber used, but also on the way in which the wood is sawn. Quarter-sawn (also called rift-sawn) lumber resists warping and generally has straight, dense, consistent graining. Quarter-sawn oak is characterized by shimmering "rays" that cross the grain. Plain-sawn (also called flat-sawn) lumber typically features a varied, wide and narrow grain pattern. Plain-sawn lumber was typical of the historic New England random-width floorboards. In the Southeast, quarter-sawn pine was dominant. More board feet can be produced with plain sawing, hence its current popularity.

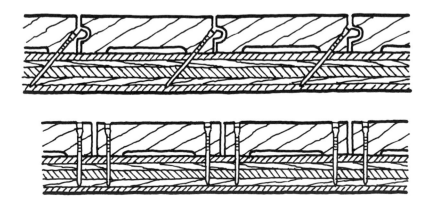

Blind and face nailing

Until the early nineteenth century, most flooring was *face nailed* (nailed through the top face) with wrought-iron nails and butt jointed. More sophisticated installations were joined between boards with splines or dowels. The heavy pegs sometimes seen in new flooring purporting to have a "historic look" were generally not found in the American colonies. *Shiplap* boards, although not common, allowed flooring to be *blind nailed* (nailed through the spline or tongue). Now standard, tongue-and-groove flooring, which also allowed floorboards to be blind nailed, was not common until the 1830s. *Parquet* flooring was developed in France in the 1600s and popularized in America in the late nineteenth century. Parquetry incorporates small pieces of wood to form a field of squares or other geometric figures and often an elaborate border using several different species that contrasted in grain and color.

WOOD FINISHES

> *Instead of painting and graining wood to imitate oak, black walnut, or other dark woods used in the . . . joinery of country houses, a very simple and excellent substitute, for cheap cottages and villas, is that of so staining the wood as to give the color of a darker wood, and yet retain all the real appearance of the grain of the wood itself. . . . A very good effect is produced, especially in the entry and living-room, by using narrow matched floor-plank, of good quality, and staining every other plank of a dark color, like black walnut.*
>
> —Andrew Jackson Downing, *The Architecture of Country Houses* (1850)

The pine floors that graced even the wealthier colonial homes received no stain or glossy finish but were instead washed regularly with water and lye, and often swept with sand. The resulting "finish" was a matte gray-brown.[2] Even though a liberal amount of water was used to wash the floors down, the water did no damage because the heart-pine floors were tight-grained and highly resinous. Oak floors, on the other hand, will stain badly after exposure to water because of their open grain. The shiny finishes we currently associate with wooden flooring were not prevalent until a hundred years ago. As a practical rule of thumb, wooden floors should be refinished when the predominant traffic pattern begins to create a difference in the color or appearance of the floor.

The choice of appropriate finishes is the most widely debated facet of wooden flooring. Ideally, a finish should enhance and protect the flooring. A finish that inhibits moisture and dirt is also called a *sealant*. The relative durability and ease of maintenance that finishes provide are other factors to consider. Before refinishing wooden floors, outline the goals of the project. The goal of restoring a floor to its original finish and appearance will yield a different finish selection than one of withstanding heavy use with minimal maintenance. To clarify the available choices, finishes can be divided into surface (or film-forming) and penetrating finishes.

Surface finishes include traditional finishes like lacquers, shellacs, and varnishes, composed of solvents, binders, and resins. When the solvent evaporates, a clear film is left on the surface of the wood. These finishes are highly flammable and somewhat brittle. Shellac is easily damaged by water or alcohol but also easily repaired. Oil varnishes are slow drying and more supple than shellacs but tend to attract dirt. The urea-formaldehyde-based Swedish floor products are surface finishes similar to polyurethanes but are highly toxic, and were developed primarily for installation on new floors.

Paint, another surface floor finish, has been documented since colonial times, though its use was not prevalent. Floors were painted in order to seal the floor surface and to introduce a decorative motif to common pine boards. Some historic floors were stenciled; others were painted in patterns that imitated more costly carpeting. Staining floors has been a popular practice since

Colonial Williamsburg's Brush-Everard House has original yellow pine floors (1717–19). Typically in colonial homes, only formal spaces might have had doweled or splined flooring. Secondary spaces were laid in plain, deal flooring. Deal flooring could be face-nailed or blind-nailed through the sides.

the 1850s. A pine floor could be stained to imitate finer hardwoods like walnut or cherry. Stain can be added to wax or other floor sealants or applied independently. Staining can be particularly useful when trying to match a new floorboard to an existing floor. Select a staining product that is compatible with the floor finish; if possible, choose all finish/sealant products from the same manufacturer.

Since the late 1960s, polyurethane has been the surface finish most commonly applied to wood flooring. Polyurethanes belong to a family of coatings that include very different products.[3] Moisture-cured polyurethane, developed for commercial and industrial applications, produces the "gym-floor look," that of a dense, shiny film over the wooden flooring. It is a tough finish that should be applied only by professionals because of its high VOC (volatile organic compounds) content. In general moisture-cured polyurethane is inappropriate on historic wooden flooring because of its shiny plastic appearance. Oil-modified polyurethanes are often used in residential applications because they are dirt and abrasion resistant. Oil-modified polyurethane is applied in two coats, which dry relatively slowly. It is available in a range of sheens from flat to high gloss. It imparts a yellow tone to the wood, which increases with time. This product is difficult to touch up or repair, a significant drawback in light of the brittle nature of polyurethane. Because it is brittle, oil-modified polyurethane should never be used on softwood flooring (with the possible exception of heart pine) and should not be used on hardwood flooring except with an understanding of its disadvantages. When a softwood floor is dented, say by the heel of a woman's shoe, the brittle surface of an oil-modified polyurethane finish is cracked. Hardwoods are less susceptible to this failure.

The most recently developed water-based polyurethanes hold great promise. Easy to handle and to clean up, these finishes are clear and have

The silver-gray-brown color of this historic floor finish is a result of regular washing with water and pure flax soap. Historically the floor was scrubbed with lye. The floor is protected with a Wilton carpet woven in England using authentic historic patterns.

no VOCs. They share with the other urethanes toughness and resistance to abrasion, but create a lighter finish, which, when applied, may raise the grain of the wood. Water-based polyurethane is also available in different degrees of gloss. Thinner in consistency but more durable than oil-modified polyurethane, water-based polyurethane should be applied in four coats, which has perhaps discouraged its popularity among homeowners.

Advocates of the penetrating oil finishes like the deep luster of the finish, claiming that the penetrating finishes seal the wood and reduce water damage. This is not affirmed by those in the flooring industry. These products were first commercially produced in the 1930s, although linseed oil has been used on floors for more than a century and a half. Penetrating oils usually must be applied in two coats and require a long drying time (a week or more). Penetrating finishes hold dirt and must be carefully maintained, but in general they are easy to apply and easy to repair. Waxing over a penetrating finish is advised to reduce erosion and wear.

Often paste wax is applied to a finish to add luster and a pliable layer of additional protection. An optional treatment over surface finishes, wax is a required coating over penetrating oil finishes in order to protect the wood from moisture and erosion. Wax produces a low-gloss, handsome appearance, and it is inexpensive and easy for the homeowner to apply. Wax requires relatively high maintenance, however, and must be renewed regularly in areas of traffic. Wax should be installed only over a floor that has been cleaned. Dirty or built-up wax can be removed with mineral spirits or turpentine. All wax must be removed from a wooden floor before applying a new finish. Wax should be applied sparingly to reduce the risk of slipping. Wax stairs with caution. Slip-resistant wax, if not on the grocery store shelves, can be purchased through janitorial supplies.

In general, wax is a superfluous treatment over polyurethane finishes. It does not add any protection against moisture or dirt and could make the floor dangerously slick.

WOOD REPAIR: WARPS, HOLES, STAINS, SQUEAKS

Warping is usually caused by a change in the wood's moisture content. Even seasonal changes in humidity can result in warping, particularly if temperature and humidity within a house are not controlled by consistent heating and air-conditioning. A homeowner's failure to prevent wide swings and sudden changes in humidity within a home could prove to be disastrous to the finishes and dimensional stability of a parquet floor. Sustained exposure to a significant amount of water, say from a window left open during rain, or from a leaky radiator or plumbing pipe, would almost certainly cause significant damage that might be repaired only with machine sanding and refinishing or that might require complete replacement of the flooring.

If buckling of floorboards is not too extreme, it can be corrected by using a thin blade in a circular saw (set to the depth of the finish floor) to make a narrow saw cut down the middle of the warped board. The two halves of the board can be screwed down, reattaching the floorboard to the joists and

Quarter-sawn oak flooring laid in a basket-weave pattern is characterized by shimmering pith rays. A parquetry border suggests overlapping squares. The nailheads have been revealed by recent sanding. Resanding this floor would likely result in a near total loss. Instead, the floor should be refinished with a water-based polyurethane.

subfloor, and eliminating the unevenness. The screw heads should be set and filled with putty tinted to match the floorboards.

A persistent squeak in flooring is the likely result of a separation of the flooring from the subfloor or separation of the subfloor from the floor joists. First try squirting powdered graphite or talcum powder in the joints. *Glazing points* (tiny sheet-metal triangles used to hold glass in a window sash) can be installed every six inches along the joints separating flooring boards. Set the points below the surface of the joint using a putty knife or a narrow sheet of metal. If the squeak persists and is in a ground-floor location, the floor (or subfloor) can be reattached easily from below without damaging finishes. Select screws that, when installed from below, will reach no closer than one-quarter inch from the finish floor level. If it is not possible to reanchor the flooring to the subfloor and floor structure from below, it may be necessary to screw (using three-inch trim-head screws) through the flooring itself, after locating the floor joist(s) with a stud finder. The screws should be countersunk and the hole filled using a wood putty tinted to match the flooring.[4] Using screws will provide more effective anchoring, and fewer screws than nails will be needed to do the job. A handyman homeowner could accomplish this.

Use carefully matched pieces of wood to fill wide cracks or holes in historic wooden floors. Wood fillers can be used effectively to fill nail holes, but the inherent movement in wooden floors, in combination with seasonal changes in wood dimensions, discourage against the use of fillers in large areas. Also, fillers tend to look plastic and monolithic in contrast to adjacent wooden members.

If, because of extensive stains, warping, or other irreparable damage, some of the boards require replacement, that work should be planned for the spring or fall, when humidity is more stable. The work should be done after painting and other refinishing work is complete (allow any wet plaster to cure for at least a week before installing any new flooring). The new wood should be stored in the house prior to installation (for two or more weeks, if possible) to bring it to the same humidity level as the existing flooring.

Homeowners are often too quick to call a flooring contractor in to resand a wooden floor. Sanding should be a measure of the last resort, taken only when all other efforts have failed. Sanding a floor usually results in the removal of one-quarter inch of the section of the wood (or one-fourth to one-half of its total thickness). Sanding, especially of parquet floors, often reveals unsightly nailheads. Often all that is needed to renew a wooden floor is complete refinishing, which can be achieved with minimal loss of material. Old paste wax can be removed using a cloth saturated with turpentine, although, because both the wax and the turpentine are highly flammable, the area should be well ventilated. Cloths used for the cleaning should be removed from the house and stored in a closed metal container to prevent spontaneous combustion and a house fire.

CERAMIC TILE

> For the floors of halls, we greatly prefer tiles of marble or pottery to carpet or oil-cloth—as far more durable and characteristic, and, in the end, much more economical. . . . Beautiful patterns of encaustic tiles, which have a good effect, are now manufactured at very moderate cost. The colors are chiefly browns, enriched with patterns and figures of fawn or blue.
>
> —Downing, *The Architecture of Country Houses*

Ceramic tile has been used since the colonial era to surface floors in damp areas like kitchens, dairies, entries, and in cellars and basements, "where dampness militated against the use of wood flooring."[5] Plain, undecorated tile was probably produced early on in colonial America, but highly decorated tiles had to be imported until about 1870.[6] By the turn of the century, tiles were increasingly promoted as being easy to clean and maintain, especially in kitchens and bathrooms. Their durability and decorative qualities also made them popular in entry halls and porches.

Ceramic tiles can be divided into glazed and unglazed varieties. Most historic floor tiles (except those used to beautify fireplace hearths) were unglazed. The color of an unglazed tile is determined by the color of the clay and the oxides or pigments added to the clay itself. Utilitarian quarry tile pavers, usually six inches square or larger, were (and continue to be) made of clay or shale. Encaustic tiles (dust-pressed and fired at very high temperatures) are usually highly decorated with colorful, inlaid patterns and molded in a variety of geometric shapes. Single-colored encaustic tiles, less costly to produce, are often referred to as geometric tiles. Encaustic and geometric tiles were produced in a range of colors from taupes, ochers, and beiges to blues, deep reds, and black. Ceramic mosaic tiles are typically smaller than the encaustics and more economical.

The color of glazed tiles was determined by matte or glossy glaze applied to the tile surface. Because they can be scuffed and scratched by constant use, these tiles, when used as flooring, were placed in areas of lower traffic. Glazed tiles dominate today's market. Though modern lead-free glazes are more vulnerable to damage, historic-replica tiles are readily available.

Historically, tile was set in a mortar bed (often called a "mud" setting bed) that was at least an inch deep. Recent decades have seen the introduction of thin-set methods and tile board (Wonderboard is one proprietary name).[7] Thin-set methods reduce the time and the weight of modern tile installations without detracting from their durability. With mud-set installations (which should be done professionally), the tiles must be soaked for hours prior to installation in the mortar bed. In both thin-set and mud-set methods, the tile is usually laid from the center out, then leveled with a straightedge. Grouting of pure sand and cement (sometimes colored) is used to fill the joints between tiles.

Unglazed brick pavers, sometimes thinner in section but often the same size as the face brick used to construct walls, have been used for centuries to floor kitchens, entries, and porches. Because brick flooring is usually slightly uneven, its popularity in public areas is limited. For interior installations, brick would be mud set. For exterior porches, terraces, or walkways, brick could be mud set or, more often, set in a bed of sand or stone dust.

CERAMIC TILE MAINTENANCE AND REPAIR

Historic tile floors require little maintenance other than regular dust mopping and occasional damp mopping. Prewetting tiles prior to cleaning can help to lift any stains from the tiles and grouting. There is no need to wax or seal ceramic tile; waxing will change the historic appearance and add unnecessary steps to routine maintenance requirements. With brick pavers, however, a penetrating sealer is usually recommended. Over time grout may erode and need replacement. Precisely describe the age and appearance of your tile and grout to a local distributor of tile products before purchasing replacement grout (usually a mixture of sand, portland cement, and pigment), or hire a reputable tile contractor to regrout your floor. If a tile becomes loose, remove it before it is lost, and store it in a labeled, sealable plastic bag until it can be reinstalled using a matching grout. Trying to remove a tile that is still partially grouted will often result in breaking the tile. Before regrouting, vacuum the area to remove dirt and loose grout.

The best way to prevent damage to a tile floor is to avoid the impact of sudden heavy loads or regular vibration. Water that sits on ceramic tile can erode grout and contribute to staining. Use of harsh cleaning chemicals can also damage tile irreparably, either etching the glaze or loosening the grout.

Careless removal and reinstallation of plumbing fixtures will inevitably result in destroying tiles that might be impossible to replace.

A historic ceramic-tile floor may be so damaged that partial replacement is required. Some historic porches suffer from the settlement of the fill supporting the porch floor. As a result, beautiful patterned encaustic tile floors have collapsed, cracking and destroying the field tile but leaving an elaborate tile border intact. Once the porch is restabilized and the porch floor supported with new fill, or joists and a subfloor, the decorative border can be salvaged and reintegrated with a new field tile. The border will need to be cut away from the remaining field tile using diamond blades. This kind of salvage operation requires advance planning and a skilled and willing contractor.

Finding replacement tile will likely necessitate a trip to your local tile distributor and to a local salvage yard. If you must order new tile, order several samples so that you may compare the optional replacement tiles with the existing historic tile. If at all possible, take a sample of the historic tile with you during your search for replacements.

STONE AND TERRAZZO

These [stone or marble] floors, associated in the minds of most Americans with shivering expeditions through damp Italian palaces, are in reality perfectly suited to the dry American climate, and even the most anaemic person could hardly object to brick or marble covered by heavy rugs.

—Wharton, *The Decoration of Houses*

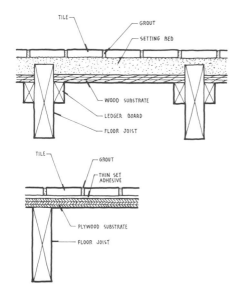

Stone floors have been used in significant public spaces for centuries. In colonial and Federal-era homes stone or masonry floors would have been found in entry halls or kitchens. At the end of the nineteenth century and during the American Renaissance period (c. 1890–1920), wealthy Americans enriched porches, terraces, and entry halls with marble, *terrazzo* (marble chips suspended in a cement matrix), granite, slate, and other polished stones. The most elaborate stone floors are the marble mosaics, which consist of *tesserae* (usually small, varicolored marble squares) hand-set in decorative patterns or illustrations.

Similar to those of ceramic tile, interior masonry floors more than twenty years old would most often have a mud setting bed an inch or more thick. Once placed in the setting bed, the stone floor would be grouted with a mixture of sand and cement (today, acrylics are sometimes added to the grout). Monolithic terrazzo floors have either metal (often bronze or zinc) or plastic joints.

MAINTENANCE OF STONE AND TERAZZO
Stone flooring is durable and beautiful, actually improving with age. Like all historic or significant materials, however, it must be carefully and appropriately maintained. Each type of stone has its strengths and weaknesses. Granite, an igneous stone, is least vulnerable to staining and other damage. Marble, which is metamorphic, found in a wide range of colors and veining, is softer, more porous, and therefore more vulnerable to staining and wear than granite. Other metamorphic stone pavers, like slate, greenstone, and bluestone, tend to scratch and show wear, and require greater maintenance. Limestone and sandstone are also vulnerable to abrasion.

Stone or terrazzo, if worn or abraded, should be reground or repolished professionally. Before polishing a stone floor, any

This glazed tile was imported from Italy to enhance the portico of an urban palazzo designed for Richmond, Virginia's leading stockbroker in the early 1900s. Unfortunately, the owner's attempt to replace worn tile with modern materials has not proven entirely successful. Today's glazes are not as durable as those made with lead a century ago; the glaze of the new tile has whitened considerably. The tile has suffered from constant exposure to pollen and debris falling from the overgrown landscaping that surrounds the portico.

The original terrazzo tiles are combined with quarry tiles on this late Victorian porch. The rich combination of materials is typical of this stylistically eclectic period. Despite exposure to weather and heavy wear, the tile and grout have held up well.

Opposite:

Top: This porch floor is tiled with a combination of patterned and geometric encaustics. The neutral buff colors of the field tile are combined with vivid blue and Indian red accents. The greatest threat to the integrity of this floor is settlement of the fill dirt supporting the porch.

Center: Mud- and thin-set tile

Bottom: Ceramic mosaic tiles have proven to be a durable flooring material in both interior and exterior installations. Fortunately the appearance of ceramic mosaic tiles has changed little in the past 125 years; replacement tiles matching many historic ceramic mosaic tiles are widely available.

loose stones should be regrouted to fix them in place and to achieve an even finish. After grinding or polishing, it is usually necessary to regrout the entire floor. When a terrazzo floor is regrouted, it must be polished once more using an 80-grit stone.[8] A properly maintained stone or terrazzo floor should not require mechanical grinding or polishing except after decades of wear.

Stone flooring keeps best with penetrating rather than surface sealants. An annual application of sealant should be adequate. An exception to the rule is terrazzo flooring; due to the porosity of the cement matrix, it should receive both a surface and penetrating sealer. Daily dusting or vacuuming, regular damp mopping, and occasional scrubbing with a neutral detergent solution are the most important steps in an effective maintenance regimen for stone floors.

LINOLEUM AND OTHER RESILIENT SHEET AND TILE GOODS

The first resilient flooring developed was linoleum, a product that combines ground cork or wood dust, linseed oil, and other organic resins and powdered pigments. Invented in 1860 by Englishman Frederick Walton, linoleum enjoyed wide popularity in the early decades of the twentieth century, and is now seeing renewed interest by homeowners, although new linoleum must be imported (U.S. manufacturers ceased production of linoleum in the 1970s, when the more economical vinyls consumed the market). Linoleum should be protected with a sealer. Even sealed, linoleums are particularly vulnerable to water damage and to alkaline conditions and have an expected lifetime of between twenty and thirty years.

Linoleum was superseded first by asphalt tile in the 1930s and then by vinyl asbestos tiles beginning in 1945. The durability and economy of vinyl flooring resulted in that material's dominance in both commercial and residential markets. Most resilient flooring materials, including the adhesives and underlayment, manufactured prior to 1986 are likely to contain asbestos. When damaged to the point of crumbling, these materials can release airborne asbestos fibers, which are extremely hazardous. It is mandatory that you consult your state or local public safety office for guidelines in dealing with asbestos. When removing or repairing existing resilient flooring, it is critical that safety precautions are followed. At a minimum, you will need to wear a face mask and use a wet-dry HEPA vacuum if you are working with old vinyl or asphalt-tile flooring. If not crumbling, old vinyl floor tile is not hazardous and can be disposed of by the homeowner far more easily than by a contractor.

Damaged resilient tiles can be replaced following careful removal. Heating the surface of the tile using an iron placed on a folded towel or other fabric will help loosen the adhesive and make the tile more flexible. After lifting a corner of the tile, a putty knife can be used to pry the tile gently from the subfloor. Old adhesive should be removed from subflooring prior to installing the replacement tile over a thin troweled bed of latex adhesive.

Now ubiquitous, vinyl tiles and sheet goods are durable and economical flooring materials that hold up well under the most arduous conditions. Even stubborn stains can be removed by scouring (first try a plastic scouring pad, then steel wool) with a mild detergent or an appropriate cleanser, such as ammonia (but do not mix ammonia with household cleansers containing chlorine bleaches). Asphalt and vinyl tiles can be waxed and polished using common paste wax.

SEEKING SOURCES FOR HISTORICALLY ACCURATE MATERIALS

Due to a steady increase in the popularity of historic preservation, manufacturers have flooded the market with a variety of historically appropriate flooring materials. *Old-House Journal, Traditional Building,* and *Fine Home*

❧ Recommended Floor Finishes and Maintenance ❧

Materials	Finishes			Maintenance		
Wood	**Surface**	**Penetrating**	**Waxes**	**Daily**	**Weekly**	**Monthly**
Hardwood: such as oak, maple, walnut, cherry	Water-based polyurethane (shellac is more historic but is brittle and stains)	"Special formulas," which combine linseed oil, pigment, and other components; need wax finish	Paste wax recommended over shellac or penetrating finish. No wax with polyurethane	Dust mop	Vacuum	Wax or buff if needed. Damp mop when dirt is not removed by vacuuming
Softwood: such as pine, cypress, or fir	Water-based polyurethane or oil-based varnish (varnish will hold dirt)	"Special formulas," which combine linseed oil, pigment, and other components; need wax finish	Paste wax recommended over varnish or penetrating finish. No wax with polyurethane	Dust mop	Vacuum	Wax or buff if needed. Damp mop when dirt is not removed by vacuuming
Ceramic						
Glazed and unglazed ceramic tile	None recommended	None recommended	Use with caution when wear is a serious problem	Dust mop	Vacuum. Damp mop as needed	Use neutral detergents; rinse thoroughly
Stone/ Masonry						
Stone	Not recommended	Apply a penetrating sealer annually (not for granite)	Not recommended	Dust mop	Vacuum. Damp mop as needed	Use neutral detergents; rinse thoroughly
Terrazzo	Not recommended	Apply a penetrating sealer annually	Not recommended	Dust mop	Vacuum. Damp mop as needed	Use neutral detergents; rinse thoroughly
Brick	Not recommended	Apply a penetrating sealer annually	Not recommended	Sweep	Vacuum. Damp mop as needed	Use neutral detergents; rinse thoroughly
Resilient Floors						
Linoleum	Not recommended	Apply penetrating acrylic sealer	Recommended to prolong life of floor	Dust mop	Vacuum. Damp mop as needed	Rewax and buff as necessary
Cork	Water-based polyurethane, or prefinished	Only applied by manufacturer	Not necessary with prefinished product	Dust mop	Vacuum. Damp mop as needed	No wet mopping
Vinyl	Acrylic finish acceptable, except for no-wax products	Not recommended	Recommended, except for no-wax products	Sweep or dust mop	Vacuum. Damp mop as needed	Use neutral detergents; rinse thoroughly. Rewax if necessary

Building magazines publish product information and lists of manufacturers who specialize in high-quality materials for maintenance and restoration of historic buildings.

Local salvage yards are often good sources of flooring (and other materials) removed from historic properties. Ceramic or masonry flooring retrieved from a salvage yard may need to be cleaned, not only of surface dirt, but also of mortar. Similarly, salvaged wooden flooring should be carefully examined for nails and any traces of old finishes, which should be removed. Despite the need for this extra work, salvage yards are invaluable if you are looking for flooring to be used in a patch. Purchase only wood that has been stored in a dry interior space, and remember to store the new lumber in your home for one or two weeks prior to installing it so that the humidity level of the replacement flooring can approximate that of the existing flooring.

Some lumberyards have developed a specialty in historic materials salvaged from demolished historic structures. For the most part, old-growth southern longleaf heart pine is available only through these sources. Heart-pine lumber from old warehouses, mills, and barns, remilled (and newly kiln-dried), is tighter and straighter in its grain and more resistant to insect and moisture damage than plain-sawn white or yellow pine, and is ideal for flooring and casework in new and old homes.

EVALUATING A PROPOSAL FROM A CONTRACTOR

When seeking proposals for floor repair or refinishing, look for reputable flooring contractors with demonstrated experience in the type of flooring being repaired. It is almost always advisable to contact at least three qualified contractors and to get a list of references from each. To ensure that the contractor is not only qualified to complete the repair job, but also professional in his or her business and work habits, contact the references to ask about the quality of the finished work, how well it has held up, how well the contractor cleaned the jobsite each day, and how closely the contractor was able to match the original time and cost estimates for the job. Making detailed inquiries concerning the contractor you are considering hiring is particularly crucial if you and others plan to continue occupying the house while the floor repairs and refinishing are under way. For further help, see the list of organizational resources given at the end of this book.

Notes

1. J. Henry Chambers, Cyclical Maintenance for Historic Buildings (Washington, D.C.: National Park Service, 1976), 53.

2. The authors are grateful to Mark J. Wenger, director of Colonial Williamsburg's Facilities Maintenance Department, for this information.

3. Michael W. Purser, "Historical Wood Floor Finishes and Contemporary Wood Floor Finishes," in The Interiors Handbook for Historic Buildings (Washington, D.C.: Historic Preservation Education Foundation, 1988), 3–35. Purser's discussion of wooden-flooring finishes is clear and comprehensive, an excellent source for anyone exploring which product to use. His explanation of the different polyurethanes is particularly helpful.

4. Floors and Stairways (Alexandria, Va.: Time-Life Books, 1995), 8–10.

5. Carl Lounsbury, An Illustrated Glossary of Early Southern Architecture and Landscape (New York: Oxford University Press, 1994), 263.

6. Anne Grimmer and Kimberly A. Konrad, Preservation Brief No. 40: Preserving Historic Ceramic Tile Floors (Washington, D.C.: National Park Service, 1996). This is a thorough study of tile use in America and a comprehensive guide to preserving historic tiles.

7. The Tile Council of America publishes excellent guidelines and specifications for ceramic tile installations. See Preservation Resources.

8. The authors are indebted to H. E. Satterwhite for information concerning terrazzo maintenance; to Norman Bobbitt of Costen Floors for information concerning wooden-floor finishes; and to John Williams of Mountain Lumber for information related to heart pine.

Heating, Cooling, and Ventilating Systems

William B. Rose

Many preservationists are uneasy around mechanical systems. For one thing, the systems seem to demand a specialized knowledge that is not part of design or preservation training. For another, it is never clear whether the systems are an integral part of the historic house, or whether their role is simply support. Should mechanical systems—heating, cooling, and ventilating —be preserved, or should they be replaced? The answer to this question goes to the heart of the preservation philosophy of an individual, a community, or a society. There are several reasons for wanting to replace a mechanical system in an old house:

- The mechanical system itself is an upgrade of earlier equipment.
- Repair, operation, and maintenance are no longer feasible or cost-effective.
- The system is unforgivably inefficient.
- Standards of comfort have changed.
- Conservation of objects or collections argues for greater temperature and humidity control.

Often this list is persuasive, and preservationists opt to gut a mechanical system and replace it with one more suited to buildings with modern uses. But against the press for modernization, it is important to recognize preservation issues and apply them to the equipment that is on hand:

- Does the equipment represent a significant step in mechanical history?
- Is there a peculiarity that makes this mechanical system unique to this building?
- What is the wisdom embodied in the present system?
- Will the building respond differently or perform differently with a replacement system?
- If removal or demolition is planned, has the mechanical system been recorded or documented?

Moreover, the indoor environment of old houses may be charming and peculiar, with irregularities of temperature distribution, odor, and airflow. The environment provided by new equipment tends to be more uniform, more free from pollutants and odors, and, some would say, more bland.

All systems are repairable, given a sufficient level of diligence and care. And all systems are replaceable with newer systems. All systems new or old provide some comfort, and all systems are exasperating, for one reason or another. There is no escape from the chores of operation, maintenance, and repair of even the most modern mechanical systems. In order to guide you in making appropriate decisions for your house, this chapter will provide an overview of both old and new systems for heating, cooling, and ventilating historic houses. See other relevant chapters in this book for discussions of plumbing, electrical, security, fire-suppression, and communication systems, which are often grouped under the term "mechanical" systems.

COMFORT

Mechanical systems were introduced for comfort. The human comfort zone may be considered to range between 65 and 75 degrees Fahrenheit and between 20 and 70 percent relative humidity. Humans are much more sensitive to temperature than to humidity. During summer, however, lowered humidity can be quite comfortable and can offset high indoor temperatures. The ventilation of buildings is for both health and human comfort,

The Vanderbilt Mansion in Hyde Park, New York, used an ingenious combination of hydronic and air distribution.

particularly for the removal of odors and pollutants, and, during summer, for the cooling effect of air movement over the skin.

Most historic houses have indoor environments that vary seasonally and daily, and from place to place within the building. Such an environment is often suitable for most of the common objects that can be found inside. But in many historic houses, particularly those incorporating fragile materials or with significant collections, the indoor temperature and humidity environment may need to be controlled for the sake of object preservation.[1]

Humidification during cold winters is often recommended to prevent problems from excess dryness, the most common of which is the opening of wooden joints in furniture and interior trim; however, too much humidification during winter can be harmful to the walls, windows, and attics. A good indication of excess humidity is window condensation. A film of frost or dew on single-pane windows at the beginning of cold weather rarely does any harm; streaming water from window condensation is a clear sign of excess humidification.

HEATING SYSTEMS

Fireplaces and stoves were the first domestic heating devices. The fire hazard and indoor air pollution these systems present, to say nothing of the inconvenience of providing fuel, argues forcefully against their use as a primary system of heating in historic houses. Subsequent mechanical systems for houses were derived from engineered mechanical systems in larger public or industrial buildings. They were simply adapted and scaled down.[2]

STEAM SYSTEMS

The earliest mechanical home heating systems were introduced in the late 1800s. They were designed to rely on steam or on the differing densities between hot and cold fluids (water or air) for distribution. These were called "gravity" systems. Electricity, now commonly used for pumps and fans, was not widely available when these systems were introduced. Steam had two distinct advantages: 1) the temperature of the radiator was constant and dependable (as long as the steam actually got to the radiator), and 2) the steam-production process was somewhat self-regulating—as steam pressure rose in the pipes, the temperature required to boil water rose as well.

In the largest cities, "district" steam was provided as a utility from a central steam plant. At the turn of the century, some city steam systems heated radiators in homes and tenements. Much more common, however, were basement steam boilers, fired usually by coal. The earliest were one-pipe systems, in which large pipes (commonly two inches in diameter) carried steam upward from the boiler and carried the returning *condensate*, the liquid water that forms when the steam condenses on the colder radiator, back to the boiler by gravity in the same pipe.

One-pipe systems are easily identified by having only one pipe connected to each radiator. Such systems were terribly inconvenient. The boiler would be fired at the beginning of winter and, regardless of weather changes, usually continued in operation until spring. There was no modulation of indoor temperature, except by opening windows. A valve was provided so that the radiator could be all on or all off, but if the valve was left partly closed, the condensate trying to escape out through the valve was met by the steam coming in. The steam would slam the slug of condensate water against the far side of the radiator, resulting in a very bothersome hammering noise.

The steam systems usually operated at three to five pounds of steam pressure; if the pressure went down (for failure to stoke the boiler perhaps), then the farthest radiators would turn cold. And even though steam systems were touted as silent heating systems, the pipes were often noisy, as steam and condensate passed in separate directions in the same pipe, especially if displacement of a

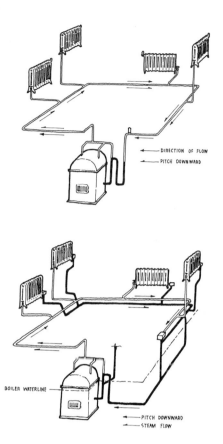

Early steam-heating layouts. In the one-pipe layout above, the pipes are large and carry both steam and the returning water condensate. The two-pipe layout shows one pipe carrying steam and the other pipe carrying the returning condensate.

pipe caused it to trap water. Displacement was common, because steel piping would expand considerably (one-quarter inch in ten feet) and sag as piping changed from room temperature to steam temperature.

The two-pipe steam system was an improvement. Here, two pipes were connected to each radiator. Condensate would be drained away from the radiator by the lower of the two pipes. A steam valve at the inlet could be throttled to reduce the flow at a radiator, so the temperature in a two-pipe system could be modulated.

Radiators in steam systems have vent valves intended to exhaust air (not steam) from the system. They are thermostatically controlled to be open at lower temperatures and closed when the temperature is that of steam. In a steam system, vents should be located low on the radiator (air can collect in the radiator below the vent), but not so low that condensate will flood it.

A further disadvantage of steam systems was the possibility of catastrophic failure. Even though boilers were equipped with safety devices to prevent excessively high pressures at low water levels (indicated by a pressure gauge and a water-level indicator), they required an operator to observe and respond. In many cities today, boiler operation requires a license and many automatic safety devices designed to shut down the burners, including a low-water-level cutoff and a high-pressure cutoff.

When electricity was introduced into houses (throughout the period from 1900 up until World War II in rural areas), it was used to operate condensate pumps. This allowed, for the first time, radiators to be placed at levels within the building other than above the elevation of the boiler.

HOT-WATER HEATING SYSTEMS

For a designer, the principal drawback to steam systems was the requirement that all of the piping allow for all the condensate to be drained by gravity back to the boiler (or to the condensate pump). For a user, the principal drawback to steam heat was that it was difficult to modulate from a fixed, very high temperature. Both of these complaints were addressed with hot-water systems, which used the same elements as steam—boiler, piping, radiators—but circulated hot water rather than steam.

The first hot-water systems were gravity-derived, relying on the lower density of hot water to effect circulation. This density difference is minuscule, so productive operation required large pipes to reduce friction. The problem of efficient distribution was most difficult for radiators located slightly above the boiler but horizontally distant.

As soon as electricity became available, gravity hot-water systems gave way to hot-water systems with circulating pumps. The piping could snake as needed through the structure, over or around obstacles. Very precise modulation was possible by thermostatically controlled valves for zones or individual radiators. Today, electrically pumped hot water has become a common and efficient means of providing heat, although the radiators themselves gave way to convectors and finned baseboard units (see below).

As we learned from gravity systems, water expands when it is heated. To accommodate a fixed amount of water within a confined distribution system, an air cushion is required; this can be seen above any hot-water boiler as an expansion tank. The boiler in a hot-water system will usually have automatic safety controls, including a shutoff for excessively high temperatures and water pressures.

RADIATORS AND COILS

Steam radiators were designed with large interior cavities to prevent the noise of steam and condensate trying to pass one another in a small passage. But large cavities meant reduced surface area. With hot water, the cavity size in the radiator could be reduced, thus increasing the radiating surface. Steam radiators required a vent, usually tapped low into the unit; hot-water radiators require a bleeder valve located at the top of the unit. Radiators provide heat to a room both by radiation and by air convection circulating through the radiator up into the room. The color of the radiator makes little difference, unless the color happens to be shiny metallic, which reduces the heat-radiating efficiency of the surface drastically and so reduces the radiation of heat into the room. Radiator covers reduce both the convective and radiative transfer to the room; to offset this effect, a radiator cover may contain a convector fan that forces air through the unit.

Radiators are usually located beneath windows. The two principal reasons for this placement are to overcome drafts in rooms, as the air near windows is chilled by the outdoors and tends to fall downward and create cold drafts at foot level; and to prevent window condensation by providing heat to the otherwise cold window surface. Recently, it has been noted that windows are the site of a considerable amount of air leakage and of a considerable amount of rain entry into wall systems. Perhaps the placement of the radiators beneath windows has mitigated the otherwise destructive effects of leakage of humid air outward and concentrated rainwater inward, by overheating the wall area beneath the windows and drying out any water that might have otherwise collected there. Radiators may have played a helpful role that goes beyond the obvious and ostensible reasons.

Radiators have been replaced, in modern installations, by finned-coil heaters. The heated pipe is surrounded by thin metal fins, and air is heated as it passes by the tubes and fins. A long coil located near the floor is the baseboard unit. If the coil is contained within a housing that is designed to allow air in at the bottom and out the top, and which works from natural buoyancy, it is called an *induction* unit. If the airflow in an induction unit is assisted by a fan, it is called a *convection* heater. If the coil can be switched from heating to cooling mode, it is usually called a *fan-coil* unit (see below). In some new construction, the water can loop through tubing located in floor or ceiling panels, which become the radiators. Radiant-heat tubing is usually a flexible plastic such as polybutylene, although, in some historically significant installations used from the 1920s through the 1950s (notably by Frank Lloyd Wright), copper or other metal piping was used in concrete slabs.

Steam systems can, in principle, be converted to hot-water systems. Steam radiators can be reused in a conversion, provided they are inspected and found safe and free from leaks. The work would consist of checking the radiators for leaks, removing the steam valves and traps and replacing with bleeder valves (which may require plugging of openings if the vents were located low), and adding return piping from each radiator if the steam system were a one-pipe system. It would be necessary to add a hot-water boiler, pump, expansion tank, pressure-relief and purge valves, and other required or desired safety devices, and to remove much of the piping from around the boiler and plug unused openings.

A steam boiler can, in principle, be reused as a hot-water boiler, if the conversion is done by a competent service person or mechanical engineer. One argument against the reuse of a boiler is that its condition may not be easy to determine. Another argument is the likely presence of asbestos on old boilers.

AIR SYSTEMS

Air movement through risers and ducts was known through the latter half of the nineteenth century. The Vanderbilt Mansion in Hyde Park, New York, designed in 1889 by architects McKim, Mead, and White, used an ingenious combination of hydronic and air distribution. The boilers were located in the subbasement. Steam was provided to a ring of radiators around the perimeter of the basement. Immediately below the steam radiators was a loop duct that could provide a dampered proportion of outdoor air or return air. The loop duct supplied air to the radiators, and the air rose through natural buoyancy up through the risers that were designed within the three-foot-thick stone exterior walls. This air moved from the tops of the risers directly into the rooms. The ingenuity of this system lies in self-regulation: the colder the indoor air, the greater the buoyancy difference that would drive the heated air upward.

A natural progression led from the fireplace in the room to the forced-air furnace that is common today. One of the principal steps in this progression was the gravity warm-air heating system. The basic elements were a firepot where the combustion took place, a casing that allowed an airspace around the firepot, and a bonnet at the top that arranged the distribution of air to the various supply ducts. Gravity furnaces were usually, but not always, provided with return-air ductwork. The furnace looked like a large octopus, occupying a central position in the house, with fat supply ducts extending outward and upward. Dampers in the individual supply ducts allowed the system to be balanced. Otherwise, the principal element of the design was to allow the smoothest flow of air possible, free of any bottlenecks or extended lateral flows, although some lateral flows were desirable to get the discharge out near the windows, as discussed above. Unfortunately, most of the early supply grilles were located near the interior of the house, thereby reinforcing rather than impeding the circular drafts that were known to cause cold feet.

The gravity warm-air furnace could operate without electricity, but as soon as electricity became available, it was used to provide booster fans. The fans were located either in the bonnet, to pull air across the firepot and swish it out the supply ducts, or in the return duct, pushing air into the space between the casing and the firepot. Of the two locations, the safer by far was having the fan located in the return. For one thing, a fan in-line with the return was not located immediately above the very hot firepot, where it could melt or burn. Perhaps more important, with a bonnet fan, any cracks in the firepot caused unsafe air movement from the combustion air into the room-supply air. Even with a crack in the firepot, a pressurizing return fan would promote safe air movement from the room air into the combustion air. The return fan served as the basis for the common modern forced-air systems.

True forced-air furnaces became common in houses after World War II. From the 1940s through the 1960s, the basic principle of duct design for forced-air furnaces was to reduce friction losses by providing smooth flow through divided airstreams and bends. By the 1970s, air-conditioning, which required insulation more than streamlining and sheet-metal craftsmanship, began to dictate ductwork, which paid less attention to friction losses and more to preventing condensation on the chilled duct surfaces. The ductwork up to the 1970s usually looked sleek and curved; modern ductwork is composed of clunkier elements of clad fiberglass ductboard and round plastic-covered flexible duct.

FUELS AND CHIMNEYS

All of the systems described so far burn fuel. Wood, the first common fuel, was replaced around the turn of the century, particularly in urban areas, by coal and coke. Hand-firing stoves and boilers was a common disagreeable task at the outset. Automatic stokers became available in the 1920s; the coal stoker was usually a screw *auger* that carried properly sized coal from a hopper to the stove or boiler. A stoker fan was part of the stoking process—it gave a boost to combustion gases going up the chimney. Removing the ash (or removing the clinkers in a mechanically stoked unit) remained a common chore. Fuel oil began to compete with coal in the 1930s. After World War II, natural gas began to be distributed widely. These are the two common fuels now, their selection usually governed by regional economics.

Approximately twenty pounds of air are needed to burn one pound of coal under normal conditions; the process could be described as one in which air is burned and a small amount of hydrocarbon is added to accomplish it. The chimney allows the escape of the combustion gases, which are hot and moist and contain noxious, irritating, and even toxic gases and solid pollutants. Any system that allows the release of combustion gases into the house (backdrafting) must be counted a failure. Flues, therefore, must move a lot of air.

The operation of chimneys is based on the buoyancy of hot gases, where there is a slight difference in pressure between the hotter, lighter gases escaping out the top of the chimney and the denser fuel gas pushing in from below. The pressure difference is so slight that it can be overcome by drafts or by solid accumulation in the flue, as well as during periods when the flue is heating up and cooling down or during mild weather. A good flow is helped by hotter combustion gases, by tall chimneys, and by wind (provided the chimney is not so stubby as it protrudes from the roof that the roof shape could force air down the chimney rather than across the top of it).

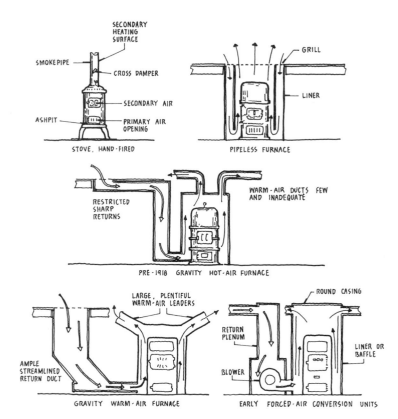

Prior to World War II, several researchers agreed that the maximum allowable efficiency of a furnace or boiler should be 80 percent. Their reasoning was that, since chimney construction was unregulated, the manufacturers were obliged to provide safety by ensuring that the combustion gases were hot—hot enough to ensure that they would safely move up the flue. The oil shock of the 1970s changed that, and new furnaces have higher efficiencies.

If a high-efficiency furnace or boiler is simply attached to an existing chimney in an old house, the consequences could be grave. For one thing, the furnace draft would be lowered considerably. Imagine a furnace at 100 percent efficiency. All of its heat would go to heating the space, so none of the heat would be available to buoy the combustion products up the chimney. For an-

Sketch of early developments in the first decades after 1900 that preceded the forced warm-air furnace. These steps began with the stove, which increased the heated radiating surface for the same combustion. The stove was moved to the basement, creating an opening in the floor for air to convect upward. An added stove surround prevented radiant loss to the basement walls and thereby enhanced the convective flow. Return-and-supply ducts were created to better distribute the flow in the living space, assisting the distribution with booster fans. The blower was integrated for fully powered distribution. These furnaces relied on the buoyancy of heated air to transport the heat. It was difficult to provide heat to rooms that were at a distance from the furnace.

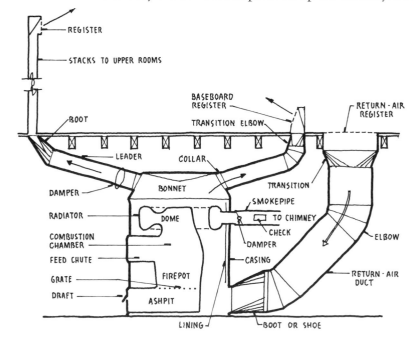

The parts of a gravity warm-air furnace

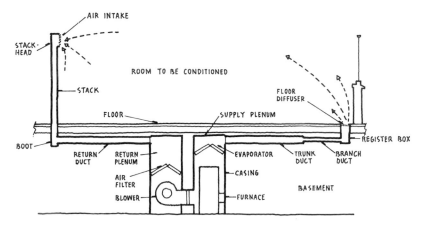

The principal elements of a forced-air system include: return-air ductwork (many building codes allow framing cavities to be used as return plenums); air filter, which serves not only to purify the air for occupants, but also to protect the blower from dust; blower (axial propeller units are called fans, while centrifugal units, or squirrel cages, are called blowers); heat exchanger, the convoluted assembly that exchanges heat between the combustion airstream and the room airstream; supply ductwork and room diffusers; burner, in the combustion airstream; operating controls, based usually on a thermostat that shuts the burner on and off; safety controls, which shut off the burner in case of overheating; a flue, for exhausting the combustion products. The evaporator is the cooling coil of an air-conditioning system.

Gravity warm-air furnace from Research Residence No. 1, Urbana, Illinois. The rod in the vertical portion of the return air duct at the right was used to hold a vane anemometer to measure the thermally induced airflow. The inclined instrument at the front is a manometer for measuring air-pressure differences.

other thing, one of the major combustion products is water; others are acidic compounds of sulfur and nitrogen. At lowered flue temperatures, more moisture would condense on the flue lining, and, if the condensate were acidic, could lead to rapid deterioration of the masonry materials of the chimney.

Many owners have opted for high-efficiency heating equipment only to encounter significant chimney damage. The chimney may need a liner designed to withstand the lower temperatures and higher corrosion potential of high-efficiency combustion equipment. Some modern heating equipment is of the "condensing" type, which maintains the combustion gases well below the melting point of PVC pipe and thus allows a powered discharge of the combustion gases to the outdoors through a simple plastic flue while the acidic condensate collects at the bottom. It should be noted that this condensate is quite corrosive and its disposal should be handled very carefully.

In a furnace or boiler with natural chimney draft, the firebox and burners are connected to the chimney by the smoke pipe. The smoke pipe must be sloped upward toward the chimney, and it should contain a draft hood, a large opening in the smoke pipe that allows indoor air to be induced up the chimney with the combustion gases. Its primary purpose is to dilute the moisture of the gas in the chimney and so help prevent condensation on the lining of the chimney. It also helps prevent wind gusts from blowing out the pilot light.

HUMIDIFICATION

Prior to the introduction of forced-air systems, wintertime humidification usually consisted of a kettle on the stove or a pan of water on the radiator. An exception is the air washer, described below. Humidification is sought for comfort, to reduce the likelihood of sparks as occupants create static electricity walking on rugs, and to help keep the joints of furniture from opening. The soundboards of musical instruments also benefit from stabilized humidity.

There are cases where evaporation pans were incorporated into the bonnets of early gravity warm-air systems. In time, humidifiers became quite popular as a side accessory to forced-air systems. These humidifiers consisted of a water pan with a float-controlled level. A motor would rotate a fabric through the water bath, allowing it to evaporate water into the airstream. A humidifier might run continuously, but more often it was controlled by humidistats, which regulated the motor operation. Units that were designed for residential use rarely performed with accuracy, and occasionally they would run amok and saturate the indoors with humidity. In any case, humidifiers require a considerable amount of care and maintenance if they are to be used properly (see below under Maintenance and Care).

Occasionally, steam was used for humidification, though this was more common in public buildings and rarely used in houses. The main problem was that water used in steam-heating systems was usually treated with chemicals to reduce the likelihood of corrosion on the boiler and the piping. These same treatment chemicals are not suitable for general discharge into the indoor environment.

COOLING SYSTEMS

The earliest cooling systems relied on simple means. In the tropics, buildings were painted white, and comfort was a matter of shade and taking advantage of any winds. Ceiling fans created slight airflow that gave some assistance to natural evaporation from the skin.

The first air-conditioned residence was Residence No. 1 at the University of Illinois in Urbana. During the summer of 1936, the dust bowl summer during which the temperature did not drop below 105 degrees Fahrenheit for one week, Professor Seichi Konzo and his wife lived at that residence in relative comfort from large blocks of ice and a fan that circulated air from these blocks throughout the house. It is from heavy ice blocks such as these that the basic unit of air-conditioning came to be called the ton. Refrigeration by compressed gases became widespread around the turn of the century. Willis Carrier of Buffalo was the first engineer to apply refrigeration principles to the conditioning of indoor air in public buildings.

Air-conditioning uses compounds called *refrigerants,* which can change from liquid to gas at normal temperatures, as a function of pressure. Ammonia was used in early refrigerators. For several decades, the refrigerants most commonly used were Freon gases, classified as chlorofluorocarbons (CFCs). Their production has been halted under the Montreal Protocols. The new refrigerant gases, hydrochlorofluorocarbons (HCFCs), pose less risk to the ozone layer. The changes in refrigerants have necessitated some changes in equipment design and sizing. This is not a conflict for most historic homes as there are few if any pieces of air-conditioning equipment of historic value.

DIRECT EXPANSION

The two common types of air-conditioning systems are *chiller-based* and *direct expansion* (DX). Chiller systems use absorption technology to produce cold water, which is distributed to air-handling or fan-coil units. They are meant for large installations and they are always engineered. DX equipment is the typical residential-scale system and is often installed by heating-and-cooling service companies.

DX air-conditioning systems work by compression of the refrigerant gases. A common compressor unit is a *reciprocating compressor,* which is usually driven by an electric motor and makes a familiar putt-putt sound. As the pressure of the gas rises, the temperature rises.

A *condenser* is a coil that cools the hot compressed gases. As the gas cools at high pressure, it condenses and continues to be pushed forward through the piping as a liquid. There are many kinds of condensers, the most common being an air-cooled condenser, in which a large fan blows outdoor air across the coil. In large buildings, the condenser coil is cooled with water, and the water is cooled in a cooling tower outdoors. Recently, water-cooled condensers have become common (see below).

An *expansion valve* is a tight orifice that opens and closes in response to temperature or pressure, or it may be a capillary tube. The compressed liquid backs up behind the tight orifice, and, as it is discharged through the opening, the refrigerant cools and becomes part liquid, part gas.

An *evaporator,* or cooling coil, is a heat-exchange surface through which the cooled liquid refrigerant passes. The coil is an arrangement of tubes and fins that is put into the stream of air that is being cooled. A blower or fan is used to blow the warm room air across the coil, cooling the air. The refrigerant vaporizes as it cools and returns to the compressor from the evaporator coil.

The work of air-conditioning is done at the cooling coil. The cooling coil will reduce the temperature of the air passing over it—this is called *sensible* cooling. If the coil temperature is below the dew-point temperature of the air, the coil will also remove water from the air—this is called *latent* cooling. The amount of sensible and latent cooling that is done by the equipment depends in a very complex way on the coil temperature, the rate at which air passes over the coil, and the conditions of the incoming air. Any air conditioner that does

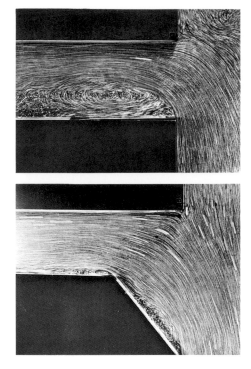

If a branch duct takes off from a trunk duct at a strict right angle, as shown at top, inefficient eddies are formed in the branch. If the takeoff is modified with an angled corner, as above, the flow is much more efficient. These photographs were taken using a water table.

Research Residence No. 1, Urbana, Illinois, was constructed in 1924. It was the only air-conditioned residence in the United States during the dust bowl summer of 1936.

The parts of a refrigerant-based air-conditioning system are shown in this schematic design. As refrigerant flows from the compressor and through the expansion valve, it changes from vapor to liquid under high pressure, and back again under low pressure.

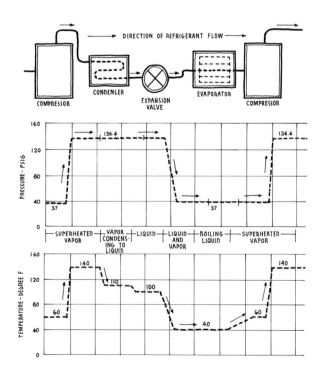

latent cooling produces condensate that drips by gravity from the evaporator or cooling coil. One of the chores of system design is ensuring the safe and effective removal of condensate from the area immediately below the cooling coil.

The simplest form of air conditioner is a window (or through-the-wall) unit, in which the condenser and the evaporator are practically side-by-side (evaporator inside and condenser outside). They are effective and inexpensive but often unsightly. A recent modification is called a *split-pack* or *mini-split* unit, where the evaporator is placed in a housing within the room space and is connected to the compressor and condenser outside. The cooling coil is usually located near an outside wall for easy condensate removal. Recently designed small units sling the condensate, which is a pure distilled water, from the cooling coil onto the compressor coil, thus greatly improving the unit efficiency.

Air-conditioning units are usually part of a ducted forced-air distribution system. In any historic house, duct design is critical. Ducts are often big, and they gobble space for both horizontal and vertical distribution. Their size and location often challenge the preservation notion of minimum intervention. The critical criteria that usually determine the size of the duct are noise and uniform distribution. Undesirable noises occur with high air velocities in ducts, particularly at turns and bends. By keeping the duct section large, the necessary quantities of air can be delivered at lower velocities. Also, if duct sections are small, then minor conditions of turns and splits can have a big effect on the dependability of the air distribution. The duct system that leads air from the equipment to the room is termed *supply*, while the system from the room back to the equipment is called *return*. Any part of the ductwork for chilled air that passes unconditioned spaces like basements or attics must be insulated and vapor-proofed, otherwise condensation would form on the inside surface of the duct and leak outward. Several manufacturers offer high-velocity air-distribution systems for air-conditioning, which use small-diameter (two inches or so) round plastic piping for distribution, and which make use of a muffler attachment at the air outlet for noise reduction.

The room termination of supply ductwork for air-conditioning is called a *diffuser*. Diffusers "throw" the air out into the room; thus they must be appropriate to the geometry of the room and to their location in the room. *Return-air grilles* are not directional, as diffusers are.

Residential air-conditioning equipment is usually controlled by a thermostat, which keeps the temperature between the limits set. Thermostat control is not designed to provide humidity control. Engineered summertime dehumidification requires additional sophistication in the equipment. It usually requires *reheat*, which means running the air across a cold coil, which will lower the dew-point temperature of the air down to the temperature of the cooling coil, then reheat the air so that it is not uncomfortably cold. This operation can be costly, but some newer equipment borrows heat from the condenser coil to provide the reheat.

Air-conditioned buildings may, at times, feel cold and clammy. This occurs most often with equipment that is oversized for the area being cooled. The thermostat's call for lowered temperatures will be met quickly, before much water can be removed from the air. Then any of the condensate remaining on the coil may be reevaporated back into the room. The net effect of cooling the air without removing much water will be to raise the relative humidity, and discomfort. Equipment that is not oversized will run for a longer period of time, removing water the entire time. To assist water removal, the fan speed can be reduced (but not down to where the cooling coil risks freezing).

Some installations consist of a small cooling unit that operates continuously to keep the indoor humidity low, and a larger, central unit that meets the sensible load. Obviously, it is difficult to provide comfortable air-conditioned air unless the building envelope is rather tight and prevents excessive exchange of indoor and outdoor air. Nevertheless, minimum fresh-air requirements can and should be expected of any system.

CHILLED-WATER SYSTEMS

In historic houses, it may simply be impossible to allow space for horizontal and vertical ductwork that will permit the movement of enough air at a low enough velocity. Another way of cooling the interior air is by circulating chilled water to coils in the interior space. The water is delivered usually to fan-coil units (that have a powered fan or blower) rather than to baseboard or induction units. This is because 1) the cold coil forms condensate, which requires a pan to collect it and discharge it out and away; and 2) natural buoyancy works well in heating mode but quite poorly in cooling, principally because of the low difference in temperature between the air and the coil. The water can be chilled by either DX equipment or a chiller. The water temperature must be above freezing, of course, and is usually delivered at a temperature around 40 to 45 degrees Fahrenheit. The services of a mechanical engineer are required to develop the most appropriate system for a particular house.

The fan-coil unit may be a two- or four-pipe unit. The coil of a two-pipe unit has one supply pipe and one return pipe attached. During winter, the boiler supplies hot water to the coil, and the thermostat would regulate either the flow rate of hot water through the coil or the on/off time of the coil with the valve fully open. A two-pipe system has a low initial cost and requires minimum intervention in the building, but it also has two serious disadvantages: 1) the system is designed to switch once a year between heating and cooling mode, and either heating or cooling may be temporarily unavailable when it is needed, so it works poorly during the changeover seasons of spring and fall, and 2) dehumidification is practically impossible.

In the most common version of the four-pipe system, there are, in effect, two parallel sets of pipes and coils—one from the chiller and one from the boiler. During swing seasons, both the chiller and the boiler may be in operation and both heating and cooling are available. Fan-coil systems have several serious drawbacks: 1) they do not allow filtration of the air, 2) they are prone to problems of condensate backup, 3) they require a lot of maintenance, repair, and cleaning, 4) they cannot provide effective dehumidification, and 5) they do not not provide fresh air or effective air distribution in the room.

HEAT PUMP

A heat pump is a reversible DX air conditioner. Heat pumps are useful where there is need for substantial cooling and occasional heating from the same piece of equipment, or where electricity is the energy source. You may recall that a window air conditioner exhausts heat to the outside from its condenser coil, as it cools the indoors. Imagine the same piece of equipment turned around to provide wintertime heating. For a heat pump, the "turning around" is achieved by using a four-way valve, which causes the condenser and evaporator coils to, in effect, change places.

Heat pumps are not capable of providing great quantities of heat during wintertime, because, among other things, they require the outdoor coil to discharge cooling to a potentially cold outside. To compensate, they usually have a booster heating unit, which often uses electric resistance heating during colder weather.

A heat pump may be useful in warm climates for a building extension or outbuilding, or where an attic or basement has been converted to use, especially where the addition of ductwork through the building is not desired.

VENTILATION

"Vitiated air" is air already breathed by someone else. "Vitiated air produces deformity, imbecility and idiocy"; it also encourages "pusillanimity and cowardice . . . vice . . . intemperance in the use of intoxicating drinks. . . . It produces inaptitude for study and, therefore, ignorance."[3] The foregoing was quoted from an 1850 physician in a 1923 article intended to update the issue. The article continues: "Air flushing alone will not always remove odors. . . . If there is a dung heap in the room it must be removed. It is no good trying to blow away the smell. . . . It is much more effective to wash dirty bodies and dirty clothes with water than with air."

In criticizing the hysterical attitude of the previous century related to invisible threats, the 1923 author quoted above was stating the basis of modern ventilation practice, that is, we need fresh air primarily to remove odors and to stabilize temperature. Otherwise, there are no human-generated pollutants that require mechanical dilution. Subsequent experts would add the importance of diluting the outgas products of some construction materials, or avoiding conditions that could grow mold, but, now as then, we ventilate primarily against odors.

In addition to the air-supply system described earlier, the Vanderbilt Mansion in Hyde Park has the air-supply system described above. It also has a separate duct system, with a grille located high in each bathroom rising up to the attic, which is vented to the outside. The framing of the attic is concrete, so it resists moisture damage. Had the attic framing been of wood, the passive bathroom ventilation system may have rotted the roof framing materials.

The turn of the century was a time of considerable air pollution in the cities, a product of coal-gas lighting. Soot was a common nuisance, indoors and out. The Museum of Natural History in London used tall towers to create a buoyant suction to move air through the building, but there was no filtration. The first powered ventilating systems were air-washer systems, intended to reduce indoors the black fog that pervaded the outdoors from coal burning and manufacturing of gas for street lighting. These systems had large, electrically powered fans that drew air through a water spray, and they were quite effective. Besides cleaning the air, they stabilized the indoor humidity, provided they were served by water of a relatively constant temperature. They were used first in industry, then in commercial buildings and museums to clean soot from the air. Despite the growth of several air washer manufacturers all through the early part of the twentieth century, no residential air washer ever found common use.

Most old buildings are leaky; ventilation occurs by natural air movement through cracks under wind, stack, and combustion pressures. Stack pressures work in any building, but particularly in tall buildings, such that, in winter, air infiltrates at the lower floors and exfiltrates at the upper floors. (That is why upper floors are more likely to see window condensation during winter than lower floors: drier outdoor air passes in around the lower windows, while the more humid indoor air is pressed against the windows at the upper floors.) Combustion exchange of air occurs when indoor air is used for the burning of fuel and the hot gases are exhausted through the chimney. Fresh "new" air will enter the building, primarily through the larger openings.

Old buildings with hydronic heat (steam or hot water) rarely had mechanical ventilation. Many residences had powered exhaust fans in bathrooms, and perhaps a range hood with a powered exhaust in the kitchen. In extreme climates, it is wise to "precondition" incoming air using a *heat exchanger*. In cold climates, air-to-air heat exchangers use the heat of the exhausting airstream to warm up the incoming airstream. In hot, humid climates, an *enthalpy exchanger* can be used to both cool down and dry out the incoming airstream using the coolness and dryness of the exhausting airstream. Enthalpy is the energy of sensible heat combined with the energy it takes to remove moisture from the air.

MECHANICAL-SYSTEM CONTROLS AND ZONING

The simplest control mechanism is a thermostat, which turns equipment on when the indoor conditions drift out of the desired range and back off once the need for heating or cooling is satisfied. Switch thermostats may have sophisticated capabilities, allowing setbacks on a daily, weekly, or seasonal basis.

Independent humidifiers are usually controlled by a humidistat. The humidistats usually sold with residential-level humidifying equipment may read humidity very poorly, and this may cause humidifying equipment to operate inappropriately. Any instrument designed to read humidity requires frequent calibration—at least yearly—to ensure the measured humidity values are accurate. High-quality humidity instrumentation is quite expensive, requires calibration and care, and may be subject to contamination if used in the wrong environment.

Commercial HVAC systems have historically used pneumatic controls for the pumps, chillers, boilers, blowers, dampers, and other operating pieces of equipment. Those are giving way to direct digital control (DDC) equipment, which uses electronic sensors and communicates by digital transfer of data among the components of the system. DDC allows a sophisticated (and often flashy) computer readout of conditions within the space and operation of the equipment and may have an alarm mode for operation or conditions that require alerts. While DDC is rapidly replacing pneumatic controls in engineered HVAC installations, homes and small museums may continue to rely on thermostats.

Zoning refers to breaking up the interior of the building so that different parts of it are controlled individually. The zoning controls may operate 1) individual equipment, 2) hydronic valves that govern flow rates of warm or chilled water, or 3) supply airflow to a space, either by dampering or mixing. Adequate partitioning is required to separate one zone from another. If the conditions are widely different between two zones, a museum exhibit space and a staff room, for example, then the separation should be a doorway with a mechanical closer.

Homeowners and managers of historic buildings, however, should not seek excessively tight control of the indoor environments. For one thing, uniform conditions can occur only in enclosures designed specifically for temperature and moisture control, and that excludes old buildings. For another, some "float" of the indoor conditions is beneficial to the building, where the indoor temperature and humidity are allowed to tend away from a single set point and toward the outdoor conditions.

MAINTENANCE AND CARE

All mechanical systems need maintenance. Many of the recent capital outlays for large and sophisticated equipment in older buildings might have been unnecessary had a sufficient level of care in operation and maintenance been exercised. A well-made building should serve for at least a century. Well-maintained equipment of high quality could serve for a century as well, even if it appears to be out-of-date. Perhaps the concept of a health maintenance organization needs to be transposed from the medical field to building management.

Well-maintained mechanical systems have the appearance, the "feel," even the smell of cleanliness. Mechanical rooms should be clean, comfortable, safe, and well lighted and ventilated. All pipes and ducts should be identified for the benefit of repair personnel who may be unfamiliar with the equipment. Manuals, specifications, and catalogues that describe the equipment should be kept in a handy but safe location. Safety procedures in case of disaster should be thought out in advance, and there should be preparedness training for building users in case of trouble.

Notes

1. Fragile objects should probably be placed in special cases. A good discussion of this subject is in Caring for Your Collections: Preserving and Protecting Your Art and Other Collectibles *(New York: Harry N. Abrams, Inc., 1992). In particular, see Steven Weintraub, "Creating and Maintaining the Right Environment," 19–29.*

2. S. Konzo, with Marylee MacDonald, The Quiet Indoor Revolution *(Chicago: Small Homes Council–Building Research Council, University of Illinois, 1992); S. Konzo, J. R. Carroll, and H. D. Bareither,* Winter Air Conditioning *(New York: Industrial Press, 1958); and S. Konzo, J. R. Carroll, and H. D. Bareither,* Summer Air Conditioning *(Chicago: Windsor Press, 1958).*

3. G. T. Palmer, "Modern Tendencies of Ventilation Practice," ASHRAE Transactions 29, *no. 643 (1923).*

Most residential heating and cooling systems are installed and serviced by heating and cooling contractors. In such firms, the term *serviceman* designates someone with a working familiarity with different kinds of equipment who is capable of troubleshooting and repair. A mechanical engineer is a professional capable of designing commercial installations, which would then be installed by a mechanical contractor. Experience counts heavily in the mechanical equipment business, so professional help should be judged primarily on their familiarity with the equipment and with work in historic houses.

FILTERS

Changing and maintaining filters is the principal maintenance activity for forced-air heating and cooling systems. Filters not only help to purify the air for better respiration and housekeeping, they also help to prevent collection of dust and dirt on the equipment. Fans and blowers, in particular, need to be kept clean for effective operation.

The most common filter uses a fiberglass mat. A fiberglass filter will do a good job of removing much of the dust and larger particles from the air. In order to remove smaller particulates such as pollen or soot, a "high-efficiency" filter is needed. These may be formed, usually with accordion pleating, of cellulose (cardboard) or polymer sheets with openings so small that light barely passes through. The finer the filter, the more likely it is to clog and the more often it must be changed. It is good practice to place filters in series of increasing fineness to cut down on the cost of replacing high-efficiency filters.

Electrostatic or electronic air cleaners are not filters, per se, because they do not actually remove solid particles from the airstream. Electronic air cleaners trap small airborne particles and reduce them in size. The removal of gaseous pollutants, as in high-quality museum environments, requires filtration of the air through activated charcoal or potassium permanganate.

Other regular chores associated with forced-air systems include seasonal cleaning of the blower or fan; checking the belt tension for any belt-driven machinery; having a professional check the condition of the heat exchanger in a furnace; checking the refrigerant pressure in air-conditioning systems; checking the cleanliness of ductwork and cleaning when necessary.

Any air-conditioner evaporator unit may produce condensate. This water is drained by gravity to a safe site for discharge. It is important to keep condensate drain lines open. In units where the cold coil is located in a critical spot, such as above the ceiling of an important room, the unit should sit in a pan, or a pan within a pan, to provide added assurance that condensate water will be discharged away from valuable parts of the building.

Steam boilers require professional maintenance to ensure that the requisite safety devices are in place and are functioning properly. Hot-water systems require that radiators be bled (i.e., removal of air trapped at high spots) at the start of each heating season, or as necessary. At the same time, one should also check the condition of the motor and pump, and look for leaks, repairing where necessary.

The control systems of many buildings may already receive attention and care. Building users know to go to the thermostat if the conditions feel too hot or too cold. In engineered buildings where the temperature control may not be easily accessible, the users may need to consult a building engineer in the event of problems.

The primary rules in maintenance are cleanliness and keeping the senses tuned to good mechanical operation. Building users should listen for sounds and look for stains or other indications of change in equipment performance. Users of the building, even those who are unfamiliar with mechanical systems, should not be shy about inquiring how the systems work. The payoff in preservation, particularly for care of valuable equipment, is enormous.

KITCHENS AND BATHROOMS

RICHARD O. BYRNE

As a kid I dug the trench for the new copper pipe that ran from our pump house to the kitchen. It set aside forever the pail that had carried every drop of water our family used. That trench is part of my heritage, and I have appreciated running water ever since. We may have already forgotten, but much of rural America was plumbed as recently as forty years ago, and our cities hardly a hundred years ago. Joseph Campbell, the great gatherer of myths, recounts a summer he spent in the depths of the Depression staying in a chicken coop–like place in Woodstock, New York, that a wonderful old man rented out at twenty dollars a year to those who he thought might have a future in the arts. He told Campbell that he wouldn't install running water "because he didn't like the class of people it attracted." Today his coops would remain empty at any price. We have come to demand our comforts.

"Authentic" restored kitchens and bathrooms are found only in house-museum settings. They are great to look at, and perhaps to "play house" in, but as a practical matter, we set down our chamber pots and turned on the taps of continued refreshment as quickly as we could. To paraphrase Kahlil Gibran, we truly do invite comfort into our homes as a guest, and we pride ourselves on how soon it becomes the master. Few today would suffer the heat, the work, and the inconvenience of even a mid-nineteenth-century kitchen. We, like all the generations before us, have gone modern.

Continued design and technological revolution in our kitchens and the addition of bathrooms to our homes during the past century have fundamentally changed how we use our homes and how we order our lives. Few old houses were designed with a modern kitchen in mind, and fewer still had the hint of a bathroom. Inserting a new bathroom or kitchen into an old building so that the new design utilizes the assets of the historic house, and thus maintaining it with a minimum of needless change, is perhaps one of the greatest challenges facing a historic property. That is not to say modern chrome elements are not an option. They have their place too, but old houses are much more than just places with "neat" woodwork and wonderful fittings. They are dictionaries of visual and social values that have been passed on from generation to generation. The next generation should be able to extract as much joy from the building as you do as its current caretaker. A house that speaks clearly to you should teach lessons that can be expressed in a sympathetic visual voice in a new bathroom or kitchen. These two rooms are often the test of the owner's ability to master visual literacy.

An old house doesn't have to be made to look "new." You probably would not buy hot pants as a gift for your grandmother; you would look for something appropriate to her personality. Try to respect the "personality" of your house. First, look at the condition of your existing woodwork, and floors and cupboards and plumbing fittings. Our architectural heritage is not something that gets bigger with passing time. Too much is thrown out that is perfectly good, that is perfectly well designed, that, if cleaned up and well maintained, would go on serving future generations without causing a puff of pollution or wasted resource.

The butler's pantry at Carter's Grove in Williamsburg, Virginia, was restored in the 1920s by private owners and then again following the 1960s acquisition by the Colonial Williamsburg Foundation. As with most old kitchens, the table is the focus of the room, not only for eating but also for food preparation. Fireplaces were common in eighteenth- and nineteenth-century kitchens, making them hospitable places for between-meal activities as well.

Some positive qualities may be hidden under layers of change. Wainscoting may be painted over, covering beautiful woods such as maple and black walnut. Are the details of the moldings so plugged with paint that you can no longer enjoy the shadow lines they were meant to have? Has beaded paneling become blurred as grooves have filled with layers of paint? And can you open the windows with ease? Your woodwork may simply need cleaning. The original elements of your house were designed with care and probably have the best of materials in them—materials you could not obtain at any price today. (A common old door, custom made in clear pine, can easily cost in excess of six hundred dollars today. Think twice before you chuck yours.)

Do not be taken in by fast solutions. America is replete with fast cures for almost every building ailment, and common to them all is that someone is making a buck off the solution. They and their company are often long gone when the nature of the problem they created (not solved) has raised its head. Be wary of the quick and cheap solution to your bathroom and kitchen problems. The original is often a lot better piece of goods than what you can replace it with.

Appliances are usually exceptions to this rule. Keeping old appliances is a tough sell. Safety, efficiency, and parts replacement are major concerns. Electrical appliances are prone to electrical-insulation breakdown, with resulting fire and shock hazards. The plasticizers in plastic elements vanish over time, and knobs and the like crumble. Plastic and rubber seals turn brittle and no longer do their job. That is not to say that some kitchen appliances cannot be rebuilt, but finding replacement parts might prove impossible. As the sophistication of oven timers and switches has increased, their repairability has decreased. Contact points burn off or become pitted. Winding springs weaken and no longer drive the timer. And to be perfectly honest, the labor- and energy-saving features of many of our new appliances are miles ahead of their counterparts of, say, the 1930s. One can always go back to wood-burning stoves for cooking—new ones are still made—but most cooks prefer modern gas or electric ovens and cooking surfaces. Common sense, and full understanding of any inherent risks, are vital to the keeping of older appliances.

That said, some heritage features such as cast-iron sinks with drainboards or cast-iron tubs are still very useful. The challenge is to fit them into the design vocabulary of a new kitchen or bathroom. It can be done.

Remember that you are not alone in your old home. There are all sorts of people to help you sort out what it is that you have. Anybody who claims to have "restored" a building all alone is either fibbing or walking on water. Tradespeople, architects, museum curators, antique collectors, historical societies—all are there waiting to lend a hand and to exchange ideas with you on what it is that you have and how you might go about saving and caring for it.

EARLY SOURCES OF WATER IN THE HOME

Getting water into a house was simple once. One used a pail that was filled at the well or a springhouse. Many of these early hand-dug wells are still in use in rural America. They should be tested from time to time by your local health authority to ensure that the water remains safe to drink. Also, care should be taken around hand-dug wells. Since they are not very deep, groundwater enters them rather quickly and the use of pesticides, herbicides, and fertilizer along with termite-control poisons must be strictly controlled. We don't use our farmlands as we once did, and what your grandfather did as a farmer is far removed from the intensive feedlots and massive chemical additives common to farming today. Also remember that wells are dangerous places if they are not kept well capped. Many is the child that has fallen through rotted planks into the well or cistern below.

Deep-drilled wells are a much safer water source, but one must also use care not to pollute them. You might be getting your water from two hundred eighty feet down instead of thirty feet, but surface pollution still can filter down that deep, and from farther away. One should also expect the rubber pressure bladder that supplies a constant water pressure from your well to deteriorate over time—ten to fifteen years might be expected—after which it and the pressure tank it is in will have to be replaced. Expect the same for the well pump motor and the pump control switches.

The other source of water historically, now almost forgotten, is rainwater from a cistern, either external to the building or in the basement or attic. Nothing is quite as memorable as bathing in a rainstorm with water from a downspout. One of the great things about many historic homes is that the cisterns are still there. They might need repair, and you might have to install an electric or hand pump to get this water to where you want it, but the reward is more than worth it. And if you don't have a cistern, you can have one built quite cheaply, and the filter system needed to get the rainwater from the roof into the cistern does not have to be elaborate. A good sand and gravel filter will do most of it.

Modern Plumbing and the Historic House

One must take into account a number of practical considerations when inserting a bathroom or kitchen into an old house, and first on the list is plumbing. New plumbing systems inserted into an old house must be carefully designed, installed, and maintained if one is to ensure that the building is not damaged—either aesthetically or in terms of the building's basic structural elements.

I have yet to see a building's plumbing installed with any thought as to how that system is to be maintained or replaced. Pipes do wear out, and sooner or later the copper or iron pipes buried in the living-room ceiling are going to leak. The challenge then is to replace the pipes without destroying the ceiling. Perhaps the installation of inspection trapdoors or ports in a ceiling or a wall would be a start in that direction. At least when there is a problem, one can get to it without destroying half of the house. Another useful maintenance tool for both plumbing and wiring systems is a complete photographic record of all walls and ceilings before they are closed in during construction.

Consult a carpenter, architect, or engineer knowledgeable about old buildings before you cut into your building's existing structural system. Over the past thirty years I have inspected hundreds of heritage structures, and by far the greatest damage one sees is that caused by uncontrolled water or by compromising primary structural systems to insert a toilet or some other pipe. More than once I have seen an eight-by-eight-inch main-support timber that has been cut in two so that a drainpipe could be inserted. The number of floor joists cut off to allow a toilet to sit in a particular spot are legion, yet in many cases, moving the toilet a few inches would avoid such damage. A toilet with a six-inch-thick dummy wall behind it would bring the toilet out just enough to miss a joist below and also provide a nice shelf: this is an example of spatial planning. Unless I knew the plumber extremely well I would never allow a plumber to install drainpipes in an old house without being present to supervise personally exactly how pipes went in and what was cut to get them into place. Drawings on paper often do not fit reality.

Plumbing Maintenance and Repair

Many fine books have been written on how to install and repair plumbing elements, if you feel inclined to do your own work. Regardless of who does the work, however, every homeowner should have a basic understanding of what is involved to ensure that a minimum of damage is done to a house by plumbing systems that are already in place and that the house is maintained with a minimum of damage to its original details.

Two new copper pipes fitted with foam insulation use the path cut out of a joist in a previous plumbing effort. The joist was cut off to allow a toilet to be seated above it. Note that the hole in the floor above has been repaired with the insertion of a wooden dutchman, or carefully fitted wooden plug.

Pipe Systems

One of the reasons we have a national building and plumbing code is that our forefathers made every mistake possible in fitting up their dwellings. Our building codes are the result of this vast background experience. Old plumbing systems, often installed by amateurs, have a few strange anomalies, such as poisonous lead pipes, or copper pipes hung to the ceiling with iron straps or hooked directly onto steel pipes, creating an accelerated bimetal corrosion system with resulting leaks and flooding. Use copper hangers on copper pipes, and use isolation fittings between copper and steel plumbing systems. Replace the lead water pipes as quickly as possible. Lead drainpipes won't hurt you immediately, but they too should be replaced as they contribute to the total pollution of our water supply.

In cities and towns, some water mains that enter many older buildings are made out of lead. If you have a lead main into your house, it would be prudent to let the water run for a few minutes before drinking it. Lead pipe is easy to identify. Look closely where the pipe enters the basement from the wall. Nick the metal with a knife. If it is soft lead, it will nick easily and will shine like new silver. Lead pipe elsewhere in a house is also easy to spot. Fortunately, streets are often repaved, and when yours is worked on it might be a good time to invest in having the water main replaced, where feasible. If nothing else, you will feel better about yourself and your family. In cold climates, some plumbing shops and public utilities have a high-amperage device they can put on your water-main pipe so that, if your water main freezes from the street (or the well), it can be thawed out without having to dig the whole thing up.

Once drainpipes are in an old house, people tend to forget them, often until serious damage has been wrought by underground leaks that have washed out soils under footings and foundations. If you drive down almost any street in America that has old homes with brick or stone foundations you will often see a curious sight: rows of houses that have cracked and sagging foundations, usually under a window. What has happened is that the drain tile that goes under the footing of the basement wall has been leaking gallons of water over the years and has washed out the soils from under the footing. The drain may have become broken from frost heaving it, or roots defiling it, or the weight of the house on the footings crushing it. The solution is drain replacement and then repair of the wall.

Septic Systems

Homeowners who are connected to septic systems have a variety of problems to attend to with good preventive maintenance. First of all, use care and good sense when flushing items down a toilet. The whole septic system consists of a holding tank for solids and a drainage field for fluids. The system stays healthy through biological breakdown of the waste and the timely cleaning out of the solids, usually every three to five years. If you pour chemicals in your drain that kill off the bacteria that break down the waste, or leave the solids in the holding tank so long that they spill out into the drainage field and plug it, then you have created a real problem. Acids, photographic-developing chemicals, paints and solvents, and the like should never be poured into the drain as they will kill off the bacteria needed to make the system work. Nor should one put cotton swabs, sanitary napkins, grease, or plastic items into the system. Care should also be taken to keep from driving cars and trucks over drain tiles, or from planting trees and shrubs around drain tiles as their roots will plug them. If you are lax in your septic cleanout schedule and your drain tiles become plugged, they will have to be dug up and replaced, a truly costly undertaking.

Another concern in the waste system is the vent stack that vents sewer gas above the roof. The vent not only allows sewer gas to escape, it also allows water to flow away into the drain without causing a vacuum to develop as the

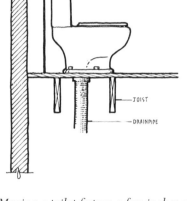

Moving a toilet fixture a few inches will often save having to cut a joist or beam below. In this instance, moving the toilet also provides a useful shelf.

water swishes away. If the vent is too small, in cold climates frost will form on the inside of the vent pipe and close it off. When this occurs, your drains will pull against a vacuum and you may find that your toilet does not flush properly. Cast-iron vent pipes sometimes get filled with rust scale and seal themselves off, causing the same problem. And I have seen improperly designed plastic-pipe vent systems (next to a bedroom window) that have been capped off because of the stench. When the cap was removed the entire inside of the plastic pipe was distorted from the power of the entrapped gases.

One should also look at the rubber or lead sleeve through which the vent pipe passes through the roof. Over time the vent may move, so that the sleeve is no longer watertight, leaving a leak alongside the vent. Entering rainwater will eventually cause extensive damage to plaster and wooden elements below. A simple silicone caulking application around the seal is all that is needed to avoid this problem. As with all maintenance, you have to look at the system from time to time to identify the problem.

COMMON PLUMBING PROBLEMS AND SOLUTIONS

LEAKS

One must be not only extremely careful in how a plumbing system is inserted into a building, one must also be extremely vigilant to see that it does not leak and spoil all that is around it. Repair all leaks immediately, and watch out for additional sources of water damage. Everyone is familiar, for example, with water condensing on a glass that has a cold drink inside. The same condensation occurs on plumbing fixtures, particularly cold-water pipes and toilet tanks. This condensate then drips onto wooden floors and into ceilings, leading to rot and continued decay. A simple solution is available: insulate the toilet tank with foam plastic from kits bought at a hardware store; pipe condensation can be controlled with foam insulation tubes available at any good building-supply center. Another useful maintenance tip is to install the toilet at least one inch away from the wall so that mildew does not form on the wall. A narrow horizontal wooden support strip can be placed between the tank and the wall to give the tank firm support.

Sweating on the outside of this toilet tank has been stopped by the foam insulative blanket fitted to its inside walls. The knife blade is in between the foam and the tank wall.

The other source of water at a toilet that can do damage is when the toilet overflows. The quicker the problem is solved, the less damage to the historic floor. There should be a water-cutoff valve to the toilet, and, more important, adults in the home should know how to reach inside a toilet tank and close the float valve that closes the tank to the toilet. (If this prospect inspires disgust, perhaps a good cleaning of the toilet tank is in order. Pour in a bottle of vinegar and some dish detergent, and then scrub it out with a brush.) And don't expect the toilet float mechanism to last forever. Several wonderful new replacement float designs are available at hardware stores. If nothing else, you will enjoy their ingenuity.

If water does get onto the floor, wipe it up immediately. It is at this time that you will appreciate the value of caulking between the base of the toilet and the floor. Like all other protective caulking systems, it should be inspected periodically to ensure that it still forms a seal to the floor. Remember, there is a great difference in movement between a wooden floor and a ceramic toilet being continually joggled about by use, and this caulk bead is under constant stress. It will need renewal from time to time.

WATER VAPOR

Inserting bathrooms and kitchens into older homes injects another water burden besides that brought by the pipes and faucets: steam, or water vapor. The placement of a vapor barrier on the inside of exterior walls is required by the building code in new construction. Warm air flows toward cold surfaces and condenses moisture out if the dew point is reached. If you can seal an exterior wall so that no interior air migrates into it, then no moisture can condense inside the wall cavity. If condensation does take place inside the wall cavity, the result will be soggy insulation or blocks of ice forming between studs in winter. Condensation on or in the exterior siding will cause the exterior paint to peel.

Most old houses do not have vapor barriers under the plaster wall surface. Not only are vapor barriers missing, the nature of the insulation in many retroinsulated walls is the perfect material to form soggy messes when moisture gets into it. Often when one inspects an older building, one sees the effect of moisture penetration in localized spots—such as exterior bathroom and kitchen walls, and even sometimes where a large number of plants are kept—clearly denoted by peeling exterior paint.

Thus it is critical to reduce the moisture level in walls. One can apply aluminum-based paints on the inside walls before your decorator color or wallpaper is applied. Apply the aluminum paint to the surface of the plaster, followed by a thorough caulking of all cracks and joints in the wall and between the wall and its adjacent woodwork and flooring. A vinyl-coated paper is another option. These are not as effective as a plastic vapor barrier but certainly are a step in the right direction. A careful caulking between baseboards and floors and between woodwork and plaster interfaces will also help. Electric boxes should be caulked tight. Cut the electric power to the box before you attend to the caulking. And for those with plastic vapor barriers already in place, remember they too will deteriorate and fail over time. I doubt they will last fifty years, probably quite a bit less.

Another way to lessen the moisture burden in a room is to install timer-switched vent fans to the outside (not the attic). Set the timer for an extra twenty minutes after you leave the bathroom. If the vent above your stove goes outside, it can also remove moisture. Many kitchen vents only pass air through a filter to remove grease. You can further decrease the vapor burden in the bathroom by taking shorter showers and hanging large wet towels elsewhere to dry, such as in a laundry room, or outside. In the kitchen, keep boiling water covered. And for those really "wet" events such as bathing the cat or making spaghetti for twenty, a dehumidifier would be useful. If you still see paint peeling off the outside of the house, you probably face a larger water problem (see pages 16–17).

FREEZING PIPES

A properly installed plumbing system's pipes can be drained in case of needed repairs or threatened freezing conditions. And it is critical that the homeowner know where the main water-cutoff valve is so that the entire system can be stopped quickly. Pipes should be installed so that the entire water-supply system can be drained back to the basement or out a faucet. This means all pipes need a back slope with no sags. Your pipe drainage efforts will also come in handy when you have to drain the lines to remove air buildups that are causing the pipes to "pound."

Special in-line cutoff valves with drain *petcocks* should be available in the basement to drain every water line in the house if one is faced with possible freezing conditions. Every plumbing fixture should have hot- and cold-water line cutoff valves at the fixture. Both drain valves and cutoff valves are inexpensive and easy to use. And to complete the cold weather emergency kit, a gallon of recreational vehicle water-line antifreeze (standard automobile antifreeze is a deadly poison and should never be used in a plumbing system) should be on hand to pour into the toilet and every drain to keep them from bursting if a freezing condition develops. Don't forget the tank on the toilet.

If you face problems with extremely cold exterior walls and less than ideal insulation (as many old houses do), wrapping heater tapes around the water pipes may save you the grief of frozen and cracked pipes and flooding water inside walls. If you can't get a heater tape wrapped around an already installed pipe, perhaps a small porthole into which hot air can be blown with a hair dryer might help avoid disaster. Remember that hot-air dryers can get very hot up close, so take care not to overheat the opening. And if you do have a frozen pipe inside a wall, do not use an open-flame torch to thaw it—countless houses have burned to the ground from this procedure. Use a heat gun, and even then be careful. Keep a fire extinguisher immediately at hand.

CLOGGED PIPES

Sometimes pipes plug up with mineral deposits and must be replaced. It is impossible to clean them out. Gradual reduction in water pressure may indicate that your pipes are indeed plugging solid. But before you tear the house apart, check the pressure tank (if you have your own well), or check with the city waterworks to ensure they are not the cause of the pressure drop. Pressure loss can also be the result of a small bit of solder that has broken loose and plugged the faucet. The pressure drop in that case will be sudden and not at all like the slow diminution of pressure caused by years of mineral buildup. Removal of solder bits is a minor repair that requires shutting off the water, taking apart the faucet, and fishing or flushing the solder out. If it is not in the faucet, the solder might be found down at the fixture's cutoff valve. Chemical drain cleaners should be used with great care, if at all. Most sink drains plugged with hair and soap can be cleaned out by taking the drain apart using the slip fitting under the sink. Bathtub drains can usually be cleaned by removing the cap to the drain.

SAFETY PRECAUTIONS IN KITCHEN AND BATHROOM

One of the most serious of bathroom and kitchen hazards exists when electrical outlets in these two rooms are not equipped with ground fault circuit interrupters (GFCI). Sinks and water pipes are grounded extremely well (usually less than 3 ohms to true earth), and if you are touching one of these and somehow come in contact with a hot electrical plug, wire, or appliance, you are going to glow if not be killed outright. Our modern electrical code requires GFCIs near any sink or bathroom fixture, but many older homes do not have them. Install them. It will be money well spent. (See also pages 193–94 for general guidance on electrical safety.)

Another aspect of basic safety, temperature-compensating bath and shower faucets are required in new construction. With these faucets, if someone flushes the toilet while you are in the shower, you don't have to worry about being scalded by hot water. Older style shower faucets can be a real hazard.

A few words should also be said about water heaters. Water heaters are expensive to operate. Keep them well insulated as recommended by your gas or electric utility. Consider a self-cleaning water heater (there are several on the market) for long-term energy savings. (It is very expensive to heat up lime deposits before you finally get to heating the water.)

Gas water heaters are for the most part cheaper to run than electric water heaters. However, gas heaters require a pilot light, which can cause explosions when heavy combustible solvents such as gasoline or paint thinner waft across basement floors and are ignited. Most of these fires could be prevented if the water heater were placed on a pedestal eighteen inches off the floor above the fumes. The greatest piece of maintenance you will ever do is when you keep your house from burning down and perhaps even save a life.

Two areas of the kitchen or bathroom may require locks. Cabinets that contain medications or chemical cleaners dangerous to small children who might have access to the rooms should be installed with childproof locks. The other lockable item is the bathroom door. It is dangerous to put a dead bolt or hook on the inside of a bathroom door. Any lock on a bathroom door should be operable from the outside with a special key or screwdriver. Thus, if there is an accident in the bathroom, or a child becomes locked in the room, you can rapidly open the door and perhaps avert a disaster.

MAINTAINING BATHROOM FIXTURES AND DETAILS

Original bathroom fixtures are often discarded because of ignorance as to how to revitalize them. A faucet is a simple device and, if it is cared for, little can go wrong with it that can't be fixed. Chrome plating can be redone at a plating shop (look for someone who rebuilds old lighting fixtures). The rubber washer inside the faucet can be replaced time and again. What is really damaging to a faucet is to let it drip for a long time; the leaking water will cut a channel into the brass seat that the rubber washer rests against. Tightening the faucet handle, though it may make you feel good, is not going to solve the problem. If a water channel is worn into the brass seat, the faucet will have to have a new seat milled into it with a special tool. But a leak is not cause to pitch out a handsome faucet. Fortunately, because of the demand for historic-style replacement faucets, fittings, and fixtures, a wide variety of replacement bathroom parts are available. (See Further Reading for magazines that carry plumbing fixture advertisements.)

If you have the good fortune to own a cast-iron tub (which keeps water hot much longer than thin steel or fiberglass does), but it is not quite up to par, several options are available. Layers of paint on the outside can be removed to reveal crisp decorative details. Be careful removing the paint as lead may be present. You might also consider removing the bathtub and having the exterior sandblasted clean.

Chipped white tub enamel can be touched up with the same paint-on enamel used for stove repairs. A variety of tints are available. Iron rust stains come out nicely with oxalic acid. Follow the manufacturer's instructions carefully, and protect your eyes and skin with gloves and safety glasses or a face shield. All of the scum and mineral deposits found in sinks, tubs, toilets, and showers are quickly softened with special mineral/soap-scum cleaners found in any grocery store. Really heavy mineral deposits inside toilets can be removed by stopping the toilet up (after it has been taken outside) and then filling it with a weak mix of water and muriatic acid or applying to the area of deposit a papier-mâché poultice wet with the acid solution. The acid will not hurt the ceramic glaze, but it will rapidly remove the mineral deposit. Be certain to wear protective clothing and a face shield.

Do not use strong acid solutions on cast-iron fixtures as you will damage them. If the enamel surface on a cast-iron fixture is badly scuffed, it can be buffed up to some extent with tin oxide, which is used for polishing marble. One could also try fine polishing compounds used to rub out car paints. Take care not to wear a hole in the enamel surface. Ceramic sinks and the like can be buffed up in the same manner. Do not use kitchen cleansers as they contain abrasives that will dull enamel surfaces.

In addition to creating unsightly mineral buildup, leaving slippery soap films on shower and tub surfaces may create a serious hazard. Be certain to rinse them off well. Also, check regularly to see that handles and the other supports people use to enter and leave bathtubs are secure. Often they pull loose because the backing plaster or drywall behind tile has failed.

From time to time, one should inspect all those places where water pipes come through walls and ceilings, such as those that connect into the shower stall or bathtub and those that run through kitchen countertops. If leaks are present or seals and caulks broken, rot will soon follow. Also, be sure that your plumber has connected the shower pipes with a solid attachment inside the wall. Otherwise, every time you turn on the shower the whole pipe system moves about, and no caulking system will long withstand such abuse. You can be certain that water will be inside the wall in a very short time.

Many bathrooms have been outfitted with improper drywall materials surrounding tubs and shower areas. Regular drywall (gypsum with gray paper) disintegrates rapidly when wet. More effective is a water-resistant drywall (with green paper), which may not have been available when the shower was built into your house. This "green board" has now been replaced with a very workable "cement board" that eliminates much of the subplaster deterioration problems in shower and tub areas. If your tiled plaster has failed, your best solution is to tear out the whole mess and start over again. The damage you will find as you open up the wall will be greater than you think. You may even find rotted two-by-fours and other serious damage.

Plaster and drywall damage can often be avoided in tubs and showers by the careful maintenance of grouted tile on its surface. The tile itself seldom goes bad as it is a fired ceramic product, usually with a glasslike glaze. What does happen is that the grout will develop hairline cracks that will wick water into the wall though capillary attraction. A hairline crack will probably cause more damage than a quarter-inch crack because the quarter-inch crack will drain out and dry whereas the hairline crack will not. If your grout is laced with tiny cracks next to tile or within itself, it should be cut out and replaced, or the wall behind it will suffer.

Decorative bathroom paints and wallpapers should be washable, i.e., wallpapers with plastic coatings and semigloss or gloss paints. Matte paints are difficult to wash clean.

Anyone who watches American television should be an expert on cleaning supplies. We have watched an army of little guys march down countless drains. What is surprising, perhaps, is that most of the cleaners thus promoted do work. Ceramic-tile grout really can be freshened with fungal growth killers and bleach. Toilets can be kept immaculate with various disinfecting inserts hung in their tanks.

The marketplace is filled with miracle tub coatings that are promoted as enamel surfaces. They are actually resin coatings that will last, at best, fifteen to twenty years, after which time your tub is ready for the junk pile, as there is no way to renew or remove the epoxy coating. Resin coatings may have their place, but it is not on a tub designed to last for generations.

A common feature of bathrooms in old houses is a wooden-framed window directly in the center of the wall above the tub. In time, a shower may have been added, which may have led to peeling paint and, eventually, rotting wood. What to do? There are no ideal solutions as the water load on the wooden members of the window is just too great. Reduce this water load as much as possible by redirecting the shower or by using a handheld shower head. And be sure that the surfaces are carefully maintained. Plastic fabrication shops might be able to construct a custom-fitted clear plastic box that fits over the window and all of its woodwork. It should not be sealed to the wall as condensation will eventually form inside the box and really cause a rot situation. Hinges or pins can be used to hang the plastic box. Another possible solution is to have a custom-fitted copper flashing made to protect the wood. Be careful in its design to ensure water cannot get under the flashing. The copper can be left to tarnish or polished to your liking. Look at the bathroom window as a high-maintenance item that is going to need constant care if wood rot and paint failure are to be avoided.

KITCHEN DESIGN AND MAINTENANCE

The evolution of kitchen design is perhaps the greatest area of change that affects our day-to-day lives. Not only cupboards and refrigerators but also spatial relationships have changed. The design of many old kitchens made them

Late nineteenth-century American bathrooms often have fixtures that are still quite serviceable. The cast-iron tub seen here is original to the house. Note the small protrusion from the far wall that hides the vent pipe. The workmanship that refurbished this simple bathroom is outstanding, yet the cost was minimal.

The original windows flood this kitchen with light. Family heirlooms are in full view but protected from kitchen grease by glass doors. The kitchen table remains a central aspect of historic kitchen design.

Except for the track lights, this cleaned-up 1852 summer kitchen is exactly as it was built: same colors, moldings, and floor. Layers of paint were removed, the hardware was repaired, the floor was scrubbed and painted (not sanded), and the chimney was rebuilt. It needed no "design" work, just care, to carry it forward for another century. Modern appliances are located at the other end of the room.

the axis of all that transpired in the home. My boyhood kitchen had a door to the stairwell, one to the living room, one to my parents' bedroom, one to the front porch, one to the woodshed, one to the pantry, and one to the scullery. That adds up to seven doors, plus two windows, all opening into one room with a large wood-burning stove, a kitchen table, and a couple of freestanding hutches and work counters. Today the challenge is to put a modern kitchen into such a space and not destroy all that the house brings to us. To do so we must look at more than a floor plan. A real understanding of that kitchen also takes in its social context and how it helped mold a family.

We bring expectations and needs to our kitchens that go beyond efficiency. Historically, kitchens were vastly more than the sterile areas we have structured into our space-efficient apartments and contemporary homes. Kitchens were places of family gathering, of cooking and canning, of generational exchange while seeking warmth, companionship, and sustenance. Individuals became family members in kitchens. We often learned our manners there, and it was from the kitchen that all of family life radiated.

Designing a kitchen with these thoughts in mind will allow one to respect the house as it was built. That is not to say there should be no change, for we define ourselves from generation to generation in terms of change—change that always comes back to a certain stasis. But the ideas presented here are intended to encourage you to look beyond kitchen design criteria centered on efficient spatial relationships and a golden step-saving triangle of stove, sink, and refrigerator. When it was built, your kitchen was very likely planned by someone with both practical considerations and less tangible needs of the inhabitants in mind. Before you tear something out, consider first what its original purpose may have been, and whether what you are replacing it with is worth what you are giving up.

When replacements are needed, beautifully detailed kitchen cupboards and countertops—both traditional and contemporary—are available. Look for high-quality hinges and drawer slides when you consider buying cabinets; you are going to give them a good workout, so buy for the long term. The difference between a great cupboard and a slam-bang job is often found in little details, such as doors that are set flush with the cabinet frame as opposed to being lipped over the opening, which results in a sloppy fit and bad hinge work. Many good cabinetmakers in America would welcome a knowledgeable client and the chance to build something using traditional designs, materials, and methods. Their skills are part of our heritage too, and it is important that they be continued. To find a good cabinetmaker, check around to see who in your community is making hand-built traditional furniture. Be extra cautious of "kitchen cabinet shops," which are often sales outlets for factories and will not provide the same carefully thought-through design followed by careful execution of a traditional cabinetmaker.

If you are having custom cabinets made, give some thought as to how you are going to incorporate windows next to countertops. Often the countertop with its back rail is pushed right up to the window without any thought as to how the window is to be used or, even more important, how the dead flies and other unpleasantries are going to be cleaned out of the narrow slot formed between the countertop and the window. Perhaps a three-inch-wide ledge along the wall will move the cabinet out enough while at the same time giving you a useful ledge for spices and jars. Then the window becomes an asset.

Be wary of products that claim you can reface your cupboards "magically." If you have really good old cabinets to begin with, consider simply having them refinished and the hardware cleaned, oiled, and polished. You may well end up with better cupboards at a lower cost than would be possible with a new suite of expensive replacement cupboards.

The selection of countertops and sinks can affect not only your purse but also your health and the longevity of your glassware and china. Granite, marble, and tile surfaces are extremely hard and can chip dishes and stemware quite easily, whereas some of the synthetic molded tops are much softer and may make more sense if, like me, you are a bit clumsy.

Almost all countertops can be "repristinated" (as the English say) by using very fine polishing compounds. Tile countertops will need their grout bleached out from time to time for reasons of both health and aesthetics.

Stainless-steel sinks have a little more "bounce" to them than cast-iron or stone sinks. All sinks can be made more dish friendly with a rubber-mesh bottom lining made for that purpose and used in most museum conservation laboratories. It can be inserted for the washing of crystal and the like as the need arises. You might also look for stainless-steel sinks with their own drainboard. They are common in Europe and are starting to become available in North America.

Kitchens pose special cleaning and insect-control problems that can be lessened with the proper selection of finishes. In response to folk wisdom that flies were repelled by the color blue, some kitchens at one time were painted blue. Flies were also kept at bay with asparagus boughs hung in appropriate places, such as above the stove where grease collects. Bronze-mesh screening can be more expensive than standard screens, but it is extremely durable.

A tremendous amount of grease becomes airborne during cooking. The fewer nooks and crannies it can settle in, the better. Paint and wallpaper surfaces should be scrubbable, and details such as plate rails, moldings, and the like should be "open" enough in their detailing so that they can be wiped clean easily. In the kitchen, set aside oil and wax finishes in favor of varnishes or semigloss paints, which can be wiped clean more easily. And when you are happy with how clean and tidy and well ordered your life has become in your kitchen and bathroom, stop and thank again the man who dug the trench that brought you the wonderful comfort of running water.

I truly believe that buildings and spaces can speak in compelling human terms. There are buildings and spaces that draw you in and calm you, that speak to your innermost thoughts just as a hearth fire does, or a stream, or the stillness of a star-filled sky. Perhaps more than anything else, your historic home should address not just the "physical" heritage found in boards and paint, but also the cultural heritage that can be read within the structure. You are part of your home's heritage. To maintain the spirit of a building is perhaps the most difficult piece of maintenance of all, but it can be done. And perhaps, just perhaps, the home you cherish will become part of our patrimony worth saving by the next generation.

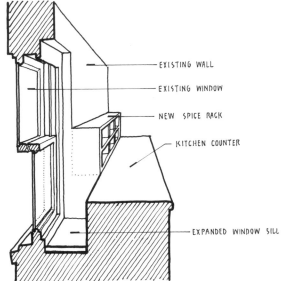

EXISTING WALL

EXISTING WINDOW

NEW SPICE RACK

KITCHEN COUNTER

EXPANDED WINDOW SILL

A narrow window opening has been enlarged by moving the kitchen cupboards forward, thus creating a spice shelf, a window ledge suitable for small plants, and easy access to the window for cleaning.

Lighting and Electrical Systems

Gordon Bock

By the 1920s, electric utilities were mounting campaigns to gain customers by offering basic wiring in existing houses at affordable rates. This ad is from a streetcar display card.

Providing light inside a house has been a goal of builders since before written time. For centuries, natural light was the main source, and devising bigger and better windows was one of the driving concerns of architecture. Artificial light, too, has long been used—in the form of torches, candles, and oil lamps —but these relatively primitive, self-contained, highly mobile forms were closer to furnishings or accessories rather than parts of the building.

All this changed with the advent of modern lighting in the last century. Electric lighting and its direct precursor, gas lighting, were large-scale systems in which the illuminating power was created far from the point of final consumption. Furthermore, in order to work, these systems, with their pipes, wires, and control equipment, had to be integrated carefully into the structure of a house. Maintaining them became part of the regular maintenance of the building.

While gas lighting in buildings is no longer used except under museum conditions, gas-lighting systems are left in the walls of thousands of historic houses. Their impact is evident still in the design of rooms and placement of windows, moldings, ornaments, and today's lighting fixtures. Electrical systems, of course, are an integral part of modern life. Originally harnessed in houses to produce light, electricity today makes possible countless marvels— clean, quiet, easily managed mechanical power from electric motors; telecommunications of every kind; heat for cooking and comfort. Understanding the evolution of these systems and the basics of how they work can help the historic-house owner not only recognize the age (and potential problems) of the house's original power sources, but also offer some useful background for creating historically appropriate lighting schemes.

Lighting Systems and Their Evolution

Gas Systems

In the late eighteenth century, experiments in the coal-producing regions of Europe—particularly in England—demonstrated that it was both safe and practical to burn gas for factory and municipal lighting. By 1816, the city of Baltimore had set up the first gas system in America for street lighting. Within forty years, gas lighting on both a residential and commercial scale was available in some three hundred communities, large and small, from the Carolinas to California. This coal gas was the primary—as well as the original—central lighting system in America for nearly one hundred years.

Often called manufactured gas, coal gas was produced at a central plant by heating coal in large vessels called *retorts*—a much different source from today's piped-in natural gas or bottled propane. Besides being a dangerous process, gas-making produced a smell so foul that gasworks were invariably sited in a remote, industrial section of town. The gas had to be "scrubbed" and filtered to reduce these noxious odors, as well as undesirable by-products (ammonia, tar, sulfur gas), before it was stored in a large, variable-volume tank called a *gasometer*. From here the gas was distributed through the town via a system of mains and pipes, much the same as modern networks.

When it reached the house, the gas had to pass through the much-maligned meter. Early wet-type gas meters, employing a drum suspended in liquid, had a reputation for being unreliable. (A common gaslight-era slur was to say someone "lied like a gas meter.") The dry-type meter, which used a system of bellows and clockwork, became common in the 1890s and is essentially still in use today. Wrought-iron pipe carried the gas to the principal rooms of the house, where it was controlled by a *cock* (valve) on the fixture.

GASLIGHT FIXTURES

Fixtures made for gas lighting took many forms as their bodies altered to meet decorative fashions and their burners and shades improved to maximize light output, cleanliness, and gas economy. By today's lighting standards, the average house had only a few fixtures strategically placed on first-floor walls and ceilings. (Gaslights were less common on the second floor.) Grand, public rooms, such as the parlor and dining room, might be lavished with an elaborate *gasolier* (chandelier) fitted with crystal globes and reflectors designed to enhance the light's effect. A gasolier equipped with counterbalancing weights and a special gas seal in the ceiling was known as a *waterslide*. It could be raised and lowered with the touch of a hand for lighting.

Strictly functional light for a kitchen or hall came from a bare-bones pendant—a simple, inverted T-shaped pipe with a naked burner at each end. Wall brackets often appeared in pairs flanking a window. They were either fixed or movable, with hinged arms that folded and swung to position the light. Table lamps, which had to be supplied with a hose from overhead fixtures and wall cocks, were an option only after vulcanized rubber became available in the 1850s.

Gas lighting survived—and in many ways surpassed—the parade of oil-burning Argand, solar, and kerosene lamps that each had their heyday in the nineteenth century. Nonetheless, the actual light output of gas was always relatively small—between 17 and 20 candlepower, or about the shine of a modern electric night-light. The final flowering of gaslight came in 1885 with the invention of the Welsbach burner.

Familiar to us now in the form of portable camp lanterns and neo-Victorian streetlights, the Welsbach system used a circular Bunsen burner (nearly the same as that used in laboratories) that was covered with a fiber mantle. When lit, the mantle turned into an incandescent cone that produced nearly fifteen times as much light as a naked gas flame. It also burned whiter with less flicker. The Welsbach burner gave gas lighting a renewed, but ultimately limited, lease on life. By 1900, gas companies were seeing their business threatened by electric lighting, which was becoming brighter and more reliable. The Welsbach burner gave them a temporary market advantage until after World War I, when economic and social changes spelled the end of residential gas lighting in most areas.

ELECTRICAL SYSTEMS

Gas lighting reigned supreme until 1879, when Thomas Edison perfected the incandescent electric light. Inventors across the globe had been toying with electricity as a light source for years—arc lighting, in fact, was at work in 1860 for street lighting in New York, Cleveland, and San Jose—but it took the Wizard of Menlo Park to put together a lamp practical enough for houses. With characteristic cheek, Edison announced, "I will make electric light so cheap only the rich will be able to afford candles!"

Edison's genius went beyond creating a light source that was hardy and bright enough to be more than a laboratory novelty. He conceived of his lamp as an inexpensive, disposable part of a centralized system (deliberately modeled on gas-lighting systems), designed to bring electrical power to whole communities and cities. Edison's lighting systems, first installed in New York City,

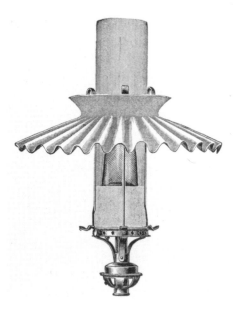

The Welsbach burner was a dramatic improvement over earlier gas-lighting burners. Instead of producing light from a naked flame, the Bunsen-type burner (tube in lower part of drawing) mixed gas and air in such a way that it burned at high temperatures, heating the mantle (center in drawing) to incandescence.

were powered by direct current (DC)—basically the same kind of power produced by batteries.

The nature of DC required installation techniques and materials that are now obsolete, although they are occasionally evident in old houses. In Edison's system, the power ran in three wires that, like water piping, reduced in size as they moved up the floors in a house—a method called "tree" wiring. The wiring was usually an *exposed* system—that is, wires were mounted in open view using wooden cleats placed every three feet or so. The electrical flow was controlled by knife switches or key-type switches resembling today's lamp sockets. Later came rotary snap switches—spring-loaded knobs comparable to an oven dial—that were designed to minimize the sparking inherent in DC electricity.

THE KNOB-AND-TUBE SYSTEM

In the late nineteenth century, competing telephone, telegraph, and electrical systems were locked in technological tugs-of-war eerily reminiscent of today's computer and Internet races. By 1900, Edison's direct current had pretty much been overtaken by alternating current (AC), which remains the standard source of power today. The pioneer of alternating current was Nikola Tesla, an early employee of Edison's who emigrated from Austria-Hungary. Tesla's inventions, such as the induction motor and high-tension power transmission, made electricity practical for far more uses than were possible with direct current. Tesla designed the first great hydroelectric power plant at Niagara Falls, New York.

Many houses originally electrified for DC were converted to AC using the same exposed wiring, snap switches, and other primitive components. Push-button wall switches, introduced in the 1890s during the DC era, readily made the transition to AC and continued to be the most widely used residential switch for another forty years. However, as electrical service grew more popular, there was a need for equipment that was more attractive, better standardized (in 1901 more than one hundred different styles of light sockets were in use), and, not least, safer.

Knob-and-tube, the first widely used system, was common from the late 1890s to after 1920. This was a two-wire *concealed* system, where wires were hidden in walls and under floors. Nonconducting porcelain knobs held the wires one inch off the surface of studs and joists, where they could be installed in open runs; porcelain tubes protected the wires where they had to penetrate framing or cross other wires. Electrical connections were made by wrapping one wire around another, then soldering and taping the joint. Wires that terminated in outlets, switches, and the like were protected with *loom*—a tube of woven fabric. The knob-and-tube system incorporated no ground-leg conductor as we know it today, and outlets were *unpolarized*—that is, you could turn the plug 180 degrees and still insert it.

THE ADVENT OF APPLIANCES

The rapid advances in AC engineering that took place in the late nineteenth century spawned the inventions that made possible other uses of electricity in the home. The perfection of the AC induction motor in the late 1880s made electric fans common by the next decade, both as tabletop units and as wall- or ceiling-mounted fixtures. (The "electrolier fan," which married an electric-light fixture to a ceiling fan, was advertised in 1894.) Obtaining heat from electricity was a difficult business until 1905, when Albert L. Marsh was granted a patent for an alloy of chromium and nickel. Able to withstand wide temperature swings, this new metal could be made into wires, paving the way for a cornucopia of appliances based on heating elements—toasters, coffeepots, laundry irons, waffle irons, hair curlers, and auxiliary space heaters. By 1927, manufacturers were promoting early versions of all the appliances we

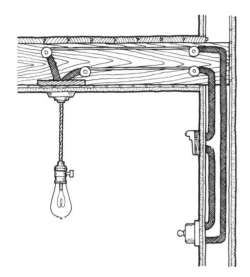

In knob-and-tube wiring, loom was added to shield insulated wires at critical spots such as where they passed through a ceiling rosette (A), for a basic electric-light pendant, or connected to a light switch (C). Concealed knob-and-tube systems were often combined with surface wooden moldings (B).

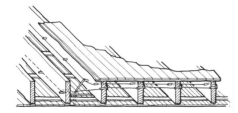

In typical knob-and-tube installations, individual rubber-insulated wires are carried at least one inch off the surface of wooden members by knobs (either solid or two-piece) and tubes (always hollow) made of porcelain.

rely on today—washing machines, refrigerators, electric ranges, and portable vacuum cleaners—as "new servants" that would aid the suburban housewife with most of the chores formerly performed by domestic help.

WIRING EXISTING BUILDINGS

While gas-lighting installations required skilled fitting of pipes and mains inside wall cavities, making the system cumbersome at best to add to an existing building, electrical service was well adapted to retrofitting, especially in wooden-frame houses. After leaving the street pole and entering the house through a drop lead, the electrician installed a basic 20- or 30-ampere service panel—essentially a meter and two screw-in fuses that would serve the rudimentary power requirements of a lifestyle before the invention of air-conditioning or color television. From here, the electrician would typically open up twelve inches or so of flooring on the second story to create one or more troughs. These he would use to gain overhead access to the main rooms of the first floor. By boring through floor joists and wall studs with a brace and bit (or a remote, chain-operated drill made for this purpose), he could install porcelain tubes to transverse structural members and wire in a central ceiling fixture in each room. Changing direction to run with the structural bays required only knobs. Wall switches and outlets—harder to install, and less necessary in an era with few appliances—were kept to a minimum.

WOODEN AND METAL SURFACE MOLDINGS

Wiring existing houses was a good business in the early days of electricity, but the cost of installing a concealed system like knob-and-tube put it out of reach of some households. A much cheaper alternative was one of the two basic *surface* systems, in use from about 1900 to 1930. Wooden moldings carried two or three wires in a grooved strip that was attached to the wall. When covered with a cap (usually beaded or ribbed with a decorative design and painted or stained to match the decor), it looked enough like picture molding to allow the electrician to plan the layout so that it coordinated with the other trim inside the house. An alternative system, metal moldings, employed the same base-and-cap method and is still used today. Though not as decorative as wood, metal moldings could be painted to blend in with baseboards and walls.

METAL CONDUITS AND CABLES

Just as it is today, protecting wires from accidental damage was a big concern with early electricity, especially in the days of primitive cloth-and-rubber insulation. Almost from the beginning, iron and steel gas piping was put to use as *rigid conduit* by running wires inside the empty pipe. Though an excellent barrier to cuts, sunlight, and animal bites, rigid conduit was expensive and hard to install. An improvement was *flexible-steel* (also known as *Greenfield*) *conduit* developed at the turn of the century. Essentially galvanized steel strips wrapped into a tube, flexible steel conduit was easy to snake into the walls and floors of houses, typically before inserting a bundle of two or three insulated wires.

The next logical innovation was *armored cable,* whose wires came from the factory bound in a continuous spiral strip of galvanized metal. Often called BX or BXL (the latter a damp-location version incorporating lead), armored cable was made possible by the improved insulation materials of the 1930s and 1940s. Although nonmetallic cables with thermoplastic insulation and jackets have been the standards for wiring houses since the 1960s, modern forms of metal conduits and cables are still in use.

GROUNDED SYSTEMS

In the 1950s, the National Electrical Code (a set of model requirements first published in 1897) started to require domestic wiring to be grounded

---

INDEPENDENT GAS AND ELECTRIC SYSTEMS

By the 1870s, gas lighting was successful enough to be the standard independent of municipal systems. Large houses and hotels beyond the reach of city gas mains could be equipped with their own gas generators. Rather than burning manufactured coal gas, these systems typically either ran on vaporized fuels, such as gasoline and benzine, or they produced acetylene gas by combining calcium carbide granules and water.

As a safety measure, the generator—an assemblage of tanks and regulators, often powered by a weight- or spring-driven pump—was stationed in the basement, an underground room, or off in an outbuilding some distance from the main house. With the exception of burners and jets designed specifically for the different kinds of gas, lighting fixtures were essentially the same as for city gas.

It was not until the rural electrification program (REA) of the 1930s that even basic electric service reached large parts of the country. Yet, much like independent gas systems, electric light could be had for those beyond the reach of a city grid. From the 1890s to well into this century, the owner of any size home might get electricity from gasoline-powered motor-generator packs. Placed in the basement or an outdoor shed, these systems were self-contained; many, like the popular Delco brand, produced direct-current electricity. Small hydroelectric plants were also developed in this same period for lighting individual properties.

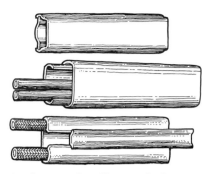

Surface metal moldings, which are still in use today, employ a two-piece base-and-cap system and come in a variety of designs.

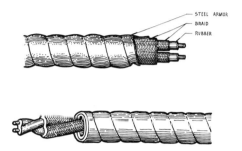

STEEL ARMOR
BRAID
RUBBER

Armored cable, which wrapped a galvanized steel band around a bundle of insulated wires, offered more protection than knob-and-tube wiring, and more flexibility than rigid conduit.

with a dedicated third wire. This wire, usually insulated and of lighter gauge than the other conductors (or, in the case of armored cable, a bare bonding wire), was required to create a continuous connection between the ground lug on all three-pin outlets. This connection, in turn, becomes a safety path to ground for electricity, in the event there is a defective appliance or damage to the wiring.

Although some later armored cables, as well as all nonmetallic cables, included a ground wire when they were manufactured, generally cable and conduit systems made before 1940 do not. Many of these systems were later upgraded, however, simply by attaching a lug to the metal conduit or armor and using it as a conductor. This practice is permitted by most local codes if the connection offers a continuous electrical path, unbroken, for instance, by nonmetallic connectors.

SYSTEMS CARE

Safety is the primary concern with electrical—and gas—systems. Generally, the best policy for questionable wiring or equipment is replacement with new materials according to current code. While building inspectors will permit the operation of older systems if they are in good working order, any construction activity usually requires bringing the wiring up to current code. The major concerns are loose or broken connections and worn insulation that will allow one leg of the circuit to touch another, causing a *short circuit*, resulting in low resistance and high current flow. In the best situation, this will cause a fuse to blow. In the worst, the resulting heat will cause a fire. Maintenance and service upgrades of electrical systems should be performed by a licensed electrician. However, the homeowner can bear the following points in mind when evaluating the conditions in his or her historic building:

Make sure electrical devices bear a stamp or sticker denoting that the product has been rated by Underwriters Laboratories, Inc. (UL) according to their electrical hazard and safety tests. Use only UL-listed parts and appliances.

Watch for gas and electrical service that is installed in tandem. At the turn of the century and later, it was common practice to spiral electrical lines around gas pipes. Typically, these pipes are grounded where they pass belowground, so that if the insulation fails on adjacent wiring, they can create a potential for short circuits.

Consider the age of knob-and-tube wiring. Generally, even the youngest knob-and-tube system is now well beyond its expected life and ready for replacement. Rubber insulation—the standard before 1930 and probably always the weakest link in the system—clearly loses its flexibility after twenty-five years. It can crack and break off, leaving bare wiring prone to short-circuit and cause fire, particularly at fixtures and switches. The original soldered joints too sometimes age, making poor connections or potential fire hazards.

Do not use thermal insulation—i.e., fiberglass batts or cellulose fill—around knob-and-tube wiring. The one inch or more of ambient air around the wiring is part of its electrical insulating capability. Packing or blowing in thermal insulation around these wires creates the potential for moisture collection, which may short-circuit aged wiring. (Packing insulation may also cause a fire hazard from modern wiring and light fixtures that are buried in thermal insulation.)

Replace wooden-molding installations. Wooden moldings have not met code since the 1930s. Over and above the fact that they were often subjected to nails by homeowners who mistook them for solid wood, early electricians often cut corners on the quality of installations.

Watch for deteriorating insulation. Rubber wiring, especially, tends to age the most in open air. The result is that wiring protected in cable and conduit systems may be intact, but, where the wiring exits in switches, light fixtures, and terminal boxes, the insulation may be very brittle and fall off under any movement. Use extreme caution when inspecting such installations. When new wiring is installed the old wire should be pulled completely out of existing fixtures and switch boxes or fittings that are reused.

Correct wiring in damp environments by removing or relocating it to a dry location and fixing the source of moisture. Unless designed for such service, no electrical equipment will operate safely where there is moisture. Older wiring is even more vulnerable to the effects of dampness and water. Corroded fixtures, switches, and boxes should be replaced.

Do not overload old wiring. The branch circuits of most pre-1940 electrical systems have a limited current-carrying capacity. Most systems are no. 14 wire, which is rated to carry not more than 15 amperes of load. (By way of comparison, today's houses are regularly wired with no. 12 wire, a size larger, and the total service of the house may be 100 amps or more.) If your house cannot support your power needs—that is, you tend to blow fuses—reduce the number or wattage rating of the appliances at your outlets until you can have an electrician upgrade your service.

Check the ground continuity of grounding outlets and circuits. Systems where grounds were added later may be compromised by poor connections or age. (Rusting of armored cable can add resistance to the ground path.) Good hardware stores sell inexpensive, user-friendly, three-wire circuit testers that check outlets by inserting the tester like a plug, then reading a set of lights to evaluate its condition.

Install tamperproof fuses. A screw-in fuse box is still a viable safety device if in good working order, but if it uses plug fuses (with bases similar to that of a small lamp), its protection can be defeated by using fuses with today's higher current ratings. Type S fuses have a different base diameter for each rating so they cannot be interchanged. Plug-fuse boxes can be upgraded to Type S by inserting special adapters (which are not removable).

Install GFCIs at appropriate locations. *Ground fault circuit interrupters* are state-of-the-art safety devices designed to prevent electrocution. They detect very low current levels, comparing the electricity in with the electricity out. If there is any difference—which might mean electricity is finding its way to ground through a human body—the device interrupts the circuit.

Receptacle-type GFCIs at point-of-use outlets are the most often seen, although they can also be incorporated in circuit-breaker panels. The National Electrical Code now requires GFCI receptacles anywhere there is a countertop or a water source within four feet of the outlet—specifically, in kitchens, bathrooms, garages, crawl spaces, basements, and outdoors.

GAS AND ELECTRIC LIGHTING FIXTURES

The year 1900 marked a very real cusp in the evolution of residential artificial lighting. Gas lighting, while limited and potentially dangerous to our late twentieth-century eyes, was then a more reliable system than electricity; plus it had reached a new level of "perfection" with the Welsbach mantle. In the eastern United States, gas was also cheaper than electricity. For homeowners before World War I, gas seemed sure to serve well into the future.

Electric lighting, however, was growing in use and sophistication as the network of poles and wires expanded block by block in many cities and new suburbs. Service improved as "the power" stayed on longer (round-the-clock service was not common at first), with fewer interruptions and low-voltage brownouts. The progressive young architect Frank Lloyd Wright was typical of new-house builders who had an eye on the future and a soft spot for the wonders of new technology. Like many, he saw electricity as safe enough to gamble on wiring his house even before service was available.

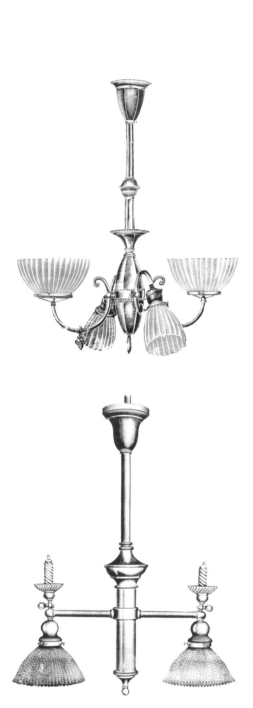

Combination Fixtures

New-home builders were not alone. Light-fixture manufacturers, forced to reconcile the two services (or at least hedge their bets on their future markets), took the most logical approach: they produced combination fixtures offering both gas and electric light sources. At first, these gasolier/electroliers were essentially standard gas fixtures upgraded with one or two electrified arms. Gas burners, by nature, had to account for the by-products of heat and exhaust, so they were typically pointed up in the normal manner. Electric lights, of course, worked well in most any position, so they were pointed down. Tastemakers cautioned that simple patterns—two electric lights, one gas—were best, although many large combination fixtures of four, six, and eight lights were made.

After 1913, as gas slowly lost its dominance to electricity, the positions of these lights on fixtures tended to switch. The Welsbach mantle, which could be piped to burn up or down, provided the freedom to put gaslights below electric lights on a combination fixture. In 1914, one architect advised home builders to "use inverted gaslights as much as possible, for they are far ahead of ordinary upright lights." Candle fixtures—small, mantleless gas burners masquerading as colonial tapers—also appeared at this time, either alone or as backup lights on primarily electric fixtures.

Early All-Electric Fixtures

Combination gas/electric fixtures remained in the catalogues of manufacturers as late as 1912, but by this time they were sharing their pages with all-electric fixtures. At their most basic, early electric fixtures were starkly utilitarian. Compared to gas, electricity required no shades or chimneys to protect an open flame—indeed, the modest light output of early equipment was best left unobscured. Furthermore, flameless electric light was such a novelty that it demanded no further visual enhancement. A *pendant,* for example, was simply a naked lamp in a key-switch socket dangling by a braided electrical cord. Ceiling-mounted *pan* and *husk* fixtures were spun-metal disks housing one or more lamps—unadorned except for an occasional ring of metal leaves wreathing their sockets. Perhaps most unusual to our eyes was the *femme-fleur.* Very often perched on a side table or the newel post at the bottom of a staircase, this mythical-looking fixture was a cast-metal woman sprouting a half-dozen sockets on sinewy tubes ornamented to look like flowers.

As the quality of electric light improved and fixture manufacturers woke up to its many applications, a new breed of all-electric lighting began to appear. These lights dispensed with the pipes, oil fonts, and shades required for the heat, flame, and fuel of earlier lighting. For example, one critic noted that "modern designers of fixtures for ceiling lights are getting away from the stiff, gas-pipe pendants which prevailed years ago." By doing so, these designers also jettisoned many of the historical design associations with candles and oil lamps. Ironically, as the light output of electricity increased after 1905, they had to deal with the—literally—harsh realities of unfrosted lamps: glare and shadows. Fitting for a completely modern light source, these new electric lights were based on "scientific" models and took the form of three general illumination systems:

The most straightforward and familiar of the three, *direct illumination* was light directed (or reflected) in one direction, usually downward. Fixtures in this category were chandeliers, brackets, floor lamps, or table lamps, especially with dark shades. Direct illumination was deemed most appropriate for living rooms, dining rooms, dens, and music rooms because it produced a mix of shadows and bright light—poor for work areas, but ideal for "comfort" rooms.

The supposed opposite of direct illumination, *indirect illumination* required a new type of fixture. Typically this was an opaque, inverted bowl fitted

Combination gas-and-electric lighting fixtures were widespread after 1900 and came in many configurations, styles, and decorative finishes. These two vaguely Colonial Revival models represent typical arrangements: pairs of electric lights and standard (pre-Welsbach) gas fitters on separate arms (top), or gas candles over electric lights on the same arms (above). On the latter, note the prismatic glass shades and the fixture's central pipe.

with a silvered reflector that directed light to the ceiling, from where it was reflected back down into the room. Suspended bowl fixtures in the middle of service rooms such as pantries, sewing rooms, and basements were the common examples. Indirect illumination was especially appropriate for the kitchen because food preparation required evenly distributed light, rather than a single bright source. Experts cautioned that it was important to have ceilings painted white or in light colors for maximum effect; reflectors also had to be cleaned regularly.

Similar to indirect illumination, except that the bowl and reflector were translucent, *semi-indirect illumination* permitted a portion of the output to be cast down as direct illumination as well as indirect illumination. These fixtures might also be overhead inverted bowls, or even cleverly designed floor lamps and wall brackets. They were recommended for bathrooms, bedrooms, dressing rooms, and billiard rooms, where light was needed without a need to "reveal the source."

FIXTURE CARE

Early electric lighting, while an advance over gas and oil-burning systems, was substantially less bright than what we are accustomed to today. The early lamps not only had lower *lumen* (light) output, there also were fewer of them in even the most aggressively lit houses. As late as 1920, the prevailing wisdom held that "there is seldom need for larger sizes than 15, 25, or 40 watts in any home." Today's lifestyles and lighting habits are still influenced by the "ample lighting" affluence of the 1960s—an era of cheap electricity when artificial lighting was pushed (by the power and electrical lamp manufacturers) as better and nearly as affordable as natural light. Yet you can achieve the effects and ambience of period lighting consistent with a historic house interior, not to mention

Once electric light came into its own after the turn of the century, perfection of a better lamp—or lightbulb—became the Holy Grail of the industry. This display, c. 1919, shows the range of early lamp shades, sizes, and filaments, all without frosting.

energy and cost savings. Try using some of the following simple methods and guidelines:

Use multiple light sources. While a lone ceiling fixture may be historically correct, it may not provide sufficient light for modern tastes and needs. Consider increasing the number and variety of sources. Where appropriate, wall sconces and brackets will add to the ambient light level without upstaging the ceiling fixture. Floor and table lamps are easily added and could have been present in the past. Balancing lower ambient light levels with task lighting to illuminate work or reading areas will also save energy.

Adding SCR-type dimmer switches (that is, compact, solid-state silicone-controlled rectifier units) to your lighting fixtures will provide two noteworthy and practical advantages. First, they are an easy way to simulate the low light level and orangy glow of early carbon-filament lamps. Use unfrosted tungsten

Electricity has been turned to lighting in many ways, such as carbon arcs for street illumination, but it was the incandescent lamp—commonly called the lightbulb—that made residential electric light practical and affordable. The nature of these early electric lamps was a critical influence on the design of the fixtures made to hold them.

Carbon-filament lamps, the first mass-produced lamps, were meticulously handcrafted versions of Edison's lab model—that is, the legendary loop of carbonized bamboo sealed in an orb of evacuated glass. The glass was clear, not frosted, and the now-famous pear shape terminated in a characteristic tip where it was sealed. Carbon-filament lamps were delicate and hard to standardize, and they gave off a soft orangy light that was far from bright—not unlike the decorative lights of a Christmas tree. Still, they were manufactured until around 1920.

Almost as soon as carbonized bamboo proved practical, the search was on for better lamps. Besides being far from brilliant, carbon filaments had a tendency to darken the glass envelope as they aged. Adding multiple filaments improved light output some, but after 1900, even Edison felt the carbon filament had reached its peak. Experiments with rare metals, such as osmium and tantalum, and advances in manufacturing yielded a parade of improved lamps. One of the most successful was the GEM lamp (for General Electric Metalized filament). Burning brighter and longer than a plain carbon filament, GEM lamps were sold from 1905 to about 1930.

In 1909, tungsten-filament lamps were introduced under the General Electric trade name Mazda—the Persian goddess of light. The classic zigzag filament produced more than twice the light output of a GEM lamp, especially through the unfrosted, straight-sided glass envelope. Tungsten lamps were manufactured with tips until about 1922, when a seal in the stem base was perfected. Although frosted tips had been tried in the 1910s, frosting inside the envelope had to wait until about 1924.

lamps and run them at about one-fourth output on the dimmer. Second, when you need a modern light level from the fixture, either occasionally or normally, it is a simple matter to turn the dimmer to full output. Appropriate dimmer switches are readily purchased at hardware and lighting-supply stores for wiring into wall boxes or inserting between the outlet and lamp's power cord.

Use appropriate lamps (see above and illustration opposite). Nothing compromises the effect of a historic lighting fixture like a lamp that is too large, too bright, or too frosted. Reproduction carbon-filament lamps have been made for some time by specialty manufacturers and can be purchased through many reproduction-fixture suppliers. It is even easier to find acceptable substitutes for historic lamps at a good hardware store. Use low-wattage ornamental or special-purpose lamps that are unfrosted. Don't overlook service-type lamps, such as those used in refrigerators and garage-door openers, that may approximate the shape or size of the lamp you seek.

Do not assume shades are always necessary. While shades and globes of glass, mica, parchment, and other materials were necessary for mitigating the glare of early unfrosted lamps, many fixtures—especially those designed for carbon-filament lamps—were intended to be shadeless. Consider instead fitting them with an appropriate lamp—usually one of low intensity. Ceiling-mounted pan lights, for example, are often mistakenly fitted with standard 60- or 75-watt lamps—funny looking and way too bright. Actually, they were designed for small, round globe lamps (still widely available) in the 15- to 40-watt range that would be left bare. Ornamental fixtures, too, typically were not intended for shades. Many had small lamps, often with a candelabra-style base.

Ceiling fixtures of the past often hung much lower than what is standard today. Gas fixtures in particular had to be within easy reach so they could be lit. Early electric fixtures too were frequently turned on at the unit, not at the wall as is customary today. Later, when semi-indirect lighting became fashionable, the distance from the ceiling was important for correct operation of the lamp. These distances, however, sometimes conflict with modern lifestyles or clearances needed for room traffic or decor, particularly where ceiling height is not ample.

As a rule-of-thumb compromise, try a distance of eighty inches between floor and fixture bottom for open rooms. In dining rooms or similar areas where the fixture will be suspended over a table, try sixty-five inches. At the very least, when you are ordering or installing a ceiling fixture, start with dimensions that are on the long side. It is much easier to shorten chains and tubes if you find the fixture hangs too low than to make them longer.

Upgrade inverted sockets. The heat produced by an incandescent lamp is substantial and, where the lamp is inverted (that is, oriented base up), it contributes to the aging of the fixture's socket base. When you have the option of ordering socket bases for new fixtures, choose porcelain bases, which are more heat resistant and durable than those made from phenolic plastic. It is also possible to retrofit many existing fixtures with porcelain bases if you have access to a good lamp-parts store with a broad inventory of fittings. (Note, however, that most porcelain bases are keyless; if the fixture is operated with a key or chain switch, you will have to stick to a phenolic base.)

WHEN WIRING WEARS OUT

Like house wiring, the electrical parts of a light fixture have a finite life (up to twenty years for wiring, often less time for sockets and switches, depending upon service), but their failure should not spell doom for a historic fixture. Electric lights are readily rewired with some simple caveats:

First, make sure the fixture is disconnected from the power source before you do anything to the fixture. As you disassemble the fixture, document how all the parts go together with photographs or sketches. Continue to make notes as any parts are disassembled.

Replace a failed lamp socket by prying off the shell with a small screwdriver (usually at a point marked Press Here). To prevent shorts, when the new socket is connected, make sure the wire wraps clockwise around the terminals and there is a cardboard insulator between the socket and shell.

When removing old wiring with cracked or dry insulation, first lubricate the fixture insides with silicone spray, and don't force the wiring (it may break). Use 18- or 20-gauge lamp cord for replacement.

GLOBES, SHADES, AND REFLECTORS

Throughout most of its history, electric light has always been mated with some sort of glass, mica, or metal surround to maximize or concentrate its output. In the age of the carbon-filament lamp, Holophane shades, popular from roughly 1907 to 1920, were invented to make the most of the yellow-orange glow of carbon-filament lamps. Clear glass cast in prismatic ribs, they redirected the light for aesthetic, as well as practical, benefits.

By the tungsten-filament era, the problem had reversed. "The naked filament of a modern electric lamp is not beautiful to look at and it is injurious to the eyes," wrote an electrical columnist in 1920. The solution recommended was to "enclose every lamp in some appropriate glassware." The duties of a shade were to 1) enclose the lamp enough to hide the filament, 2) reflect the light in the right direction, and 3) not absorb excessive amounts of light. Indeed, the amount of light absorbed by the glass was regarded as critical information for the homeowner to consider because it required a correspondingly larger lamp. At 10 to 20 percent absorption, sand-blasted and alabaster globes were the next best thing to clear glass; ribbed- and ground-glass globes were slightly less effective at 15 to 30 percent; ruby and cobalt blue globes would "steal" light at 85 to 95 percent, "just as blotting paper soaks up ink."

Well into the 1940s, bedrooms and other rooms with ceilings too low (or too commonplace) for hanging fixtures were often lit by pan lights. These plain-Jane fixtures were intended to be shadeless and use small, round lamps. Called globe lamps, they are still widely available.

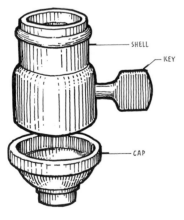

Keyed lamp sockets have changed little since the 1920s. The brass shell is held in the cap by projections, which can be pried apart to open the socket for repairs.

CARE OF FINISHES

Especially before 1920, an amazing variety of decorative metal finishes were highly popular for light fixtures of all sorts. The surface might be plated (nickel plate over a brass base was very durable and common), plated and treated (copperplate treated to brown-black, then sporadically buffed, produced a very popular "antique copper" effect), or highly polished solid metal, such as brass. Regardless of the finish, the surface is likely to be lacquer-coated to protect it from oxidation.

Before assuming a fixture needs polishing or other surface restoration, inspect it closely to determine as much as possible the original finish. Check the back or hidden parts of the fixture for clues. Put a magnet to various areas (to locate steel or plated-iron parts), and scratch it with a sharp awl in an inconspicuous spot (to identify base metals under plate). Cleaning the surface gently with a mild detergent will usually remove loose dirt and improve the looks. If the lacquer has failed or the metal finish has corroded, consider taking the fixture to a reputable metal-finishing shop.

With barely a century of history behind them, lighting and electrical systems may well be some of the most recent services to be found in a historic house—which can be perhaps one hundred twenty, one hundred seventy, or two hundred years old in many parts of North America. The primary purpose of care for these systems is to ensure their safe operation, but it is also important for maintaining their contribution as cultural artifacts. Early lights and the systems that power them are as much a part of a building's historic fabric and architectural intent as a plaster ceiling medallion or stained-glass window. When we lose them through ignorance or lack of care, we lose an original part of the building and its unique record of a time now past.

Caring for the Landscape

BARBARA WYATT

A house and its setting are partners in creating a historic property. A historic house is composed of the exterior of the house, the interior, the immediate setting, and the neighborhood setting. The parts of this composition originally formed an interrelated design continuum. This harmony should continue to prevail today.

Too often neglected or put on the back burner in home restoration or rehabilitation plans, the landscape or yard of a historic house is a resource with distinct value and significance, as well as the setting for the house. As a setting, the landscape should complement the historic nature of the house and flatter restoration efforts. Proper maintenance is as important to the yard as it is to the house. It can result in an improved appearance, a healthier yard, and enhancement of the historic elements of both house and yard.

Tending the yard of any house requires fundamental care, such as mowing, pruning, and weeding. Maintaining the landscape of a historic house, however, presents distinct considerations. Removals and alterations must be evaluated carefully for their effect on the historic setting. The impact of the landscape on the fabric of the historic house needs to be considered. Historically accurate design features and plant materials can be maintenance intensive. In this chapter, the discussion will focus on maintaining an established yard, as well as making choices that are compatible with a historic house, and the owner's lifestyle and interest in gardening. For specific advice regarding appropriate design for various periods, reference books or a design professional with expertise in historic landscapes should be consulted.

THE FUNDAMENTAL HISTORIC CHARACTER OF THE SETTING

Every historic house has a setting that is as vital to its character as the fabric of its walls or the pitch of its roof. Unlike relatively stable architectural elements, many aspects of the setting are fluid—changing with the seasons and the times. With each new generation of occupants, a new function for the landscape might be perceived. Plant materials die and plant preferences may change. Thus, the carriage house may become a garage, the vegetable garden a spot for the swing set, and the clothes-drying area the site of a patio. The old elm might die, the hollyhocks might disappear, and the big lilac might be taken out to make room for a shed.

Each setting has some core characteristics—natural features, spatial relationships, or built elements—that do not change easily. These core characteristics are unique for every house—they might include a stream or view of the mountains, the relationship of the house to a street, the location and alignment of walks, old trees and other plant materials, and outbuildings and the spaces created by their placement.

Architectural style should influence landscape choices involving historic houses. Although there are no firm rules for landscaping each style, general trends in landscape design for a period and in a region can be applied. For instance, a nineteenth-century adobe house in California would have had a stark setting, with an absence of turf and ornamental plants but a few trees to provide shade. A Tudor Revival house of the 1920s might have achieved an inviting appearance of intimacy by incorporating a winding path, clusters of evergreens, and vine-covered walls. Above, the exuberant and varied fence border harmonizes with this late Queen Anne–style house.

The elements that are essential to the fundamental historic character of the landscape should be preserved and integrated with new elements. Usually a property owner can readily determine some core historic characteristics; however, sometimes the evidence is subtle—a nearly vanished path or a walkway revealed by the placement of the garage. Because many landscape elements are irreplaceable, nothing should be removed or greatly altered until the owner is convinced that its contribution to the landscape is not essential to historic character.

NEW CONSTRUCTION: DESIGN AND FABRIC

New construction often is necessary to increase enjoyment of the yard, enhance its historic nature, or facilitate maintenance. For example, chronic maintenance problems such as poor site drainage and inhospitable soil can be remedied by building retaining walls or raised beds. Problems with marauding wildlife (and neighborhood pets) and some safety concerns can be addressed with fencing. In some cases it is effective to screen or diminish a nonhistoric or utilitarian element or an undesirable view with fencing. Perhaps a patio or shed would add comfort or convenience.

The design of built components should be considerate of the historic nature of the property in form, material, and color. By placement and prominence on the landscape, they should not overwhelm historic elements. Exact duplication of historic elements can be reserved for museum-quality restorations; however, some reference to historic motifs or stylized versions of historic patterns can be effective. For example, an exact replica of a historic fence may require custom milling that would be cost prohibitive. Instead, a fence of a similar design and proportion can be built of readily available materials. Often, an honest expression of modern elements is best, for example as a reflection of modern needs or to accommodate modern utilities. Thus, outdoor security lighting does not have to resemble historic lamps mounted on period posts, nor does a screen around an air conditioner require a colonial appearance.

The fabric of new elements should blend with the house and other landscape elements. Look to the house for appropriate materials to use for landscape elements like paving, retaining walls, and raised beds. The house should provide a cue regarding the color, texture, and scale of materials to use in constructing landscape elements. Materials and techniques that have become popular in the late twentieth century, such as retaining-wall systems, should be avoided.

Consider historic references. If fieldstone was used historically for walls, it still may be a good choice. When choices are limited by a lack of materials or artisans, a complementary material or alternative construction methods that mimic the historic can be used. In place of fieldstone, a concrete retaining wall might be faced with a stone veneer.

ASSESSING THE LANDSCAPE

Assessing the natural and human-made features of the landscape always should precede a landscape restoration or rehabilitation, and it is the first step in de-

Steps should be taken to preserve historic landscape features, including plants and built elements such as fencing. They lend an extraordinary character to the landscape that has evolved over time.

Opposite:
Earlier occupants of a historic house often had different relationships with the yard than people do today. The backyard may have been a service area rather than an outdoor living space. The front yard or porch, in fact, was the preferred outdoor sitting area—a friendly way to meet and greet neighbors. Historically, the front porch became an extension of the living room during the summer, and sometimes was the most decorated part of the yard. Today's owners of historic houses should consider growing flowering plants in containers if garden flowers are too difficult or time consuming.

veloping a landscape maintenance plan. For a historic home, an important aspect of the assessment is determining the plants and landscape features that have historic significance or help define the building's historic character. It also should result in the identification of problems that need to be corrected, assets that enhance the landscape, elements to be screened, and conditions that affect the choice of plant materials. The process requires owners to think carefully about how the family wants to use the yard. An overriding consideration should be enhancing the historic character and maintaining a strong relationship between the house and the landscape.

Ideally, the inventory or assessment should be done with the assistance of a landscape professional. If the budget precludes this, the homeowner can make lists and sketches of the existing conditions and desired outcome. Several books are available to guide a homeowner through this process.[1] The point is to evaluate existing conditions and identify assets, problems, and needs before major changes are made.

It is important to understand the natural environment of the setting so that sound design decisions will be made and appropriate plants will be selected. A program of maintenance that will foster optimum health of the landscape and its components must be developed. An essential step is to evaluate the quality of the soil, which can then be amended to establish an optimum growing medium for specific situations (such as lawn or garden). Homeowners can test the pH, nitrogen, phosphorous, and potassium with home test kits purchased at garden centers. The kits usually provide general recommendations for treatment depending on the test results. More accurate and thorough tests can be conducted by soil-testing laboratories operated privately or by public agencies.

Assess the various exposures of the setting—areas of shade, sun, and partial shade—and the potential effect of existing wind patterns. Also look at the general health of the lawn and trees and shrubs, as well as the condition and content of beds. Check that the drainage patterns (from the house and through the lot) work effectively.

Finally, look for the presence of any historic elements that should be preserved and nonhistoric elements that may need to be removed or replaced. Owners may need the help of a historic-landscape specialist to determine the historical significance of landscape elements. If such expertise is not available, look for a qualified landscape professional who can at least appreciate historic elements. In this case, you as owner will need to help identify the site's historic character and components.

Problems that threaten the health of plants or that are dangerous should be taken care of immediately. Solutions for nonhazardous conditions should be determined in the planning stages. Look for damp areas due to poor drainage or runoff; thin or patchy lawn; too many weeds; overgrown or dead vegetation; limbs that overhang the house, garage, or patio; and too much shade. Check also for aesthetic weaknesses: unattractive views that may require screening or shabby architectural elements such as an unsightly retaining wall or shed. Also, look for functional problems: poor access between the house and yard or between the house and garage or driveway; lack of a compost area; lack of a play area or the presence of an unnecessary play area; or an inconvenient grade.

To make sure all needs are accommodated by a plan, determine how you want to use your yard, what is needed for comfort and enjoyment there, and spaces that need to be created or eliminated. It is equally important to consider needs related to maintaining the yard. Such considerations might include areas for sitting and eating, parking, and storage; spaces for favorite plants or specialty gardens (such as vegetable, herb, perennial, rose); lawn and/or paved spaces for play areas; and paths or other means to facilitate access. You may also need to consider placement of a compost area or a new septic system.

Every yard has some positive attributes; building on and preserving these assets are important aspects of the planning process. Existing vegetation can make an important contribution, whether mature trees, specimen plants (such as a flowering tree or shrub), or desirable collections of plant materials, such as groves, hedges, or flower beds. Your yard may provide gorgeous views or advantageous exposures or possess historic architectural features.

FOSTERING A HEALTHY ENVIRONMENT FOR A HISTORIC HOUSE

A house's setting should promote the health of its occupants and the health of the house itself. As much or more than newer architecture, historic buildings must be surrounded by a space that promotes conservation of the building fabric. The following three basic rules provide fundamental guidelines for promoting a healthy environment:

1. MAINTAIN GOOD DRAINAGE

Most homeowners know that keeping water away from a house is beneficial to the structure of the house and fosters comfort for its occupants. A damp house can result in dank conditions, odors, and discomfort for allergy-prone occupants. It can provide a good habitat for insects and breed mildew and mold, eventually leading to deterioration of the building's fabric. With the frequent presence of moisture, wooden components of the house can decay, and poured concrete foundations and mortar joints can begin to break down, providing entry points for insects, rodents, and more water. Outside, soggy conditions can result in challenging planting conditions.

DRAINAGE FROM THE HOUSE

Water shed from the roof can be the source of enormous amounts of moisture near the house. Except in arid climates, most houses have a system of gutters and downspouts to keep rainwater and melting snow from falling off the house in sheets and to carry water away from the house. Without gutters, or with clogged gutters, a trench can be created where the water falls from the roof. It can disturb plant growth and hold water that will work its way back toward the house. Well-maintained gutters with extensions from the downspouts should carry the roof runoff away from the house in a positive direction and an appropriate distance to allow continued drainage away from the house. The ground should slope away from a house to direct water away from it. Ideally, the slope should be gentle enough to allow some moisture absorption in the process of runoff. With steeper grades, less water will be absorbed, soil can be eroded, and vegetation may be difficult to establish.

As much water as possible should be absorbed on the site, and residual water should be directed toward the storm sewer system or dry well. The rate at which the discharge flows through the yard is influenced by the amount of runoff, degree of slope, type of soil, and presence of paving and plants.

DEALING WITH SLOPE

Some historic houses have been built at the base of or on a slope because of the sheltered conditions offered or simply because of the existing terrain. Over time, measures that were taken to keep water from running toward the house can break down (or perhaps they never were effective). The problem might have been dealt with originally by creating trenches or lower areas around the house to divert runoff, or by building into the slope and grading to encourage water to drain around one or both sides of the house.

The solution to runoff problems should begin by improving the grade, stabilizing it with plantings, and incorporating measures to divert water or slow runoff. In some situations, simply redistributing the existing soil to create a good slope will be sufficient. In other cases, soil will need to be added because over the years so much has been lost. Raised beds can be an effective means of controlling the grade around masonry buildings. The problem with this method on wooden buildings, however, is apparent.

Plants play an important role in stabilizing slopes by breaking the impact of falling water and utilizing available groundwater. Generally, plants that are lower to the ground are better at breaking the impact of falling water.

Improvements to a surface or subsurface drainage system might be needed, or a new system may need to be installed. Drainage tiles might be installed at the foundation or a French drain might be installed to handle surface runoff (see page 48). Terraces created by retaining walls can be the most effective means of treating a slope, both practically and aesthetically. They can slow runoff and provide a greater area for water absorption. By improving the planting area, terraces encourage plants to play a greater role in the drainage process. Usually, measures need to be taken to drain the groundwater that accumulates behind retaining walls. Weep holes in the wall will alleviate the pressure that could heave the wall forward. Their size and spacing depend on soil conditions and the size of the wall. A lateral drain behind the wall might also be required.

The scale and fabric of the walls should be in keeping with those of the house. Landscape timbers, large-scale boulders, and cast-concrete systems are not appropriate materials for handling grade changes in historic settings. Yet, because they can be the least-expensive choice, they are often favored. If at all, they should be used in a series of lower walls that can be concealed with plant materials instead of a single, higher wall. Generally, from an aesthetic and practical perspective, retaining walls should be less than three feet tall. The beds are easier to work from both sides and low walls can double as sitting space. If a series of terraces is needed to accommodate the slope, each should be at least three feet wide to provide a good planting bed.

REMOVING LARGE PLANTS

New drainage problems can be created when trees or shrubs with well-developed root systems are removed from the vicinity of the house. Roots help bind soil together and promote the infiltration of water into the soil, thus reducing runoff. The moisture in the soil is used by the plants, so the soil does not become overly saturated. The dynamic between roots and soil is lost when a tree dies or is removed and the roots stop functioning. The soil absorbs less water, and dries out. This drying is manifested by cracking on the soil surface, which will vary with the clay content of the soil (higher clay content leads to greater shrinking and cracking). Cracking also can occur in walks, walls, and foundations.

As roots break down, they add humus to the soil, which will promote soil stability. If a large plant or tree does have to be removed, enough good soil should be added to ameliorate settling, and a ground cover, shrub, or new tree should be planted in its place. At the very least, even if not replanted, the area surrounding the lost tree should be mulched so the soil will not dry excessively. A slow watering technique, such as the drip method, will allow better absorption of moisture.

2. KEEP VEGETATION AT BAY

There is no question that shrubs, flowers, and trees surrounding a house lend an attractive appearance. However, everyone has seen examples of "too much of a good thing." A house enshrouded in overgrown shrubs, trees, and vines simply looks unkempt. Too much vegetation creates an environment that can be unhealthy for the house and garden and uncomfortable for humans.

Vegetation that is overgrown, crowded, or too close to the house can limit the amount of circulating air and sun that reaches the house. The resulting damp, dark conditions can lead to moisture problems on and in the house. If the tree and shrub canopy is dense, limited sun will hit the ground plane, creating challenging conditions for many plants. Following are suggestions regarding trees, shrubs, and vines in the vicinity of historic houses.

TREES

Trees in a yard are almost always an asset. As the "bones" of a garden plan, they provide structure for other garden elements. Mature trees convey stateliness and a sense of age and stability to a property, and provide valuable shade. Well-placed trees in a yard can increase comfort inside and outside and can reduce heating and air-conditioning costs.[2] Attention should be paid to the health and vitality of all trees in the yard, but those at close range to the house require particular vigilance. If trees are diseased or decaying, they can harbor insects, such as carpenter ants, that thrive on damp, dead wood. The insects may find wooden portions of the house equally attractive.

Branches on trees with compromised health may be more susceptible to falling off, particularly during storms. In the process, they may injure people and damage the house and other plant materials. Homeowners should be careful to trim dead branches before this can happen. Even healthy tree limbs that overhang houses should be removed. The debris that drops on the roof can accelerate its aging and clog the gutters, heavy shade on the roof can lead to fungal growth, and limbs that fall directly on the roof can cause damage. New trees should be planted far enough away from the house to avoid future problems. Small trees should be no closer than eight feet and large trees should be fifteen to twenty feet from an outside wall.[3]

The root structure of a tree may be weakened by disease or age. If this is the case, the tree may be subject to suddenly falling over. A certified arborist should be consulted on a regular basis to examine old trees, particularly those that may be hazardous. Trees that pose dangers should be removed immediately.

SHRUBS

A house surrounded by shrubbery at its foundation has become the standard image of homeyness and proper attention to landscape detail. It has become an ingrained aesthetic that the base of a house needs to be softened or concealed with shrubs—so the house can float above a green base. It is hard to believe that this prevalent image is a fairly recent phenomenon, springing from a desire in the mid- to late nineteenth century to conceal raised foundations, and becoming endemic in the vast post–World War II subdivisions, where shrubs were used to provide a quick, economical landscape treatment.

Shrubs can effectively accent the foundation and should have a prominent role in most gardens. Rarely, however, should a shrub border completely engulf a foundation, with breaks only for the doors to the house. This does a disservice to the landscape and the architecture. It can be a tedious design and promote damp conditions. If shrubs are too tall, they can spoil the proportions of a house. Even fairly low shrubs can hide interesting details, for example a water table on a masonry house. A better practice is to use shrubs as accents around the house—at corners, angles, and doorways. Ground covers, perennials, and annuals, interspersed between the shrubs, can provide a low and airy base.

Shrubs can be reduced in size if they have become so overgrown that they eliminate light into the house, obscure too much of the house, or simply look ungainly. *Renewal pruning* can be used on some shrubs to allow them to assume a more attractive form and to maintain shrubs once a good shape is achieved. It is an effective procedure for most broad-leaf shrubs, but narrow-leaf evergreens may respond poorly. With renewal pruning, the oldest stems are removed at their base, which promotes the growth of new shoots and allows light to penetrate the interior of the shrub for denser foliage. Severe pruning should be done when the plant is still dormant in late winter. This timing should protect new growth from being killed by frost.[4]

The absence of foundation plantings, or shrubs, allowed an uninterrupted view of the entire architectural composition.

VINES

Vines may be part of the historic landscape fabric on or near the house, and they have practical and aesthetic benefits as well. If grown on the sunny side of a building, they have a cooling effect in the summer by shading the surface. Conversely, they warm the building in the winter by breaking the flow of air. The color and texture of vines can add year-round interest. Unfortunately, vines can cause damage to the house by holding moisture close to the walls and penetrating paint and mortar. The resulting conditions can lead to the growth of fungus and deterioration of the walls.

Whether vines are grown for historic, aesthetic, or practical reasons, the damage they cause can be minimized. The key is to use a system of support that allows airflow between the vines and the building. It is important to select a type of vine and a support system that work well together. The support structure must be strong enough for the weight of the vine yet must not damage the house. Wire for twining vines, like honeysuckle and wisteria, can be strung on anchors attached to the house. Clinging vines, like ivy and Virginia creeper, also can be given a trellis to cling to instead of the house walls. The trellis should be installed so that it can be pulled away and laid on the ground at any time to allow inspection and maintenance of the walls. Both systems allow air to circulate more freely between the house and vines and eliminate direct contact with the house.

3. ELIMINATE PEST HABITATS

Nature has evolved with the coexistence and codependence of creatures and plants, and the complete absence of creeping, crawling, and flying creatures in a yard could be devastating. Bees, for example, play a vital role in pollinating many plants. However, some creatures cause a great deal of damage by eating or burrowing, often descending in very large numbers. Many a garden has suffered from the presence of insects, rodents, deer, and other creatures with a proprietary interest in the garden they love to eat or dig. In terms of gardens, these creatures are pests.

Pests not only damage a garden, they also can damage a house and spoil the historic setting. Pests can best be controlled by eliminating the factors that make the yard an appealing habitat or food source. Pest control can be a very local issue, from an environmental and control perspective. Therefore, homeowners should seek specific information from pest-control specialists in their area. This discussion is limited to general advice regarding the control of insects, some small animals, and deer.

INSECTS

Bothersome or damaging insects usually are controlled by selecting plant varieties that are resistant and by using biological controls, either commercial pesticides or homemade remedies. Another approach is to minimize the insects' food source. Many insects, like flies, mosquitoes, and wasps, thrive on organic matter. To keep their food source at a minimum:

- Keep trash containers tightly covered—use lids that will stay on when tipped over by raccoons and dogs. Seal wet organic material in plastic bags.
- Keep the yard free of dog feces.
- Remove pet-food containers when the animal is finished eating.
- Keep gutters on the house clean. Debris in gutters can provide an attractive, damp habitat for many types of insects.
- Do not allow water to collect in containers, puddles, or pools on the ground (any standing water can serve as a breeding place for mosquitoes).
- Rake and remove leaves with *galls* (swelled growths caused by insects laying eggs or feeding) to reduce the insect population next year.

SMALL ANIMALS

Homeowners can inadvertently create ideal habitats for rodents and other small animals that damage gardens and may find their way into houses. Damage can be caused in all seasons as animals use plants for food or cover. Limit your yard's appeal as habitat:

- Remember woodpiles can provide rodent habitat and attract insects associated with decaying wood. Woodpiles should not be placed close to house walls where they can create damp conditions and allow the tenants they harbor close to the house. Wood that has decayed beyond usefulness as firewood should be removed from the yard.
- Brush should not be allowed to accumulate in piles. It can provide a habitat for rodents and other small animals, attract insects, and kill the plant materials it covers.
- Avoid dense and persistent vegetation near houses, which provide nesting places and cover. Vegetation that is a food source is particularly attractive.
- Do not include meat, dairy, or oily foods in compost piles because of their appeal to small animals. Other compost food scraps should be mixed into the center of the pile and buried several inches.

Some small animals will occupy a yard to be near appealing food sources. Take measures to discourage their access. For example, fences can discourage rabbits from gardens. A low, three-quarter-inch wire-mesh fence trenched into the soil should keep rabbits out. Later in the growing season, when other food sources become available, a decorative fence may do the job.

Mice, voles, and squirrels can be discouraged from gnawing the bark of young trees by wrapping the trunks with wire or plastic mesh. Keeping ground cover low and mulch minimal around trees will make the area a less attractive habitat.

In yards where squirrels are unwelcome, block their access to the bird feeder through strategic placement of the feeder and the installation of barriers. Several commercial barriers are available. Squirrels can be deterred from digging up recently planted flower bulbs by planting species they tend to avoid, such as daffodils, allium, and anemones. The bulb bed can also be covered with chicken wire weighted at the corners, which plants can grow through in the spring (they may need a little guidance). Wire mesh also can be used on flower and vegetable gardens to discourage squirrels.

Unlike many other small garden animals, moles eat insects, not garden plants. They can damage a garden mightily by tunneling through the soil to pursue grubs. Probably a range of techniques will need to be utilized to rid a garden of moles. Pesticides can kill the food source (and other good insects); barriers can be used to keep them out of special areas; they can be trapped or poisoned; and repellents are sometimes effective. Each of these techniques has its advantages and drawbacks. Homeowners should consult with local experts for advice on effective techniques for their area.

LARGE ANIMALS

Of the large animals that invade yards, deer especially can wreak havoc on gardens located in the vicinity of their habitat. Because of their size and, in many places, their large populations, deer can be one of the most difficult animals to discourage from the garden. Plant choice and barrier techniques can be used to make a yard less appealing and accessible to deer. Homemade or commercial sprays applied to leaves are intended to deter deer, but they are not foolproof and need to be reapplied frequently. Other homemade remedies, such as hanging human hair from trees (in mesh bags) or hanging bars of deodorant soap left in the wrapper, can be effective. Electric fences can provide a barrier. They should be four to five feet high, with wires spaced about eight inches apart. Consult with local experts for advice on deer-resistant plants and the best practices for discouraging deer in a given area.[5]

LANDSCAPING TO DETER FIRE

Many fires associated with old houses are linked to faulty wiring or other electrical problems. Fire also can come from outside sources—forest, brush, or range fires that begin in the yard or sweep through an area. With thoughtful landscape design, the area surrounding a house can serve as a barrier to fire, or at least minimize its intensity, spread, and speed. This practice often is described as *firescaping*. Although most commonly applied to western landscapes, where arid conditions and winds can fuel devastating wildfires, the technique can be applied to many parts of the country.

The landscape should be planted to minimize the amount of fuel available to an encroaching fire. Generally, vegetation should be planted in zones surrounding the house, the plants in each zone being progressively more fire-resistant as they are placed closer to the house. Fire-resistant trees and shrubs should comprise the outermost zone, with shrubs and perennials comprising the next zone. A greenbelt of fire-resistant ground cover should surround the house, and the most fire-resistant plants available should be planted next to the house.[6]

In wooded neighborhoods throughout the country, residents would be wise to take steps to protect their homes from forest fires. Fires can be deterred by keeping brush and vegetation off the house, cleaning up plant litter in the yard, and pruning and trimming dead growth. Mulching and watering during dry spells keep soils moist as an added deterrent. Plants with a low oil content and moisture-holding foliage and stems can help discourage fire. Native plants often are a good choice.[7]

ESSENTIAL MAINTENANCE

An attractive garden—whether the setting for an old or new house—requires routine maintenance to make it thrive and retain its healthy appearance. Garden chores naturally fall into seasonal patterns. Most tasks, if done at the optimum time, contribute to the improved appearance and health of plants, promote disease resistance, cut down on plant loss, and minimize work later.

The extent of maintenance needed on a property and the time needed to accomplish maintenance tasks is variable. Homeowners must assess their level of interest and time available for garden maintenance in the planning stages. The garden can lose its charm if owners feel overly burdened with its upkeep. The property owner can control the level of maintenance in a yard to a certain extent through design and plant selection. Environmental factors, such as soil and climate conditions, should affect plant choices. The placement of plants in the yard depends on wind patterns, light, and water availability. To decrease the need for extensive soil amending and seasonal plant protection, it is easiest to select native plant materials or species well adapted to local conditions.

If a lot is large, consider keeping a portion of it in a state that reflects the natural habitat of the area, such as woods or prairie. Although natural areas are not maintenance free, typically they require less intensive work once they are established. Managers of natural areas need to decide if succession will be allowed to proceed naturally or if aggressive management policies need to be implemented to maintain a certain population of plants. Large lots are amenable to subdivision into sections, usually with the area closest to the house often the most de-

Increasingly, homeowners are minimizing lawn in favor of perennial plantings. The garden in this yard presents an array of textures and colors that harmonizes with the Queen Anne style.

Hosta provides an appealing alternative to foundation shrubs.

signed and requiring the most maintenance. Outlying parts can incorporate the native vegetation and be less formal, less detailed, and less work.

Garden beds—whether flower, herb, rose, or vegetable—require maintenance throughout the year except in the coldest months, but they contribute enormously to a landscape. Besides color and texture, they are an excellent means of decreasing lawn area and increasing plant diversity. Eliminating some lawn area can reduce the use of fertilizers containing nitrogen and phosphorus that, as a component of runoff, can cause environmental pollution. Because most beds require regular upkeep, homeowners should decide how much time they are willing to spend on this maintenance task (versus mowing a larger lawn area).

The following section presents routine garden tasks for each season. Generally, these tasks pertain to many parts of the United States; however, because of inevitable regional variation, consult local experts, particularly on fertilizing and watering. Through trial and error, homeowners will discover what works best in their own yard.

FALL

• *Lawn:* Fall is the single most important time to fertilize cool-season grasses (Kentucky bluegrass, Fescue). Apply fertilizer after the average daily temperatures are 50 degrees Fahrenheit. Warm-season grasses (Bermuda, zoysia, St. Augustine) should be fertilized lightly in fall and spring. Fall is also the time to plant cool-season grass seed or lay sod; aerate compacted areas; rake to remove leaves and dethatch grass; apply lime to acidic soils and sulfur to alkaline soils; and mow regularly as long as grass is growing.

• *Trees and Shrubs:* Prune fruit trees after leaves have fallen. Protect lower bark of tree trunks from rodent and rabbit damage by wrapping with wire or plastic mesh. Trim back tall roses and mulch after several frosts. In northern regions, protect roses from frost with cones or burlap.

The aloe garden at Lotusland in Santa Barbara, California, demonstrates an effective use of arid-climate plants, which are low maintenance.

Fertilize trees and shrubs, particularly those that were not fertilized in the spring, with bonemeal or rock phosphate. If nitrogen fertilizer is needed, apply late in the fall or wait until spring. Where winters are severe, spray antidesiccant to protect tender flower buds.

Plant peonies and bare-root roses. Plant deciduous trees and shrubs. Early fall is the optimum time to plant evergreens.

• *Perennial and Annual Flowers, Herbs, and Vegetables:* Remove and compost annual flower and vegetable plants. Check the pH of the soil in beds and amend as needed with organic matter, lime, sulfur, or fertilizer (but not nitrogen fertilizers).

Plant perennials and biennials, but mulch only after the ground freezes to protect plants from severe cold. Cover mums and other fall bloomers at night so they will last longer. Continue to water if conditions are dry.

Plant spring flowering bulbs and some onions, garlic, and allium. Dig and store tender bulbs, corms, and tubers, such as gladiolus and dahlias. Divide perennials that seem crowded, including iris rhizomes, lilies, and daylilies. Sow annual rye or other cover crops in vegetable gardens. In some climates, cool-tolerant vegetables, such as lettuce, can be planted in the fall.

• *Other:* Clean gutters and downspouts after leaves have dropped. Drain gasoline from mowers and other power tools, and run the engine out of gas. This is a good time to change spark plugs and oil, clean air filters and blade housings, and lubricate cylinders of mowers and other equipment. Turn the compost pile and add debris from garden cleanup.

WINTER

• *Trees and Shrubs:* Prune trees, including fruit trees, and remove dead, broken, and diseased branches. Prune summer flowering shrubs and evergreens, except pines (see Summer), at the end of winter, just before spring growth begins. Remove canes of everbearing raspberries, blackberries, currants, and gooseberries.

SPRING

- *Lawn:* Fertilize poor lawns of cool-season grasses at the first sign of new growth; fertilize warm-season grasses with 50 percent of their annual dose. Apply preemergence herbicide if crabgrass was a problem the previous year.

Rake grass to remove thatch, and seed bare spots. Dig and pull weeds when the ground is damp, or spray with a selective herbicide.

- *Trees and Shrubs:* Remove dead limbs and branches on trees, except for oaks, which should never be pruned between April and September. Prune spring-blooming shrubs after flowers fade.

Fertilize shade trees with signs of poor health in early spring. Plant deciduous trees and evergreens.

- *Perennial and Annual Flowers, Herbs, and Vegetables:* Clean leaves and debris out of beds and remove winter mulch from perennials and roses. Till cover crops in vegetable beds before they go to seed.

Get a head start on weed control in beds: pull perennial weeds, like violets, before they set seed; remove annual weeds as they begin to appear, and stir up the soil to expose seeds. Divide perennials that were not thinned in the fall. Plant new perennials and annuals. Apply organic mulches (such as bark, cocoa-bean hulls, or pine needles) to control weeds, retain moisture, and cool soil temperatures.

- *Other:* Clean gutters and downspouts on house. Service lawn mower and other power equipment as needed.

SUMMER

- *Lawn:* Water as needed to promote grass and discourage weeds; water in the morning until the soil is moist four to six inches down. (The time to achieve this penetration will vary with different soils.) Keep cool-season lawns mowed at about a three-inch height and warm-season lawns at two inches or shorter. Dig and pull or spray weeds.

- *Trees and Shrubs:* In early summer, trim about two-thirds of new growth on pines. During midsummer, evergreens other than some pines can be pruned again. Some evergreens also can be planted in summer, but water demands must be met.

- *Perennial and Annual Flowers, Herbs, and Vegetables:* Check soil moisture and plant symptoms to determine when watering is needed. Keep beds weeded. Fertilize flowers until mid-August as needed in response to soil tests and poor performance.

Although equipment, frequency, and standards have changed over the years, cut grass has long been considered important to the well-maintained yard.

MINIMIZING MAINTENANCE

Plant choices and the manner in which plants are tended can have a great bearing on the maintenance level of a yard. Low-maintenance plants are hardy in the region, well adapted to local soil conditions, disease and mildew resistant, and in need of little supplemental watering. Not surprisingly, native plants are typically a low-maintenance choice. Some plants with otherwise low-maintenance characteristics are "messy," however. They drop fruit or seeds. Their foliage is dense and tends to mat when it falls, or they have weak wood so limbs break easily. Because cleaning up after messy plants can take much of a gardener's time, even native plants should be screened for the work they may entail.

The style in which plants are maintained and the design of a yard have maintenance consequences too. Formally trimmed hedges require more tending than shrubs allowed to assume a more natural form. The juncture of beds and lawn takes longer to maintain if it requires hand clipping. Some plants and garden features require quite a bit of maintenance in the first few years but very little once they are well established. Usually the long-term savings in time is worth the additional work in the first years. Assuming that plants and landscape treatments under consideration are well suited to the soil, exposure, and climate, those with a high level of maintenance include shaped trees and shrubs, especially topiary; roses (some varieties and in some climates); fruit trees; recently installed perennial gardens (first two to three years); lawns; and vegetable gardens. Medium-maintenance features include well-established perennial gardens filled with sun-loving flowers and herbs and their shade-tolerant cousins; recently established ground covers, such as periwinkle, pachysandra, or ajuga; deciduous trees; and annual flowers and herbs. Among low-maintenance choices are well-established ground covers; evergreen trees; and drought-tolerant plants (if tolerant of the climate).

Various other techniques can be used to decrease landscape maintenance and promote environmental health, with attractive results that reflect the historic character of the house. Implementing any of the five practices suggested here will help control the level of maintenance.

1. DECREASE LAWN AREA
Replacing lawn with perennial beds and ground covers will increase the work in the first couple of years, but plants well adapted to the area, with few watering and fertilizer requirements, can require less maintenance than lawn when well established. Pay particular attention to mulching and watering these plants in the first few years. Shrub borders also can be a substitute for some of the lawn, or an area or path can be attractively paved.

2. ADD COLOR WITH TREES AND SHRUBS
Flowers should not be the only source of color in a garden. Flowering trees and shrubs should be used to provide color in various seasons, texture, and seasonal scents. The color from trees and shrubs comes from leaf color, flowers, fruit, seeds, and bark. Each season brings a different appearance: plants change dramatically with dormancy, new and mature growth, and with seasonal changes in patterns of light and shadow. A mix of evergreen and deciduous plants provides wonderful diversity in texture and color throughout the year.

3. INCORPORATE PRACTICES OF XERISCAPING
Xeriscaping refers to a landscape plan designed to decrease the amount of watering required. An important element of Xeriscaping is the use of plants native to the area. Historically, native plants were readily available, affordable, and proven survivors that adjusted naturally to the setting of a house. Often, they came with the property and constituted its initial landscaping. Because they are well adapted to the soil and climate in which they naturally occur, native plants require minimal fertilizing, winter protection, and watering. Nonnative low-water plants also can work well if soil and climate conditions are amenable.

Besides plant choice, ample mulching and reduced lawn are keys to successful Xeriscaping. The practice also suggests grouping plants by water needs. For example, plants that require the most moisture should be grouped where they naturally receive more water. Supplemental watering should be facilitated by a water-saving technique, such as a drip irrigation system.

Water conservation is an issue at times in all parts of the country. In areas that are not naturally arid, much of an inappropriately planted landscape can be destroyed in drought years. Several books have been written on gardening to conserve water. Information on drought-tolerant plants also may be available from extension agents, other state organizations, or garden retail centers.[8]

4. Mulch

Mulch is a covering applied to beds and around trees and shrubs to help control weeds, retain moisture, enhance ground temperatures, and reduce erosion. Around trees, mulch can eliminate injury caused by mowing. Common organic and inert mulches include bark, pine needles, cocoa beans, gravel or pebbles, peanut hulls, and leaves. Synthetic mulches are various weights of plastic or polypropylene. The synthetic mulches typically are used to warm the soil in spring in cold climates or to underlay organic or inert mulches in permanent plant beds. Usually, mulch is applied two to three inches deep; those that tend to mat, such as leaves, should be only about one inch deep. Mulch should be shallower around young plants.

The type of mulch selected should be based on the effect on available nutrients, availability, and aesthetic preference. The time of application is based on regional variation: in cold climates, mulch should be applied after the first frost and renewed in the spring before the ground gets too dry. In warm climates, mulch usually is applied in the spring.

5. Take Advantage of Available Tools and Technology

Labor-saving tools and chemicals are constantly being developed for the home gardener. Jobs can be done more efficiently with the right tool for the job, and certain chores can be virtually eliminated with new developments. Basic to efficient gardening are a stable garden cart or wheelbarrow; sharp pruning shears and small saw; a shovel, spade, rake, hoe, and spading fork; a hand trowel, small fork, and cultivator; a lawn mower; and equipment to water all parts of the garden.

Proper watering equipment eliminates a great deal of work and produces superior results. An automated sprinkler system can get water to a garden on a regular schedule without the need to drag hoses through the yard. Drip irrigation systems installed in nonlawn areas can promote the health of plants, conserve water, and ease the watering task.

Mowing is also less onerous with well-maintained equipment. Regular mowing to the height recommended for the climate and type of grass helps deter weed growth and eliminates the need to rake. Cut grass left on the lawn is a good source of lawn nutrition. Mulching lawn mowers cut the grass into smaller pieces so the cut grass will filter down and decay more quickly.

The setting of a historic property presents landscape challenges unlike those related to newer lots. The first is to complement the historic design and internal spaces of the house. Another is to fit today's preferences and needs within a space designed to accommodate different activities. A third is to deal with mature and large-scale plant materials. Each of these challenges presents special maintenance consequences.

Developing a maintenance schedule will help clarify the work implications of a landscape plan and should be integral to the planning process for a historic setting. Modifications can then be made according to time constraints and the degree of interest in landscape maintenance. For example, if an owner is daunted by the amount of time it takes to tend several large flower beds, ground cover or a shrub border could reduce the area. A maintenance schedule can also be a helpful guide for an existing landscape by establishing a checklist of tasks to accomplish.

With some forethought, both those who enjoy gardening and lavish much of their spare time on their yard and those who simply want to create a historically appropriate setting for their old house can achieve a compatible level of maintenance. In either case, the overall goal should be to create a setting that enhances the health of the house and to maintain the yard so it contributes to the health of the immediate setting and wider environment.

Notes

1. One of the best sources for historic properties is Charles A. Birnbaum, ASLA, Preservation Brief No. 36: Protecting Cultural Landscapes: Planning Treatment and Management of Historic Landscapes (Washington, D.C.: National Park Service, Preservation Assistance Division, 1994).

2. For further guidance regarding the assets of shade, see Tree City USA Bulletin, no. 21, The National Arbor Day Foundation, 100 Arbor Avenue, Nebraska City, NE 68410.

3. For further guidance on tree spacing, see Tree City USA Bulletin, no. 4, The National Arbor Day Foundation, 100 Arbor Avenue, Nebraska City, NE 68410.

4. Regional guidelines are available for the appropriate pruning of specific shrubs. A good guide to pruning common shrubs in the northern United States is E. R. Hasselkus, "Caring for Deciduous Shrubs," Publication A1771, Cooperative Extensions, University of Wisconsin-Extension, 1996. It can be ordered from Cooperative Extension Publications, 630 W. Mifflin Street, Madison, WI 53703-2636; phone: (608) 262-3346.

5. Kathy Piper, "Living with Deer," Flower and Garden (October–November 1993): 35. This article lists trees, shrubs, bulbs, vines, annuals, and perennials that do not appeal to deer.

6. See City of Santa Barbara Firescapes Demonstration Garden, City of Santa Barbara Fire Department.

7. See Carol L. Rice and Susan D'Alcamo, "Natives to Reduce Fire Hazard," Horticulture (October 1992): 18.

8. The Rancho Santa Ana Botanic Garden has published a bibliography that lists hundreds of sources concerned with landscaping to conserve water. The book, published in June 1990, is available by writing to the botanic garden at 1500 North College Avenue, Claremont, CA 91711-3101; or by calling (909) 625-8767.

FIRE PROTECTION

MARILYN E. KAPLAN

Historic houses are vulnerable to damage due to the predominance of flammable building materials used in their construction. These buildings are best protected from the ravages of fire by eliminating hazards and rigorously applying appropriate housekeeping techniques. Ironically, most fires in historic structures occur during construction.

Fire can damage a site in minutes and destroy it within a few hours. Thus, effective fire protection is essential for a historic house. Such protection should combine architectural and engineering solutions, which entail some addition or physical change to a building, and careful management and maintenance, which are all too often overlooked. Given the uniqueness of each historic property, specific approaches to fire protection vary according to budget, the significance of the building and its contents, and the building's configuration.

In the twentieth century, the field of fire protection generally focuses on saving lives before property. For the historic house, where the protection of irreplaceable property is also important, the goal is to provide the highest degree of life safety possible *and* retain historic materials and character. To achieve this ideal, the unique physical characteristics and particular fire risks of the historic house must be considered. This approach is necessarily different from that practiced on new construction, where construction materials and building configurations are highly standardized.

FIRE: IDENTIFYING THE RISKS

Each historic house presents a unique set of fire risks that can best be addressed following an analysis of the fire risks and evaluation of the impact of potential improvements. Ideally, a fire-protection engineer should conduct the analysis. Since most fire-protection engineers do not have expertise in historic preservation, a preservation architect or other historic preservation specialist should also be part of the consultant team. In the absence of these professionals, private homeowners and small-house museums can make use of the local fire department and reputable suppliers of fire-protection equipment; relevant publications and checklists can also be of assistance (see Further Reading).

Most historic houses were built with combustible materials and contain flammable finishes, wood paneling, tapestries, furnishings, paintings, and books with inherently high fire loads. Fire is most often caused by defective or overloaded electrical equipment, construction operations, careless or illicit smoking, or arson. The combustibility of dry construction materials, the lack of fire and smoke barriers between rooms and through floors, the presence of concealed routes in wall and ceiling cavities, and the low fire-resistance ratings of floors, walls, and doors all contribute to the rapid spread of fire. Monumental open spaces and stairways, and complex networks of stairs and uncompartmented corridors that are inadequately sized or configured, create opportunities for fire spread as well as obstacles to safe building evacuation. The location of the building can also present additional hazards: sites in remote locations may have poor or unreliable water supplies and be far from the fire service, while those in urban areas may be prone to arson and vandalism.

Historic houses, their barns, and other ancillary structures may also be susceptible to lightning. Particularly vulnerable are those structures located on high ground in rural or beach areas. Lightning can ignite wood, splinter or shear structural members, blow out window glass, cause trees and other objects to split or become dislodged, melt holes in metal roofs and decks, and damage electrical equipment. Objects can be struck by lightning more than once, and in rapid succession. A building need not be hit to be damaged: a strike at overhead electrical wires can incur extensive damage to adjacent structures.

Due to budget constraints and aesthetic and conservation concerns, historic houses often contain antiquated or overloaded mechanical and electrical equipment. Certain elements of the building's electrical system can be particularly hazardous: deteriorated insulation and conductors at ceiling fixtures, deteriorated receptacles with loose connections or lack of grounding connectors, and circuits that are inadequately protected from overload. Additionally, many historic houses have not been upgraded with adequate fire-protection systems.

CREATING A FIRE-SAFE ENVIRONMENT

In order to provide effective protection for the historic building, it is vitally important that the historic-house owner or site supervisor have a complete familiarity with every aspect of the house's structure, contents, and systems, and a carefully considered plan for maintaining them (see Getting to Know Your House and Establishing a Maintenance Program). On this basis, fire safety can be achieved by a combination of building improvements, in some cases mandated by building and fire codes, and the installation of fire-protection systems and observance of sound inspection and maintenance practices.

BUILDING AND FIRE CODES

Code compliance can be problematic for historic buildings constructed long ago with materials and configurations that differ from the standardized requirements of new construction. Thus, most building and fire codes are applicable only to new construction and rehabilitation projects undergoing a change of occupancy or a substantial financial investment, or to houses that are open to the public. Few building-code requirements are retroactive, with the exception of those related to fire protection.

Most states and municipalities in the United States follow one of the three model building codes: the *Standard Building Code* in the Southeast; the *Uniform Building Code* in the West; and the *Basic Building Code* in the Northeast. Each code currently has special provisions for existing buildings: the *Standard Existing Building Code*, the *Uniform Code for Building Conservation*, and chapter 34 of the *National Building Code*, respectively. The states of Georgia, Massachusetts, California, and Wisconsin, among others, have adopted separate historic preservation codes or special requirements to address the unique circumstances faced by historic structures.

States and municipalities that adopt the model codes can amend the requirements to address local conditions and concerns. As a result, great inconsistencies between codes exist. However, currently being developed, under the aegis of the International Code Council, is a national-building code, the International Building Code, anticipated to be adopted by all states when published in 2000. Additional requirements for existing buildings can be found in the National Fire Protection Association's (NFPA) *NFPA 101, Code for Safety to Life in Buildings and Structures*, and the *NFPA 101A, Guide on Alternative Approaches to Life Safety*.

Fire marshals or code officials charged with local enforcement are most often the arbiters of the conflict between preservation goals and prevailing safety standards. These officials are limited by the absence of generally accepted methods to predict the performance of a building in a catastrophic situation and the lack of accepted standards of practice with which to evaluate alternative code solutions. Their work, when focused on the historic building, is also hampered by the codes' focus on life safety and slant toward new construction principles. Moreover, historic preservation is neither the primary mission of code officials nor a value reflected in most code documents. Even if

Following the destruction by fire of his previous home in Cazenovia, New York, John Lincklaen constructed this mansion between 1807 and 1808 using construction materials and techniques intended to produce a fire-resistant building. The mansion, named Lorenzo, is built entirely of brick, and has two-inch plaster ceilings and iron-lined fireplaces. The building is now owned by the New York State Office of Parks, Recreation, and Historic Preservation.

A decorative iron-lined fireplace, one of the fire-resistant features at Lorenzo.

supportive of preservation, the code official is often granted limited discretion by the regulations to vary from the code. The code official may also be concerned with the precedent-setting implications of each decision and personal-liability exposure, an anxiety fed by the litigious construction climate.

Some code conflicts can be remedied by modifications likely to have minimal aesthetic impact, for example, changing the direction of a door swing or introducing of exit lights. Unfortunately, many code-required modifications related to fire protection mandate the removal or alteration of historic materials and spaces in a manner that would compromise the architectural and historic integrity of the building. For example, the codes' requirements to limit the spread of fire and maintain safe means of egress in a monumental open and unprotected stairway present no simple, aesthetically acceptable remedy.

A wide-open attic is a place where a fire can spread rapidly undetected. Fire-safety practices may include the construction of fire-rated partitions or the installation of detectors. In this example, a sprinkler system has been installed.

In addition to physical conflicts, regulatory discrepancies can develop when a project must comply with both building and fire codes and local, state, or federal preservation guidelines. Most often, the preservation guidelines used are *The Secretary of the Interior's Standards for the Treatment of Historic Properties* (Secretary's Standards), written by the Department of the Interior to provide guidance on appropriate preservation treatments (see also Getting to Know Your House). Building codes and the Secretary's Standards are different in their philosophy and approach. The codes provide exact specifications for building construction or performance; the Secretary's Standards use nontechnical language to outline a philosophy for the appropriate treatment of historic resources. Glaring contradiction exists between the code requirement that mandates the removal of original materials and the preservation guidelines that require their retention. Resolving such conflict can be difficult when multiple regulatory entities, such as the building- and/or fire-code official, the local historic-review commission, the state historic preservation agency, and one or more federal preservation agencies are involved.

FIRE SEPARATIONS

The basic principles of fire protection are to eliminate fire spread while providing safe evacuation of occupants and safe access for the fire service. To accomplish this, areas of a building can be separated by the installation of fire-resistant barriers at walls, ceilings, and floors; fire dampers in ducts and chases; and fire stopping within walls and attic areas. A wide range of modern fire-stopping materials for large and small openings are available to help create fire-resistant compartments within the building. Regulations designed to eliminate fire spread between buildings include setback requirements in zoning and building ordinances and specifications mandating the use of fire-resistant materials at exterior walls. Guidance on the effective fire ratings of materials and systems no longer commonly used, first published by HUD as *Volume 8: Fire Ratings of Archaic Materials and Assemblies* of its *Rehabilitation Guidelines*, is now included in *NFPA 914.*

FIRE-RETARDANT COATINGS

Flame-retardant coatings have existed since the Romans applied mixtures of limestone and loam to building materials to minimize fire spread. Now applied through impregnation or surface application, flame-retardant treatments are used to hinder fire development or smother a fire. In a historic building, the use of a fire-retardant material impregnated at the factory is generally limited to applications where new wood is used.

Most commonly used on historic buildings are *intumescent* coatings, a type of fire-retardant coating that melts when in contact with heat and forms a carbon char that insulates and protects the wood underneath. Another coating often used is a retardant made of antimony oxide, which cannot be used in moist environments. A number of surface coatings can be applied on-site by brush or spray. Some intumescent coatings require overpainting to minimize their sensitivity to moisture; up to two coats of conventional paint can be used over the intumescent coat without a loss of flame retardancy. These coatings are more expensive and less readily available than conventional paints. A further disadvantage is that coatings damaged by sawing or scraping require reapplication.

LIGHTNING PROTECTION

The most conventional approach to lightning protection is to mount grounded rods or masts (air terminals) at the highest point of a building and to attach these to copper or aluminum conductors that connect the terminals with each other and to the ground. The conductors are placed along ridges and edges of sloping and flat roofs and extend vertically to the ground. With the exception of building features such as spires and poles, most structures have at least two vertical down conductors, usually placed at diagonal corners to each other.

Grounding arrangements depend on soil conditions: the conductor can be extended into the ground, or, when the building is complex or the conditions are not ideal, extensive designs with wire networks or concrete-encased electrodes can be used. The location of water pipes and other metallic elements, the ground resistance, and the likelihood of people or animals being near the ground electrode during a storm are factors in determining optimum placement. Other means of providing lightning protection consider electrical bonding, surge suppression, and circuit-design techniques. In lightning-prone areas, consider lightning protection for trees that overhang the building or have historic significance.

The design and installation of any system should be undertaken by reputable contractors following the *NFPA 78 Lightning Protection Code.* Proper maintenance is critical, as rods can break, corrode, or be stolen. Lightning-protection features should not be used for other purposes, such as antennas or flagpoles.

FIRE DETECTION, ALARM, AND SUPPRESSION

The selection of a protection system must be based on the fire-safety objectives established for the individual historic structure. Generic solutions do not provide adequate protection and are particularly ill suited for the historic house where the aesthetic and physical impact on historic materials are of primary concern. The system must be adequate to the building risk, be relatively easy to operate and maintain, and have a low false-alarm rate. To the extent possible, equipment in historic buildings should be invisible and not detract from the historic character. One exception is the equipment that must be visible and easily accessible in case of emergency, such as manual call boxes from which a building occupant can sound an alarm or indicator panels that communicate a fire's location to security and firefighting personnel.

The most critical stage of a fire is the initial moments. Detection and alarm systems are designed to provide the earliest possible warning for initiating fire-suppression efforts and for evacuating building occupants. The basic components of an alarm and detection system are initiating devices (detectors or manual call boxes); control and indicating equipment; a primary power supply, usually connected to the local utility; emergency backup power provided by a

---

FIRE-PREVENTION FACTORS

HEAT SOURCES
- Fixed equipment
- Portable equipment
- Torches and other tools
- Smoking materials and associated lighting implements
- Explosives
- Natural causes
- Exposure to other fires

FORMS AND TYPES OF IGNITABLE MATERIALS
- Building materials
- Interior and exterior finishes
- Contents and furnishings
- Stored materials and supplies
- Trash, lint, and dust
- Combustible or flammable gases or liquids
- Volatile solids

FACTORS THAT BRING HEAT AND IGNITABLE MATERIAL TOGETHER
- Arson
- Misuse of heat source
- Misuse of ignitable material
- Mechanical or electrical failure
- Design, construction, or installation deficiency
- Error in operating equipment
- Natural causes
- Exposure

PRACTICES THAT CAN AFFECT PREVENTION SUCCESS
- Housekeeping
- Security
- Education of occupants
- Control of fuel type, quantity, and distribution
- Control of heat-energy sources

From *Fire Protection Handbook*, 18th ed., National Fire Protection Association, Quincy, Massachusetts.

storage battery and/or generator; the alarm-indicating appliance; and wiring, or the capability of transmitting an alarm to the fire department by radio, either directly or via a remote station. Wiring connects the initiating device to alarm-indicating appliance circuits, to which local alarms (bells, horns, speakers) and/or off-premises alarms are connected. In some cases, interface with other building equipment, such as air-conditioning, door-release units, or elevators, is provided. The control panel, the heart of the system, provides twenty-four-hour monitoring.

The control panel must be tolerant of interference yet intelligent enough to identify most false alarms—a characteristic expected of all fire-protection equipment. Upon notification from a sensor device, a silent or audible alarm is generated. The alarm can be transferred to an off-site location from which the fire service is notified; it can also activate an automatic-suppression system or cause building occupants to initiate manual fire extinguishing.

Fire-detection and alarm systems are defined by the complexity of their control unit. A *conventional system*, for small and medium-size installations, uses copper wiring installed in a closed loop for each zone circuit to provide basic alarm and supervisory-signal information. Most modern systems are *microprocessor based*, which is similar to the conventional system but with additional features, including smoke-detector alarm verification and identification of the fire's location within one of the building's established zones. *Addressable multiplex systems* provide even more detailed information. In these systems, each detection device has its own address unit and identification code, so that the exact location of an alarm can be identified immediately. *Addressable analog multiplex systems*, also known as *smart computer-based systems*, are similar, except that the smoke and heat detectors are connected to analog devices that send continuous information to the control panel.

Wireless systems use battery-powered initiating devices and radio signals to link detectors and manual stations with control equipment. These can be used where hardwiring is infeasible or undesirable. Detectors contain a battery-powered transmitter that sends alarm signals or signals indicating fault notification or low-battery warning. Installation of a wireless system involves no wiring, minimal drilling, and no follow-up cosmetic repairs; detectors are simply installed to a backplate that is attached to the wall.

DETECTORS

Detection units recognize the fire signatures of smoke, flame, or heat. They must be selected for the specific fire risk (such as grease fires in a kitchen or electrical fires caused by overloaded circuits), the available firefighting facilities and anticipated speed of response of the fire service, the type and quantity of fuel load in the room, the possible ignition sources, the volume and configuration of the space, the significance of the space and its collections, and the fire-protection objective to be achieved. Detector selection must also consider ambient environmental conditions that could cause false alarms, the owner's tolerance of such alarms, budget, and aesthetic concerns regarding placement and appearance.

Heat detectors, the first and least expensive detectors available, have been used since the nineteenth century. They have the lowest rate of false alarm but are the slowest to respond to a fire. Heat detectors are most appropriate for small confined spaces, directly over a hazard where a rapidly spreading, high-heat fire could occur, where the speed of detection is not critical, or where environmental conditions prohibit other detection types. Heat detectors are either fixed-temperature units, which respond when the operating element reaches a predetermined temperature, or rate-of-rise detectors, which respond when the temperature rises at a rate exceeding a predetermined value. Some combination detectors incorporate both fixed-temperature and rate-of-rise principles.

Smoke detectors provide earlier warning of fire than heat detectors, since in most fires measurable amounts of smoke are produced prior to measurable amounts of heat. Smoke detectors respond to both visible and invisible smoke particles and are generally more expensive than heat detectors. *Ionization-type* smoke detectors have the fastest response to open flames, while *photoelectric* smoke detectors are best used where smoldering fires are anticipated, although these are extremely sensitive to tobacco smoke. The several types of photoelectric smoke detectors work on either light-obscuring, light-scattering, or cloud-chamber smoke-detection principles. *Air-sampling* detectors use pumps or fans to draw air samples through small wires or pneumatic tubes that protrude slightly through a small hole in a ceiling or ornate plaster decoration, to a remotely located sampling chamber. Special applications include smoke detectors installed in air ducts and detectors that automatically close hold-open devices on smoke doors.

Infrared- and *ultraviolet-flame* detectors are line-of-sight detectors that respond to radiant energy. They have an extremely fast response time, although false-alarm rates can be high due to their sensitivity. Flame-detection units are relatively expensive. They provide excellent protection where flammable vapors or dusts are usually present and are commonly used in high-hazard industrial areas. Infrared-flame detectors are valuable in high ceiling spaces, where they can be installed high on the wall in order to minimize the visual impact a ceiling-mounted unit would have.

CHOICE AND PLACEMENT OF DETECTORS

Most smoke and heat detectors are available as *spot detectors,* which detect fire at a specific point within a volume of space, or *linear detectors,* which use wires, pneumatic tubes, and photoelectric beams to define a line through the space. Both spot and linear detectors can be mounted on a ceiling or on a sidewall surface near the ceiling. The light transmitter and receiver of linear detectors can be located at corners or opposite ends of a room and are generally unobtrusive in large rooms where a high decorative or vaulted ceiling exists. For smaller rooms or spaces with unusual conditions, linear detectors that contain the transmitter and receiver in a single unit are available. The most unobtrusive detection units are the air-sampling type, although other low-profile designs and special finishes are increasingly available.

Photoelectric smoke detectors are often used in egress routes and rooms opening to them, in particular those containing sleeping accommodations. They are also well suited for use in large open spaces. These and other smoke detectors are not recommended in or close to kitchens, bathrooms, laundry rooms, or boiler rooms due to the possibility of false alarm.

While most detectors are located at ceilings, installation at upper wall areas is also possible. In both cases, detectors are placed at least four inches from the corner of the wall and ceiling intersection. Spot detectors are generally placed at the center of the ceiling or at regular intervals on a grid according to manufacturers' recommendations. Heat detectors are also installed in a grid pattern; closer spacing can decrease response time or accommodate high or irregular ceilings. The placement of smoke detectors installed on a grid may require modification to accommodate prevailing air currents. The placement of smoke detectors is critical since in an air-conditioned or ventilated building, stratified smoke can be diluted from air-supply diffusers before reaching the detector. The location of line-of-sight detectors, in particular flame-detection units, is also critical since their function can be compromised by opaque or solid obstructions.

Wiring for detection and alarm systems is usually protected in concealed, mineral-insulated copper-sheathed cable or, in larger buildings, metal raceways. The feasibility of concealed wiring may determine the location of the manual stations and detectors. When no alternatives to exposed cable exist, custom colors or finishes may help camouflage the installation.

For all detectors, the frequency of false alarms must be minimal. Sophisticated detectors can generally differentiate between genuinely adverse factors and the insignificant changes that occur daily. All new systems should be certified and regularly maintained by the manufacturer and/or installer. Some detection units must be serviced following each activation.

ALARMS

Alarms range from simple localized systems that alert building occupants to the presence of a fire to complex systems that automatically transmit the alarm, initiate fire suppression, and interact with other building systems. Alarms are triggered by the activation of a manual wall pull or break-glass station, by a fire detector, or by water flow in a sprinkler system. Manual wall pull and break-glass stations are single-action devices for use by building occupants, usually located at exits and stairs. Their exact placement is not critical although they must be accessible and easily identifiable; special finishes are available to minimize their presence.

Alarm systems vary in their method of reporting an alarm. *Localized systems* sound only in the protected building using a local fire alarm or emergency voice/alarm communication system and thus are beneficial only when the building is occupied. *Central, remote,* and *proprietary systems* use telephone lines connected to a constantly attended central station. When an alarm is activated, the central station notifies the fire service directly. Central stations are operated by commercial services or by a private organization, which usually is monitoring more than one property.

In an *auxiliary fire-alarm system,* the alarm is connected directly to a public fire-communications switchboard through the master fire-alarm box or using a dedicated telephone line. This system can be connected to an *emergency voice/alarm communication system,* in which speakers throughout the building direct occupants to evacuation routes or to areas of refuge within the building.

Alarm signals are classified as *trouble* or *supervisory.* Trouble signals indicate any open or short circuit in the wiring caused by a disarrangement of wiring or failure of the primary power source. Supervisory signals, further classified as *protective systems* or *guard patrols,* indicate when some feature of the fire-protection system is not registering as normal and can monitor the manual inputting of the fire/security patrol.

INTEGRATED SECURITY SYSTEMS

Arson and theft, significant dangers to the historic building, are generally controlled by a single approach to security. Unwanted entry to the building must be made as difficult as possible. Traditional security measures, including solid doors with quality locks and bars and shutters or security glazing at windows and skylights, are strongly recommended for any historic house. When these are not appropriate due to their aesthetic impact, alternative solutions include strengthening of existing interior wooden shutters to increase their impact resistance; installing new interior wooden or steel shutters unobtrusively; adding attractive, compatibly designed steel security bars at windows and doors; and the use of secondary glazing units constructed of steel or hardwood frames and laminate glass or polycarbonate glazing. If security installations such as grates, bars, and dead-bolt locks would prohibit occupant escape and create difficult access for the fire service, fire bolts (panic hardware) on doors and quick-release mechanisms on windows and doors can be installed.

The security system consists of sensors placed at possible points of entry—doors, windows, and skylights—and possibly at key site-perimeter locations. A wide selection of active and passive detection units are available. They use magnetic or mechanical switches or electronic detectors (based on active or passive infrared, ultrasonic, or electromagnetic Doppler radar, seismic, or acoustic principles) to provide point, linear, or volumetric protection. A high level of security can be achieved with systems that use keys or digital keypads and display information about the protected zones at a central location. Microprocessor units include a memory and can be programmed readily to accept changes in site usage.

The security system is often integrated with the control unit that receives signals from fire-protection equipment. Modern integrated systems can also link security functions with closed-circuit television, watch patrols, or other services. The selection of an integrated system is based on the scale, nature, and value of the house and its contents; budget; and the insurer's requirements. Selection of a reputable supplier and installer is critical since standardized installation guidelines often are not available. (See page 33 for guidance in selecting professional consultants.)

FIRE SUPPRESSION

Portable extinguishers, introduced in the late nineteenth century, have long been the first line of defense for on-site fire protection. If detected early enough, most fires can be extinguished by a portable extinguisher. The extinguisher must be in working condition, visible and clearly labeled in a location immediately accessible to the fire, and properly marked with the type of fire it works against and instructions for its use. Extinguishers must be regularly maintained, and their pressure gauges should be checked as part of general house maintenance.

Dry chemicals—such as sodium or potassium bicarbonate, potassium chloride, or ammonium phosphate—are the most typical medium used in portable extinguishers. Most common is the ABC extinguisher, which can extinguish fires of ordinary combustible materials (class A), flammable or combustible liquids and gases (class B), and live electrical lines (class C). Class D extinguishers are intended for select, less common combustible metals. In the future, the popularity of carbon dioxide extinguishers may increase due to the recent removal of halon from the marketplace.[1]

AUTOMATIC FIRE-EXTINGUISHING SYSTEMS

Automatic extinguishing systems were used in mills and warehouses in the United States as early as the late nineteenth century and have since become standard components of fire-protection installations. The systems automatically identify and begin to extinguish a developing fire, often before the arrival of the fire service.

Automatic extinguishing systems are composed of piping and individual, heat-sensitive sprinklers (heads) that, on detecting a fire, automatically discharge water or another fire-suppression medium. In a *glass-bulb sprinkler*, the rising temperature from a fire causes the liquid inside the bulb to expand and burst, allowing the release of the valve that prevented the escape of water or (in a dry-pipe system) air. In a *fusible-link sprinkler*, the fire's heat softens the soldered plates, causing the release of the valve that holds back the water or air in the piping. The sprinklers are attached in a uniform pattern to overhead piping that is connected to a water supply via a control valve. Only sprinklers in the vicinity of the fire will activate.

Water is provided to the piping from a municipal or private water-distribution system that includes gravity or suction tanks, fire pumps, or pressure tanks. The water source must be clean, adequate for the expected demand, dependable, and protected against frost. The water supply into the sprinkler system is controlled by a main stop valve and an alarm valve. The stop valve is operated manually by the fire service. The alarm valve is designed to stop

Some components of the historic house, such as these independent gas-generating machines used for lighting structures in the late nineteenth century, present a fire risk far too great to warrant their operation today. However, the equipment may be disconnected and left in place to serve as a historical record.

backflow and causes an alarm to sound as soon as a sprinkler opens and water flows into the system. The systems to be considered for the historic property include *wet-pipe, dry-pipe, preaction,* and *water-mist systems.*[2]

Wet-pipe systems are permanently piped pressurized-water systems that rely on the same basic principles used by their nineteenth-century predecessors. When exposed to high heat, each sprinkler discharges water immediately and individually. Wet-pipe systems are often selected based on their relatively low cost. They are extremely simple, reliable, and durable but cannot be used in spaces subject to freezing.

In *dry-pipe systems,* the sprinklers are attached to a piping system that contains pressurized air. When a sprinkler is actuated by heat, the air pressure is reduced and causes the dry-pipe valve to open and water to flow through any opened sprinkler. A dry-pipe system can be used in areas subject to extreme heat or freezing conditions, although the water supply, control valves, and water-filled pipes must be located in a heated area. Since the response time of the basic dry-pipe system is slower than that of a wet-pipe system, more sprinklers are likely to open in a fire; to compensate, the dry-pipe system may also have a *water accelerator* or an *exhaust mechanism* to reduce the time delay. *Alternate (wet-and-dry-pipe)* systems can operate as a dry-pipe sprinkler in the winter and a wet-pipe system in the months when freezing will not occur.

Preaction systems are a variation of dry-pipe systems that have a supplemental fire-detection system, usually ionization-type smoke detectors, installed in the same area as the sprinklers. As a result, the normally dry system can react to a fire as quickly as a wet-pipe system. The actuation of a detector opens a valve that allows water to flow into the piping and to be discharged from any sprinkler that has been opened by the heat from the fire. A preaction system can be installed in areas subject to freezing. In a cross-zoned alarm system, two detectors must be actuated in order to open the sprinkler valve. While preaction systems may reduce unnecessary water discharge, they require more maintenance than wet-pipe systems. However, they are an option for the historic house, where the avoidance of any accidental discharge of water is extremely important.

Clean-agent systems use permanent piping, discharge nozzles, and gaseous extinguishers under pressure, actuated by a detection system, to flood an enclosed space with an extinguishing agent. The agent must be tightly contained within a room to achieve an effective concentration. Extinguishing agents do not chemically damage most artifacts, are low in toxicity, and leave no residue, but they can be hazardous and occupant evacuation is critical. Clean agents are particularly effective on surface fires on paper and fabrics and are best used as protection for the contents of a room rather than as protection of the building.

Residential sprinklers were introduced in the 1970s to prevent injuries and fatalities in residential properties due to the time lag associated with conventional sprinklers. Residential sprinklers have become so popular that, since the early 1980s, many municipalities have passed legislation requiring sprinkler installations in new houses or houses undergoing major renovation.

The residential sprinkler activates under certain minimum life-safety thresholds with respect to carbon monoxide levels and ceiling and eye-level temperatures. In small compartments, residential sprinklers respond up to six times faster than regular sprinklers to smoldering and fast-developing fires and can often suppress a fire with the actuation of a single sprinkler. Residential sprinkler systems share the water supply with the domestic water service, typically twenty to thirty gallons per minute. They require a one-inch water meter; residential sprinkler heads; and steel, copper, or plastic piping. The same valve that controls the water supply into the building serves as a control valve for the sprinklers. Residential sprinklers usually include a backflow-prevention valve and may have devices to regulate water pressure. They deserve serious consideration for installation in smaller historic houses and house museums.

Quick-response sprinklers, available since the 1980s, are an offshoot of the quick-response sprinkler system designed for residential occupancies. Although various types of quick-response sprinklers are currently under development for a range of occupancies, they are currently used only in hotels, motels, offices, and other commercial buildings to enhance life safety.

Water-mist sprinklers are a recent development, initially conceived as an alternative to halon. Water-mist systems discharge fine water spray (fifty to two hundred microns in size as compared with the thousand microns of a normal sprinkler spray). An expensive alternative to a conventional water system (as much as three times in cost), water-mist sprinklers have great potential where limited water is available or where sensitivity to water damage is high. In tests, water-mist systems have used less than 10 percent of the water used by a conventional water-based system.[3]

SELECTION OF A SUPPRESSION SYSTEM

The potential for water damage to valuable materials has contributed to a long-held bias against water-based suppression systems in historic buildings; however, many professionals now concur with fire-protection engineers that the potential for water damage in a sprinklered building is much less than that in its nonsprinklered counterpart. Each sprinkler delivers approximately 15 gallons of water per minute, compared with the 250 gallons a minute a fire department hose is capable of dispensing. Additionally, most fires are controlled by the operation of fewer than five sprinklers and the incidence of unwarranted discharge is very low. In fully sprinklered buildings, more than 95 percent of fires are suppressed or controlled by sprinklers, and, with the advent of quick-response sprinklers, even higher performance will be available.

The primary considerations in selecting an automatic suppression system are cost and visual impact. Contemporary sprinklers are much smaller than those used thirty years ago, and a wide array of special colors and finishes is available. Even so, in most historic buildings, with the exception of large barns and other simple or unfinished structures, systems with concealed piping are strongly preferred. In *recessed sprinklers* and *flush-type sprinklers*, most of the sprinkler is housed above the ceiling. In *concealed sprinklers*, the entire body of the sprinkler is above the ceiling, and the unit is concealed by a plate at the ceiling line that drops when the fusible link softens at a predetermined temperature that is lower than the sprinkler's operating temperature.

One-story buildings often allow the easiest access to the attic or concealed ceiling spaces for the installation of piping and equipment. In ornate, high-ceilinged spaces, exposed piping and sprinklers can sometimes be camouflaged by a custom finish and the discreet location of pipework and sprinklers. However, air drafts in high ceiling spaces, unprotected vertical openings, and open areas such as monumental stairways can carry heat away from sprinklers located immediately over a fire. The subsequent delay in water discharge can cause additional sprinklers to activate. In cases where an exposed system would be visually undesirable, quick-response sprinklers placed on walls some distance down from the ceiling may provide adequate protection.

The physical difficulty of installation has been one of the impediments to a wider use of fire-suppression systems in historic houses. Planning the installation can be difficult when no architectural drawings are available: even when drawings do exist, they may not be sufficiently detailed to identify concealed vertical and horizontal locations where piping could be accommodated.

Plastic pipework is commonly used for retrofit projects. CPVC (chlorinated polyvinyl chloride) pipe sections are relatively inexpensive and easily joined without special tools. Polybutylene pipe is more flexible than CPVC pipe and can be preassembled and snaked through a building's walls and ceilings. In tight spaces, where traditional pipe sizes cannot be accommodated, special looped or dual-feed systems can reduce the diameter of piping. Copper is increasingly used due to new techniques that minimize the number of fittings and joints and the industry's acceptance of reduced pipe and fitting sizes.

These technical advances are not a substitute for the continued need for great care in the design and installation of the system. It is essential that an acceptance test be conducted after the system's installation, and the installer should provide semiannual maintenance. Owners and site personnel should have a working knowledge of the system in order to undertake weekly and quarterly checks and should ensure that appropriate precautions are taken when construction work occurs near pipework and sprinklers.

DISASTER-PREPAREDNESS PLANNING

No matter how elaborate the fire-protection system, careful planning is also essential for protecting a historic house during and after a fire. Planning should consist of contingency measures to be followed in the case of an emergency and mitigating measures to be followed to minimize the loss.

Guidance for the development of a disaster-preparedness plan can be obtained in reviewing the plans of similar historic buildings and from local and national disaster agencies. The written plan should include priorities for protection and recovery of significant spaces and property; identification of outside resources and supplies that will be necessary; and sources of assistance, identified by name, address, and telephone number. The plan must be simple, flexible, and allow quick action by those who will carry it out.

The disaster-preparedness plan for a private owner will focus on safe evacuation of family members first and protection of the building second. The historic-house museum should have an emergency response team, led by a key staff member who has the authority and the capability to implement the plan. The plan should establish the lines of communication for the team and identify the individuals who will be involved in the salvage, documentation, and restoration of materials damaged in the fire. The team should receive periodic training on the implementation of the plan. Training should include drills, after which the plan is analyzed and revised as necessary. On an annual basis, the plan should be reviewed to reflect current staffing, changes to the building, and the status of the collection. Local fire-service or other emergency-management officials should be asked to assist with the preparation of the plan and to evaluate its adequacy.

The fire service is one of the most important elements in protecting the historic house. Since it is the fire service that will fight the fire should one occur, that organization's familiarity with the historic house is critical to extinguishing a fire with the least damage to the contents and structure. The fire service should visit a house museum annually for general inspection and fire drills. Key fire-service representatives should be aware of the most significant holdings of the collection and be familiar with staff and physical changes at the site.[4] Homeowners may also be able to arrange for the local fire service to provide regular inspections that can uncover potentially hazardous conditions.

FIRE PROTECTION DURING CONSTRUCTION

The historic house is most vulnerable when construction work is undertaken: many individuals may have access to the site; hot-work operations such as cutting, welding, brazing, and soldering require heat guns, torches, or bitumen boilers (for roofing); flammable materials are stored on-site; and fire-protection systems are often turned off. Work during this period should be carefully supervised by the building owner or a designated fire-safety coordinator. Regular communication with the fire service and the property insurer throughout the length of the project is also important, as is having a disaster-preparedness plan in place in the event of an emergency.

One should never assume that the contractor(s) will provide adequate fire protection. Instead, the owner or staff should be prepared to inspect fire-protection equipment, construction work areas, egress routes, and fire-fighting access daily, one hour after the construction work is complete. The following guidelines should help to determine whether the contractor is taking adequate safety precautions.

Be sure that contractors and their staffs are aware of egress routes and the location and operation of existing fire-extinguishing equipment, manual stations, and telephones for summoning the fire service. Insist that a no-smoking policy be strictly enforced in the construction area. Confirm with the contractors that construction schedules are organized to minimize the impact on the building's existing fire-protection system and to ensure that the equipment is fully operational during hazardous operations such as hot work, which is the greatest construction-related risk for historic houses. Hot-air and electric tools are generally safer than those using open flames. If possible, hot operations such as pipe fitting should be moved to a workshop or a single controlled location. Hot operations should occur only when fire-protection equipment is operational.

The contractor must rest and dispose of hot equipment safely during and following the work. Workers should wear shields to protect against the long-distance travel of sparks and hot metal and also use noncombustible blankets or screens as needed to ensure that materials adjacent to the work area are not ignited. Be sure that boilers for roofing are attended at all times and located on a noncombustible base, and that the contractor has made provisions in advance in case of an overflow of hot material. Workers should use extreme caution when working in or adjacent to concealed spaces such as window and floor cavities where sparks can easily go undetected. The workers should also inspect regularly all equipment for leakage or damage to cables and wiring. At least two crew members should be present with fire-fighting equipment during these operations and for at least one hour after the work has stopped.

Temporary walls to isolate areas of the building opened up during construction can limit the potential spread of a fire through the building. However, since temporary partitions can impact the effectiveness of sprinklers and detectors, careful oversight is important.

Make sure that during the construction period fire extinguishers are easily accessible adjacent to all work areas, any temporary wiring is installed by qualified electricians, and all equipment is unplugged when not in use. Do not allow existing electrical circuits to be overloaded with portable equipment. Be sure that any gas supplies are turned off after use.

To minimize the potential fire load within a building, only construction materials to be used in two days of work should be stored inside. Check to see that manufacturers' storage recommendations are followed and, to the extent possible, flammable materials are kept off-site or in fire-resistant cabinets. Flammable liquids and propane gas must be stored separately from oxygen and materials that would increase the toxicity of a fire. Post storage areas with visible signs indicating relevant safety risks, such as Highly Flammable Liquids or No Smoking. Be sure that waste products are removed from the site daily and oily rags and combustible materials are stored separately in enclosed metal bins; that no burning of waste occurs on-site; and that all spillages of flammable liquids are cleaned immediately. Any temporary construction or storage structure should be noncombustible, located as far from the historic building as possible, and should not obstruct routes for egress and fire service access.

At the end of each workday, workers should remove all combustible materials from floors. Combustible floors not susceptible to water damage should be wet down and covered with sheets of noncombustible materials, and openings in walls and combustible materials that cannot be moved should be

The use and storage of flammable materials should receive particular attention. Such items should be stored outside of the house or, when not possible, in metal cabinets specially designed for this purpose.

❈ Fire Prevention Checklist ❈

Electrical Equipment

- No makeshift wiring
- Extension cords serviceable
- Motors and tools free of dirt and grease
- Lights clear of combustibles
- Circuits properly fused or otherwise protected
- Equipment approved for use in hazardous areas (if required)
- Ground connections clean and tight and have electrical continuity

Friction

- Machinery properly lubricated
- Machinery properly adjusted and/or aligned

Special Fire-Hazard Materials

- Storage of special flammables isolated
- Nonmetal stock free of tramp metal

Welding and Cutting

- Area surveyed for fire safety
- Combustibles removed or covered
- Permit issued

Open Flames

- Kept away from spray rooms and booths
- Portable torches clear of flammable surfaces
- No gas leaks

Portable Heaters

- Set up with ample horizontal and overhead clearances
- Safely mounted on noncombustible surface
- Secured against tipping or upset
- Not used as rubbish burners
- Combustibles removed or covered
- Use of steel drums prohibited

Hot Surfaces

- Hot pipes clear of combustible materials
- Ample clearance around boilers and furnaces
- Soldering irons kept off combustible surfaces
- Ashes in metal containers

Smoking and Matches

- No Smoking and Smoking areas clearly marked
- No discarded smoking materials in prohibited areas
- Butt containers available and serviceable

Spontaneous Ignition

- Flammable waste material in closed, metal containers
- Piled material, cool, dry, and well ventilated
- Flammable waste material containers emptied frequently
- Trash receptacles emptied daily

Static Electricity

- Flammable-liquid vessels grounded or bonded
- Proper humidity maintained
- Moving machinery grounded

Housekeeping

- No accumulations of rubbish
- Safe storage of flammables
- Passageways clear of obstacles
- Automatic sprinklers unobstructed
- Premises free of unnecessary combustible materials
- No leaks or dripping of flammables and floor free of spills
- Fire doors unblocked and operating freely with fusible links intact

Extinguishing Equipment

- Proper type
- In working order
- In proper location
- Service date current
- Access unobstructed
- Personnel trained in use of equipment
- Clearly marked

From *Fire Protection Handbook*, 18th ed., National Fire Protection Association, Quincy, Massachusetts.

covered. Equipment should be tested for flammable concentrations of vapor and dust, and all gas cylinders should be secured. The operation of the alarm, detection, and suppression systems should be checked, and all work and adjacent areas to which heat and sparks may have spread should be inspected. Clear access to the site and all fire hydrants for the fire service's use should be maintained and the building should have posted accurate egress routes, changed as necessary as the construction project proceeds.

MAINTENANCE AND HOUSEKEEPING

Many historic-house museums have the advantage of full-time personnel dedicated to the building and its collections. When trained in the function of fire-protection equipment and emergency procedures, these staff members can provide an unsurpassable level of care and attention. The same principles of maintaining a safe environment apply equally to the homeowner.

Historic houses require general architectural assessments undertaken at five-year intervals to identify potentially dangerous conditions. Have all air-conditioning, heating, and electrical systems permanently and professionally installed and regularly maintained.

Change filters regularly, particularly those that are part of the building's ventilation system. Be sure that adequate ventilation exists in special-use areas, such as a painting studio or conservation or maintenance workshop. Establish adequate and secure facilities for handling and storage of special materials, in particular those that are flammable and hazardous. The same precautions for storage and removal of hazardous materials at a construction site can also be helpful here. To the extent possible, relocate high-fire-risk activities to separate, nonhistoric buildings.

Keep all tools, motors, and lights clean and free of dirt and all electrical circuits protected. Make sure that ground connections are clean, tight, and uninterrupted. Avoid temporary wiring, and check that all electrical cords, including extension cords, are unfrayed and appropriate to their electrical load. If portable heating equipment is used on a temporary basis, allow adequate horizontal and vertical clearances and place it so that it will not tip or touch noncombustible surfaces. Have ample clearance around boilers and furnaces, and keep hot pipes clear of combustible materials.

Good-housekeeping practices are important to keeping any house clean and orderly and for controlling flammable waste; poor housekeeping creates opportunities for fires to start and spread. Choose cleaning agents carefully. Water-based floor waxes are generally preferable to waxes with low-flash-point solvents, which can be particularly dangerous when used with electric polishers. Also avoid furniture polishes containing oils that are subject to spontaneous heating, and be sure that saturated rags and other combustible materials are properly disposed of.

Keep insurance plans current, and establish a budget for the installation, upgrade, and maintenance of fire-protection equipment, including a contingency fund to provide emergency repairs in the event of a fire. Document the house and its contents as fully as possible and store architectural drawings and photographs at a secure or off-site location.

Protection of the historic house from fire is a complex task that ranges from basic housekeeping to the installation of sophisticated and expensive equipment. There is no generic approach that is appropriate to all sites, and the unique characteristics of each historic house play a part in planning its fire-protection program. Sophisticated systems alone cannot do the entire job; instead, it is the careful integration of physical improvements, fire-protection equipment, and maintenance practices that provide the historic house the level of protection of which it is worthy.

Notes

1. *Halon systems gained popularity in the 1950s, but have been phased out due to halon's adverse environmental effects and the curtailing, since 1987, of the production of halon. The search for replacement agents that reuse the piping and nozzle systems installed with Halon 1301 systems has had limited success. Other extinguishing systems that are not applicable to historic houses include those using carbon dioxide, chemical, or high-expansion foams.*

2. *Standpipe and hose systems, composed of piping and fittings connected to the building's main water supply, supplement the hoses brought to the site by the fire service. These systems are generally used in tall and large buildings and are not applicable to the smaller historic house.*

3. *Exterior sprinklers have been used since the nineteenth century to minimize the spread of fire from one structure to another. They are typically variations of deluge systems, which are designed without valve caps or heat-responsive elements in order to apply water immediately to the entire area in which a fire originates. Generally mounted on the roof or cornice line of a building, exterior sprinklers have had minimal use on historic buildings.*

4. *Some historic sites have taken extraordinary measures to ensure this familiarity and strengthen the relationship, including extending to fire-service personnel complimentary invitations to visit the site and opening the site to fire-service functions.*

Appraisals, Insurance, Preservation Easements, and Estate Planning

Thomas A. Coughlin

This chapter begins where historic-house restoration ends.[1] Whether the restored historic house is located in an urban historic district, in a rural village, or on a family farm, the owner faces several common concerns. These include:

- What is the market value of a fully restored historic house and how is it determined? We consider the appraisal of historic houses in part 1 below.
- Is the standard homeowner's insurance policy sufficient to insure a restored historic house? If not, are endorsements available to cover risks unique to the historic house? Is there a special policy designed specifically for the historic-house market? Issues unique to insuring the historic house are discussed in part 2 below.
- Is there any way the owner can protect a historic house after it has been sold? Can the current owner prevent a future owner's ill-conceived addition, application of artificial siding, or wholesale removal of architectural detailing in an effort to "update" the house? A preservation easement, as explained in part 3 below, may offer some measure of protection, as well as potential income-, property-, and estate-tax savings.
- Are there ways the owner of a historic house can keep the historic house in the family for benefit of future generations? Some of the basic estate-planning techniques that have been used successfully to retain historic property in continued family ownership are discussed in part 4 below.

1. Appraising the Historic House

Since the beginning of the preservation movement, one of the most vexing questions has been, What price history? Time and again, in such disparate areas as Savannah's Victorian District, Boston's Beacon Hill, Baltimore's Bolton Hill, Seattle's Pioneer Square, and Washington, D.C.'s Capitol Hill, Logan Circle, or Georgetown neighborhoods, I have seen a restored historic house described as "priceless."

Before restoration, that same house—or its immediate neighbors—might well have been described by local realtors as an "unfinished shell," a "handyman's special," or some similar euphemism. Those who have undertaken historic restoration know well that the real-estate market consistently underestimates the cost, time, and effort necessary to realize a prospective purchaser's vision of bringing a shell back to the condition of a fully restored, "priceless" historic house.

The economic value of the historic-house shell before restoration may well be "priceless" simply because the work necessary to effect restoration far exceeds what the marketplace would be willing to pay. In this case, "priceless" may be tantamount to "valueless." Any value associated with such a shell might be land value, with a discount for the costs of demolishing the shell to achieve vacant, buildable status.

After restoration, the market regards the historic property differently. In its restored condition, the historic house has a number of values. It has the "priceless" value of being a unique structure with architectural finishes and detailing that set it apart from its neighbors. It may have associative historic value if it was the former home of a prominent person or if events of historic importance occurred there. It also has economic value, whether as a property held for investment or as a single-family residence.

The appraisal process is integral to documenting a property's value for mortgage underwriting, as a baseline for insurance analysis, for real-estate property-tax assessment, for charitable gifting, and for estate taxation. Many people, including some in the appraisal and legal community, perceive that historic properties are more difficult to appraise and, in some instances, may indeed be "priceless" simply because of the appraiser's inability to define the scope of the appraisal assignment. This part of the chapter is intended to provide the owner with a basic understanding of the appraisal process in the hope that, by being better informed, he or she will be able to select and work with an appraisal professional who is indeed qualified and capable of completing the appraisal of the historic house.

DEFINITION OF FAIR MARKET VALUE

We begin with the concept of *fair market value,* the economic value of a restored historic property. Fair market value is critically important. It establishes the price at which a property should sell in the marketplace and the value of the property for local property-tax purposes. Fair market value is used as the measure for calculating the value of a charitable contribution if the owner chooses to donate the property to a preservation organization or other charitable institution. It is used to measure damage to the property in case of a condemnation or insurance loss. And, finally, fair market value is the measure for computing the estate and gift taxes payable when the owner dies or makes a taxable gift of the historic house during his or her lifetime.

For federal tax purposes, fair market value is defined as "the price at which the property would change hands between a willing buyer and a willing seller, neither being under any compulsion to buy or sell and both having reasonable knowledge of relevant facts."[2] Real estate appraisers, however, generally follow the definition of fair market value promulgated by the Appraisal Institute of the National Association of Real Estate Appraisers, which is "the most probable price in cash . . . for which the appraised property will sell in a competitive market under all conditions requisite to fair sale, with the buyer and seller each acting prudently, knowledgeably, and for self-interest, and assuming that neither is under undue duress."[3]

USE OF THE REAL ESTATE APPRAISAL PROCESS TO DERIVE FAIR MARKET VALUE

A property's fair market value is derived through the real estate appraisal process. This process is intended to provide a reasoned estimate of the value of a given property at a certain point in time. An appraisal begins with research and analysis of market trends, including national, regional, community, and neighborhood factors that influence value. This research provides an understanding of the forces and factors that affect property in a given area. It also provides raw data from which the appraiser extracts numerical market trends.

The ultimate goal of an appraisal is a well-supported conclusion that reflects the appraiser's study of the influences of the market on the value of the property being appraised. The analysis involves three related steps: 1) identification of the property's "highest and best use," 2) analysis of the property by the three recognized approaches to value, and 3) a final reconciliation and conclusion of value.

HIGHEST AND BEST USE

The highest and best use of a property is that reasonable and probable use that will support the highest present value for the property as a whole on the date of the appraisal. The highest and best use must be physically possible, legally permissible, economically feasible, and yield the highest return on the investment over time.

In determining highest and best use for a historic house, the appraiser must first analyze the land as if it were vacant. Thereafter, the appraiser considers the entire property as it is currently improved and decides whether the highest and best use would involve retention or demolition of the existing house.[4]

In an area containing a number of vacant, derelict buildings, the market may place no value on existing buildings in the area, even if they are in a historic district. This is especially true in transition areas where demolition of smaller buildings for new and larger construction is the dominant practice.

When the cost of adapting a historic shell to contemporary requirements exceeds the costs of demolition and new construction, the shell is said to have reached the end of its economic life. In such cases, also, existing historic improvements have no contributory value. The highest and best use of the property would be for new construction.

By contrast, if a strong preservation ordinance is in place, alongside a healthy demand for owner-occupied or rental historic houses, the highest and best use for an existing historic shell may well be for rehabilitation. In these cases, one can expect that the value of the shell will be recognized in the total value of the property.

THE THREE APPROACHES TO VALUE

The three approaches an appraiser uses in valuing a property are described by the National Trust for Historic Preservation and the Land Trust Alliance in the book *Appraising Easements: Guidelines for Valuation of Historic Preservation and Land Conservation Easements.* A brief summary of those descriptions is provided below.

The *comparable-sales approach* involves direct comparisons of the historic property with other properties that have recently been sold in the same or in a similar market in order to derive an indication of the market value of the subject. This approach assumes that for each comparable sale, the buyer and seller act prudently and knowledgeably and that the price is not affected by unique circumstances, such as unusual financing terms or property conditions. The comparable-sales approach is considered most reliable where there exist active markets for properties of the type being appraised.[5]

The *cost approach* to value is used on improved properties as an independent indicator of value and to test and support the other two approaches to value. It is generally inappropriate for valuing vacant land. The basic premise in the cost approach is that an improved property will sell at a price reasonably related to the depreciated cost of a newly constructed version of itself. A modified form of this approach—looking to cost of reproduction rather than simple replacement—may be warranted in the appraisal of special-purpose and historic properties.

Replacement cost is an appraisal term referring to the expense of replacing an existing building with an equivalent one using contemporary building materials and design. *Reproduction cost* refers to the expense of constructing a replica of an existing building, using the same construction and design techniques. For many historic properties, the owner will want the appraiser to estimate both the reproduction and the replacement costs.

In making a valuation, the appraiser will determine which type of cost for each improvement to the property is appropriate. For market-value analysis, the appraiser will favor replacement cost, unless the local market recognizes a premium for historic finishes, in which case reproduction cost might be appropriate. For insurance purposes, the owner may wish to rely on the reproduction cost to be certain to have sufficient funds available to reproduce existing improvements with a materially identical replica using current prices for labor, material, profits, and overhead (see Establishing a Maintenance Program).

Under either the replacement- or reproduction-cost approach, after calculating the cost to reconstruct the existing improvements, the appraiser must deduct from this estimate the accrued depreciation from physical deterioration, as well as functional and economic obsolescence, and add the market value of the land to the depreciated cost of improvements to arrive at a final indication of value.[6]

The *income approach* provides an indication of the value of property by capitalizing the net operating income that a property generates at an appropriate capitalization rate. The income method applies only to properties that are suitable for use as income-producing properties.[7] Since the focus of this chapter is the owner-occupied historic house, we will not consider the income approach further.

RECONCILIATION OF VALUE INDICATIONS AND CONCLUSIONS

After studying the property using the three approaches to value, the appraiser's next step is to reconcile all the value indications to arrive at a final conclusion and opinion of the property's fair market value. This must include the appraisal's analysis of the property's highest and best use and the appropriateness of the existing improvements to such highest and best use. Only then can the appraiser express an opinion as to the property's fair market value.

HOW TO FIND A QUALIFIED APPRAISER

Professional accreditation is not required to qualify an appraiser for federal tax purposes. The tax law merely requires assurance that appraisers are independent of both the former and new owners of the property being appraised. Further, they may not have an interest in the property or base their fees on a percentage of the value of the property being appraised. In addition, appraisers are required to hold themselves out to the public as being in the business of appraising property of the type in question and to append to the appraisal report a statement of qualifications, including "the appraiser's background, experience, education, and membership, if any, in professional appraisal associations."[8] A number of professionals—for example, local real estate or mortgage brokers, real estate attorneys, even architects or developers specializing in historic properties—could conceivably satisfy the Internal Revenue Service's broad definition of an appraiser. For the historic-house owner, however, only a certified real estate appraiser has the professional training necessary to render a qualified opinion as to historic-property valuation.

The principal accrediting service for real estate appraisers is the Appraisal Institute of the National Association of Real Estate Appraisers. Appraisers who complete the institute's training program are entitled to use the designation MAI—Member of the Appraisal Institute—following their name. In addition, some real estate appraisers who specialize primarily in residential property may hold SRPA, SREA, SRA, or RM designations.

The best source of information about experienced appraisers of historic properties is the local historic preservation organization, followed by the state historic preservation agency for the state in which the property is located. If no appraisers working in historic preservation are listed in the local market, consult the local Yellow Pages directory under the heading Real Estate Appraisers. Those with access to the Internet can contact the Appraisal Institute's Web page at http://www.appraisalinstitute.org for a list of members. Finally, the regional office of the National Trust for Historic Preservation may have a list of professionals knowledgeable in the appraisal of historic property. Once you have compiled a list of appraisers, interview several and check all references before making a decision.

2. INSURING THE HISTORIC HOUSE

The question, What price history? is equally relevant to insuring the historic house. In this part we discuss some of the special coverages that the historic-house owner can purchase, either by endorsement to a standard homeowner's policy or through a specialized insurance product designed for the historic-house market. As a practical matter, both avenues are equally satisfactory, so long as the owner addresses the insurance issues discussed below.

COINSURANCE

We have seen that a qualified real estate appraiser can determine the fair market value of a historic house with a minimum of guidance. Many insurance agents begin and end their insurance analysis by confirming that the property is insured for at least 80 percent of its fair market value. Unfortunately, fair market value rarely bears any relationship to the true value of a historic house for insurance purposes.

The problem stems from the fact that most homeowner's policies require the owner to maintain insurance equal to at least 80 percent of the *replacement cost* of the property. This is referred to as the *coinsurance clause*. If a property is not insured to 80 percent of its *replacement cost,* it is under-insured. We have seen, however, that the term *replacement cost* is itself a variable concept when dealing with a historic property. An appraiser generally uses the term to describe the cost to replace a given structure with a structure of similar size and function but using contemporary building techniques and finishes. Yet the cost to "replace" a historic house with a replica—a true replacement in kind—is frequently far in excess of the property's fair market value.

In the event of a complete loss to an underinsured property, the insurer may pay the face amount of the policy; however, if the property is insured for less than 80 percent of its replacement cost—or, say, $150,000 when the actual cost to replace the house is $250,000—the owner will have to supply the additional $100,000 necessary to cover the actual costs of a total loss.

If instead of a complete loss, the owner suffers a partial loss, the full amount of the partial loss will not be covered if the house is underinsured, even if the partial loss is less than the face amount of the policy. Assume our homeowner above had a loss of $100,000 as a result of a kitchen fire. The homeowner's policy was written in a face amount of $150,000, but subsequent estimates required by the fire indicate that this amount actually represents only 60 percent of the replacement cost. If the property had been fully insured, the insurance carrier would have paid $100,000 for the partial loss. Since the property was insured only to 60 percent of its replace-ment cost, the insurance carrier is required to pay only $60,000, or 60 percent of the total cost of repairs, the equivalent percentage at which the homeowner was insured.

Above and opposite:
Proper planning for adequate insurance coverage is essential to enable historically appropriate repairs after sustaining damage in natural disasters. The damage to these homes in Charleston, South Carolina, was caused by Hurricane Hugo in 1989.

The only way to be assured of full coverage in case of a partial loss under a standard homeowner's policy with an 80-percent-of-replacement-cost co-insurance clause is to insure the property to its full reproduction cost. Thus, when considering insurance for a historic structure, one must decide up to what financial limit it is worth seeking insurance for full reproduction cost in the event of a partial loss. For example, a historic property may contain archi-tectural detailing that could not be reproduced affordably if destroyed, mak-ing the cost of adequate insurance prohibitive.

AGREED-AMOUNT ENDORSEMENTS

In some cases, the homeowner may elect to incur the expense necessary to insure the property to its full reproduction cost in order to be fully insured under the coinsurance clause. In others, the homeowner may determine that it would not be worthwhile to reproduce the property if it were destroyed. In case of a partial loss, the homeowner could decide that replacement of historic wet-plaster walls and moldings with contemporary materials such as drywall and stock wooden trim would be an acceptable compromise.

In these instances, the owner may be able to negotiate an *agreed-amount endorsement* with the insurer. Under an agreed-amount endorsement, the insur-ance carrier agrees to insure the property to a specified "agreed amount," which generally represents the property's fair market value. In the event of a total loss, the maximum amount the insurance company would be required to pay would be the face amount of the policy. While the fair market value might be consider-ably less than what would be required to reproduce the property, it might enable the owner to purchase a comparable historic house in the local market.

In case of a partial loss, the agreed-amount endorsement would cover the full amount of the loss, up to the agreed amount. Given the expense of reproducing historical finishes, an agreed-amount endorsement represents a useful compromise for the homeowner unable or unwilling to pay the

additional insurance costs necessary to cover full reproduction cost.

ORDINANCE-OR-LAW ENDORSEMENTS

The standard homeowner's policy excludes coverage for any loss caused by enforcement of ordinances or laws regulating construction, repair, or demolition. For example, a local ordinance may *require* demolition in cases where more than 50 percent of a property is destroyed. Alternatively, the ordinance may require the homeowner to bring the *entire* house into conformity with contemporary building codes if more than a specified percentage (typically 25 or 50 percent) of the house is to be recon- structed. This could entail installation of upgraded wiring, widening of hall- ways and doorways, or installation of fire-protection devices (see also Fire Protection). The specified percentage could be either expressed as a percent- age of the value of repairs to the market value of the house or based on a per- centage of the total square footage that is affected by the reconstruction.

Thus, a homeowner with a traditional homeowner's policy faces an enormous problem in the case of a partial loss requiring reconstruction work that triggers a local ordinance's requirement to demolish or upgrade to contemporary code requirements. Under the ordinance-or-law exclusion, this policy may not pro- vide coverage for the costs of demolition. Similarly, the traditional homeowner's policy will not cover the costs of new construction that may be required to bring the building into conformity with current building-code requirements. To offset the problem, some insurance companies now offer an ordinance-or-law endorse- ment, which operates in a manner similar to the agreed-amount endorsement, to provide coverage where demolition or additional construction work is required in nonaffected spaces solely to comply with current code requirements.

LIABILITY PROTECTION

Most homeowner's policies provide liability coverage for "slip and fall"–type accident claims. However, coverage may not be provided if the historic house is held open to the general public for even a nominal fee, such as in connec- tion with Historic Preservation Week or a local historic-house tour. Similarly, liability coverage may not be provided for volunteer work or unpaid service on the board of directors of a nonprofit organization. Because individual home- owner's policies vary greatly in the scope of coverage offered, it is not enough to ask the agent to confirm that adequate liability coverage is provided. The homeowner must examine the fine print of the policy and, if necessary, request an *extension of coverage* for risks to third parties.

SPECIALIZED POLICIES

When confronted with a restrictive extension-of-coverage policy for liability to third parties, or the need for both an agreed-amount and ordinance-and-law endorsement, the historic-house owner might rightly question whether he or she should seek a policy that is designed especially for the historic-house market rather than seeking incremental additional coverage to a standard homeowner's policy. The answer will vary depending upon the state insurance commission's practices and the ability of the insurance agent. Outlets for insurance specifi- cally designed for the historic house are limited.

A knowledgeable insurance broker and a skilled appraiser are central to providing adequate and affordable insurance coverage either with specialized policies designed for the historic house or through endorsements to a standard homeowner's policy to cover gaps commonly overlooked. Start with your existing insurance broker and homeowner's policy. If you cannot satisfy yourself that you are fully covered, it may be time to look beyond your existing policy to a new insurance program.

3. PRESERVATION EASEMENTS AND THE HISTORIC HOUSE

A preservation easement is a legal instrument by which a historic-house owner can limit the extent to which future owners may modify the house and/or surrounding property. Preservation easements can have favorable tax ramifications as well. Although it may be possible to create a preservation easement for a specific term of years, such an easement would not qualify for favorable tax treatment. Thus, most preservation easements are granted "in perpetuity." Legally, the term *perpetuity* means an estate of indefinite duration. Perpetuity does not mean forever. It does require that, at the time the easement is created, neither grantor nor grantee anticipate that the easement would be released.

Because the easement is granted in perpetuity, it is not an agreement to be entered lightly. Discussed below are how an easement works, how it compares with protections afforded under local zoning or historic-district ordinances, and the income- and estate-tax treatment accorded charitable gifts of preservation easements that meet the requirements of federal tax law.

HOW EASEMENTS WORK

A preservation easement is a two-party instrument created by a deed. In the easement deed, the originating owner, or grantor, conveys to a nonprofit historic preservation organization or a unit of government ("the holding organization") the right to enforce specified restrictions on the property, including prohibitions against subdivision, alteration of significant architectural details, and demolition. The easement also regulates permitted uses, such as alterations to less significant elevations, and may permit construction of additions with the prior approval of the holding organization. In order to be tax deductible, the easement must be granted to a publicly supported charity or unit of government. Because the easement imposes in-perpetuity burdens and responsibilities on the holding organization—including the duty to confer with the owner concerning proposed changes and property-maintenance issues, to inspect periodically to confirm compliance with the easement, and to seek enforcement in the event of noncompliance with the easement terms—it must be accepted by the grantee in order to be valid.

In addition to legal terms, restrictions, and conditions governing permitted and prohibited uses of the property, the easement contains a detailed set of background information about the property. This background information, referred to as *baseline data,* establishes the condition of the property on the date the easement is created. Depending upon local practice, the baseline data may be recorded with the easement, or original counterparts of the baseline data may be retained by the grantor and the holding organization. The baseline data consist of photographs of all elevations of the house in sufficient detail to show clearly all architecturally important elements that the easement is designed to protect. In addition, if the property is listed in the National Register of Historic Places or a local inventory of historic resources, that listing will be included in the baseline data. Finally, a survey or site plan detailing the location of the house and any significant land features will be included in the baseline data.

Once the easement terms have been negotiated and documented and the baseline data completed, a deed of preservation easement is executed by the grantor and holding organization. Following execution by both parties, the deed of easement is recorded among the land records for the county or city where the property is located.

Once recorded, the easement provides *record notice* of its terms. Because the terms of the easement will be discovered in any title search of the property, record notice is often sufficient to protect the property against threats of sale for demolition, subdivision, or assemblage. This protection is self-enforcing because no prospective purchaser or lender will advance funds contemplating demolition or subdivision in the face of a recorded legal agreement that prohibits such a use. If the holding organization is working closely with the building-permit department of local government, any work that requires a building permit may also become largely self-enforcing if the permit office agrees to condition issuance of a permit on receipt of evidence that the holding organization has reviewed and approved the proposed work.

Other elements of easement protection, such as the need for prior consultation and permission of the holding organization before alterations to architectural features are permitted, may not be self-enforcing. Yet experience to date indicates that the owner who initiates an easement typically complies fully with its terms. Enforcement difficulties may arise with future owners who may not understand fully the requirements of the easement or be as willing to abide by its terms. On occasion, holding organizations have needed to go to court to enforce compliance with the terms of a preservation easement. Courts in at least two jurisdictions, the District of Columbia and Pennsylvania, have required owners who constructed improvements in violation of the terms of an easement to remove such improvements at the owner's expense. The author is aware of no instance in which a court has refused to enforce the terms of a preservation easement when presented with evidence of flagrant violation.

HOW EASEMENTS COMPARE WITH ZONING AND HISTORIC-PRESERVATION ORDINANCES

A preservation easement is a voluntary, negotiated agreement between a property owner committed to preserving and protecting a historic property and a knowledgeable preservation organization that shares the owner's preservation objectives. Given such commonality of interest and experience, a preservation easement often is custom-tailored to the unique needs of a given historic property. With an easement, it is possible to establish protections that the government could never achieve through its zoning and regulatory powers.

Local zoning or historic-preservation ordinances are enacted under the state's power to regulate land use for the common good in terms of public health and safety. Central to zoning is the requirement that similarly situated properties be treated similarly. Also, a preservation ordinance must avoid undue regulation to avoid a *takings claim*—an assertion that, through excessive regulation, the government has deprived a property owner of his or her property without compensation.

To avoid a takings claim, historic-preservation ordinances contain a procedure to enable an affected property owner to demonstrate that application of the ordinance would work an economic hardship. An owner who believes that application of a preservation ordinance is unfair is entitled to a hearing to prove hardship. If, after a hearing, it is found that application of a zoning or historic-preservation regulation would result in special hardship to a particular property, the provisions of the ordinance will not be enforced. Because a hardship exception is based on *economic* hardship, it has the potential to undermine totally preservation protections in a given instance. Some ordinances also permit nonpreservation factors to be considered. For example, the District of Columbia's Landmarks Preservation Ordinance has an exception for "projects of special merit," which permits the mayor's office to circumvent the landmarks ordinance to further some other planning goal.

Because a preservation easement is created voluntarily, there is no required hardship procedure, no exception for projects of special merit, and no poten-

tial for political influence. Thus, a preservation easement has the potential to afford a higher level of protection than would be available under local zoning or preservation ordinances.

FEDERAL TAX TREATMENT OF PRESERVATION EASEMENTS

To encourage protection of historic properties through preservation easements, federal tax law provides a charitable-contribution deduction for the value of a preservation easement granted in perpetuity to a publicly supported charity or unit of government. There are a number of requirements to qualify.

The property must be an eligible property. The holding organization must be an eligible organization. And finally, the conservation purposes of the gift must be protected in perpetuity. The income-tax benefits of an easement are limited by the value of the gift and percentage-of-income restrictions that limit the amount of a charitable-contribution deduction a taxpayer can use to a specified percentage of the taxpayer's annual adjusted gross income (see also page 238). Each of these terms is discussed below.

ELIGIBLE PROPERTIES

In order to qualify for an easement, the property must be listed in the National Register of Historic Places or be located in a "registered historic district" and be certified by the National Park Service as being of historic significance to the district. A registered historic district is any district either listed in the National Register of Historic Places or created under a preservation ordinance or statute that is certified by the Secretary of the Interior as being consistent with National Register guidelines and containing provisions calculated to encourage the protection of properties within the district.[9]

If a property is neither listed in the National Register nor located in a registered historic district, it may still qualify for an easement donation. The tax law also recognizes a deduction for an open-space easement granted "for the scenic enjoyment of the general public" or pursuant to a "clearly delineated governmental conservation policy." The implementing regulations illustrate scenic enjoyment by including an example of an urban easement where scenic enjoyment is satisfied because the easement preserves the diversity of architectural styles and provides relief from urban closeness. A clearly delineated governmental conservation policy includes local zoning ordinances and other regulations intended to promote open-space protection or historic preservation, even if such an ordinance is not certified by the Secretary of the Interior.[10]

The Virginia Department of Historic Resources holds an easement for the house and lot of the Mahlon Meyers Cottage in Waterford, Virginia, which was built in 1808. Founded in 1733 by Quaker settlers, Waterford has become a modern community while preserving its historical architecture and pastoral setting. The Waterford Foundation, Inc., created in 1943, is one of the oldest community-preservation organizations in the country. It has worked with the citizens to develop one of the nation's most comprehensive easement programs for the protection of architectural and scenic resources. Sixty-seven properties are protected by easements. In 1970 the entire town and its surrounding farmland were designated a National Historic Landmark District.

ELIGIBLE HOLDING ORGANIZATION

The tax law limits eligible recipients of preservation easements to publicly supported charities and units of government. Most preservation organizations will qualify as a publicly supported charity. When considering an organization as a potential easement grantee, the grantor should ask to be provided with copies of the organization's tax-exemption letters. These letters from the Internal Revenue Service will confirm the organization's status as a publicly supported charitable organization.

The term *unit of government* is not as straightforward as it sounds. Legally, a unit of government is confined to those governmental entities that have legislative authority—federal, state, county, and municipal governments. The gift of a preservation easement to a local park authority would not be a gift to an eligible grantee because the park authority lacks legislative authority. On the other hand, a gift to a local municipality that will benefit the local park authority or be administered and enforced by the park authority will qualify because the gift is made to the governmental unit itself and not an agency of the governmental unit.

PROTECTION IN PERPETUITY

A tax deduction will be allowable only if there is assurance that the preservation purposes of the easement donation will be protected in perpetuity. This requires compliance with two conditions.

First, if the easement granted is over mortgaged property, the holder of the mortgage must agree to subordinate its mortgage to the rights of the holding organization to enforce the easement. Otherwise, the easement could be extinguished in the case of a foreclosure, and the preservation purpose would not be protected in perpetuity.

Second, if the easement is ever extinguished as a result of changed circumstances, the easement must grant the holding organization a right to receive a share of the sales proceeds in an amount equal to the fractional value the easement bears to the unrestricted fair market value of the property at the time the easement was granted (see below). If a historic house was worth $50,000 and the easement worth $5,000 at the time the easement was granted, the easement would be worth 10 percent of the property's fair market value. Thereafter, if the historic house were to burn down and the easement were to be extinguished at a time when the property's unrestricted fair market value had increased to $100,000, the holding organization would be entitled to receive the increased cash value of its easement—$10,000 (still 10 percent of the property's fair market value)—if the property were sold. Note, however, that, if the easement were to continue to restrict the size and scale of the replacement structure (through conversion from a historic-preservation easement to a scenic easement, for example), there would be no requirement to extinguish the easement and no requirement to share proceeds of sale with the holding organization.

FAIR MARKET VALUE OF A PRESERVATION EASEMENT

The fair market value of a preservation easement is determined by appraisal. The IRS directs that the *before-and-after* method must be used to determine the value of a preservation easement.[11] Under the before-and-after method, the appraiser conducts two appraisals of the property. The first appraisal—the *before value*—is conducted to determine the property's fair market value immediately before the easement is imposed. The *after-*

value appraisal considers the value of the property at the same point in time but assuming that the preservation easement had been imposed. The difference in value between the two appraisals is the value of the preservation easement.

TAX RULES GOVERNING CHARITABLE GIFTS OF HISTORIC PROPERTY

In order to appreciate the potential benefit of an easement donation, the historic-house owner must have a general understanding of the tax rules governing charitable contributions. Summarized below are the principal tax rules governing charitable contributions as they relate to the charitable gift of a historic preservation easement.

CHARITABLE CONTRIBUTIONS FOR INCOME-TAX PURPOSES

GIFTS OF CASH AND ORDINARY-INCOME PROPERTY

Charitable contributions of cash and other property that has been held by the taxpayer for fewer than twelve months (called *ordinary-income* property) at the time of donation are deductible against up to 50 percent of a taxpayer's adjusted gross income in the year of contribution. If the value of a taxpayer's charitable contributions of cash and ordinary-income property exceeds 50 percent of adjusted gross income, the excess value must be carried forward to the next tax year and can be applied to reduce tax liability in up to five carry-forward years.

GIFTS OF APPRECIATED LONG-TERM-CAPITAL-GAIN PROPERTY

A gift of appreciated property that has been held by the taxpayer for longer than twelve months is limited to 30 percent of the taxpayer's adjusted gross income in the year of donation. Again, any value that exceeds 30 percent of adjusted gross income in the year of donation may be carried forward for up to five carry-forward years.

Gifts of cash seldom approach the 50 percent ceiling. In the second category, however, gifts of substantially appreciated assets, like land, a historic house, or a preservation easement, can often exceed the 30 percent ceiling. In these cases, the excess value may be carried forward for not more than five carry-forward years. Any value remaining at the end of the five-year carry-forward period is lost for income-tax purposes.

For example: Mr. and Mrs. Smith have an adjusted gross income of $100,000 per year and expect their income to remain constant for the foreseeable future. They make a charitable contribution of appreciated property valued at $40,000. Applying the 30-percent-of-adjusted-gross-income ceiling means the Smiths could deduct no more than $30,000 in charitable gifts of appreciated property in the year of the gift. Thus, of the $40,000 gift, $30,000 will be allowed in the year of contribution. The remaining $10,000 must be carried forward to the next tax year when it will be deductible in full, assuming the Smiths make no other gifts of appreciated property.

The income-tax savings that can be achieved from a charitable contribution of a preservation easement or other valuable real estate holding may be nominal when compared with the market value of the gift. The after-tax saving for a taxpayer depends upon the taxpayer's marginal tax bracket. In the preceding example, if the Smiths made their gift in 1997, they would be in the 31 percent tax bracket. We saw that the portion of their $40,000 gift that would be allowable in 1997 was limited to $30,000—30 percent of their $100,000 adjusted gross income. The economic benefit of their $40,000 gift would be $9,300 in 1997—31 percent of the $30,000 that was allowed under the percentage-of-income ceiling. Although the after-tax benefits of a charitable contribution may increase as the taxpayer's income increases, income-tax savings alone are rarely sufficient to create a strong incentive to a taxpayer who is not already highly motivated to protect his or her property.

CHARITABLE GIFTS FOR ESTATE- AND GIFT-TAX PURPOSES

The rules governing charitable gifts for estate- and gift-tax purposes are similar except there is no percentage-of-income limitation. Thus, the full value of a charitable gift is deductible for estate- and gift-tax purposes. The gift of an easement also removes the full value of the easement from the decedent's estate. Although an easement gift by itself may not protect the property from forced sale, it does reduce the estate-tax burden and increases the chance that the family can continue to retain ownership of the property. If the family does not want to retain continued ownership, the easement ensures that the land will be protected in perpetuity.

Note that the estate- and gift-tax benefits from an easement gift may increase over time. Frequently, the greatest appreciation occurs on land that has development potential. Once the easement is donated, the potential for exploitive development through subdivision, assemblage, or demolition for new construction is removed from the property. Over time, the easement will ensure that any future appreciation in the property's value will be attributable to its intrinsic value as a single-family residence or other nonintense usage compatible with the property's historic or environmental importance. Appreciation attributable to the property's speculative value for development is totally removed. Thus, although the easement donation may generate relatively modest immediate income-tax savings, the gift has dramatic potential for generating estate- and gift-tax savings while making it easier to retain the property in continued family ownership. The estate-tax savings possible through use of a preservation easement are discussed below.

PRESERVATION EASEMENTS AND LOCAL PROPERTY TAXES

In most states, property-tax assessments are based on the fair market value of the property. If the fair market value of a property protected by a preservation easement is less than a comparably situated property that is not burdened by an easement, the tax assessment for the property protected by easement *should* be commensurately lower, although this argument does not always convince the local tax assessor. Depending upon the community, an appeal to lower a historic house's assessed value for property taxes may be received favorably. Legally, such an appeal should win. Frequently, however, the local tax assessor will refuse to recognize any reduction in value in an effort to protect the local tax base.

4. ESTATE PLANNING FOR THE HISTORIC-HOUSE OWNER

Historic properties offer unique estate-planning challenges. A historic house may have passed from generation to generation within a family. With the diffusion of wealth over time, it may come to represent a disproportionate share of the assets in one branch of a family. Typically, this occurs because of the need in prior generations to balance the size of bequests among family members and the need to pay estate and gift taxes as each generation succeeds to ownership. The concentration of wealth attributable to a historic house can cause substantial *illiquidity*, or the absence of cash or readily salable securities or other personal property, which leaves the historic house vulnerable to forced sale to satisfy estate taxes that must be paid, in cash, generally within nine months of death. Planning techniques are available to facilitate retention of the historic house within the family, despite the federal estate tax. To take advantage of them, historic-house owners must understand the federal estate- and gift-tax system and how it will apply to their situation. The following discussion presents ways to prepare for and in some cases lessen the burden of estate and gift taxes.

Historic preservation easements have enabled this urban historic home to retain a significant portion of its original lot. The lot encompasses nearly one quarter of a block and includes a stable and carriage house.

Overview of the Federal Estate- and Gift-Tax System

The federal estate tax and the federal gift tax are actually two separate taxes, each of which is assessed at the same nominal rate. The gift tax applies to all gifts made during the taxpayer's lifetime, with limited exceptions.[12] For the historic-property owner and his or her family, the most important exceptions to the estate and gift tax are the unlimited marital deduction and the $10,000 annual exclusion. Each of these is discussed in detail below.

The federal estate tax is assessed against the fair market value of all property includable in a person's estate at death.[13] This includes the fair market value of all property the decedent owned outright as well as the fair market value of the decedent's share of jointly titled property (even if such property passes by operation of law to a designated survivor outside the decedent's will). It includes the value of all life-insurance policies owned by the decedent or to which the decedent had an incident of ownership.[14] *Incidents of ownership* include the ability to borrow against the policy, to change the beneficiary, or to surrender the policy for its cash value. The decedent's taxable estate also includes the value of any IRAs, qualified pension plans, or other retirement savings.

Calculation of Gift and Estate Taxes

Because there is an unlimited marital deduction for interspousal gifts,[15] a taxpayer can leave all of his or her assets to the surviving spouse. It is in gifts to the next generation, or to anyone other than a spouse, that gift and estate taxes are incurred. At that point, federal estate and gift taxes are assessed at a single progressive rate of tax on the cumulative total of all lifetime and testamentary transfers.[16]

Estate- or gift-tax liability is determined by first computing the gross amount of the tax, after which a statutory unified credit is applied against the gross amount of tax to determine the estate or gift tax payable. The tax credit is equivalent to the tax that would be payable on the first $600,000 in a decedent's estate (see sidebar). In addition, property owners, during their lifetime, can give away their property gradually over an unlimited number of years, taking advantage of the $10,000 annual gift-tax exclusion for the gift of a present interest in property.[17] In the case of couples, *each* spouse may make separate gifts up to $10,000, for a total annual exclusion of up to $20,000. For lifetime gifts that exceed this $10,000 annual gift-tax exclusion, a gift tax is imposed on the cumulative total value of all current and prior taxable lifetime transfers.[18] Although a gift may exceed the $10,000 annual gift-tax exclusion, tax will not be payable on the transfer until the $600,000 unified credit against estate and gift taxes is exhausted. Regardless, gifts in excess of $10,000 in any calendar year must be reported by a gift-tax return filed in the quarter the gift is made.[19]

Use of Family- and Marital-Trust Planning to Shelter Up to $1.2 Million from Federal Estate and Gift Taxes

There is no federal estate tax for decedents who leave an estate of less than $600,000 because up to $600,000 is sheltered by the unified credit.[20] Thus, if a family has less than $600,000 in total assets, with minimal planning, the entire value of the historic house and other assets can be left to younger family members without any federal estate tax. If the family has between $600,000 and $1.2 million in assets, according to the current rate schedule, taxation will begin at 37 percent for the first dollar above $600,000 and is sharply progressive.[21] The total federal estate-tax cost for a family with $1.2 million in assets and no estate- or gift-tax planning would be $235,000. With minimal planning, this heavy tax burden could be totally sheltered.

Calculating Estate- and/or Gift-Tax Credits

After this chapter was written, Congress increased the maximum amount that could be sheltered from estate taxes from $600,000 to $1,000,000 over a period of years, ending in 2006 as follows:

FOR DECEDENTS DYING IN	THE APPLICABLE EXCLUSION AMOUNT IS
1998	$ 625,000
1999	$ 650,000
2000, 2001	$ 675,000
2002, 2003	$ 700,000
2004	$ 850,000
2005	$ 950,000
2006 or thereafter	$1,000,000

Many couples rely on a simple "I love you" will to leave all their assets to the surviving spouse. Such a will is often accompanied by jointly titled property, with provisions that on the death of the first to die, title will pass to the surviving spouse. Such an estate plan will result in no estate taxes on the death of the first spouse because all assets pass to the surviving spouse. However, on the second death, all assets will be fully exposed to taxation.

If, instead, the couple had used a two-trust family- and marital-trust system, on the first death, $600,000 in assets would have been titled in the name of a family trust. Any assets in excess of $600,000 would pass to the surviving spouse, either outright or in trust. The transfer of assets to the surviving spouse would be without tax because of the unlimited marital deduction. The transfer of the first $600,000 to the family trust would be without tax because transfers up to $600,000 are sheltered by the first spouse's unified credit.

After the first spouse's death, under the two-trust system, the Internal Revenue Code allows the surviving spouse to receive all of the trust income and as much of the principal in the family trust as is necessary for his or her "health, education, maintenance, and support," without causing the principal of the trust to be includable in the surviving spouse's estate at death.[22] What this means is that the surviving spouse can have full access to the deceased spouse's principal that was left in the family trust to support the family in the style to which they were accustomed at the time of the death without causing those assets to be included in the surviving spouse's estate. Thus, on the surviving spouse's death, if the estate had totaled $1.2 million, the entire estate could pass completely free of federal estate and gift taxes. The $600,000 in the family trust created under the first decedent's estate plan would pass according to its terms to the couple's children on the death of the surviving spouse. And the surviving spouse's $600,000 would pass tax free because it is sheltered by the surviving spouse's unified credit. In the case of larger estates, taxes would be incurred on sums beyond $1.2 million, yet other strategies are available to prepare for this eventuality.

USE OF THE SECOND-TO-DIE WEALTH-REPLACEMENT TRUST TO PROVIDE NEEDED FUNDS TO PAY ESTATE TAXES

We have seen that estate taxes can be deferred until the second spouse dies because of the unlimited marital deduction. The first $600,000 in assets owned by the first spouse to die should be placed in a family trust to keep those assets that were treated as having been taxed on the death of the first spouse out of the estate of the surviving spouse. Any assets in excess of $600,000 may be left to the surviving spouse without estate tax because of the unlimited marital deduction. At the death of the surviving spouse, however, it will no longer be possible to defer estate taxes because there typically is no surviving spouse. (Widows and widowers who remarry should consult their tax adviser regarding additional tax planning beyond the scope of this chapter.) The estate tax is payable within nine months of the death of the second spouse to die.

To take advantage of the marital-deduction estate-tax deferral and to provide funds when they are most needed, the insurance industry introduced a *second-to-die* insurance policy. Unlike the single-life policy, which is intended to replace lost income on the death of a wage earner, the second-to-die policy is designed to provide cash needed at the second death to pay estate taxes. In effect, the second-to-die policy replaces the wealth that is exacted by the tax system on the second death. Since the policy is underwritten on the basis of two lives, the mortality rates, and hence the premium costs, are substantially lower than with a single-life policy.

Since life insurance owned by the decedent is includable in his or her estate at death, the second-to-die policy may not be owned by either spouse.

The best vehicle to hold such a policy is an irrevocable life-insurance trust. The irrevocable life-insurance trust ensures that neither spouse possesses any incidents of ownership in the policy. Since the policy is excludable from both spouses' estates, the full value of the second-to-die insurance policy will be available at the second death.

At the death of the surviving spouse (the second insured life), the trustee of the life-insurance trust is able to lend money to the executor of the decedent's estate or to purchase assets from the decedent's estate to pay the decedent's estate taxes. A second-to-die policy is an extremely efficient way to provide funds to pay estate-tax obligations. Without it, the executor of the decedent's estate may be forced to sell assets (including the family's historic house) at a discount simply to raise the funds needed to pay estate taxes within the nine-month deadline.

USE OF A QUALIFIED PERSONAL-RESIDENCE TRUST TO REDUCE TRANSFER TAXES

A qualified personal-residence trust (QPRT) should be considered by every owner of a historic house where the house is used as the owner's principal or vacation residence and the owner will have a taxable estate (i.e., where a single owner will have an estate of at least $600,000 or where a married couple will have an estate in excess of $1.2 million).

A qualified personal-residence trust is an irrevocable trust created to hold legal title to the grantor's personal residence.[23] The term *personal residence* is confined to the grantor's principal residence or a vacation property that is used by the grantor as a personal residence. During the term of the trust, the grantor retains complete control of the property and is treated for tax purposes as though he or she were the owner of the property. Thus, all property taxes and costs associated with the property flow through to and are payable by the grantor.

There are several reasons why the owner of a historic house might want to enter such an arrangement. First, because the beneficiaries' entitlement to occupy the house is deferred, the value of the property that is being transferred (here referred to as the *value of a remainder interest*) must be discounted to reflect the value of the occupancy term retained by the grantor. This enables the grantor to transfer the historic house today at a fraction of its fair market value. Any future appreciation following transfer to the trust will pass to the beneficiaries without additional tax. The grantor can continue to live in and control the house during the trust term. Following expiration of the trust term, the grantor can continue to occupy the house so long as he or she pays the beneficiaries the fair-market rental value of the house. Payment of this rent removes more assets from the grantor's estate. Finally, the full value of the historic house and any appreciation is removed from the grantor's estate *provided* he or she survives the trust term. If the grantor dies during the trust term, the personal-residence trust will terminate and the full value of the property will be taxable in the grantor's estate, with an offsetting tax credit for gift taxes previously paid.

VALUING THE REMAINDER INTEREST

The value of a remainder interest in a qualified personal-residence trust is based on the actuarial life expectancy of the grantor, the length of the trust term, and a discount rate derived from Treasury tables using 120 percent of the applicable federal rate (AFR) for the month the trust is created. The following example illustrates the operation of a qualified personal residence trust:

Catherine Johnson is seventy years old with a taxable estate of $2.5 million, consisting of her historic house, which has a fair market value of $500,000, and various investments and retirement-plan assets valued at $2 million. Real estate in her neighborhood has been appreciating at the rate of 7.2 percent per year. If current appreciation continues, Catherine's home will be worth $1 million in ten years. She desires to leave her house and estate to her son John. Catherine is considering establishing a trust for a ten-year term at a time when the AFR is 7 percent.

If Catherine were to make an outright gift of her home to John, the value of the gift would be its fair market value—$500,000. If Catherine were to establish a qualified personal-residence trust for a ten-year term, the value of the gift would be the value of the remainder interest—$160,815. At the end of the trust term, the value of the residence will be $1,000,000, assuming the property continues to appreciate at the rate of 7.2 percent a year during the ten-year trust term.

If Catherine survives the ten-year trust term, she will have succeeded in transferring $1 million of value from her estate at a value for gift-tax purposes of $160,815. Note that if Catherine waited until her death to transfer her home, her estate would be in the 55 percent tax bracket because the full appreciated value of her home ($1 million ten years in the future) would be added to the $2 million present value of her other assets. By using the QPRT, Catherine is able to transfer her home to her son at a gift-tax value of only $160,815 and an effective transfer-tax cost of $78,799 (based on a 49 percent marginal estate-tax rate for an estate of $2.16 million multiplied by the $160,815 value of remainder interest discounted for the value of Catherine's ten-year retained term). The trust enabled Catherine to reduce her estate by $1,000,000, to use her home for ten additional years, to use only $78,799 of her unified credit to transfer ownership of a $1,000,000 asset to her son, and to remove additional assets from her estate in the future if she elects to rent the property from her son following expiration of the trust term.

ISSUES TO CONSIDER IN USING THE PERSONAL-RESIDENCE TRUST

A number of issues surround the use of qualified personal-residence trusts. Most significant is that the grantor should reasonably expect to survive the term of the trust. The risk of death during the term can be covered with a second-to-die or term life-insurance policy held in an irrevocable life-insurance trust.

Because the transfer of property is a gift in trust, it does not qualify for the $10,000 annual gift-tax exclusion. The grantor will need to file a gift-tax return and use a portion of the estate's unified credit to shelter the gift from immediate tax. In addition, because the transfer is a taxable gift, it is imperative that the value of the property be substantiated with a good appraisal report.

The beneficiaries of a qualified personal-residence trust do not receive a step up in tax basis at the death of the grantors. Although the property's fair market value is used for assessing gift taxes, the beneficiary of the trust takes the grantor's basis, increased by the amount of gift taxes paid. Thus, upon sale, a beneficiary will pay higher capital-gains taxes than if the property were received at death. Generally, this is an acceptable cost, since the tax on long-term capital gains is 20 percent, while the maximum estate-tax rate is currently 50 percent.

USE OF A PRESERVATION EASEMENT TO DEFLECT UNWANTED DEVELOPMENT VALUE FROM A DECEDENT'S ESTATE

We have previously seen how a preservation easement could be used to obtain an income-tax charitable-contribution deduction for the value of unwanted development rights. In many ways, the real value of the preservation easement is found at death, when the full value of the easement is allowable as a charitable deduction for estate-tax purposes. Consider the following example.

In 1980, John and Mary Smith purchased Oakdale, a hundred-acre national historic landmark located in a rapidly developing metropolitan area, for

$100,000, or $1,000 per acre. Because of development pressure, the property is currently worth $1 million, or $10,000 per acre, as the site for a hundred-unit residential subdivision. A preservation easement precluding subdivision of the land and demolition or alteration of the historic house would reduce the value of the property to $500,000. The $500,000 value of the preservation easement, measured as the difference between the fair market value of the property before imposition of the easement ($1 million) and the value of the property after imposition of the easement ($500,000), would be deductible currently as a charitable contribution for income-, gift-, and estate-tax purposes.

Mr. Smith is currently sixty years old and has an adjusted gross income of $100,000 per year, which he expects to maintain until retirement at age seventy. Because Oakdale has appreciated in value and is treated as long-term-capital-gain property for tax purposes, Mr. Smith would be allowed to deduct the $500,000 value of the preservation easement against 30 percent of his adjusted gross income in the year of donation, with five-year carry-forward rights for the remainder.

Although Mr. Smith would have made a charitable gift of $500,000, he would be able to take advantage of only $180,000 of that gift ($30,000 allowable in the year of donation under the percentage-of-income ceiling, and $30,000 allowable in each of the succeeding five carry-forward years). A substantial portion of the charitable-contribution deduction will be lost for income-tax purposes because of the percentage-of-income ceiling.

Now consider the estate-tax consequences of the same easement donation. If the easement had not been granted, the fair market value of Oakdale would be based on its $1 million value for subdivision and development. With the easement, the value of Oakdale is $500,000, its value for continued use as a single-family residence and farm. The entire $500,000 easement value will be excluded from Mr. Smith's estate upon death. For a decedent whose estate is in the 50 percent marginal tax bracket, the easement gift will generate estate-tax savings of $250,000.[24]

Equally important, the value reduction attributable to the easement will continue as long as the easement is in place. Thus, by reducing the value of Oakdale through the preservation easement—literally extinguishing further development possibilities for the property—Mr. Smith has made it less likely that his decedents will be forced to sell all or a portion of the property to pay estate taxes based on Oakdale's speculative value for subdivision and development.

Over time, the easement donation will ensure that the future appreciation in the property's value will be attributable to its intrinsic value as a single-family residence or other nonintense usage compatible with the property's historic or environmental importance. The appreciation attributable to the property's speculative value for development is totally removed. Thus, although the easement donation may generate relatively modest current income-tax savings, the gift has dramatic potential for generating estate- and gift-tax savings while making it easier to retain the property in continued family ownership.

If a family does not believe it can afford to forgo the monetary value represented by a property's excess development potential, it may be possible to use the income-tax savings generated by the easement donation to purchase a second-to-die life insurance policy to be held by an irrevocable life-insurance trust. On the death of the second spouse, the proceeds from the second-to-die life-insurance trust could be paid to the children to replace the value lost in the easement donation. Further, the deflection of unwanted development pressure would make it more likely that the property could be retained in continued family ownership: the estate-tax burden would be reduced, and the loss in value represented by the preservation easement would be replaced or reduced by insurance proceeds. And in any case, the historic-house owner would have assurance that the property was preserved following his or her death.

Notes

1. This chapter focuses on owner-occupied historic houses that have been completely rehabilitated. Readers interested in learning more about insuring the historic house during restoration should contact the National Trust for Historic Preservation. Readers interested in learning about tax issues specific to historic income-producing properties should contact their state historic preservation office, the Heritage Preservation Services Program of the National Park Service, the National Trust for Historic Preservation, or the American Association of Museums in Washington, D.C.

2. Treasury Regulations § 1.170A-1(c)(2).

3. The Appraisal of Real Estate (8th ed.), 33.

4. Appraising Easements—Guidelines for Valuation of Historic Preservation and Land Conservation Easements (Washington, D.C.: National Trust for Historic Preservation and the Land Trust Alliance, 1984, 1990), 16.

5. Ibid., p. 24.

6. Ibid., at 25–26.

7. Ibid., at 27–28.

8. Treas. Reg. § 1.170A-13(c)(5).

9. Treas. Reg. 170(h)(4)(A) and (B).

10. Treas. Reg. §1.170A-14.

11. Treas. Reg. 1.170A-14; Rev. Rul. 73-339; Rev. Rul. 76-376. See also Appraising Easements.

12. Internal Revenue Code (I.R.C.) § 2501.

13. I.R.C. § 2001.

14. I.R.C. § 2042.

15. I.R.C. § 2523(a).

16. I.R.C. § 2001(c).

17. I.R.C. § 2503(b).

18. I.R.C. § 2501.

19. I.R.C. § 6901(a); Treas. Reg. § 25.6019-1(a); Instructions for Form 709.

20. I.R.C. § 2010.

21. The current estate-tax rate for estates between $600,000 and $750,000 is 37 percent; the marginal rate from $750,000 to $1 million is 39 percent; the rate from $1 million to $1,250,000 is 41 percent; and so on, up to a maximum rate of 55 percent.

22. I.R.C. § 2041(b).

23. See I.R.C. § 2702; Treas. Reg. § 25.2702.

24. The Taxpayer Relief Act of 1997 enacted a unique estate-tax exclusion for certain open-space easements given on properties located within twenty-five miles of a "Standard Metropolitan Statistical Area" or a national park. I.R.C. § 2031(c). For decedents dying in 2002 and later, when the exclusion is fully phased in, the first $500,000 in value of property subject to easement will be excluded from federal estate tax. The exclusion is not available for historic houses, but may prove useful for owners of historic properties with substantial open space.

PRESERVATION RESOURCES

Selection of materials and people for the care and repair of your historic house can be difficult because they need to be right for you and the special nature of your house and its needs. Lists of resources, such as the Yellow Pages, do not describe the suitability of the material or the skills of the people offering services. However, a lot of help is available for the asking.

Because myriad manufacturers and suppliers of materials for historic houses exist, it would be impossible to list a fair representation here. Numerous professional and public-service organizations for historic preservation are available for guidance. Many of these are membership organizations that publish and hold conferences and workshops. A few are listed below, with subgroups listed as appropriate. These resource organizations, particularly your State Historic Preservation Office, may be able to help you locate contractors, consultants, and suppliers in your region. Additionally, statewide and local historic preservation organizations and landmarks commissions may be of assistance.

The best resources are satisfied historic-house owners who can share experiences and suggest sources of materials, contractors, and consultants. They usually are very willing to help and share their pride in their homes.

The Alliance for Historic Landscape
Preservation
82 Wall Street, Suite 1005
New York, NY 10005
www.mindspring.com/~ahlp

American Association for State
and Local History
530 Church Street, Suite 600
Nashville, TN 37219
(615) 255–2971
www.aaslh.org

American Institute for Conservation
1717 K Street, NW, Suite 301
Washington, DC 20006
(202) 452–9545
palimpsest.stanford.edu/aic
Conservation Services Referral System

The American Institute of Architects
1735 New York Avenue, NW
Washington, DC 20006–5292
(202) 626–7300
www.aiaonline.com
Many state societies and local chapters of AIA have Historic Resources Committees.

American Society for Testing and Materials
100 Barr Harbor Drive
West Conshohocken, PA 19428
(610) 832–9500
www.astm.org

American Society of Landscape Architects
636 Eye Street, NW
Washington, DC 20001–3736
(202) 898–2444
www.asla.org
Open Committee on Historic Preservation;
Landscape Architecture *Magazine*

Association for Preservation Technology
International
P.O. Box 3511
Williamsburg, VA 23187
(540) 373–1621

*The Catalog of Landscape Records
in the United States*
Wave Hill
675 West 252nd Street
Bronx, NY 10471
(718) 549–3200

Construction Specifications Institute
601 Madison Street
Alexandria, VA 22314–1791
(703) 684–0300

Heritage Preservation
1730 K Street, NW, Suite 566
Washington, DC 20006
(202) 634–1422
www.heritagepreservation.org

Historic Preservation Education
Foundation
P.O. Box 77160
Washington, DC 20013
(202) 828–0096

National Conference of State Historic
Preservation Officers
444 North Capitol Street, NW, Suite 342
Washington, DC 20001–1512
(202) 624–5465
Can provide addresses of state offices.

National Fire Protection Association
1 Battery March Park
Quincy, MA 02269
(617) 770–3000
www.nfpa.org
Cultural Resources Committee

National Park Service
Heritage Preservation Services
1849 C Street, NW, Suite NC200
Washington, DC 20240
(202) 343–9578
www2.cr.nps.gov
Technical Preservation Services
(Preservation Briefs); *National Register
of Historic Places* (Preservation Tech
Notes); CRM Bulletin, *Federal Historic
Preservation Tax Incentives Program*

National Trust for Historic Preservation
1785 Massachusetts Avenue, NW
Washington, DC 20036
(202) 588–6000
www.nthp.org

National Trust for Historic Preservation
Library Collection
University of Maryland
McKeldin Library
College Park, MD 20742
(301) 405–6320
www.lib.umd.edu/UMCP/NTL/ntl.html

Old-House Journal (bimonthly)
Old-House Interiors (quarterly)
2 Main Street
Gloucester, MA 01930
(978) 283–3200
www.oldhousejournal.com
www.oldhouseinteriors.com

OHJ *also publishes the* Old-House
Journal Restoration Directory, *an
annual sourcebook of suppliers.*

Seed Savers Exchange/Flower and
Herb Exchange
R.R. 3 Box 239
Decorah, IA 52101
(319) 382–5990

Thomas Jefferson Center for
Historic Plants
Monticello
P.O. Box 316
Charlottesville, VA 22902
(804) 984–9816
Twinleaf *catalogue*

Tile Council of America, Inc.
P.O. Box 1787
Clemson, SC 29633
(864) 646–8453
www.tileusa.com

Traditional Building (bimonthly)
69A Seventh Avenue
Brooklyn, NY 11217
(718) 636–0788
www.traditional-building.com

FURTHER READING

An ever-growing literature, books and articles, can be found on historic preservation and the care and treatment of historic buildings. A caring historic-house owner should be conversant with this literature and develop a reference shelf and file. Unfortunately, many of these books are hard to find, but there are bookstores that specialize in architecture and construction books in major cities in the United States, Canada, and England. (The English have particularly good books about building conditions and treatment of building problems.) Learn to use your local libraries and encourage them and local historic preservation agencies and organizations to develop resource centers for historic-property owners.

Answers to your questions about your historic house exist in print, but it is important to know your house well enough to determine if those answers are appropriate solutions to your problems. Remember that mistakes can occur due not only to a lack of information but also the nonapplication or misapplication of available information. The following selected reading list can help you expand your knowledge and better understand the care of your historic house.

GENERAL

Ashurst, John, and Nicola Ashurst. *Practical Building Conservation.* 5 vols. Hants, England: Gower Tower Press, 1988.

Becker, Norman. *The Complete Book of Home Inspection.* 2nd ed. Summit, Pa.: McGraw-Hill, 1993.

Blumenson, John J. G. *Identifying American Architecture: Pictorial Guide for Styles and Terms, 1600–1945.* Nashville: American Association for State and Local History, 1981.

Brand, Stewart. *How Buildings Learn.* New York: Viking, 1994.

Brown, Robert Wade. *Residential Foundations.* New York: Van Nostrand Reinhold, 1984.

Bucher, Ward. *Dictionary of Building Preservation.* New York: The Preservation Press, 1996.

Chambers, J. Henry. *Cyclical Maintenance for Historic Buildings.* Washington, D.C.: National Park Service, 1976.

Dietz, Albert G. H. *Dwelling House Construction.* 5th ed. Cambridge, Mass.: MIT Press, 1991.

Feilden, Bernard M. *Conservation of Historic Buildings.* London: Butterworth, 1982.

Frens, Dale H. *Preservation Tech Notes, Temporary Protection No. 2: Specifying Temporary Protection of Historic Interiors during Construction and Repair.* Washington, D.C.: National Park Service, 1993.

Hale, R. W., Jr. *Methods of Research for the Amateur Historian.* Nashville: American Association for State and Local History, 1969.

Historic Building Interiors: An Annotated Bibliography. Vols. 1 and 2. Compiled by Anne E. Grimmer. Washington, D.C.: National Park Service, Technical Preservation Services, 1994.

Howard, Hugh. *How Old Is This House?* New York: Farrar, Straus and Giroux, Noonday Press, 1989.

Jester, Thomas C., ed. *Twentieth Century Building Materials: History and Conservation.* New York: McGraw-Hill, 1995.

Kitchen, Judith L. *Caring for Your Old House.* Washington, D.C.: The Preservation Press, 1991.

Knight, Paul, and John Porterfield. *Mechanical Systems Retrofit Manual.* New York: Van Nostrand Reinhold, 1987.

Kyvig, David E., and Myron A. Marty. *Nearby History: Exploring the Past Around You.* Nashville: American Association for State and Local History, 1982.

Lafever, Minard. *The Beauties of Modern Architecture.* New York: DaCapo, 1968.

Liska, Roger W. *Means Facilities Maintenance Standards.* Kingston, Mass.: R. S. Means Company, Inc., 1988.

Lounsbury, Carl. *An Illustrated Glossary of Early Southern Architecture and Landscape.* New York: Oxford University Press, 1994.

McAlester, Virginia, and Lee McAlester. *A Field Guide to American Houses.* New York: Alfred A. Knopf, 1984.

Magee, Gregory H. *Facilities Maintenance Management.* Kingston, Mass.: R. S. Means Company, Inc., 1988.

Melville, Ian, and Ian Gordon. *The Repair and Maintenance of Houses.* London: The Estates Gazette Ltd., 1979.

Moss, Roger W., ed. *Paint in America: The Colors of Historic Buildings.* Washington, D.C.: The Preservation Press, 1994.

National Institute for the Conservation of Cultural Property (now Heritage Preservation). *Caring For Your Collections: Preserving and Protecting Your Art and Other Collectibles.* Edited by Arthur W. Schultz. New York: Harry N. Abrams, Inc., 1992.

National Register Bulletin No. 15: How to Apply the National Register Criteria for Evaluation. Washington, D.C.: National Park Service, 1991.

The National Trust Manual of Housekeeping. Compiled by Hermione Sandwith and Sheila Stainton. Harmondsworth, England: Penguin Books Ltd., 1984.

Nelson, Lee H., FAIA. *Preservation Briefs No. 17: Architectural Character: Identifying the Visual Aspects of Historic Buildings as an Aid to Preserving Their Character.* Washington, D.C.: National Park Service, Technical Preservation Services, 1988.

O'Donnell, Eleanor. *National Register Bulletin No. 39: Researching a Historic Property.* Washington, D.C.: National Park Service, 1991.

Poore, Patricia, ed. *Guide to Restoration.* Dutton, N.Y.: The Old-House Journal, 1992.

Ransom, W. H. *Building Failures—Diagnosis and Avoidance.* New York: Methune, Inc., 1981.

Seaquist, E. O. O. *Diagnosing and Repairing House Structure Problems.* New York: McGraw-Hill, 1980.

Walker, Lester. *American Shelter: An Illustrated Encyclopedia of the American Home.* Woodstock, N.Y.: Overlook Press, 1981.

Weaver, Martin E. *Conserving Buildings: A Guide to Techniques and Materials.* New York: John Wiley and Sons, 1993.

Weeks, Kay D., and Anne E. Grimmer. *The Secretary of the Interior's Standards for the Treatment of Historic Properties with Guidelines for Preserving, Rehabilitating, Restoring & Reconstructing Historic Buildings.* Washington, D.C.: National Park Service, Technical Preservation Services, 1995.

Yapp, Bob, and Rich Binsacca. *About Your House with Bob Yapp.* San Francisco: Bay Books, 1997.

ROOFS

Architectural Sheet Metal Manual. Vienna, Va.: Sheet Metal and Air Conditioning Contractors National Association, Inc., 1979.

Bock, Gordon. "Composition Shingles of the 1920s and 1930s." *Old-House Journal* 18, no. 3 (May/June 1990): 28–31.

———. "Making Sense of Metal Roofs." *Old-House Journal* 20, no. 4 (July/August 1992): 30–33.

———. "Slate & Shingle Lookalikes: Manmade Substitutes for Natural Roofing." *Old-House Journal* 22, no. 6 (September/October 1994): 46–49.

———. "Wood-Shingle Roof Care." *Old-House Journal* 18, no. 3 (May/June 1990): 36–38.

Byrne, Richard. "On the Roof: How to Inspect and Maintain It." *Canadian Heritage* (February 1982): 38–40.

Copper & Common Sense — Sheet Copper Design Principles and Construction Techniques. 7th ed. Rome, N.Y.: Revere Copper Products, 1982.

Design and Application Manual for New Roof Construction. Bellevue, Wash.: Cedar Shake and Shingle Bureau. Available by calling (206) 453–1323.

Garskof, Josh. "Wood Shingle Report." *Old-House Journal* 22, no. 6 (September/October 1994): 50–51.

Gayle, Margot, David W. Look, AIA, and John G. Waite, AIA. *Metals in America's Historic Buildings: Use and Preservation Treatments.* Washington, D.C.: National Park Service, Technical Preservation Services, 1980. Revised edition, 1992.

Grimmer, Anne E., and Paul K. Williams. *Preservation Briefs No. 30: The Preservation and Repair of Historic Clay Tile Roofs.* Washington, D.C.: National Park Service, Technical Preservation Services, 1993.

Leeke, John. "Making Wood Shingles Last." *Old-House Journal* 18, no. 3 (May/June 1990): 39–41.

Levine, Jeffrey S. "Slate Quarrying and Shingle Manufacture." *Fine Home Building* (January 1992): 64–68.

———. *Preservation Briefs No. 29: The Repair, Replacement, and Maintenance of Historic Slate Roofs.* Washington, D.C.: National Park Service, Technical Preservation Services, 1993.

National Slate Association. *Slate Roofs.* 1925. Reprint, Fair Haven, Vt.: Vermont Structural Slate Co., Inc., 1977.

Old-House Journal Technical Staff. "Wood Shingle Roofs." *Old-House Journal* 18, no. 3 (May/June 1990): 34–38.

Park, Sharon. *Preservation Briefs No. 19: The Repair and Replacement of Historic Wooden Shingle Roofs.* Washington, D.C.: National Park Service, Technical Preservation Services, 1989.

Sweetser, Sarah M. *Preservation Briefs No. 4: Roofing for Historic Buildings.* Washington, D.C.: National Park Service, Technical Preservation Services, 1975.

209 RR-86 Residential Asphalt Roofing Manual. Rockville, Md.: Asphalt Roofing Manufacturers Association, 1984, 1993.

Waite, Diana S. *Nineteenth Century Tin Roofing and Its Use at Hyde Hall.* Albany, N.Y.: New York State Parks and Recreation Division for Historic Preservation, 1975.

EXTERIOR MAINTENANCE

Fisher, Charles E., III, ed. *The Window Handbook: Successful Strategies for Rehabilitating Windows in Historic Buildings.* Washington, D.C.: National Park Service, Technical Preservation Services and The Center for Architectural Conservation, College of Architecture, Georgia Institute of Technology, Atlanta, 1986.

Fisher, Charles E., III, Deborah Slaton, and Rebecca A. Shiffer, eds. *Window Rehabilitation Guide for Historic Buildings.* Washington, D.C.: Historic Preservation Education Foundation, 1997.

Leeke, John. *The Practical Restoration Report* series. In particular: "Managing Maintenance," "Exterior Woodwork Details," "Epoxy Repairs for Exterior Wood," "Exterior Wood Columns," "Mouldings," and "Wood Gutters." Available by calling (207) 773–2306.

London, Mark. *Masonry: How to Care for Old and Historic Brick and Stone.* Washington, D.C.: The Preservation Press, 1988.

Moss, Roger. *Century of Color.* Watkins Glen, N.Y.: American Life Foundation, 1981.

Moss, Roger, and Gail Winkler. *Victorian Exterior Decoration.* New York: Henry Holt & Co., 1987.

Sloan, Samuel. *The Model Architect.* 1852. Reprint, Mineola, N.Y.: Dover Publications, 1980.

Weeks, Kay D. *Preservation Briefs No. 14: New Exterior Additions to Historic Buildings: Preservation Concerns.* Washington, D.C.: National Park Service, Technical Preservation Services, 1986.

Weeks, Kay D., and David W. Look, AIA. *Preservation Briefs No. 10: Exterior Paint Problems on Historic Woodwork.* Washington, D.C.: National Park Service, Technical Preservation Services, 1982.

Window Directory for Historic Buildings. Compiled by Brooks Prueher. Washington, D.C.: National Park Service, Technical Preservation Services, 1996.

The Window Workbook for Historic Buildings. Washington, D.C.: Historic Preservation Education Foundation, 1986.

INTERIOR MAINTENANCE

Auer, Michael J., Charles E. Fisher, III, Thomas C. Jester, and Marilyn E. Kaplan, eds. *The Interiors Handbook for Historic Buildings, Volume II.* Washington, D.C.: Historic Preservation Education Foundation, 1993.

Benjamin, Asher. *The American Builder's Companion.* New York: Dover Publications, 1969.

Cavelle, Simon. *The Encyclopedia of Decorative Paint Techniques.* Philadelphia: Running Press, 1994.

Cohn, Marjorie, ed. "Conservation of Historic Wallpaper." *Journal of the American Institute for Conservation* 20, no. 2 (1981): 51–151.

Dalton, Byron William. *Practical Plastering and Cement Finishing and Related Subjects.* Chicago: Byron William Dalton, 1949.

Flaharty, David. "The Old Merchant's House Ceiling Medallions." *CRM (Cultural Resources Management) Bulletin* [U.S. Department of the Interior, National Park Service] 16, no. 8 (September 1993): 18–19.

———. "Ornamental Plaster Restoration." *Fine Homebuilding* 57 (January 1990): 38–42.

———. *Preservation Briefs No. 23: Preserving Historic Ornamental Plaster.* Washington, D.C.: National Park Service, Technical Preservation Services, 1990.

Floors and Stairways. Alexandria, Va.: Time-Life Books, 1995.

Garrison, John Mark. "Decorative Plaster: Running Cornices." *Old-House Journal* 12, no. 10 (December 1984): 213.

Gere, Charlotte. *Nineteenth-Century Decoration: The Art of the Interior.* New York: Harry N. Abrams, Inc., 1989.

Goodier, J. H. *Dictionary of Painting and Decorating.* London: Charles Griffin & Company, 1987.

Goodier, J. H., and A. E. Hurst. *Painting and Decorating.* London: Charles Griffin & Company, 1980.

Grimmer, Anne E., and Kimberly A. Konrad. *Preservation Briefs No. 40: Preserving Historic Ceramic Tile Floors.* Washington, D.C.: National Park Service, Technical Preservation Services, 1996.

Gypsum Construction Handbook. Chicago: The United States Gypsum Company, 1986.

Hamburg, H. R., and W. M. Morgans. *Hess's Paint Film Defects: Their Causes and Cure.* London: Chapman and Hall, 1979.

Hoskins, Lesley, ed. *The Papered Wall: History, Pattern, Technique.* New York: Harry N. Abrams, Inc., 1994.

Lynn, Catherine. *Wallpaper in America.* New York: Barra Foundation/Cooper Hewitt Museum, 1980.

MacDonald, Marylee. *Preservation Briefs No. 21: Repairing Historic Flat Plaster Walls and Ceilings.* Washington, D.C.: National Park Service, Technical Preservation Services, 1989.

Masonry, Carpentry, Joinery. Scranton, Pa.: The International Textbook Company, 1899. Reprint, Chicago: Chicago Review Press, 1980.

Nouvel-Kammerer, Odile, ed. *Papiers Peints Panoramique.* Paris: Musée des Arts Décoratifs, 1991.

Nylander, Richard. *Wallpapers for Historic Buildings.* Washington, D.C.: The Preservation Press, 1992.

Nylander, Richard, Elizabeth Redmond, and Penny Sander. *Wallpaper in New England.* Boston: Society for the Preservation of New England Antiquities, 1986.

Oman, Charles C., and Jean Hamilton. *Wallpapers: An International History and Illustrated Survey from the Victoria and Albert Museum.* New York: Harry N. Abrams, Inc., 1982.

Phillips, Morgan. "Adhesives for the Reattachment of Loose Plaster." *The Association for Preservation Technology Bulletin* 12, no. 2 (1980): 37–63.

Porter, Tom. *Architectural Color: A Design Guide to Using Color on Buildings.* New York: Watson-Guptill Publications, 1982.

Purser, Michael W. "Historical Wood Floor Finishes and Contemporary Wood Floor Finishes." In *The Interiors Handbook for Historic Buildings.* Washington, D.C.: Historic Preservation Education Foundation, 1988.

Rickman, Catherine. "Wallpaper Conservation: The Support." In *Traitement des Supports: Travaux Interdisciplinaires.* 217–27. Paris: Association des Restaurateurs D'Art et D'Archeologie de Formation Universitaire, 1989.

Shivers, Natalie. *Respectful Rehabilitation: Walls and Molding.* Washington, D.C.: The Preservation Press, 1990.

———. *Walls and Moulding: How to Care for Old and Historic Wood and Plaster.* Washington, D.C.: National Trust for Historic Preservation, 1989.

Van den Branden, F., and Thomas L. Hartsell. *Plastering Skills.* Homewood, Ill.: American Technical Publishers, 1984.

Wallpaper Reproduction News. Lee, Mass.: WRN Associates. Available by calling (413) 243–3489.

Weber, Pauline, and Merryl Huxtable. "The Conservation of Eighteenth Century Chinese Wallpapers in the United Kingdom." In *The Conservation of Far Eastern Art*, edited by J. S. Mills et al. 52–58. London: International Institute for the Conservation of Historic and Artistic Works, 1988.

Weismantel, Guy E. *Paint Handbook.* New York: McGraw-Hill, 1981.

MECHANICAL AND ELECTRICAL SYSTEMS

Cook, Arthur L. *Interior Wiring.* 2nd ed. New York: John Wiley & Sons, 1923.

Croft, Terrel. *Wiring of Finished Buildings.* Various editions. New York: McGraw-Hill, 1915 to 1920s.

Ferro, Maximilian L., and Melissa Cook. *Electrical Wiring and Lighting in Historic American Buildings.* New Bedford, Mass.: AFC/Nortec, 1984.

Konzo, S., with Marylee MacDonald. *The Quiet Indoor Revolution.* Champaign, Ill.: Small Homes Council/Building Research Council, University of Illinois, 1992.

Konzo, S., J. R. Carroll, and H. D. Bareither. *Summer Air Conditioning.* Chicago: Windsor Press, 1958.

———. *Winter Air Conditioning.* New York: Industrial Press, 1958.

National Electrical Code Handbook. Quincy, Mass.: National Fire Protection Association, 1996.

Palmer, G. T. "Modern Tendencies of Ventilation Practice." *ASHRAE Transactions* 29, no. 643 (1923).

Patteson, Frank A. *Interior Wiring/Electric Signals.* Scranton, Pa.: International Textbook Company, 1929.

KITCHENS AND BATHROOMS

Blankenbaker, E. Keith. *Modern Plumbing.* South Holland, Ill.: Goodheard-Wilcox Co., 1992.

Garrett, Elisabeth Donaghy. *At Home: The American Family 1750–1870.* New York: Harry N. Abrams, Inc., 1990.

Marchant, Valorie J., ed. *Kitchen & Bathroom Plumbing . . . Fix It Yourself.* Alexandria, Va.: Time-Life Books, 1987.

Miller, Judith. *Period Kitchens.* London: Reed Consumer Books, 1995.

Philbins, Tom. *Costwise Bathroom Remodeling.* New York: John Wiley & Sons, 1992.

Plante, Ellen M. *The American Kitchen 1700 to the Present.* New York: Facts on File, 1995.

Seymour, John. *Forgotten Household Crafts.* New York: Alfred A. Knopf, 1987.

Thomas, Steve, and Philip Langdon. *This Old House Kitchens.* New York: Little, Brown & Co., 1992.

Wellikoff, Alan. *The Historical Supply Catalog.* Charlotte, Vt.: Camden House Publishing, 1993.

LANDSCAPES

Birnbaum, Charles A. *Preservation Briefs No. 36: Protecting Cultural Landscapes: Planning, Treatment and Management of Historic Landscapes.* Washington, D.C.: National Park Service, Technical Preservation Services, 1994.

Birnbaum, Charles A., with Christine Capella Peters. *The Secretary of the Interior's Standards for the Treatment of Historic Properties with Guidelines for the Treatment of Historic Landscapes.* Washington, D.C.: National Park Service, Heritage Preservation Services, 1996.

Birnbaum, Charles A., and Cheryl Wagner. *Making Educated Decisions: A Landscape Preservation Bibliography.* Washington, D.C.: Preservation Assistance Division, National Park Service, 1994.

Coats, Alice M. *Flowers and Their Histories.* New York: McGraw-Hill, 1971.

———. *Garden Shrubs and Their Histories.* New York: Simon and Schuster, 1992.

Favretti, Rudy J., and Gordon P. DeWolf. *Colonial Gardens.* Barre, Mass.: Barre Publishers, 1972.

Favretti, Rudy J., and Joy P. Favretti. *For Every House a Garden.* Chester, Conn.: The Pequot Press, 1977.

———. *Landscapes and Gardens for Historic Buildings.* Nashville: American Association for State and Local History, 1978.

Jabs, Carolyn. *The Heirloom Gardener.* San Francisco: Sierra Club Books, 1984.

Leighton, Ann. *American Gardens in the Eighteenth Century, For Use or Delight.* Amherst, Mass.: University of Massachusetts Press, 1987.

———. *American Gardens of the Nineteenth Century, For Comfort and Affluence.* Amherst, Mass.: University of Massachusetts Press, 1987.

———. *Early American Gardens, For Meate or Medicine.* Amherst, Mass.: University of Massachusetts Press, 1987.

Meier, Lauren. *Historic Landscape Directory.* Washington, D.C.: Preservation Assistance Division, National Park Service, 1991.

Stilgoe, John R. *The Common Landscape of America, 1580 to 1845.* New Haven, Conn.: Yale University Press, 1982.

Stuart, David, and James Sutherland. *Plants from the Past.* New York: Viking, 1987.

Tree City USA Bulletin. Nebraska City, Nebr.: National Arbor Day Foundation.

Whiteside, Katherine. *Antique Flowers.* New York: Running Heads, Inc., 1988.

FIRE PROTECTION

Ackland, Tony. "Custodians of the Past." *Fire Prevention* 267 (1994): 25–27.

Artim, Nick. "An Introduction to Water-Mist Fire Suppression Technology." *APT Bulletin* 27, no. 4: 3–6.

Bowden, Geoff. "Radio Fire Alarm Technology Moves into the Big League." *Fire Prevention* 281 (1995): 24–25.

Boyt, Arthur. "Explaining Sprinklers." *Fire Prevention* 267 (1994): 21–24.

Caloggero, John M. "Lightning Protection Systems." In *Fire Protection Handbook,* edited by Arthur E. Cote. 18th ed., sec. 3, 51–61. Quincy, Mass.: National Fire Protection Association, 1997.

"Combining Security and Fire Protection." *Fire International* (February/March 1987): 59–60.

Cote, Arthur E., and Russell P. Fleming. "Fast Response Sprinkler Technology." In *Fire Protection Handbook*, edited by Arthur E. Cote. 18th ed., sec. 6, 181–97. Quincy, Mass.: National Fire Protection Association, 1997.

"Getting the Contractors In." *Fire Prevention* 255 (1992): 23–27.

Higgins, John T. "Housekeeping Practices." In *Fire Protection Handbook,* edited by Arthur E. Cote. 18th ed., sec. 3, 64–72. Quincy, Mass.: National Fire Protection Association, 1997.

Hunter, John E. *Emergency Preparedness for Museums, Historic Sites and Archives: An Annotated Bibliography.* Nashville: American Association for State and Local History, 1979.

"Integrated Security Systems." *Fire Prevention* 198 (1987): 22–24.

Isman, Kenneth E. "Automatic Sprinklers." In *Fire Protection Handbook,* edited by Arthur E. Cote. 18th ed., sec. 6, 124–35. Quincy, Mass.: National Fire Protection Association, 1997.

Lauziere, Kenneth E. "Sprinkler Protection in Historic Buildings." *Chief Fire Executive* 3, no. 1 (January/February 1988): 20–21.

Lee, Scott. "National Library of Scotland—Protecting a Nation's Heritage." *Fire Prevention* 249 (1992): 22–26.

Levy, David. "Disappear Into the Woodwork with Radio-Based Fire Detection Systems." *Fire Prevention* 225 (1989): 33–35.

Moore, Wayne D. "Automatic Fire Detectors." In *Fire Protection Handbook,* edited by Arthur E. Cote. 18th ed., sec. 5, 12–23. Quincy, Mass.: National Fire Protection Association, 1997.

Nelson, Carl L. *Protecting the Past from Natural Disasters.* Washington, D.C.: The Preservation Press, 1991.

Scoones, Katharine. "Fires During Construction." *Fire Prevention* 248 (1991): 19–22.

Tillott, R. J. "Preserving Timber from Fire." *Fire Prevention* 240 (1991): 18–22.

APPRAISALS, INSURANCE, PRESERVATION EASEMENTS, AND ESTATE PLANNING

The Appraisal of Real Estate. 11th ed. Chicago: Appraisal Institute of the National Association of Real Estate Appraisers, 1996.

Appraising Easements—Guidelines for Valuation of Historic Preservation and Land Conservation Easements. Washington, D.C.: National Trust for Historic Preservation and the Land Trust Alliance, 1990.

Boasberg, Tersh, Thomas A. Coughlin, and Julia H. Miller. Chapter 15, "Preservation Easements and Other Voluntary Techniques to Protect Historic Property," and chapter 16, "Legal and Tax Planning Issues in the Valuation and Use of Preservation Easements," *Historic Preservation Law and Taxation.* Transnational Juris Publications, Inc., 1990.

Coughlin, Thomas A. "Easements and Other Legal Techniques to Protect Historic Property in Private Ownership." 6 *Preservation Law Reporter* (Fall/Winter 1987–88): 2031.

———. "Handling Easement Valuation Disputes Before the IRS and in the Courts." *The Practical Real Estate Lawyer* 3, no. 1 (1987): 81.

———. "Preservation Easements: Statutory and Tax Planning Issues." 1 *Preservation Law Reporter* (1982): 2011.

Diehl, Janet, and Thomas S. Barrett, eds. *The Conservation Easement Handbook.* Alexandria, Va., and San Francisco: Land Trust Exchange and Trust for Public Land, 1988.

Esperti, Robert A., and Renno L. Peterson. *Legacy.* Denver: The Esperti-Peterson Institute, 1996.

———. *The Loving Trust.* New York: Penguin, 1994.

———. *Protect Your Estate.* New York: McGraw-Hill, 1992.

Gandelot, Jon B., and Byron E. Woodman, Jr. "Keeping Vacation Property in the Family." Presented at Collegium I, Atlanta, Ga., 1996. Denver: National Network of Estate Planning Attorneys, 1996.

Hammel, Louis J., Jr. "Keeping a Family Vacation Home in the Family for Younger Generations." *Estate Planning* 23, no. 3 (March/April 1996).

Lind, Brenda. *The Conservation Easement Stewardship Guide: Designing, Monitoring and Enforcing Easements.* Washington, D.C., and Concord, N.H.: Land Trust Alliance and Trust for New Hampshire Lands, 1991.

MacDonald, Marylee. "Filling the Old House Insurance Gap." *Old-House Journal* 22, no. 5 (July/August 1994): 50.

Marshall, Tom. "Ordinance or Law Coverage." *Professional Agent* (December 1992).

———. "Replacement Costs." *Professional Agent* (January 1993).

Oldham, Sally G. "Historic Properties: Variable Valuations." *The Appraisal Journal* (July 1982).

Reynolds, Anthony, and William D. Waldron. "Historical Significance—How Much Is It Worth?" *The Appraisal Journal* (July 1969).

Reynolds, Judith. "Factors Affecting the Valuation of Historic Properties." *Information Sheet Series.* Washington, D.C.: National Trust for Historic Preservation, 1976.

———. *Historic Properties—Preservation and the Valuation Process.* American Institute of Real Estate Appraisers, 1982.

———. "Preservation Easements." *The Appraisal Journal* (July 1976).

Shlaes, Jared, and Richard J. Roddewig. "Appraising the Best Tax Shelter in History." *The Appraisal Journal* (January 1982).

Small, Stephen J. *The Federal Tax Law of Conservation Easements.* Washington, D.C.: Land Trust Exchange, 1986, supplemented in 1989 and 1996.

Snyderman, Lois, Samuel N. Stokes, and Elizabeth A. Watson. *Virginia's Heritage: A Property Owner's Guide to Protection.* Richmond, Va.: Virginia Department of Conservation and Historic Resources, 1988.

Watson, Elizabeth A. "Establishing an Easement Program." *Information Sheet Series.* Washington, D.C.: National Trust for Historic Preservation, 1982.

Timothy V. Barton is the research director for the Landmarks Division of the Chicago Department of Planning and Development. He has documented numerous buildings and historic districts for both Chicago Landmark and National Register of Historic Places designations and has written articles on Chicago history and architecture. Mr. Barton received a B.A. in political science from the University of Illinois and a law degree from Loyola University, Chicago.

Gordon Bock has been editor of *Old-House Journal* (OHJ)—a national bimonthly devoted to the restoration of historic buildings—since 1990, and a member of the editorial staff since 1987. Prior to that date he was a frequent contributor to OHJ and a variety of housing, marine, technical, and how-to periodicals. He has worked in the field on a variety of houses and industrial buildings over the years. Mr. Bock's ongoing restoration is an 1880s family homestead in eastern Pennsylvania.

James Boorstein is an architectural conservator who focuses on the restoration of historic interiors. He worked as a master restorer for The Metropolitan Museum of Art on numerous American period rooms, including the Frank Lloyd Wright and Shaker rooms, and at the J. P. Getty Museum on several French period rooms. Mr. Boorstein is a partner in Traditional Line Ltd., a restoration company that he founded in 1984. He received a B.A. in fine arts and archaeology from Colgate University and studied architectural history and engineering at Columbia University. He has written and lectured widely on topics of windows, floors, doors, finishes, as well as strategies and philosophies about restoration.

Richard O. Byrne has worked in restoration and architectural conservation for more than twenty-five years. He has held professional positions with the Canadian Conservation Institute, Parks Canada, and the Heritage Canada Foundation and has worked as a private consultant. He has written numerous articles for the Association of Preservation Technology International (APTI) *Bulletin* and for *Canadian Heritage*. Educated at the University of Wisconsin and the Centre International d'Etudes pour la Conservation et la Restauration des Biens Culturels (ICCROM), he currently lives in Virginia, where he has worked on several restoration projects, including a rural antebellum home.

Thomas A. Coughlin is a lawyer specializing in the areas of estate planning and tax and business law in Washington, D.C. Mr. Coughlin is a past chairman of the Committee on Historic Preservation and Land Conservation of the Real Property, Probate and Trust Law Section and a member of the American Bar Association's Tax Section. Before entering private practice in 1985, Mr. Coughlin served for almost ten years as tax and real estate counsel to the National Trust for Historic Preservation. While at the Trust he also served as project director and principal author of *Appraising Easements: Guidelines for the Valuation of Land Conservation and Historic Preservation Easements*, and he was principal author of the Trust's report *Federal Taxation and the Preservation of America's Heritage*. Mr. Coughlin attended Hiram College and is a graduate of Brandeis University and Boston College Law School. With his former partner Tersh Boasberg, he coauthored *Historic Preservation Law and Taxation* (1986), and is the author of numerous articles in the field.

Charles E. Fisher has worked more than twenty years for the National Park Service in programs involving the rehabilitation and restoration of historic buildings. He has written and lectured widely on the subject of building preservation and has led a national effort over the past fifteen years to improve the quality of window work in historic buildings.

David Flaharty owns a Philadelphia-based ornamental plastering studio, David Flaharty, Sculptor, which undertakes architectural conservation and restoration in addition to period design, manufacture, and installation for new construction. Trained at Rhode Island School of Design and Cranbrook Academy of Art, Mr. Flaharty specializes in eighteenth- through twentieth-century decorative enrichments and concentrates on ceiling medallions, cornices, and ornamental metals. With twenty-five years of experience in the field, Mr. Flaharty also conducts lectures and hands-on demonstrations. In addition to restorations of historic houses, significant projects include ornamental plasterwork in the American Wing period rooms at The Metropolitan Museum of Art, the Diplomatic Reception Suites at the U.S. Department of State, and the White House.

Dale H. Frens, AIA, is principal of the firm of Frens and Frens, Restoration Architects, located in West Chester, Pennsylvania. He holds a degree in history from the University of Michigan, a bachelor of architecture degree from the University of Arizona, and a master of science degree in historic preservation from Columbia University. Prior to establishing Frens and Frens in 1985, he worked with Jan Hird Pokorny Associates in New York City, and John Milner Associates, West Chester, Pennsylvania. He has extensive experience in the areas of building conservation, historic architecture, building rehabilitation and restoration, and specifications writing. He lectures frequently and his publications include *Temporary Protection, Number 2: Specifying Temporary Protection of Historic Interiors During Construction and Repair*, prepared for the National Park Service "Tech Notes" series, 1993.

Andrea M. Gilmore is director of the New England office of Building Conservation Associates, Inc. (BCA), a private consulting firm that specializes in the conservation of historic building materials. Prior to joining BCA, Ms. Gilmore worked at the Society for the Preservation of New England Antiquities, first as architectural conservator and later as director of architectural services. She also worked for eight years as an architectural conservator at the National Park Service. Ms. Gilmore holds a B.A. in history from Carleton College and a M.S. in historic preservation from Columbia University, Graduate School of Architecture, Planning and Preservation.

Jeffrey Greene is president, chief executive officer, art director, and principal-projects administrator of EverGreene Painting Studios, Inc., in New York City. He is well versed in the creation and execution of decorative finishes and possesses extensive knowledge of both the formulation of historic and modern paints as well as the history of their application. Mr. Greene often works as a consultant for the restoration of historic interior finishes, including the preparation of feasibility studies, budget estimates, and technical specifications for decorative paint restoration. His work has been featured in numerous books. He received a B.F.A. in painting from the Art Institute of Chicago. Additionally, he has been educated at the Skowhegan School of Painting and Sculpture, the Art Students League in New York City, the National Academy of Design, the School of Visual Arts, and the Nova Scotia College of Art and Design.

Marilyn E. Kaplan is architect and principal of Preservation Architecture in Valatie, New York, a firm that specializes in historic preservation projects. Prior to becoming a sole practitioner, Ms. Kaplan was Director of Historic Preservation and Research for Cannon Design and Senior Historic Sites Restoration Coordinator at the New York State Office of Parks, Recreation and Historic Preservation. She was educated at the Syracuse University School of Architecture, the Graduate School of Architecture at Rensselaer Polytechnic Institute, and ICCROM in Rome, Italy. She currently serves as president of the Historic Preservation Education Foundation. She has lectured and published widely on historic preservation issues, in particular building codes and fire protection and their relationship to historic buildings.

John Leeke is a preservation consultant from Portland, Maine, who guides owners, tradespeople, contractors, and architects in understanding and maintaining their historic buildings. He has been preserving historic buildings in New England for twenty-six years and has a national reputation as a consultant and writer on restoration and preservation topics. His articles have appeared in *Fine Homebuilding*, *The Journal of Light Construction*, *Old-House Journal* (where he is contributing editor), and other national publications and books. A well-recognized preservation craftsman, Mr. Leeke has gained a reputation as an advocate of conservation planning and maintenance programming. He has lectured and presented workshops for the Association for Preservation Technology

International, National Trust for Historic Preservation, and Restoration 1993–98 International Conferences.

T. K. McClintock is a graduate of the Cooperstown Graduate Program in the Conservation of Historic and Artistic Works. He directs a private practice in Boston that is devoted to the conservation of fine art and historic works on paper. He has supervised the examination and treatment of numerous rooms of historic wallpaper in museums, historic houses, and private homes in North America and Europe.

Hugh C. Miller, FAIA, is a graduate of the University of Pennsylvania Graduate School of Fine Arts and a registered architect noted for his work in the development of historic preservation programs. He served as the first director of the Virginia Department of Historic Resources and as State Historic Preservation Officer (1989–94). From 1979 to 1988, Mr. Miller was the Chief Historical Architect of the National Park Service (NPS). During his twenty-eight-year career in the NPS, he was responsible for preservation planning for the Chicago School Skyscrapers and Pennsylvania Avenue (in Washington, D.C.) and architectural projects such as Independence Hall. He served as executive architect for the Statue of Liberty/Ellis Island Restoration Project. He now serves as architectural consultant to several National Historic Landmarks. Mr. Miller was a director of the Association for Preservation Technology from 1974 to 1981 and was founder and past president of the APT Foundation. In 1996 he was appointed adjunct professor by Goucher College to teach building technology in its graduate historic preservation program.

Richard Pieper is an architectural conservator with broad experience in stone masonry conservation issues. Mr. Pieper has a degree in geochemistry from Cornell University (1971) and has completed studies in architectural conservation at the International Center for the Conservation of Cultural Property in Rome in 1981 and the Sixth International Course in the Preservation and Treatment of Stone in Venice in 1985. He coedited *The Deterioration and Conservation of Stone*, published by UNESCO in 1989. He currently serves on the boards of the Historic Preservation Education Foundation and the U.S. Committee of the International Council of Monuments and Sites. Mr. Pieper is director of preservation for Jan Hird Pokorny Associates in New York City, a preservation architecture firm, and is an adjunct professor in Columbia University's Graduate School of Architecture, Planning, and Historic Preservation.

William B. Rose is a research architect at the Building Research Council at the University of Illinois. From 1972 to 1980 he was a builder and restoration woodworker. In 1983 he received his master's degree in architecture from Harvard, then practiced architecture in France. He began research at the University of Illinois Small Homes Council in 1984. His current research concerns attic and cathedral ceiling construction, building foundations, and rainwater management at building sites. He is the author of both scientific and historical articles on moisture movement in buildings and building-envelope regulations. He is a consultant to several museums and historic buildings, including Independence Hall, Frank Lloyd Wright's Wingspread House, the Henry Ford Museum, and the National Gallery of Australia.

Mary Harding Sadler, AIA, received a bachelor's degree in art history at Williams College and a master's degree in architecture from the University of Virginia. Her professional career has alternated between the public and private sectors with a consistent focus on historic preservation and adaptive reuse projects. Her first position was as a project architect with SWA Architects, designing renovations of several historic Richmond landmarks. Later, as senior architect with the Virginia Department of Historic Resources, Ms. Sadler worked with state and federal government agencies to negotiate agreements that guaranteed the preservation and reuse of publicly owned historic properties. In July 1997, Ms. Sadler cofounded Sadler & Whitehead Architects, PLC, with Camden Whitehead.

Robert Silman has been president of his structural engineering firm, Robert Silman Associates, for the past thirty-two years. Mr. Silman has particular expertise in historic preservation, as evidenced by his work on Carnegie Hall and The Museum of Immigration at Ellis Island, and knowledge of construction systems in the United States dating back to our earliest building types. He has received such distinctions as, in 1989, a Certificate of Merit from the Municipal Arts Society of New York for work on landmark buildings; in 1996, a Certificate of Achievement from the New York City Landmarks Preservation Commission for developing the art of structural preservation of historic buildings; and, in 1988, election as Fellow of the American Society of Civil Engineers. He received a B.A. from Cornell University and bachelor's and master's degrees in civil engineering from New York University. He is currently Adjunct Professor of Architecture at Columbia's Graduate School of Architecture, Planning, and Preservation.

Deborah Slaton, CCS, is an architectural conservator with Wiss, Janney, Elstner Associates in Northbrook, Illinois, an interdisciplinary architectural, engineering, and materials science firm. She has served as project architectural conservator for preservation work at the Kennedy Center in Washington, D.C.; San Jacinto Monument in Houston, Texas; and the Rookery and Reliance Buildings in Chicago, among other projects. Ms. Slaton is past editor of the Association for Preservation Technology International (APTI) newsletter, *Communique*, and coauthor of "Guide to Preparing Design and Construction Documents for Historic Projects," jointly published by APT and the Construction Specifications Institute. She is vice-president of the Historic Preservation Education Foundation, and coeditor of two of their conference proceedings: *Preserving the Recent Past* (1995) and *Window Rehabilitation Guide for Historic Buildings* (1997). Ms. Slaton received a B.A. from Northwestern University, an M.A. in writing, and a master of architecture degree from the University of Illinois in Urbana-Champaign.

John R. Volz is an architect and vice-president with Volz and Associates, Inc., a firm in Austin, Texas, specializing in the restoration of historic buildings and interiors. Mr. Volz received his M.S. in historic preservation from Columbia University, and a B. Arch. from the University of Texas at Austin. Before establishing his practice, he was a restoration architect with the Texas Historical Commission, the National Trust for Historic Preservation, and the National Park Service. Two of the many notable projects in his practice are the Texas State Capitol and the Texas Governor's Mansion in Austin. Mr. Volz sits on the board of the Historic Preservation Education Foundation. He is a coauthor of three historic-district preservation plans published by the National Trust's Preservation Press and author of a comprehensive bibliography of historic-paint publications. He has been an instructor at preservation-maintenance seminars sponsored by the National Park Service and other organizations, and he has taught a graduate preservation-technology course at the University of Texas School of Architecture.

W. Camden Whitehead, AIA, designs renovations and new constructions within sensitive historic contexts. After practicing with a number of Richmond architectural firms, Mr. Whitehead joined the faculty of Virginia Commonwealth University in the Department of Interior Design, where he has taught for the past decade while continuing to design residences and residential and commercial interiors. Mr. Whitehead has a degree in fine art from Averett College and a master's degree in architecture from Virginia Polytechnic and State University. He cofounded Sadler & Whitehead Architects, PLC, in July 1997. Mr. Whitehead combines this architectural expertise with a penchant for watercolor painting. Posters he has painted on behalf of Virginia Commonwealth University, SWA Architects, and Baskervill & Son document and commemorate local history and the buildings that continue to link us to the past.

Barbara Wyatt, ASLA, is a private consultant in landscape architecture and historic preservation in Madison, Wisconsin. For eight years she was the head of survey and planning in the Division of Historic Preservation at the State Historical Society of Wisconsin. She has lectured on historic landscapes and other preservation topics. Additionally, she has published articles and taught courses on historic preservation and historic preservation planning. Wyatt has a B.S. in landscape architecture, as well as a B.A. in history and a M.S. in regional planning. She was president of The Alliance for Historic Landscape Preservation for several years.

INDEX

Numbers following the entries refer to page numbers.

sanding: of floors, 158; to strip finish, 137
scheduling, of care/repair, 15, 34–36, 79, 120–21
screens (window), 94
sealants: on exterior woodwork, 84; on floors, 155; on masonry, 76–77; for stone flooring, 162
seasons, and gardens, 209–10
second-to-die insurance policy, 241, 243, 244
second-to-die wealth-replacement trust, 241–42
security systems, 219–20
septic systems, 181–82
settling: of foundation, 43, 44; and plaster work, 109–10
shed roofs, 42
sheet iron, roofs of, 64–65
sheetrock, repainting of, 137–38
shellac, 129, 132
shifts, in masonry, 73
short circuits, 193
sinks, 188
site, 12; conditions assessment of, 30
slate, roofs of, 60–62
sling psychrometer, 142
slope: landscape, and drainage, 203–4; of roofs, and materials advised, 60
smoke detectors, 218–19
Society of Architectural Historians, 24–25
soiling, 101
solvent acrylics, 131, 133
solvent-borne paints, 130, 131–33
solvent loss (paint curing), 129
solvents (paint), 128, 129
sources: of historic records, 24–28; for historically accurate materials, 162–64
spalling, 44, 73
specialty paint, 138–39
sponging, 138
sprinkler systems, 220–23
squeaky floors, 158
staining, 135; of floors, 155–56
stains, 45; on exterior paint, 101; on floors, 158; on masonry, 72–73; on wallpaper, 123
steam boilers, 177
steam systems, 166–67, 168
steel, 43
stenciling, 138, 139
stone: care of, 77–78; flooring, 160–62; masonry, 69–70
storm windows, 94
stripping: of floor finishes, 153; of paint, 93, 101, 136–37, 148–49
structural systems, 12, 40–50; conditions assessment of, 30; problems, 43–50, 109
studs, 41
styrene butadiene paints, 131
subflooring, 154
subflorescense, 72

substrates: nonpaint, preparing historic, for repainting, 137–38; of paint, identifying, 130–33
sugaring (of limestone), 70
sulfate skins, 70
sunlight, exposure to, 126
surface finishes, 155
surface preparation, of exterior painted surfaces, 99–101
surface weathering, 83
Swedish floor products, 155
systems of a house, seen as a whole, 23–24

T

tax treatment, of preservation easements, 236–39
tempera paint, 131
temperature, and woodwork, 143
term life-insurance policy, 243
termites, 45, 83, 89, 143
terra cotta, 70
terraces, 204
terrazzo flooring, 160–62
theft, 219
thermal insulation, 193
thermal lag, 51
thermohygrometers, 142
thermostats, 176
tile: in bathrooms, 186; flooring, 152, 158–60, 162
timber roofs, 41–42
tinplate iron, roofs of, 65
touch-up painting, 105
trisodium phosphate (TSP) solution, 90, 91, 93
true arches, 41
tuck-pointing, 76

U

ultraviolet (UV) light, 142–43
unified-estate tax credit, 240
uniform-annual-cost method of economic analysis, 35, 38, 39
unlimited marital deduction, 240
urethanes, 131

V

value of a remainder interest, 242–43
vapor barriers, 182–83
varnish, 131
varnish paints, 132
vehicle (paint), 128, 129
vent fans, timer-switched, 183
vent stacks, 181–82
ventilation systems, 45, 165–77
vibration, and plasterwork, 109
vines, 53, 73, 205–6
vinyl asbestos floor tiles, 162
visible light, measurement of, 143
visual records, of historic houses, 28
VOC (Volatile organic compounds)

regulations, 102
voussoirs, 41

W

wainscoting, 140
wallpaper, 116–26
warping, in flooring, 157–58
water: and concrete, 44; and cracks, 43, 44; groundwater flow, and structural protection/repair, 48–49; and maintenance, 45–46; and material deterioration, 13, 16–17; and plasterwork, 109; visible damage by, as clue to structural problems, 45; and woodwork, 141–42. *See also* condensation; moisture
water-based paints, 130–31
water-based polyurethanes, 156–57
water conservation, and gardening, 211
water-cured urethane paints, 130
water damage, from fire suppression systems, 222
water heaters, 184
water mains, 181
water sources, in historic settings, 179–80
water vapor, 182–83
waterborne polymer emulsions, 131
waterproofing, of foundation, 78
wax, 148, 157
wax encaustic paints, 133
weather checking, 62, 83
weather envelope, 80–81, 84
weatherstripping, 94
wells, 179–80
wheat-starch paste, 121, 125, 126
whitewash, 130
wind checking, 62–63
window sash, 88–89, 91–92
windows, 87–95, 188
wiring: electrical, 198; for fire-protection systems, 218–19
wood: checking, 62–63; flooring of, 154–58; as fuel, 169; hazards to, 63, 141–43; paneling, fixing, 146–47; repainting of, 137; roofs, 62–64; windows of, 87–95
Wood Epoxy Repair (WER), 50
woodwork: as clue to historical styles, 149; exterior, 80–86; interior, 140–51
woodworking, vs. historic-house restoration, 85
wrinkled paint, 135

X

X-braces, 41
X-ray techniques, 14, 134
Xeriscaping, 211

Z

zoning: of interior systems, 176; ordinances vs. easements, 235–36; variances, 28

Photograph and Illustration Credits

Acme Gas and Electric Fixture Co. Catalog, c. 1912. Courtesy *Old-House Journal* Collection: 195 top and bottom

Jaime Ardiles-Arce: Courtesy of The Old Merchants House: 106

Timothy Barton: 24

Gordon Bock: Courtesy of *Old-House Journal:* 110, 148 top and bottom; Courtesy of Gordon Bock Collection: 199 top

David Bohl: Courtesy of the Society for the Preservation of New England Antiquities: 236

James Boorstein: 141 top and bottom, 149 bottom left; Courtesy of The Metropolitan Museum of Art: 145 top and bottom

Jack E. Boucher: HABS collection, National Park Service: 8, 10, 13, 16, 20, 35 bottom, 228, 232, 233, 239

Richard O. Byrne: 180, 182; Courtesy of Belle Hearth Bed and Breakfast, Waynesboro, Va.: 186

Courtesy of the Cambridge Historical Commission: 98 top

Courtesy of *Century Home Magazine:* 187 bottom

Courtesy of Chadds Ford Historical Society and Pennsylvania Historical and Museum Commission: 32 top and bottom

Maureen S. Clark: Courtesy of Clark's Trading Post, Rte. 3, North Woodstock, New Hampshire: 196

Courtesy of Colonial Williamsburg Foundation: 156 top and bottom, 178

Courtesy of the Commission on Chicago Landmarks: 22 top left, 22 top right, 26 top, 27

Sharon Crawford: Courtesy of Ganna Walska Lotusland Foundation: 209 bottom

Courtesy © Crown Point Cabinetry: 187 top

John Obed Curtis: 114

EverGreene Painting Studios, Inc.: 129, 130, 132, 136 top and bottom, 137 top, 138, 139; Courtesy of Hackley & Hume Historic Site, Muskegon County Museum: 127, 137 bottom

Nathaniel R. Ewan, HABS collection, National Park Service: 18

Charles E. Fisher: 87, 91 top, 95

David Flaharty: 111, 113 top and bottom

Dale H. Frens: 33 top and bottom

Andrea Gilmore: 7, 96, 100 top, center, and bottom, 101 top and bottom; Courtesy of the Cambridge Historical Commission: 98 bottom

HABS collection, National Park Service: 29

Drawn by Luc Herbots: 40, 42 bottom, 76 top and bottom, 82, 86 bottom, 93, 154 top right, 154 center, 154 bottom, 160 center, 181, 188; Adapted with permission of John Wiley & Sons, Inc. from Allen, *Fundamentals of Building Construction,* © 1985: 41; Derived from a similar diagram in *American Building,* Chicago: University of Chicago Press, 1983: 42 top; Derived from a similar diagram in *Historical Building Construction,* New York: W. W. Norton, Inc., 1995: 44; Adapted with permission of John Wiley & Sons, Inc. from Ramsey/Sleeper, *Architectural Graphic Standards,* © 1994: 46 top; Detail developed by Jan Hird Pokorny Associates, New York City, for work on the Studio at Chesterwood, a National Trust Historic Site in Stockbridge, Massachusetts: 48; Derived from similar drawings in *Masonry, Carpentry and Joinery,* reprinted by Chicago Review Press, Chicago, 1988: 107 bottom, 109; Derived from similar diagrams in *Winter Air Conditioning,* New York: Industrial Press, 1958: 167, 170 top and bottom left; Derived from similar diagrams in *Summer Air Conditioning,* Chicago: Windsor Press, 1958: 171 top, 173 bottom; Derived from a similar drawing from *Wiring Houses for Electric Light,* by Norman H. Schneider, 1911. Courtesy of *Old-House Journal* Collection:191 top; Derived from similar drawings from *Interior Wiring,* by Arthur L. Cook, 1923. Courtesy of Gordon Bock Collection: 191 bottom, 193 top and bottom, 199 bottom

Carol M. Highsmith: 152

Marilyn Kaplan: 215, 224; Courtesy of New York State Office of Parks, Recreation and Historic Preservation, Lorenzo State Historic Site, Cazenovia, N.Y.: 214 top

From Minard Lafever's *Beauties of Modern Architecture,* 1835. Courtesy of The American Institute of Architects Library and Archives, Washington, D.C.: 112

Joseph Lawton: 140 top and bottom, 149 top, 149 bottom right

John Leeke, © 1997 John C. Leeke: 80, 83 top and bottom, 84, 85 top and bottom, 86 top

David Lubarsky, © 1991 David Lubarsky: 144

T. K. McClintock: Courtesy of the Prestwould Foundation: 116, 118, 123 left and right; Courtesy of The Historical Society of the Town of Greenwich, Conn.: 119; Courtesy of the Marblehead Historical Society, Marblehead, Mass.: 122 top and bottom; Courtesy of Historic Charleston Foundation: 125; Courtesy of The Connecticut Daughters of the American Revolution, Inc., which owns and maintains the Oliver Ellsworth Homestead in Windsor, Conn.: 121

Courtesy of National Park Service: 91 bottom and right, 108

Courtesy of National Park Service, Vanderbilt Mansion National Historic Site: 165

Courtesy of New York State Office of Parks, Recreation and Historic Preservation, Lorenzo State Historic Site, Cazenovia, N.Y.: 214 bottom

Richard Nickel: Courtesy of the Richard Nickel Committee, Chicago, Illinois: 22 bottom

Courtesy *Old-House Journal:* 88

Richard Pieper: 69, 70 top and bottom, 71, 72 top and bottom, 73 bottom, 74, 75, 77; Courtesy of University at Buffalo, State University of N.Y.: 73 top

From *Practical Hot Water Heating Steam and Gas Fitting,* by James Lawler and George Hanchett, 1895. Courtesy of *Old-House Journal* Collection: 190

From Robinson's *Atlas of the City of Chicago,* E. Robinson, New York, 1886. v. 3, plate 12: 26 bottom

Sadler and Whitehead Architects, PLC: 153, 157, 160 top and bottom, 161 top left, 161 bottom right

Robert Silman: 43, 46 bottom, 49 top and bottom

Courtesy of State Historical Society of Wisconsin WHi V24 1886: 210; WHi V24 1893: 205

Courtesy of the University of Illinois Library Archives: 171 bottom, 173 top

Courtesy of the University of Illinois School of Architecture–Building Research Council Archives: 172 top and bottom

Courtesy of Virginia Department of Historic Resources, Richmond, Va.: 11

John Volz, Volz & Associates, Inc.: 2–3, 35 top, 56 top and bottom, 57 top and bottom, 213; Courtesy of Dean-Page Hall, Eufaula, Ala.: 51; Courtesy of The John Bremond House, owned and renovated by the Texas Classroom Teachers Association: 53 top; Courtesy of New York State Office of Parks, Recreation, and Historic Preservation, Olana State Historic Site: 53 bottom; Courtesy of The Ephrata Cloister, Pennsylvania Historical and Museum Commission: 61 top; Courtesy Historic Fort Worth, Inc. Eddleman-McFarland House: 52, 60 top and bottom, 61 bottom; Courtesy of the Neill-Cochran Museum House, National Society of the Colonial Dames of America in the state of Texas: 66 top and bottom

Courtesy of The Waterford Foundation Local History Collection: 237

Kay Weeks, Heritage Preservation Services, NPS: 107 top

From *Wiring of Finished Buildings,* by Terrell Croft, 1922. Courtesy of Gordon Bock Collection: 189

From *Woodward's National Architect,* by George E. Woodward, 1869. Courtesy of *Old-House Journal* Collection: 220

Barbara Wyatt: 200 top and bottom, 201, 208, 209 top